THE PORTUGUESE EMPIRE

1415–1808

Published with the support of Comissão Nacional
para as Comemorações dos Descobrimentos Portugueses
(the National Commission for the Commemoration
of the Portuguese Discoveries).

THE PORTUGUESE EMPIRE
1415–1808

A WORLD ON THE MOVE

A. J. R. RUSSELL-WOOD

THE JOHNS HOPKINS UNIVERSITY PRESS
Baltimore and London

Published in hardcover in 1992 by Carcanet Press Limited, Manchester,
England, as *A World on the Move: The Portuguese in Africa, Asia, and America,
1415–1808.*
Johns Hopkins Paperbacks edition, 1998
9 8 7 6 5 4 3 2

The Johns Hopkins University Press
2715 North Charles Street
Baltimore, Maryland 21218-4363
www.press.jhu.edu

Library of Congress Cataloging-in-Publication Data

Russell-Wood, A. J. R., 1939–
  The Portuguese empire, 1415–1808 : a world on the move /
A. J. R. Russell-Wood.
    p.   cm.
  Originally published: A world on the move : the Portuguese in Africa, Asia,
and America, 1415–1808. Manchester [England] : Carcanet, in association with
The Calouste Gulbenkian Foundation, 1992.
  Includes bibliographical references and index.
  ISBN 0-8018-5955-7 (pbk. : alk. paper)
  1. Portuguese—Foreign countries—History. 2. Civilization, Modern—
Portuguese influences. 3. Intercultural communication. I. Russell-Wood, A. J. R.,
1939–   World on the move. II. Title.
DP534.5.R86   1998   98-3736
909′.09712469—dc21   CIP

A catalog record for this book is available from the British Library.

CONTENTS

LIST OF MAPS

ILLUSTRATIONS

xi

PREFACE TO
THE JOHNS HOPKINS EDITION

The 1992 publication of *A World on the Move* inevitably made it part of a historiography associated with the Columbus quincentennial. While my purpose was neither commemorative nor celebratory, but rather to provide an exercise in compensatory history by bringing the Portuguese dimension to the fore, I did fail to mention that Columbus probably spoke Portuguese before Castilian, that he took a Portuguese woman as his wife, and that he was fully versed in Portuguese cartographic advances. The Norwegian explorer Thor Heyerdahl has even suggested that Columbus may have participated in a Portuguese-Danish expedition in 1477 from Greenland across the Davis Strait to the North American mainland. If so, this and his voyage to São Jorge da Mina in present-day Ghana would have given him the practical knowledge concerning currents and wind systems of the Atlantic to provide him with the assurance that, should he sail west from Europe, winds of the north Atlantic gyre would favor his return. Columbus could have found no better teachers, for the Portuguese were to be the first Europeans to contend with two important wind systems: the trade winds of the north and south Atlantic and the seasonal monsoonal wind systems of the Indian Ocean, Arabian Sea, Bay of Bengal, Indonesia, and East Asia. Such meteorological factors were to imbue different rhythms to communications, operations, commerce, and administration of the Portuguese Estado da India, which extended eastward from the Cape of Good Hope, and to those Portuguese colonies or enclaves washed by the waters of the Atlantic.

Of greater import than celebration or commemoration is examination of the aftermath and ramifications of landfalls, or "discoveries." So intense was the human and emotional dimension of initial contacts or encounters between peoples of different nations, races, and religions that it is easy to forget that these were contextualized to a degree probably not fully appreciated even by the participants. Such contexts were an amalgam of political, religious, commercial, military, and social considerations, and these different skeins would be woven into a tapestry of national policies and competing agendas. Regardless of differing levels of expectations, aspirations, reluctance, or rejection, such contacts between Europeans and non-Europeans inexorably heralded a new transcontinental, transoceanic, and transnational age of globalization which was to be characterized by interdependence, interaction, and exchange. These processes occurred at different levels of intensity, at different rates of acceleration, and over greater or lesser spans of time. Some European and non-European peoples were untouched by such changes and others slightly affected, whereas still others were forceful and active participants. The Portuguese were initiators, protagonists, and cultural brokers. The history of Portugal in the early modern period is the history of Portugal in the world.

This book is not intended to be a history of the many facets of the Portuguese enterprise overseas. Charles Boxer has accomplished this task magnificently in his broad-sweeping history titled *The Portuguese Seaborne Empire, 1415–1825* (London: Hutchinson & Co., 1959). Other scholars have focused on discrete aspects: missionary activities, commerce, military campaigns, and administration of empire. So too are there now available adequate histories of the Portuguese in India, China, Japan, Africa, and Brazil. Such a far-flung empire posed a challenge to metropolitan agencies of government and to the crown. This challenge was twofold. First was to assess the most effective manner in which to assert and maintain royal control over a web made up of territories including forts, trading posts, isolated islands, and landmasses such as Brazil and Angola. Over some the crown held sway and Portuguese sovereignty prevailed, in others proprietary lords had jurisdiction, others bore a marked similarity to protectorates, and in still others the Portuguese had been granted extraterritorial rights or enjoyed certain commercial rights. Some local rulers, such as the Mutapa ruler Mavhura Mhande, declared themselves vassals of the Portuguese crown. The degree of jurisdiction over Portuguese *vassalos* was absolute, but varied regarding indigenous peoples.

There was a second, intensely personal, dimension to this challenge, namely how to ensure that Portuguese nationals retained their sense of identity as Portuguese and as Catholics, and their linkage to Portugal and to the Portuguese crown, in situations in which they were often a cultural as well as demographic minority and were constantly exposed to the assimilative forces of other cultures, religions, and political leaders. There were instances of Portuguese (primarily in India) who succumbed to such pressures, serving in the military forces of non-European potentates, placing their technical skills at the service of powers that opposed the Portuguese, and apostatizing. They moved culturally, linguistically, and physically out of the Portuguese world by taking local women as wives and living in indigenous environments. This human flotsam and jetsam should not be confused with those stable communities of Portuguese on the Bay of Bengal (São Tomé de Meliapor, Hughli) and other communities of Portuguese in southeast Africa and elsewhere who effectively lived outside the political umbrella of the Estado da India. Macao was *sui generis*. While under Portuguese governance and playing a crucial commercial role, Macao was far enough removed from the preying eyes and effective control of the viceroy in Goa to afford relative security for Portuguese who, by virtue of their commercial and other activities, would not have welcomed official scrutiny. Such communities provide further examples of the human dimension of a world on the move.

The crown met this challenge by imposing an administrative structure that consisted initially in the establishment of a conciliar structure in the metropolis (notably the Overseas Council) for the administration of overseas affairs, and by having codes of law which were equally applicable overseas and in the mother country. Viceroyalties and governorships were the prime instruments for overseas administration. Institutions for the administration of fiscal and judicial matters and an accompanying bureaucracy closely followed metropolitan counterparts: *fazenda* (treasury), *relação* (appellate court), *alfândega* (customs), and *provedores da fazenda, desembargadores, ouvidores, juízes de fora*, and *meirinhos*. Of these administrative entities, probably the most important for a Portuguese-born person in Cochim, Luanda, or Mariana was the Senado da Câmara and the centrally located stone column, or *pelourinho*, which epitomized local government, recalled the role of the crown in the concession of municipal status and accompanying privileges, and whose officers held titles and performed functions virtually identical to their counterparts in the Minho, Douro, or Alentejo. Nevertheless, here it is necessary to enter the caveat that overseas institutions and bureaucrats, while closely modeled on their continental European counterparts, often deviated from them to some degree in terms of jurisdiction, membership, or functions.

The classic example is the Santa Casa da Misericórdia, whose many branches were governed initially by *Compromissos* of the parent house in Lisbon, but which developed functions and practices that reflected local conditions and priorities. The Misericórdia, the Third Orders, and the many other brotherhoods of lay men and women overseas were anchors of stability, Christian values, and charity, and they provided an institutional matrix for the Portuguese overseas. Admission to a branch of such far-flung brotherhoods carried the guarantee of membership in any branch in the Portuguese world and benefits that included financial aid, legal and hospital assistance, a Christian funeral and burial attended by the membership and settlement of the estate and implementation of the testamentary provisions of the deceased. The story I have to tell of mobility is, for the most part, in the context of such an institutional framework.

On the collective level, there were various mechanisms available to the crown to remind Portuguese far from home of their national and cultural heritage and their allegiance to God, king, and country. These took many forms: the public celebrations at the installation of a viceroy, bishop, or crown judge; joyful celebrations of a birth or marriage of a member of the royal family and public grief accompanying funeral services, eulogies, and periods of mourning at a royal death; and public punishments, which fulfilled a judicial function. These events, by their very ceremonies, brought together the king's personal representative in the person of a viceroy or governor, dignitaries of Church and State, and members of the magistracy. Law and order were preserved by soldiers under the command of officers whose letters patent had been approved by the king. Such events transcended the narrowly punitive or even the exemplary. They were corporate and public manifestations of the power of the monarchy and reminders of the importance attached by the monarch to enforcement of Portuguese laws and the heavy sanctions that would be imposed on those who transgressed moral, ethical, physical, and spiritual codes of behavior expected of those who prided themselves on being Portuguese. Other reminders of their heritage included royal coats of arms, circulation of coins bearing the royal head and Portuguese national symbols, and even controversial taxes and voluntary donations exacted of subjects of the crown. Such instruments of kingship had two characteristics: first, no Portuguese could remain indifferent to, or unaware of, their presence; second, local variations notwithstanding, they represented continuity in what was a highly volatile early modern world. The intent of the crown was to bring institutional stability to different regions of the Portuguese empire and reinforce the sense of national identity among subjects of the crown scattered through the major continents. However, it should be noted that there was another side to the centralization of authority in the king and in the metropolis: namely, the decentralization of authority that was a no less potent force in the Portuguese seaborne empire.

Kingship also placed at the disposal of the monarch a wide

gamut of forms of recognition of achievements by vassals of the Portuguese crown or as tokens of the royal expectation that a task would be undertaken or a challenge overcome. The Paulistas of Brazil, famed for their recalcitrance, reluctance, or outright hostility toward Portuguese laws and crown representatives and emissaries, proved susceptible to royal *mercês*, the concession of privileges, and other tokens of royal esteem. There were knighthoods to be granted in the Orders of Santiago and São Bento or, the most coveted, in the Order of Christ. The merchant-adventurer of seventeenth-century Portuguese Asia, Francisco Vieira de Figueiredo, whose exploits included organizing a fleet of galleys to harass vessels of the Dutch East India Company and inciting indigenous leaders to rise against the Dutch, received a knighthood in the Order of Christ for his good services. Other recipients included Henrique Dias and João Fernandes Vieira, both of African descent, who distinguished themselves in the war of liberation against the Dutch in Brazil. Such recognition could also be extended to those who had assisted the Portuguese crown by their good services. One such beneficiary of the royal goodwill was Nina Chatu, a rich quelim merchant, who greatly assisted the Portuguese before, during, and after the siege of Malacca. In 1514 Dom Manuel confirmed him as recipient of the title *bendara,* which gave him authority over all indigenous residents of the city. Another beneficiary was Francisco Mendes, a Christian and relative of the king of Macassar, whose good services as royal secretary for Portuguese affairs earned him recognition in the form of a habit of the Order of Christ.

That I have not here chosen to write a book about these administrative and institutional aspects of empire is not to deny their existence; but my intention here lies elsewhere. First and foremost, my purpose is to emphasize the global nature of the Portuguese enterprise and reinforce the notion of interconnectedness not only between the maritime and terrestrial components but also between the different spheres of activity. The Portuguese endeavor was multioceanic and multicontinental and occurred concurrently, not seriatim.

Secondly, I hope to counterbalance the proclivity (often attributable to such practical considerations as access to archives or linguistic constraints) on the part of scholars to compartmentalize the Portuguese seaborne empire into discrete geographical regions or impose sometimes artificial chronological constraints. The history of Portugal beyond Europe is vulnerable in this regard for two reasons that have more to do with the nature of historical studies and historical methodology than with the subject. There has been the tendency on the part of scholars to specialize in research into the history of the Portuguese in a single continent (Europe, Africa, Asia, America) or region, invariably to the exclusion of the others. The reader can learn much from monographs with such titles as *Portuguese Africa, Portuguese in South-East Africa, Portuguese Brazil, Portugal in China, The Portuguese in India,* and *Portuguese Rule in Ceylon.* But the price paid—and this is no less applicable to other multicontinental empires of the early modern period—is loss of sight of the whole and diminished appreciation of the global scope and interconnectedness of the imperial undertaking. Recent studies have demonstrated that the movement of—to take but three examples—bullion, spices, and textiles can only be adequately studied in the global context.

Oceanic history has gained acceptance as a valid field for scholarly enquiry. The Indian Ocean, Atlantic Ocean, and what Michael N. Pearson has termed the Afrasian Sea, which reaches from the Cape of Good Hope to the southernmost tip of India, have been recognized as units of study. The program in Atlantic History and Culture, established at the Johns Hopkins University in 1970, has inspired other like-named programs at universities in the United States and Europe. Ideally, such programs bring a comparative and interdisciplinary approach to the examination of common themes while recognizing the diversity and individualism of peoples and cultures in regions touched by the Atlantic Ocean. If a maritime dimension is inalienable from the history of Portugal overseas, yet to be fully examined is the degree to which the sea was the unifying nexus for a series of territorial holdings that were widely dispersed and rarely contiguous.

A magisterial contribution to remedy this shortcoming is Dauril Alden's *The Making of an Enterprise: The Society of Jesus in Portugal, Its Empire, and Beyond, 1540–1750* (Stanford: Stanford University Press, 1996). While discussion of the transplantation of institutions is tangential here, the comprehensive and globally encompassing study by Isabel dos Santos Guimarães of the Santas Casas da Misericórdia (*Quando o rico se faz pobre: Misericórdias, caridade e poder no império português, 1500–1800* [Lisbon: Comissão Nacional para as Comemorações dos Descobrimentos Portugueses, 1997]) underlines how, geographical and cultural diversity notwithstanding, Portuguese institutions in four continents embodied shared values and objectives. This point had already been made for town councils by Charles R. Boxer in his *Portuguese Society in the Tropics: The Municipal Councils of Goa, Macao, Bahia, and Luanda, 1510–1800* (Madison: University of Wisconsin Press, 1965).

The Portuguese empire is not the only victim of historiographical fragmentation. Historians of the Dutch overseas (Charles Boxer being a prominent exception) are largely divided between those who study the Dutch East India Company and scholars of the Dutch West India Company. For the British empire, the British historian Huw Bowen is one of the few scholars looking at the wider British empire and the transition from the Western Hemisphere to the east—a shift whose direction was diametrically opposed to what occurred in the case of Portugal—and how peripheries viewed one another and the metropolis, a comparative dimension for which the Portuguese influenced world is a fertile field of study.

The Portuguese seaborne empire has also been the victim of overzealous attempts at periodization. To link historical periodization to landfalls or military exploits is to miss the quintessence of the Portuguese overseas experience: namely, that many developments occurred concurrently in different geographical theaters. Placing undue emphasis on the fifteenth and sixteenth centuries and linking this approach to what might be termed the "contact" period or what for Europeans were "discoveries," tends to obscure the fact that, for the Portuguese, the contact period extended over several centuries. The achievements, failures, and successes of the Portuguese must be viewed over the *longue durée*. Discrete events and single encounters must be contextualized not only within the immediate period in which they occurred but also within a broader chronology. This fragmentation, be it by geography or by chronology, undermines the universal nature of the Portuguese achievement.

I also wish to stress that the Portuguese not only were the

first Europeans to establish (from a European perspective) the boundaries of the modern world, but, to a degree unmatched by any other European nation in the early modern period, came into contact, initiated exchanges, and maintained relationships with persons of a greater diversity of racial, cultural, religious, and national backgrounds. While conquest and brutality were part of Portuguese overseas history, I have sought to counterbalance the emphasis given to this dimension by pointing to examples taken from the global stage, on which Portuguese acted in concert with, not isolated from, those peoples with whom they came into contact. *Convivência* (the ability to live together) was a marked characteristic of the Portuguese overseas experience, a facet that has not received the attention it deserves. This book details numerous examples of Portuguese and non-Europeans working together in collaborative ventures that demanded mutual respect. This is not to deny that Portuguese did, on occasion, use such acquired knowledge, information, or skills for what were avowedly imperialist or mercantilist agendas. But this book draws on examples from a diversity of experiences—cartography, navigation, astronomy, marine architecture, crop husbandry, metal working, medicine, music, the decorative and graphic arts—to illustrate exchanges of information, skills, and styles. While historians have pointed to European dominance in some such relationships, I seek to emphasize the reciprocal nature of the exchanges. There was interaction in a cross-cultural context between European and non-European peoples. In this regard the Portuguese adopted leadership roles.

The reprinting of a scholarly work provides the opportunity to make limited revisions and corrections and to clarify some points. I should like to acknowledge my debt to Professors Dauril Alden, Charles R. Boxer, and Timothy Coates for their suggesting changes in the text, which are reflected in the following observations.

As regards Portuguese crown motivations for expansion beyond Europe, there was no single agenda. Domestic metropolitan circumstances on the one hand, local conditions overseas on the other, to say nothing of differing priorities at different periods for different regions, led to a variety of motivations, including evangelization, commerce, comparative military advantage, territorial acquisition or securing of extraterritorial rights, and outright conquest. But, for the earlier period, I did not include among the motivations the need to expand fishing areas and I failed to link the need for gold to the chronic deficit of wheat in Portugal. The interested reader should turn to Vitorino Magalhães Godinho's *A economia dos descobrimentos henriquinos* (Lisbon: Livraria Sá da Costa Editora, 1962) for discussion of this linkage. Nor did I make sufficiently explicit how important bullion was in Portuguese (and other European nations') trade with Asia.

Emigration from Portugal and the Atlantic islands to Africa, Asia, and Brazil; sea-based migration east of the Cape of Good Hope; and land-based (and fluvial) migration by Portuguese and their descendants within Asia, Africa, or Brazil require further research. The evidence is often absent, fragmentary, or incomplete other than for case studies or for limited periods. Readers are cautioned that figures proposed by Charles Boxer and Magalhães Godinho (p. 60) are informed estimates. What precisely constituted emigration demands clarification. My working definition was that individuals or groups who left Portugal and the Atlantic islands of their own free will, with the intention of establishing themselves overseas, were bona fide emigrants. This did not preclude the possibility of reverse migration. On the other hand, for civil servants, soldiers, and even some men of the cloth, their passages overseas were viewed initially as a relocation or temporary posting rather than emigration, although many did not return to the metropolis or to their places of origin and thus became de facto emigrants. Whereas the crown often underwrote the cost of such relocations, which can be extended to include exiles whose return was not encouraged, there were few examples of crown-sponsored bona fide emigration.

As regards the most blatant example of forced migration, namely, the Middle Passage, readers seeking further details should consult the effective synthesis by Robert E. Conrad, *World of Sorrow: The African Slave Trade to Brazil* (Baton Rouge: Louisiana State University Press, 1986). The prominence given to the forced relocation by the Portuguese of as many as 6 million African-born persons to the Americas should not blind the reader to the fact that native peoples originating from regions as remote from one another as East Africa, China, and Timor, or the Tiwi of Bathurst and Melville islands off the coast of northern Australia were forcibly transported and enslaved by the Portuguese or were purchased by the Portuguese as slaves.

I have drawn on some of the scholarship the passage of five years has seen for the revised and enlarged Portuguese language edition (Lisbon: Difel, 1998). The incentives and initiatives of the National Commission for the Commemoration of the Portuguese Discoveries have stimulated research and promoted publication of monographs that bear directly on subjects here under discussion. My comments on the transmission of fauna would have benefited from António Luis Ferronha, Mariana Bettencourt, and Rui Lourenço's *A fauna exótica dos descobrimentos* (Lisbon: Edição ELO, 1993). *Portugal e o mundo: O encontro de culturas na música/ Portugal and the World: The Encounter of Cultures in Music,* edited and organized by Salwa El-Shawan Castelo-Branco (Lisbon: Publicações Dom Quixote, 1997), contains essays bearing on the role of the Portuguese as disseminators of music in Africa, Asia, and Brazil. José Manuel Correia's *Os Portugueses no Malabar (1498–1580)* (Lisbon: Imprensa Nacional-Casa da Moeda, 1997) contains chapters on commerce, art, architecture, and the influence of the Portuguese in the formation of creole dialects and vocabulary. Walter Rossa's *Cidades Indo-Portuguesas: Indo-Portuguese Cities* (Lisbon: National Committee for the Commemoration of the Portuguese Discoveries, 1997) is a useful contribution to our understanding of Portuguese urban development on the west coast of India and the Bay of Bengal. *Portuguese Voyages to Asia and Japan in the Renaissance Period,* edited by Peter Milward (Tokyo: The Renaissance Institute, Sophia University, 1994) is more encompassing than the title would suggest, and Marco Spallanzani's *Mercanti Fiorentini nell'Asia Portoghese, 1500–1525* (Florence: Edizioni S.P.E.S., 1997) illustrates how the carracks of the Cape route carried Europeans other than Portuguese to India and beyond. Sanjay Subrahmanyam's *The Portuguese Empire in Asia, 1500–1700* (London: Longman, 1993) is indispensable. Meticulously researched, it challenges inherited "truths," provides original hypotheses, and contains information so rich that it transcends the modest subtitle "A Political and Economic History." Two books of collected essays merit attention. The perceptive essays contained in *Implicit Understandings: Observing, Reporting, and Reflecting on the Encounters between Europeans and Other*

Peoples in the Early Modern Era, edited by Stuart B. Schwartz (Cambridge: Cambridge University Press, 1994) are an important contribution to the literature on how Europeans viewed other peoples, and vice versa, and the creation of bridges between cultures. The twenty-four essays in *The Portuguese and the Pacific*, edited by Francis A. Dutra and João Camilo dos Santos (Santa Barbara: Center for Portuguese Studies, University of California, 1995) range over space (from the Straits of Melaka to the Straits of Magellan) and time, with a concentration on the sixteenth and seventeenth centuries, and include case studies and broader interpretations.

The Career and Legend of Vasco da Gama by Sanjay Subrahmanyam (Cambridge: Cambridge University Press, 1997) goes beyond an examination of the career of this noble, "discoverer," soldier, and viceroy to raise broader questions of myth-building and nationalism. These are of interest to historians of the early modern period, but hitherto the Portuguese dimension has not been part of the international debate. Whereas students of early modern Europe are familiar with the creation and rise of national states and with what has been characterized as the "expansion of Europe," other than for the period of so-called discoveries the Portuguese component has not received the attention it deserves in discussion of subsequent developments. In this regard, the historiography on Portugal overseas, no less than on the Netherlands overseas, has largely been the bailiwick of Portuguese and Dutch historians, respectively, whereas the overseas histories of England, France, and Spain are central to the ongoing international scholarly debate on comparative historical development. Most notably in America, but also in Africa and the Estado da India, Portuguese overseas experience illuminates various aspects of the phase which immediately followed initial encounters between Europeans and non-Europeans and which included conquest, physical oppression, cooperation, and colonization. The theme of dispossession predominates: of lands, cultures, belief systems, values, moral codes, and behaviors, all of which had been integral to the sense of identity among non-European peoples. A subsequent phase saw conflicts and negotiations between, on the one hand, settler populations of European birth or origins and pluralistic societies and, on the other, colonists voicing their own aspirations and crown representatives expressing metropolitan demands and expectations. Portugal has been alone among European nations in not succumbing as early or as rapidly to the disintegration of its global empire, except in America, where creole nationalism and revolts—but not wars of independence such as those that occurred in the British and Spanish colonies—provided the colonial context for a move to independence in Brazil.

Finally, by interconnecting the histories of four continents and multiple oceans and seas over the span of four centuries, my intent is here to educate those unfamiliar with Portugal and its empire about the extent and enduring nature of this enterprise and to show that this empire merits study not only per se but as a rich source for cross-cultural and comparative history. With the reincarnation of world history as an academic subdiscipline, scholars working in this field are reexamining the position of, and the role played by, the West in the history of the world: questioning and bringing new dimensions to the concept of "civilization," comparing and contrasting the waxing and waning of major cultures, attempting to explain the phenomenon of power, tracing the trajectory from birth to maturity to decline in a comparative framework, and developing an awareness of alterity, of the Other. This is leading scholars to seek non-Western iconographic and manuscript sources to arrive at a better understanding of different perspectives and thus be able to place the many histories of the past in a global context. In such scholarly debates it is important that a Portuguese voice be heard loud and clear.

A. J. R. Russell-Wood

ACKNOWLEDGEMENTS

My debt to colleagues and scholars, living and dead, will be apparent. To Professor Charles R. Boxer, I owe a special debt of gratitude. It was he who introduced me to the seductive forces of Portuguese overseas history and whose infectious enthusiasm for scholarship and historical research was irresistible. Professor Peter Russell awoke my interest in history as a discipline and showed me how my earlier pursuits of Romance philology and Portuguese literature were not aberrations such as to preclude training as a historian. From both I learnt that historical evidence is not limited to documentary and printed materials, and that historians should cast their nets wide in search of sources. Colleagues at The Johns Hopkins University, in ways of which they probably were not aware, have answered questions informally and discussions in the general seminar have opened up new avenues of enquiry. Professor Philip Curtin encouraged me in my world history approach, read part of the manuscript, and provided me with photographs of sailing craft on the Gambia. Professors Bill Rowe and Georg Krotkoff advised me on Chinese and Arabic terms respectively. Professor John Pocock answered many and diverse questions. Professor Richard Goldthwaite walked the galleries of the Uffizi in search of the portrait of Salvador Correia de Sá – unfortunately in vain. Ms Sharon Widomski, although characterizing my approach to the electronic age as 'dinosauran', unstintingly shared her knowledge of the heartbeat of the magic machine. Ms Sarah Springer, Ms Sharon McKinney and Ms Shirley Hipley have been patient beyond the call of duty. Ms Betty Whildon has been friend and pilot in navigating the shoals of bureaucracy.

The daunting task of selecting illustrations has been made less onerous because of the knowledgeable and collegial advice and assistance received from staffs of libraries and museums in the

Americas and Europe. Professor Carol Urness, Acting Curator of the James Ford Bell Library of the University of Minnesota made two trips to St Paul on my behalf and shared generously with me her knowledge of rare books and fascination for illustrative materials. Ms Susan Danforth of the John Carter Brown Library aided me in my cartographic searches. At the Smithsonian Institution, Ms Ann Yonemura and Ms Carol Bolon of the Sackler Gallery, Ms Bryna Freyer and Ms Amy Staples of the National Museum of African Art, and Ms. Laveta Emory and her able assistant Ms Elena Musterspaw, helped me with good grace. Ms Kate Ezra of The Metropolitan Museum of Art was most helpful. In Berlin, Dr Holger Stoecker of the Deutches Historiches Museum tracked down photographs of a stone pillar erected by Diogo Cão. The photographic services of the British Library, under Mr L. Alphonse, were expeditious as too was Ms Nancy Schmugge of The Pierpont Morgan Library, in providing photographs. The director of the Museu da Inconfidência in Ouro Prêto, Dr Rui Mourão, gave me free access to the collections and authorized photography. Photographers Eduardo Tropia in Ouro Prêto and Sr Joaquim in Sabará worked on my behalf in Brazil and Mr James T. Van Rensselaer of the photographic laboratory at The Johns Hopkins University made photographs of consistently high quality, often at short notice. Mr Michael Teague graciously offered me photographs from his collection on the Portuguese-speaking world. Dr James DiLisio, chairman of the Department of Geography of Towson State University, and his wife Kay not only drew the maps but painstakingly verified details. At The Johns Hopkins University, the staff of the Inter-Library Loan service dealt with daily, and sometimes hourly, requests with patience, courtesy and service. Mrs Janet Allen and Dr Robyn Marsack of the Carcanet Press have met the challenge of bringing order to the manuscript and illustrations.

This book saw its genesis as a lecture at the Library of Congress. Dr Graça Almeida Rodrigues, Cultural Counsellor at the Embassy of Portugal in Washington D.C., encouraged me to develop this into a lengthier manuscript. Dr Artur Teodoro de Matos arranged for me to visit Madeira where my host was Alberto Vieira, and the Azores, where I was lavishly entertained by Dr Avelino de Freitas de Meneses and his colleagues on São

Miguel and by Francisco dos Reis Maduro-Dias in Angra do Heroísmo. I owe to Dr Luís Adão da Fonseca intellectual support for the development of this project and to Dr Vasco Graça Moura and the Comissão Nacional para as Comemorações dos Descobrimentos Portugueses the financial support which has enabled me to complete this project earlier than would otherwise have been possible.

My family – Hannelore, Christopher, and Karsten – have shared their views and counsel with me, tolerated my impatience, and provided support and encouragement.

11 October 1991   A. J. R. Russell-Wood
                                        The Johns Hopkins University

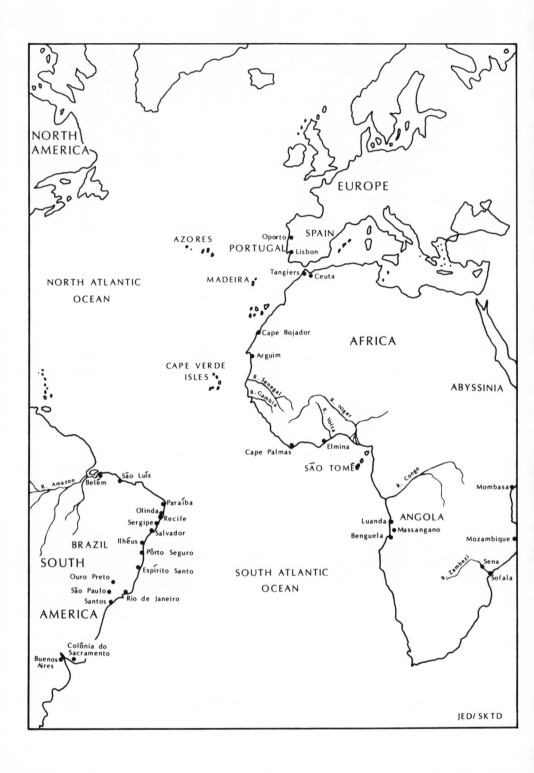

THE PORTUGUESE WORLD

ASIA

JAPAN

Hormuz

Muscat

ARABIA

Diu
Damao
Bassein
Chaul
Goa
Mangalore

INDIA

BENGAL

Hooghli

CHINA

Macao

Nagasaki Bungo

Ningpo

Cannanore
Calicut
Cranganore
Cochin
Quilon

Mannar
Colombo
Mattural

S. Thome de Meliapor

Nagappattinam
Jaffna
Okanda

CEYLON

PHILIPPINE
ISLES

Manila

Malacca

SUMATRA

BORNEO

Macassar

JAVA

FLORES

Ternate

Tidor

BANDA
ISLES

TIMOR

Malindi

INDIAN OCEAN

MADAGASCAR

AUSTRALIA

TASMANIA

COMMODITIES FLOW IN THE PORTUGUESE WORLD

LOCATIONS From → To	Commodities
1. Baltic–Portugal	cereals, amber, wheat
2. Germany–Portugal–Germany	metals, metal objects, arms, glass, armour – salt, wine, fruits, olive oil, hides
3. Portugal–Morocco	cloths, spices, lacquer
4. Morocco–Portugal	cereals, fruits, metals, coral, carpets, textiles
5. Madeira–Portugal	sugar, wines, dyes
6. Azores–Portugal	sugar, wines, wheat, cotton, dyes
7. Cape Verdes–Portugal	salt, maize, dye
8. Portugal–W. Europe	brazilwood, dyes, spices, ivory, peppers, sugar, wines, silks, salt, cloth, tobacco, dyewoods
9. W. Europe–Portugal	cereals, manufactured goods, woollens, textiles
10. Portugal–Italy	brazilwood, dyes, spices, ivory
11. Italy–Portugal	cereals, velvets, glass, faience
12. Portugal–Brazil	olive oil, flour, codfish, wines, tools, manufactured goods
13. Brazil–Portugal	brazilwood, sugar, gold, diamonds, hides, woods, resins, oils, cotton, tobacco, silver, beverages
14. E. Africa–Portugal	ebony, gold, ivory, coral
15. Portugal–E. Africa	cloth, glass beads
16. Brazil–W. Africa	tobacco, gold, brandy, hides, horses
17. W. Africa–Brazil	slaves, ivory
18. S. Brazil–La Plata	sugar, slaves, rice
19. La Plata–S. Brazil	silver
20. W. Africa–Portugal	slaves, ivory, gold, peppers, musk
21. Portugal–W. Africa	manufactured goods, textiles, blankets, metal objects, beads, bracelets, corn, horses, shells
22. Goa/Cochin–Bandas/Moluccas	cottons, copper
23. Bandas/Moluccas–Goa/Cochin	cloves, nutmeg, mace
24. Goa–East Africa	textiles
25. East Africa–Goa	slaves, gold, ivory
26. Goa–Hormuz	spices, silks
27. Hormuz–Goa	silver, horses
28. Goa–Portugal	spices, silks, cottons, porcelains, aromatic woods, chintzes, ivory, precious stones, perfumes, lacquer, medicinal plants
29. Portugal–Goa	bullion, copper, metals, European cloth & linens, European goods, lenses, clocks
30. Goa/Cochin–Malacca	Indian linens, cotton goods, European goods, spices, pepper, ivory, lenses, clocks
31. Malacca–Goa/Cochin	gold, copper, silks, musk, porcelain, pearls, medicinal plants, Japanese objects
32. Malacca–Macao	spices, pepper, woods, hides, European goods, Indian cloths, ivory, lenses, clocks
33. Macao–Malacca	pearls, medicinal plants, porcelain, musk, silks, copper, gold, Japanese objects
34. Macao–Nagasaki	European goods, gold, silks, porcelains, musk
35. Nagasaki–Macao	Japanese silver, lacquerware, furniture, screens, weapons
36. Macao–Manila	Chinese silks, Indian cottons, furniture, porcelain
37. Manila–Macao	American silver

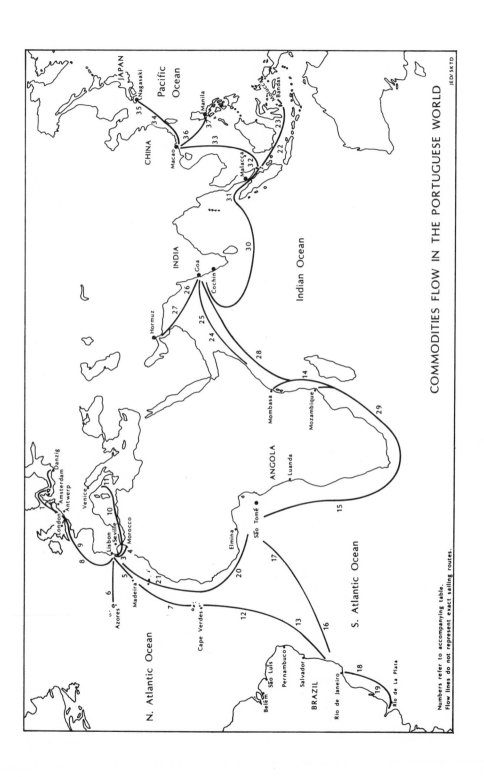

COMMODITIES FLOW IN THE PORTUGUESE WORLD

Numbers refer to accompanying table.
Flow lines do not represent exact sailing routes.

JED/SKTD

THE PORTUGUESE EMPIRE
1415–1808

INTRODUCTION:
QUINCENTENNIALS

By way of introduction, let me begin with two anecdotes. One day at breakfast, my older son Christopher (aged 11) announced: 'Daddy, I want to be a historian.' Unprepared for this conversational gambit so early in the day, undiplomatically but spontaneously, I replied: 'Good God. Why?' To which he rejoined: 'Because there is so much action.' He was right, of course. This is part of the appeal of history: people, a plot, and action. The unfailing attraction which the history of Portugal holds for me lies in the unceasing ebb and flow of people, commodities, flora and fauna, ideas, and influences, with the globe as their stage. My second anecdote derives from a recent telephone call from a composer in New York who had been commissioned to write an opera about Columbus. He asked me where it was precisely that Columbus had made his landfall. Armed with this knowledge, he would then instruct his travel agent to book him a passage so that he might compose on location. My reply was that there are at least half a dozen schools of thought as to the place of landfall but that he could vacation in the Bahamas confident that he would look out on a landscape or seascape and enjoy a climate not far removed from that experienced by Columbus and his men in 1492.

It did occur to me that no such ambiguity would have surrounded the question as to where was the first recorded landfall by Portuguese in America or, for that matter, in many parts of Africa, India, or Asia. The history of Portugal overseas is highly visible to this very day. Be it by *padrões* or other symbols, the Portuguese left records of their landfalls. *Padrões* were initially the wooden crosses, and later stone pillars, topped by a cross and bearing the royal coat of arms and an inscription, which the Portuguese placed on promontories and capes, or to mark their arrival at the mouth of a river. By so doing, they established both primacy and possession. This practice was initiated by King Dom João II with the 1482-84 voyage of Diogo Cão which revealed to the Portuguese the coasts of what are today's Gabon, Congo, and Angola. Cão placed a pillar dedicated to St George at the opening of the river Congo (still known as the Ponta do Padrão) and another pillar dedicated to St Augustine at his most southerly point (13° 25' S), the former Cabo do Lobo and now known as Cabo de Santa Maria. The traveller willing to travel to the Yellala rapids 100 miles upstream on the river Congo, can discern a carving in the rock made by Diogo Cão and his men on his second voyage (1485-86) when they reached the furthest point of their travels up-river. This depicts the arms of Portugal, a cross, an inscription, and initials and names cut in the rock. Cão set up two further pillars: one at Cabo Negro, the north headland of the bay of Porto Alexandre, and the other at Cabo Padrão (Kaap Kruis or Cape Cross) at 21° 46' South, on the north coast of today's Namibia. With the exception of the last, which was removed to Berlin by the Germans and is now in the Deutsches Historisches Museum in Berlin, fragments of the other pillars are in the Sociedade de Geografia in Lisbon. Bartolomeu Dias left three pillars and Vasco da Gama six on his first voyage to India. A visitor to Kenya can walk out on a promontory at Malindi and examine the pillar and cross raised by Vasco da Gama and still visible to this day. A mere fifteen years later, in 1514, Jorge Álvares placed a *padrão* on Lin Tin (named by the Portuguese Tamão) island in the middle of the Pearl River entrance to Canton.

Shores washed by the south Atlantic bear witness to a Portuguese presence in the early sixteenth century. In Brazil, the Cidade Alta in Pôrto Seguro is home to a marker raised in 1503 by Gonçalo Coelho on his way to India. There also are ruins of a chapel built on the Outeiro da Glória by men of the cloth who accompanied the expedition and whose charge it was to convert the Indians and minister to the Portuguese. On the other side of the Atlantic, in Congo, are the ruins of the sixteenth-century church, all that remains of the oldest European building in subequatorial Africa, together with vestiges of fortifications introduced by the Portuguese into the capital of the old kingdom of Congo, São Salvador do Congo. Chapels, churches, forts, administrative buildings – many in ruins or reduced merely to their foundations – on the coastboards of the Atlantic Ocean, Indian Ocean, South China Sea, and Pacific, bear testimony to the pioneering presence of the Portuguese.

With the quincentennial of Columbus' famous landfall in the New World receding into the recent past, it is well to bring a sense of perspective to this historical event with the realization that the years 1987 to 2000 AD embrace the quincentennials of, *inter alia*, evangelization of the Congo, opening by Europeans of the south-east passage around the Cape of Good Hope, the first maritime voyage from Europe to India, and the first contact by Europeans with the Tupinambá and Tupinikin of Brazil. In all cases, the protagonists were Portuguese. Nor need such quincentennial celebrations end in the year 2000. Future quincentennial dates can include: 2014, first European maritime trade mission (Jorge Álvares) to China; 2020, opening by the Portuguese captain Fernão de Magalhães of the south-west passage around the southernmost promontory of the South American continent; 2042-43, first landing by Europeans (Portuguese) in Japan; 2049, establishment of crown government in Brazil and the beginning of the Jesuit mission to Japan; 2052, publication of the first *Década* of João de Barros (with subsequent volumes in 1553, 1563, and 1615). It would be easy to multiply 'firsts' by Portuguese in terms of encounters with cultures hitherto unknown or only known by hearsay to Europeans: first descriptions by Europeans of other peoples, as of Bushmen of East Africa; primacy as emissaries and ambassadors to courts of princes, sultans, and emperors; first missionaries and priests to convert people to Catholicism (and sometimes train indigenous clergy) in regions where Islam, Hinayana and Mahayana Buddhism, Hinduism, Confucianism, ancestor worship, and fetishistic and shamanistic cults prevailed; first commercial envoys; first accredited European ambassadors, as to Japan in 1647; first to witness and describe customs, rites, lands and seas, flora and fauna, and objects and phenomena of scientific interest previously unknown to Europeans. By extending the 'known' world as perceived by Europeans, the Portuguese also served as agents for change who made not only Portugal and Europe, but also Africa, Asia, and America, part of a global system of exchange.

'Portugal is a province of Spain, isn't it?' 'The capital of Brazil is Buenos Aires.' 'They speak Spanish in Brazil.' 'Very few people speak Portuguese: it's a Spanish dialect.' Such statements testify to the ignorance concerning the Portuguese-speaking world. Consultation of the index of a recently published compendious (1536 pages) volume modestly entitled *A History of World Societies* (by John P. McKay, Bennett D. Hill, John Buckler. Boston: Houghton Mifflin, 1984) reveals only ten references for the span 1415-1975 under 'Portugal'. The index to the Pelican *History of the World* (Revised edition. Harmondsworth: Penguin Books, 1983) by J. M. Roberts gives a better idea of the dynamic of the Portuguese seaborne empire with references under 'Portugal' to 'trading ships', 'interest in Persia', 'trade with India', 'in China', 'in Japan', 'maritime expeditions', and 'commercial imperialism'. Labourers in the field of Latin American history are resigned to textbooks purporting to be histories of Spain and Portugal in the New World, only to discover that the Portuguese part has about the same ratio to the Spanish as has the visible part of an iceberg to the bulk under water, namely one ninth. In the 'Age of European Discoveries', how many Portuguese have not been denied the credit due to them by casual erasure of distinctions between Diego and Diogo, Juan and João, Gonzalez and Gonçalves, and Castilianization of Portuguese names. Whereas few would fail to recognize the Portuguese nationality of Vasco da Gama, that other great Portuguese who realized the dreams of Columbus by sailing west to reach the East, pioneered the south-west passage, and whose *Victoria* traversed the south-east passage to circumnavigate the globe, has become an international commodity: to the English, Ferdinand Magellan; to the Spanish, Fernando de Magallanes; whose glory was sung by an Italian squire of Vicenza named Antonio Pigafetta in an account published in French (Paris, 1525) under the title *Le Voyage et navigation, faict par les Espaignolz es Isles de Mollucques.* How many would recognize his Portuguese name of Fernão de Magalhães? Other Portuguese who sailed in the service of Castile included João Dias de Solis, killed in 1515 after reconnoitring the mouth of the Río de la Plata, the pilot Estêvão Gomes who was commissioned (1525) by Charles I of Spain to find the north-west passage in which he failed but sailed the coast of North America from Newfoundland to the Chesapeake, and João Rodrigues Cabrilho (1542-43), the Portuguese pilot who reached California and explored the San Francisco Bay. It was a native of Evora, Pedro Fernandes de Queirós, who was chief pilot for Alvaro de Mendaña in his disastrous attempt to settle the Solomon islands, but whose dream was to discover the Antarctic continent. Sailing from Callao in 1605 he failed to realize his dream, but in 1606 did 'discover' islands (Duff group) while crossing the Pacific, and the New Hebrides which he named Australia del Espirito Santo and of which he took possession in the name of King Philip III of Spain. How is it that every schoolboy of the English-speaking world can rattle off the names of Hernán Cortés, Francisco Pizarro, Hernando de Soto, that indefatigable trekker Alvar Núñez Cabeza de Vaca, Vasco Núñez de Balboa, Juan Ponce de León and his search for the 'Fountain of Youth', and others of their ilk? And yet, when questioned about the pantheon of Portuguese explorers, that selfsame schoolboy would be hard pressed to name one other than the anglicized and inappropriately named Henry 'the Navigator'.

All the blame cannot be laid at the doorstep of Winifred Sackville Stoner, Jr, whose poem (1919) 'The History of the United States' contained the immortal lines:

> In fourteen hundred and ninety-two,
> Columbus sailed the Ocean Blue.

The question of 'When did Columbus become a hero?' (and,

one might add, 'for whom, and why?') is intriguing. In the United States, the tercentennial (1792) of his voyage was celebrated in Boston and New York. The first public monument erected to Columbus in the Americas was raised in Baltimore in 1792. The Columbus Day celebration in many cities of the United States has no counterpart for a Portuguese navigator. That 1989 marked the quincentennial of 'evangelization and meeting of cultures' ('cinco séculos de evangelização e encontro de culturas') passed unnoticed outside of Portugal, where a mass was said by the Archbishop of Lisbon in the Monastery of the Jerónimos on 26 November, and the Vatican, which issued a papal announcement. Yet that was but the first step in evangelization extending from Ambon to the Amazon and whose most spectacular success – the establishment of the Japan mission which was to culminate in the conversion of some 300,000 Japanese – will celebrate its 450th anniversary in 1999. Did not Vasco da Gama issue in a new era as momentous as that heralded by the Columbus landfall in the Bahamas? In neither case were the pioneering voyages for which they are celebrated to be as important as the aftermath.

Today, when Columbomania (to coin Richard Kagan's expression) is sweeping parts of Western Europe and the American continent, and arousing an interest as consuming to some sectors of the population as the recollection of 'discovery' and its legacy is distasteful to other no less substantial sectors, my purpose here will be two-fold: first, to bring perspective by placing the voyages of Columbus within the broader framework not only of a Portuguese age of discoveries, but also of the global nature of the Portuguese series of initiatives; secondly, to emphasize the sheer dynamic of the Portuguese enterprise which transcended the limitations of individuals and constraints of time and space.

This small book is not intended to be a history of the Portuguese enterprise overseas, as implied in the sub-title, but to be precisely what the main title states, namely taking movement and mobility as a unifying theme which characterized the Portuguese in Africa, Asia, and America. In so doing, I have not focused on the military or political dimension of the Estado da India which has so occupied historians, nor on missions from the Amazon to Japan, nor on commercial ventures, and certainly not on the administration of empire. These aspects have been ably covered by others. So too are there now available adequate histories of the Portuguese in India, in Japan, in China, in Africa, and in Brazil. Taking movement as my underlying and unifying theme has freed me to cross oceans, to move from one continent to another, and escape within reason the tyranny of chronology. Selection of the themes of transportation, people, commodities, flora and fauna, and ideas, to illustrate this world on the move reflects the diversity, breadth, and balance between competing interests and priorities. By treating the Portuguese from a global perspective, I hope to counterbalance the scholarly proclivity to compartmentalize their activities into discrete geographical regions. I have also sought to emphasize that on their global stage the Portuguese acted in concert with, and not isolated from, those peoples with whom they came into contact. If I succeed in stimulating readers to share in that same sense of fascination which the history of Portuguese overseas holds for me, then this book will have served its purpose.

CHAPTER I
PORTUGAL AND THE
'AGE OF DISCOVERIES'

While it would be entertaining to include a Portuguese among the pantheon of Irish saints, Norse explorers, Welsh princes, Genoese, Castilians, Catalans, and others who – intentionally or driven by storms – travelled into the Atlantic from the eighth century onwards, for practical purposes the Portuguese voyages of exploration – official and unofficial – started in 1419. They continued, with varying degrees of intensity, and running the gamut from those well-organized under State aegis to haphazard individual enterprises, for a century and a half. It is not my purpose here to retell the story of the explorations and haven-finding skills of the Portuguese. For my immediate purpose a succinct chronological listing of how the Portuguese inexorably pushed forward the frontiers of European knowledge and established a permanent European presence in

Africa, Asia, and the Americas, will suffice.

The Portuguese made the first recorded landfalls on the uninhabited Atlantic islands of Madeira (c.1419), the Azores (c.1427), Cape Verdes (1456-60), St Helena and Ascension (1501-1502), and Tristão da Cunha (c. 1506). By 1500, they had probably voyaged to Greenland, Labrador, and Newfoundland. By the 1520s they attempted settlement on Cape Breton island, and on Nova Scotia by mid-sixteenth century. But their major achievements were in more southerly latitudes. It was the Portuguese who overcame the physical and psychological barriers of two capes: Gil Eanes who rounded the promontory of Cape Bojador (not to be confused with Cape Nun which is 200 miles northeast) in 1434, thereby opening the way to the upper Niger, Senegal, and Guinea; and the better known Bartolomeu Dias, whose rounding of the Cape of Good Hope in 1488 demonstrated that entry could be made into the Ptolemaic land-locked waters of the Indian Ocean. The Portuguese made extraordinary exploratory progress in the intervening half century, averaging slightly more than one degree southwards each year: 1435, crossed the Tropic of Cancer; 1460s, Gulf of Guinea; 1473, crossed the Equator; 1482, Congo river; 1485-6, 1° 17' North of the Tropic of Capricorn. In his outward voyage of 1497, Vasco da Gama followed in the wake of his predecessors to Santiago in the Cape Verdes, then pioneered his own route south and southwest before catching the westerlies which carried him east to make his landfall at St Helena Bay on the west coast of South Africa. He proceeded around the Cape of Good Hope, reached Natal on Christmas Day, and entered the well travelled routes of coastal East Africa. The fortuitous landfall in Brazil by Pedro Álvares Cabral in 1500 was a minor diversion in the move toward the consolidation of a Portuguese presence in India and beyond in the first quarter of the sixteenth century.[1]

The half century after Vasco da Gama's arrival in Calicut (May 1498) was characterized by trade and missionary activities rather than exploration *per se* in the East. The first commercial expedition by Europeans to the Clove Islands was Portuguese, and arrived in the Bandas and Moluccas in 1512. Two years later, Jorge Álvares headed the first European sea-based mission to Canton. Portuguese were the first Europeans to sail to New Guinea in 1525. A Portuguese was the first European to see the coast of Chosen in 1578, and Portuguese were the first Europeans to visit Korea. The case has been argued for the Portuguese having made the short hop from Timor and to have been the first Europeans to visit the east coast of Australia two and a half centuries before Captain Cook.[2] Three Portuguese were probably the first Europeans to arrive in Japan in 1542-43, passengers on a Chinese junk swept there by storm. We shall have occasion to see later that Portuguese adventurers and missionaries were probably the first Europeans to enter remote areas from the Zambezi to Tibet and from the Atlantic coast to the Andes.

This bare-bones chronology of Portuguese achievement underlines the following. First, this was a protracted effort sustained over more than a century. Secondly, it touched all continents with the exception of Antarctica and possibly Australia, and Portuguese vessels left wakes on all the oceans and major seas of the world. Thirdly, the Portuguese were exposed to a diversity of political regimes and commercial practices, as well as to all major religions. Finally, the Portuguese experienced a series of 'encounters' (as it is now fashionable to call them) over more than a century in Africa, Asia, as well as in America, whose complexity and variety makes the Spanish experience in the Americas and the Philippines pale by comparison.

If I appear to over-emphasize the time span of more than a century which may legitimately be regarded as a Portuguese age of discovery (and by this I mean the first sightings by Portuguese of what, to them, were new lands), it is to assert how important it is to consider the Portuguese global endeavour as an entity and to discourage fragmentation. The history of Portugal beyond Europe is vulnerable on this score for two reasons which have more to do with the nature of historical studies and historical methodology, than with the Portuguese. The first has been the tendency on the part of scholars to specialize in research into the history of the Portuguese experience in a single continent or region. The reader can learn much from monographs with such titles as *Portugal in Africa*, *Portuguese in South-East Africa*, *Portuguese Brazil*, *Portugal in China*, *The Portuguese in India*, and *Portuguese Rule in Ceylon*. But the price paid is loss of sight of the whole and diminished appreciation of the global scope of the Portuguese enterprise. The second results from over-zealous attempts at periodization. A sampling of such forced periodizations would include the following: to make the era of Portuguese discoveries concurrent with the life span of the infante Dom Henrique (1394-1460); to regard 1498 as the end of an era; or, arbitrarily, to posit the years 1519-22 with the global circumnavigation by the *Victoria* of Magellan's armada, as the end of the age of discoveries. Such an approach, namely linking historical periodization to landfalls, is to miss the quintessence of the Portuguese overseas experience. Many developments occurred concurrently in different geographical theatres. For the earlier period, the quest for information about Prester John and the trans-Saharan camel routes was a significant motivating force. For the later period, the breakthrough by Bartolomeu Dias into the Indian Ocean coincided with at least three less publicized but no less important overland intelligence gathering missions sent by King Dom João II to acquire information on Prester John and the spice routes.

The desire for knowledge about gold, Prester John, and spices, spurred Portuguese probings and more formal expeditions overland within continental Africa. In the 1480s, Portuguese reached Timbuktu and Mali to acquire information on the gold routes. In 1486, Dom João II dispatched João Afonso de Aveiro to penetrate the hinterland of the 'slave rivers'. He was well received by the Oba in Benin City, and it was agreed that the chief of Ughoton would accompany him back to Portugal. The Maltese-type crosses the chief carried awoke great interest at the Portuguese court and spurred hopes (unfounded) of contacts with the Prester. In 1514 and 1515, the Oba sent emissaries to Dom Manuel and in 1515 the first Portuguese missionaries arrived in Benin, one of the Oba's sons was baptized, and taught to read, and a start made on the building of a church. This, and further attempts at conversion, appear to have met with little lasting success. Other expeditions were to penetrate the Congo and Angola by the 1530s. In East Africa, stories of gold led the authorities in Sofala to dispatch António Fernandes, an exile (*degredado*), sometime ship's carpenter and carpenter of the fort at Sofala, whose special qualification was his local language skills which led him to be the official interpreter for the fort, to make two extended journeys in 1514 and 1515 through the northern part of present-day Zimbabwe and in the kingdom of Monomotapa, in all some 300 miles inland. He reported on peoples (Bushmen with 'tails'), river systems, Muslim trading fairs, the trade in copper ingots from the Congo and, most importantly, on the gold fields of Matabeleland and his recommendation of the use of the southern route along the Sabi river to penetrate the interior.[3] But, among these individual efforts or more formal expeditions, one stands out for the extent of its reach.

This was the Covilhã-Paiva intelligence gathering mission.[4] Already, at the end of 1485 or in early 1486 the king had dispatched two emissaries – one Father António de Lisboa and the other Pero de Montarroio – to make contact with the Prester. They reached Jerusalem but their inability to speak Arabic frustrated their mission and they returned to Portugal. Nothing daunted, in May of 1487 Dom João II dispatched Pero de Covilhã and Afonso de Paiva. Covilhã was superbly qualified, having an excellent knowledge of Arabic gained during several royal commissions to North Africa. They travelled, disguised as moorish merchants, to Alexandria and Cairo, reaching Aden in mid-1488. Paiva headed to Ethiopia, where he died. But, between 1487 and 1492, Covilhã took boat for Cannanore and visited Calicut and Goa, before sailing for Sofala, travelling up the coast to Hormuz and Aden, and thence to Cairo. In Cairo he met two Jewish emissaries sent in search of Paiva and Covilhã by the king – one Josepe, a shoemaker from Lamego who had already allegedly been in Baghdad and had told Dom João II of the Persian Gulf and spice trade, and the other a rabbi named Abraham from Beja. Covilhã handed his report to Josepe whose orders were to take it to the king. This report contained details of the origin of, and trade in, eastern spices, and the observation that there was a maritime route from 'the seas of Guinea' to Sofala and Madagascar. Following the royal orders, Covilhã and Abraham travelled to Aden and the Persian Gulf where they separated. Abraham left for Aleppo. Covilhã set about fulfilling his remaining royal charge, namely to go to Ethiopia. This he accomplished by way of Jiddah, Mecca, Medina, Mount Sinai, taking boat from Tor to Zeila, and then travelling through rough mountainous terrain to the court of Prester John where he was held and died in 1526.

It is not known for certain (although historians including João de Barros and Damião Peres have assumed delivery) whether Dom João received Covilhã's report or whether rabbi Abraham returned to Portugal. Already, in 1488, an Ethiopian priest had travelled from Rome to Portugal, where he was received at court, and given letters of friendship from Dom João II to the Prester. There were follow-ups to the Covilhã embassy. When the Portuguese seized Socotra in 1507, Tristão da Cunha sent the priest João Gomes to Ethiopia, where he remained.[5] An emissary named Matheus from the regent Queen Elena carrying letters including an offer of a joint military offensive against the Turks in the Red Sea, a request for technicians to divert the Nile, and presents, reached Lisbon – albeit via Chaul, Goa, and Cannanore – in February 1514. He was well received by king Dom Manuel to whom he presented a piece of the True Cross. Catholic Europe and the Portuguese court were excited by this appearance, coming on the heels of news of Albuquerque's victories in India and conquest of Malacca, and the Portuguese capture of Azemmour in Morocco in 1513. Pope Leo X sent Dom Manuel the consecrated golden rose, beatified Dona Isabel, and established the diocese of Funchal. He also issued two bulls giving the Order of Christ spiritual jurisdiction over overseas ecclesiastical benefices and confirming the royal rights over all empires, cities, coasts, and properties, already recovered or to be acquired from 'the infidels'.

In 1515, the king dispatched an embassy to Ethiopia headed by Duarte Galvão. This was delayed in India, further delayed by the death of Galvão on Kamaran island in the Red Sea, and subsequent return of Matheus and other members of the embassy to Goa. In 1520 Dom Rodrigo de Lima headed a new mission, which numbered friar Francisco Álvares and Matheus, who died shortly after landing in Ethiopia, and was well received by the Negus Lebna Dengel (David II). Dom Rodrigo de Lima and his twelve companions remained in Ethiopia for six years. In July 1527 Dom Rodrigo, friar Francisco Álvares and an Ethiopian priest Zagazabo (the emperor's emissary to the king) arrived in Lisbon. They carried four letters from the emperor which variously declared obedience to the pope, expressed surprise that no other Christian ruler had contacted the emperor, suggested joint military strikes against the Turks, and requested technical assistance. These were accompanied by a gold and silver crown for the king. Dom João III was less preoccupied with Ethiopia than had been Dom Manuel and did not respond in a timely (ten

13

years!) manner and the Negus sent a second ambassador to Lisbon who arrived by early 1538. This was a Portuguese physician, João Bermudes, who had accompanied the Lima mission and, by his own description, been appointed patriarch of the Abyssinian Coptic Church. Indirectly, this embassy and subsequent news of the death of Lebna Dengel and the prospect of domination of a Christian kingdom by Islam in the persons of Turkish troops were enough to spur the Portuguese to launch an expeditionary force in 1541 under Dom Cristóvão da Gama. This will be described later: suffice it to say here that it was ultimately to be successful after suffering heavy losses.[6]

To see the Portuguese experience solely in terms of a maritime chronology is to diminish the importance of Portuguese terrestrial initiatives. The tropical forests and local peoples of the hinterland of the Gambia and Senegal were not conducive to attempts to travel inland but, from the mid-fifteenth century onwards, there are reports of Portuguese expeditions to the interior. From an early date the Portuguese put ashore *lançados*, or exiles, who probably reached Timbuktu during the reign of Dom João II (1481-95). Emissaries were later dispatched by the king to Timbuktu, to Mali, and possibly to rulers on the upper Volta. In the 1490s, there was penetration inland in the Congo. In 1520 Dom Manuel issued a *regimento* to Baltasar de Castro and Manuel Pacheco to travel to the interior of Angola. Six years later, Baltasar de Castro reported to his monarch of his explorations on the upper Congo river. In East Africa, António Fernandes was not alone in travels to the interior. For the most part these were made by Portuguese who had become disaffected with life in the coastal forts and a report of 1528 referred to 'hundreds' of Portuguese living in the interior. Most traded, some had families, some discovered minerals, others proved themselves as warriors, but under the umbrella name of *sertanejos* ('backwoodsmen') they penetrated the interior of south-east Africa.[7] Not only in Africa, but in Persia, India, and Asia, Portuguese travelled extensively by land, even entering Tibet and Nepal. In the western hemisphere, as early as 1524 the Portuguese Aleixo Garcia, who had accompanied the ill-fated expedition of João Dias de Solis, sent back silver samples from the Incan empire eight years before the arrival of Francisco Pizarro and his 168 men in the valley of Cajamarca. Later the *bandeirantes*, or pioneers from São Paulo, carried a Portuguese presence to the Spanish viceroyalty of Peru and to the altiplano of what is now Bolivia and Colombia.

The Portuguese were entering a world, most importantly in the case of East and West Asia, which had not been in mutual isolation from western Europe, as was the case of the American continent and Australia. This does not negate the importance of what were in many cases first contacts: commercial treaties with Muslim sultans in the Moluccas; missionary activities in India, Bengal, China, and Japan; diplomatic overtures to Siam, Borneo, and a host of other states. 'Discoveries' are not measured by landfalls alone. In navigational terms, repeatedly in the early sixteenth century Portuguese crossed hitherto uncharted waters for Europeans with the assistance of native pilots: Arabs for the Indian Ocean; Arab, Gujarati, Javanese, and Malay, for voyages from Malabar ports to Ceylon, Malacca, the Sunda islands, Java, the Moluccas, Sumatra, and Siam; and Chinese for the Malacca-Macao-Japan run.[8] The Portuguese must be credited with diplomatic, commercial, and religious initiatives in West and East Africa, India, East Asia, and Indonesia, in the fifteenth and early sixteenth centuries. Such initiatives were the fruits of knowledge and experience acquired in several continents and over a protracted span of time.

The depth, breadth, and richness of intelligence-gathering by the Portuguese was a notable characteristic in the formation of their world. This has been discussed in the context of acquiring knowledge of lands, peoples, and commodities beyond Europe, but there was a storehouse of knowledge available within Europe. Much derived from a Graeco-Judeo-Arab scientific and mathematical tradition (both theoretical and applied) and knowledge of cosmography. The result was a wealth of astronomical, scientific, mathematical, and geographical knowledge, on which the Portuguese could draw. Apparently paradoxically, concurrently there existed a no less rich tradition of veneration for the marvellous, shown by the popularity of mirabilia and bestiaries: the Sea of Darkness; mythical kings; monstrous peoples; fantastic animals and birds; deaf peoples near the cataracts of the Nile. The bridge between empirical knowledge and the marvellous was fraught with pitfalls and even the best could slip between the cracks.

One such was Duarte Pacheco Pereira. His *Esmeraldo de Situ Orbis,* which ironically did not see the light of day until publication in 1892 to commemorate Columbus' landfall although probably written between 1505 and 1508, is a good example. This is a superb statement on nautical science, instrumentation, and coastal navigation, enhanced by a detailed, eye-witness account with bearings and distances of the coast from the Straits of Gibraltar to the river Gabon. And yet, accompanying all the scientific truths and first-hand accounts is an abundance of references to classical, biblical and ecclesiastical authorities and an undeniably medieval quality. Too close a reading of and trust in the classics led Pacheco Pereira to confuse the Nile and Sudanese river systems. But the sharpest contrast between the Renaissance observer and precise recorder of latitudes and distances on the one hand, and inheritor of the uncritical acceptance by medieval minds of classical excesses on the other, concerned birds and animals. After a detailed account of the Senegal and commentary within the bounds of accuracy on pythons, crocodiles, and ivory, Pacheco Pereira remarks on a monstrosity of such rarity as to be seen but once in a decade:

> There are other snakes a quarter of a league long, with thickness, eyes, mouth and teeth in proportion; there are very few of these this size, but when they reach the size I mentioned their instinct is to leave their native lakes and make for the sea. On their way thither they work much damage, and multitudes of birds fall upon them and pick at their flesh, which is of an incredible softness, and when they reach the sea they dissolve in the water.

Duarte Pacheco Pereira was here victim of his own extensive reading and knowledge.[9]

A contemporary, Father Francisco Álvares, who accompanied the Portuguese embassy to Ethiopia in 1520 and wrote an account of his travels and six years residence in the country, had no such temptation to resort to classical or mythical references. Whereas he did indeed err – as in his reference to tigers – he steered clear of the fantastic. He stated clearly in his preface where he stood:

> I decided to write down everything that happened to me on

1 Upper part of the limestone pillar (*padrão*) placed by Diogo Cão on Cabo Padrão, now Kaap Kruis, in south-west Africa during his voyage of 1485-1486. Depicts the coat of arms of the Portuguese king Dom João II (front) and an inscription in Latin and Portuguese (back).

Deutsches Historisches Museum, Berlin.

2 Lisbon.
Georg Braun and Franz Hogenberg, *Civitates Orbis Terrarum* (Cologne, 1572).

S. GEORGII Oppidum MINA nuncupatum, quod Lusitaniæ Regis iussu D. Joannis II Anno salutis, 1482 in Genea ædificatum est, quò Mauri mercatores aurum infectum apportent, recipientes à Christianis, rubrum, ac flauum, item lineum pannū, & similes ipsis gratas, conuenientesque merces.

Trium Regum

S. Iacobi

Pagus

S. Georgy

3 Elmina.
Georg Braun and Franz Hogenberg, *Civitates Orbis Terrarum* (Cologne, 1572).

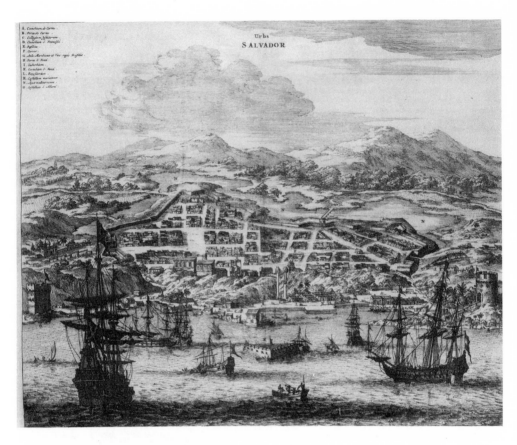

4   Salvador in 1671.
John Ogilby, *America. Being the Latest and Most Accurate Description of the New World* (London, 1671).

ORMVS.

5   Hormuz. Georg Braun and Franz Hogenberg, *Civitates Orbis Terrarum* (Cologne, 1572).

6   Calicut. (*above*) 7   Goa. (*below*)
Georg Braun and Franz Hogenberg, *Civitates Orbis Terrarum* (Cologne, 1572).

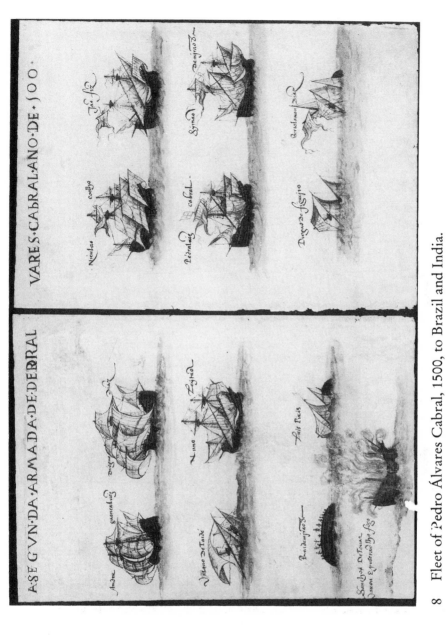

8   Fleet of Pedro Álvares Cabral, 1500, to Brazil and India.
     From 'O Livro de Lisuarte de Abreu', The Pierpont Morgan Library, New York (M. 525).

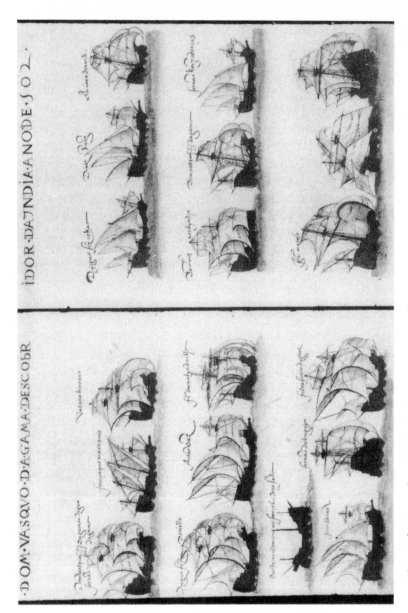

9 Fleet of Vasco da Gama, 1502 voyage to India.
From 'O Livro de Lisuarte de Abreu', The Pierpont Morgan Library, New York (M. 525).

10 Vila de Cametá on the day of arrival (19 January 1784) of Martinho de Souza e Albuquerque, governor and captain-general of the captaincies of Grão-Pará e São José do Rio Negro. Alexandre Rodrigues Ferreira, *Viagem filosófica.*

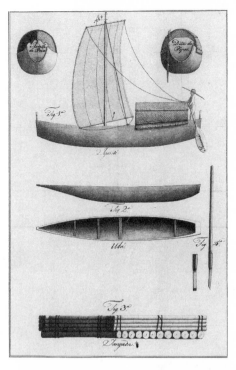

11 Native American canoes (*igarité* and *ubá*) and raft (*jangada*) in the north of Brazil.

12 Native American canoe construction in the north of Brazil.
Both from Alexandre Rodrigues Ferreira, *Viagem filosófica.*

13 A raft (*jangada*) in Brazil.

14 Crossing a river in Brazil.

15 Fishing canoe in Brazil.
  13–15 from Henry Koster, *Travels in Brazil*. 2 vols. 2nd edition (London: Longman, Hurst, Rees, Orme, and Brown, 1817).

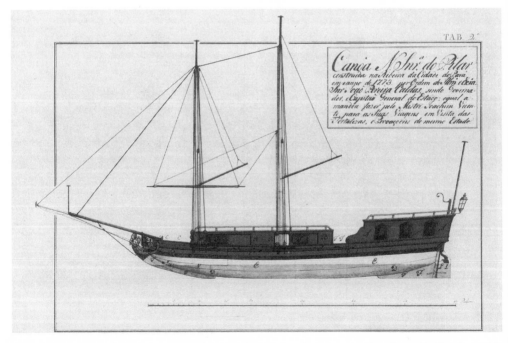

16 Canoa Nossa Senhora do Pilar, built in the ship-yard of Belém do Pará, 1773.
  Alexandre Rodrigues Ferreira, *Viagem filosófica*.

17 (*left*) Construction of a pirogue at Barra Point on the north bank of the entrance to the river Gambia.

18 (*below*) A pirogue at Barra Point on the north bank of the entrance to the river Gambia.

19 Portuguese noble lady in India being carried in a palanquin and accompanied by her slaves.
Mid-sixteenth-century water-colour by an unknown Portuguese artist. Biblioteca Casanatense, Rome. MS 1889.

20 Upper class lady being carried in a luxury *cadeirinha* by her liveried slaves, Rio de Janeiro. Late eighteenth century.
Water-colour by Carlos Julião.

21 *Cadeirinha de arruar* of late eighteenth-century Catas Altas in Minas Gerais, Brazil.
From Museu da Inconfidência, Ouro Prêto, #343.

22 *Liteira* of carved wood to carry two, reputedly owned by the Baron of Amparo, Minas Gerais, late eighteenth century.
Museu da Inconfidência, Ouro Prêto, #345.

23   Hammock slung from a pole. Early nineteenth-century Brazil.

24   Cart modified for personal use in early nineteenth-century Brazil.
     23 and 24: Drawings by Guillobel.

25 The chair and its successor the chaise in front of the British Mission, Rio de
Janeiro, 1819-1820.
From *Views and Costumes of the City and Neighbourhood of Rio de Janeiro, Brazil, from
Drawings taken by Lieutenant Chamberlain, Royal Artillery, During the Years 1819 and 1820*
(London: Columbian Press, 1822).

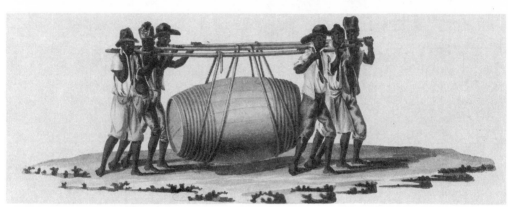

26 Dolly pushed and pulled by a team of slaves in early nineteenth-century Rio de Janeiro. (*above*)

27 Team of slaves carrying a barrel. Early nineteenth-century Rio de Janeiro. (*middle*)
Both from drawings by Guillobel.

28 *Cangalheta*. A saddle of wood and leather for transportation of gold and valuables in eighteenth-century Minas Gerais. (*left*)
Museu da Inconfidência, Ouro Prêto, #260.

29 Pedlar carrying kitchen utensils and pots. Early nineteenth-century Rio de Janeiro. (*left*)
Drawing by Guillobel.

30 Pedlars carrying sugar-cane, fruits, and birds for sale. Note the white child carried by one pedlar. Late eighteenth-century Rio de Janeiro. (*below*)
Water-colour by Carlos Julião.

31 (*above*) Pedlars in the Largo da Glória, Rio de Janeiro, in the early nineteenth century. Note the alms collector with an icon and the player of a musical instrument originating in the Congo.

32 (*below*) Pedlar and his slave in late colonial Rio de Janeiro. Note the leper with his leg wrapped in a banana leaf to reduce swelling.

33 (*above*) Muleteers (*tropeiros*) from São Paulo. Note the use of
ponchos. 34 (*below*) Ox cart on Beira da Lapa, Rio de Janeiro. Early
nineteenth century. The design for these primitive carts had been
carried from Portugal.
31–34 from *Views and Costumes of the City and Neighbourhood of Rio de Janeiro*.

35 Vasco da Gama.
    'O Livro de Lisuarte de Abreu', The Pierpont Morgan Library, New York (M.525).

36 Afonso de Albuquerque.
Sloane 197. British Library.

37 Martim Afonso de
Sousa.
'O Livro de Lisuarte de
Abreu'. The Pierpont Morgan
Library, New York (M.525).

38 Diogo do Couto, 1542-
1616.
An engraving in his *Década
VII*, 1616.

39 Portuguese noble in India, followed by entourage. Mid-sixteenth
century.
From Biblioteca Casanatense, Rome. MS 1889.

40 Convicts and galley slaves in late colonial Rio de Janeiro carrying
water and provisions for their fellow jailbirds and with bone objects
for sale.
From *Views and Costumes of the City and Neighbourhood of Rio de Janeiro*.

41 Pendant (brass) of Portuguese horseman. Nigerian-Edo. Court of
Benin. Sixteenth–eighteenth century. Height 6.25".
The Metropolitan Museum of Art 1991 (1991. 17.39).

42 Pendant with European and horse. Eighteenth–nineteenth century.
Edo peoples. Nigeria. Cast copper alloy. Height 8".
National Museum of African Art, Eliot Elisofon Archives, Smithsonian Institution
(85-19-9).

43 Plaque from Benin. Multiple figures including Europeans. Mid-sixteenth–
seventeenth century. Cast copper alloy. Height 18".
National Museum of African Art, Eliot Elisofon Archives, Smithsonian Institution (82-5-3).

44 Ivory salt cellar. Double vessel in two tiers with European figures. Bini-Portuguese style. Nigeria. Early sixteenth century. The Metropolitan Museum of Art, 1972 (1972. 63).

45 Xarafo or money changer of Kingdom of Cambay. Clients include three Portuguese. Water-colour by unknown Portuguese artist. Mid-sixteenth century.
Biblioteca Casanatense, Rome. MS 1889.

46 Akbar hears a petition with a European observer. Indian
painting attributed to Manohar. Mughal period, school of
Akbar.
Freer Gallery of Art, Smithsonian Institution, Washington D.C. (Freer
60.28).

47 Chinese as depicted in a Portuguese manuscript of
the mid-sixteenth century
Biblioteca Casanatense, Rome. MS 1889.

the journey, things seen and things found, by sea and on land, and the kingdoms, lordships and provinces, cities, country houses and places where we went, and the nations and peoples, their clothes, manners and customs, whether Christians, Moors, Jews or heathens, the customs of each of them. Whatever I have been able to learn I shall vouch for as something I saw if I saw it, and if it was something I heard I shall tell it as something I heard. So I promise and swear in my soul that I shall tell no lie, but what I write I shall vouch for as the truth. If there should be any word that is not the truth it will be a slip of the pen, and not willingly said, still less written.[10]

Such information was topographical, cartographic, navigational, commercial, political, cultural, religious, social, and ethnographic. Much was to be critical to the Portuguese in their explorations and especially maritime enterprises. In four distinct instances, the Portuguese were not themselves inventors but inherited the fruits of earlier discoveries. The positioning of a central rudder on the stern post of the keel had first appeared in the Baltic in the mid-thirteenth century. Secondly, shipboard application of the magnetic needle and compass had arrived in Portugal from the Arabs and this practice has been attributed to the Chinese as early as the beginning of the twelfth century. Thirdly, the triangular lateen sail had originated in the eastern Mediterranean in the early Middle Ages. Fourthly, the portulan chart with compass or wind roses and rhumb lines had been known to Italian seamen by the early 1300s and developed from an 8 point wind rose to a 64 point instrument.[11] Portugal was very much in contact with developments elsewhere in Europe and especially the Mediterranean area through Portuguese who travelled beyond the Pyrenees and foreigners who came to Portugal. One such was Prince Dom Pedro, Duke of Coimbra and a brother of Prince Henry. From 1425-28, he travelled extensively in Europe (London, Bruges, Cologne, Vienna, Hungary, Romania, Venice, Florence, Rome, Catalonia, Aragon, and Castile) to acquire knowledge and international exposure and experience.[12] In Portugal, there were cartographers, mathematicians, and scientists of the highest order and the Portuguese had accumulated a wealth of navigational and cartographic information enabling them to sail not only along the coast of the African Atlantic, but out of sight of land to Madeira and the Azores and subsequently across the Atlantic and into the Indian Ocean. Such information was to be incorporated into the rich sailing directions known as rutters (*roteiros*) and to be complemented by hands-on Portuguese experience in the Atlantic, Indian and Pacific Oceans, China Sea and Sea of Japan, and by technical knowledge gleaned from native pilots.

If Vasco da Gama was the first to employ an Arab pilot, by name Ahmad-Ibn-Madjid, in Malindi, to guide him across the Indian Ocean, he was but establishing a precedent to be followed by sailors of various European nationalities. In 1512 the governor of Portuguese India, Afonso de Albuquerque, sent a 'piece of map' to Dom Manuel. This had been taken from a large map by a Javanese pilot which showed the coasts of Portugal, Brazil, Cape of Good Hope, Red Sea, Persian Gulf, and the Clove Islands, and included Chinese navigation and rhumbs and routes.[13] To capture Goa, Afonso de Albuquerque was ably assisted by Hindu captains and mercenaries. In their capture (1511) of Malacca, the Portuguese were assisted by Coromandel Hindu merchants who subsequently were to be important to the Portuguese in developing trade to the Malayan archipelago. When the first Portuguese fleet bound for the Moluccas left Malacca in 1511, there were Javanese pilots on board and it was preceded by a vessel carrying an influential and wealthy Muslim from Malacca to ensure that the Portuguese would be well received.[14] The large Portuguese carracks of the Macao-Nagasaki route had Chinese pilots to assist their Portuguese counterparts. Indigenous peoples of Africa, India, and Asia, met not only the physical demands – sexual, military, transportation, and labour – of Portuguese overseas, but provided them with skills, information, and intelligence, which contributed substantially to what used to be referred to as 'the expansion of Europe'. In the India-Malacca-China commercial sphere, the Portuguese were also to depend on local sources for capital for their ventures. Two continents and half a century later, Portuguese pioneers were to forsake the Brazilian littoral and move into the *sertão* of Brazil. They depended on native American guides. This was to become established practice over the next two centuries as intrepid Portuguese pushed by rivers and overland into Goiás and Mato Grosso, northwards into the Maranhão, and along the many navigable rivers of Brazil towards the Andes.

Recognition of the importance of native lore and skills permitted the Portuguese to not only cross oceans, but to become a significant presence ('control' is too strong a word) in maritime trade routes of the East. The capture of Ceuta (1415) had provided the Portuguese with a different type of information – political and commercial – about camel caravans of the western Sudan and the gold-bearing regions of the upper Niger and Senegal. From mid-fifteenth century, Portuguese were moving into Mali and Timbuktu and were travelling inland from the West African coast. By the 1550s, Portuguese had acquired an excellent knowledge of the interior of Congo and Angola and East Africa from the coast to present-day Zimbabwe. A reading of the *Décadas* of the 'Portuguese Livy', João de Barros, serves as a constant reminder of the importance given by the Portuguese to intelligence gathering. This was gained fortuitously by questioning native sources, or gleaning information from merchants, prisoners of war, pilgrims, emissaries, sailors, and even exiles, through personal observation, exhaustive reports, and was also the fruit of systematic travels of reconnaissance as had been the case of Pero de Covilhã. Albuquerque's knowledge of Ethiopia was acquired from prisoners captured by the Turks and who then fell into Portuguese hands, and by debriefing an ambassador from the Negus. The importance Albuquerque placed on intelligence was demonstrated by the elaborate cover he gave two potential envoys whom he landed at Cape Guardafui. Both were disguised as Mohammedan (one was Mohammedan, the other Portuguese) merchants and their cover was that they had been robbed by the Portuguese. The Portuguese even underwent circumcision in Malindi in preparation for his embassy, which came to nought.[15] Diplomatic missions often had the dual purpose of gathering fresh information or confirming or denying what had hitherto been mere hearsay. Frequently they remained in their countries of destination for several years, as was the case of the Portuguese embassy headed by Dom Rodrigo de Lima to Ethiopia.

The quality of the intelligence, and richness and diversity of information, are manifested in chronicles, narratives of voyages, accounts of embassies, Jesuitical letters, diaries, and official correspondence. Dignitaries of church and state, priests, missionaries, soldiers, sailors, men of science, physicians, pilots, merchants, adventurers, miners, and agriculturalists, felt compelled to write – or have written for them – accounts of their experiences. Sometimes these were first hand, written *in situ*. Others were the fruits of memory and written on return to Europe and often after a substantial lapse of time. Others revealed a tendency to embroider experiences and indulge in fantasy. Still others bore the imprint of self-promotion, defence against slander, or a strong ideological bent. That such chronicles, histories, or personal reminiscences bore the imprint of an European perspective does not detract from their importance in painting a broad canvas of political institutions, commercial potential, military strengths, religions, and social practices. What fascinates is the detail. In sixteenth-century Japan, Luís Fróis S.J., noted that, whereas in Europe doors swing on hinges, in Japan they slide. His fellow Jesuit, João Rodrigues, was intrigued by the cleanliness of privies, rituals surrounding the taking of baths, and the *kotatsu* or sunken grate. In Canton, the Dominican friar Gaspar da Cruz had two song birds which enthralled him and which were fed 'with cooked rice wrapped in the yoke of an egg, somewhat on the dry side, which deceives them into thinking they are eating little insects'.[16] Seemingly there was no facet of the human experience which escaped the lynx eyes and keen ears of the Portuguese in their peregrinations. Among this wealth of information, there are two blatant *lacunae*: the virtual absence of narratives by women, and the scarcity of records about the Portuguese by indigenous peoples of Africa, Asia, and America. This information provided the source materials for official chroniclers and historians who not only had unrestricted access to all reports entering Portugal but could draw on the rich oral testimony of those returning from overseas. In this, they were not alone. Royal advisers, military strategists, commercial planners, and even men of the cloth, counted on these sources in reaching decisions in the best interests of crown, country, and Christianity.

This brings me to an important characteristic of the Portuguese in the fifteenth and sixteenth centuries. This was their ability to put to good use the enormous data bank they had accumulated. This often took the form of diplomacy. The history of the Estado da India (which officially came into being in 1505 and embraced Portuguese territories east of the Cape of Good Hope) is studded with references to diplomatic initiatives by the Portuguese. Five manuscript books in the Goa archives known as the *Livros das Pazes e Tratados da India* (Books of Agreements and Treaties in India) contain treaties signed by the Portuguese with rulers in India, East Africa, and Asia, as well as with European powers between 1571-1856. A further twenty-two volumes contain correspondence from 1619-1842 with the *reis vizinhos*, or 'neighbouring kings' in India. In 1456, Diogo Gomes and Cà da Mosto made a treaty of 'peace and friendship' (*paz e amizade*) with the Mandinga on the Gambia.[17] In fifteenth and sixteenth-century Africa, it was usually only as a measure of last resort that the Portuguese used force to obtain their goals. In the majority of cases, establishment of 'factories' (trading stations) or building of forts was accomplished after discussion and negotiation with local potentates. Two exceptions were Gujarat and Angola. Until the Portuguese succeeded in obtaining permission (1535) to build a fort at Diu, Gujarati-Portuguese relations were hostile. Bassein (1534) and Daman (1559) also contributed to an effective Portuguese control of the Bay of Cambay, but even into the 1560s the Portuguese considered themselves at war with Gujarat.[18] In Angola the arrival of Paulo Dias de Novais in 1575 ushered in half a century of warfare. What is so amazing, and a tribute to Lusitanian powers of negotiation and diplomacy, is how little – in comparison with other European colonizing powers – the Portuguese engaged in out-and-out war. In early sixteenth-century Brazil, the Portuguese played second fiddle to the French in establishing harmonious relations with native American peoples. Also, in counterdistinction to the English and French proclivity for signing treaties with the peoples of North and South America, rarely did the Portuguese enter into such formal agreements in Brazil.

This information proved invaluable in the planning of military offensives. Clearly, the population of Portugal did not permit the manning of a global empire, let alone its maintenance over several centuries, without the ability to plan decisively. The genius of the Portuguese lay in the following: first, accurate identification of strategic and key points, both militarily and as regarded the long distance Muslim dominated trade routes, control of which was essential to Portuguese interests; secondly, assessment of how great or how small a Portuguese presence was necessary; thirdly, recognition of options or alternatives to territorial possession, settlement, building of a fort, or establishing a trading factory, but which would still provide a Portuguese presence. That the Portuguese were able to become players in Asian and Indian Ocean trade was attributable to their conquest and occupation of Goa on the west coast of India (1510), Malacca in the Malay Straits (1511), Hormuz on the Persian Gulf (1515), and the building of a fort at Colombo in 1518. The first permitted, if not exclusive control, at least a substantial Portuguese challenge to Gujarati trade domination of the routes to the Levant. The second was the key to commerce to the east with China, Japan, Indonesia, and the Spice Islands, and to the west with subsequent distribution to the Bay of Bengal and Indian Ocean. The third controlled the routes to the Levant and Persian Gulf, and the fourth was excellently placed to monitor traffic between the Sea of Oman and the Bay of Bengal. Portuguese failure to capture Aden left open the loophole of the Red Sea to Muslim trade. Control of these key points was crucial to the maintenance of a Portuguese presence in the Indian Ocean and beyond.

These were complemented by fortified trading posts (*feitorias*) and forts in East Africa (Kilwa, Sofala, Mozambique, and Fort Jesus at Mombasa), Socotra off the Gulf of Aden, Muscat on the Gulf of Oman, on the west coast of India (Angediva, Cannanore, Cochin, Chaul, Diu, Daman, Bassein), Nagappattinam on the Coromandel coast, Ceylon, the Maldive islands, Indonesia (Pacem in Sumatra), Ternate and Tidor. By 1571, there were some 40 forts or trading posts between Sofala and Nagasaki, in Indonesia, and as far as the Moluccas. It was through negotiation that the Portuguese secured extra-territorial trading rights at San Thome of Meliapore on the Coromandel coast and at Hooghly (known to the Portuguese as Ugulim) in Bengal. In the case of Macao, Portuguese control was the result of negotiation with Cantonese officials. The rights granted to the Jesuits in Nagasaki, which became the most easterly destination in Asia for Portuguese vessels, were conditional on agreement not to have a military presence. In West Africa, the first factory had been at Arguim (1445) and others followed, to be dominated by the construction (1482) of the fort of São Jorge da Mina. In North Africa, the Portuguese had strongholds in Morocco. Madeira counted the sixteenth-century fort of São Lourenço, and on São Miguel in the Azores was the fort of São Braz (1553). Dominating the Atlantic, and comparable to Malta for the Mediterranean, was the magnificent seventeenth-century fortress of São João Baptista on the island of Terceira. The Brazilian coastline is dotted with forts and fortresses of the late sixteenth and seventeenth centuries.[19]

This Portuguese hegemony was to be whittled away in the course of the seventeenth century in India and Asia by the Dutch and the English primarily but also by local leaders who reassserted themselves. In some cases the Portuguese suffered loss through war, in others they were the victims of edicts of expulsion, and in still other instances possessions or territories were ceded as the result of decisions taken at the bargaining table. The fiery combination of commerce, religion (in this case, Islam), and politics, was not an exclusively European or Catholic prerogative. Local merchants and traders from Sofala to the Moluccas and Bandas found ways to deny the Portuguese the monopoly they sought on routes and commercial networks. The Portuguese could build forts, they could impose a pass system (*cartazes*) on shipping, they could establish settlements, they might even plunder, but their presence was not as dominant as the impressive numbers of forts and settlements suggest. Muslim and other traders were in for the long-haul and they had their hands on the pulse of interlocking trade diasporas, both local and inter-oceanic, from the Levant to the East. Even on the west coast of India, non-Portuguese trade continued. In Coromandel, where the Portuguese presence was limited to Nagappattinam and San Thome of Meliapore, and in the northern part of the Bay of Bengal where they were at Hooghly, their impact was minimal. Attempts by the Portuguese to establish any degree of hegemony were thwarted by the multiplicity of routes to which cargoes could be diverted.

The strength of the Portuguese became their Achilles tendon. Coastal forts and fortresses were eminently vulnerable to being picked off, one by one. Only in a few instances could the Portuguese throw into the breach the requisite number of soldiers, supplies from hinterlands, or immediate logistic support. Let us take two examples of this vulnerability. One required reinforcements from across an ocean; the other demanded marches over

23

rugged terrain on sometimes precipitous roads, crossing a mountain barrier, and fording flooded rivers. For the relief of Luanda in 1648 from the Dutch (aided and abetted by local support), an expeditionary force was launched from Rio de Janeiro. This comprised a Portuguese contingent mostly of Lisbon jail-birds and the products of vigorous recruiting in Brazil. There were problems of acquiring salt to preserve meat supplies and raising funds to meet the costs of the expedition. The Atlantic crossing took two months and was rough. Vessels were lost, or turned back. Final success was attributable to the leadership of Salvador Correia de Sá. In the case of the French attack on Rio de Janeiro in 1711, a force of some 6,000 men (regular and militia) was raised within a week of the alarm being sounded in Minas Gerais. By forced marches they reached Rio in a month. The city had already capitulated, and the French leader Duguay-Trouin, who was more interested in profit than settlement or conquest, was satisfied to be able to sail away with full holds. This was fortunate because the Portuguese reinforcements had no wheeled vehicles, few pack animals, and inadequate supplies of powder and shot. On arrival outside Rio, any hope of retaking the city would have been ill-founded in view of the fact that munitions consisted of only four kegs of shot and no artillery.[20]

Dutch encroachments were reflected in the remorseless sequence of captures of Portuguese forts in India and Asia and the Moluccas, whereas the English focused on Portuguese holdings around the Indian Ocean and Persian Gulf. The chronology tells the story of losses to the Dutch: 1605, Spice Islands; 1641, Malacca; 1656, Colombo; 1658, Ceylon; 1660, Nagappattinam; 1662, Cranganore and Cochin. In 1622, Hormuz was lost to the Persians with English help; in 1632 Hooghly to Mughal troops. The Ya' arubi Imans of Oman – with Dutch and British assistance – captured Muscat (1650) and Mombasa (1698), and expelled the Portuguese from the East African coastal states of Pate, Pemba, Zanzibar, and Malindi. Portuguese reassertion of control in the 1720s was fleeting and, by 1730, the Omanis were firmly back in control of the Swahili coast and Mombasa. In 1634 the Portuguese were expelled from Ethiopia and in 1639 from Japan. In 1665 Bombay was ceded to the British as the dowry of Catherine of Braganza when she married Charles II of England, as too was Tangiers. The 1737-1740 campaign of the Marathas

24

resulted in their conquest of Portuguese settlements in the Province of the North reaching from Bombay to Daman. In 1778, Fernando Pó and Annobón in the Gulf of Guinea were ceded to Spain, as too was the territory of present-day Uruguay by the Treaty of San Ildefonso.[21]

There were Portuguese successes. They held off Dutch attacks (1607, 1608) on Mozambique, on Malacca (1616, 1629), on Macao (1622, 1626), and on Goa (1603 and 1610). Although São Jorge da Mina fell to the Dutch in 1637, a 1625 Portuguese expedition had delayed the process. The 1640s and 1650s saw ebb and flow in Portuguese-Dutch rivalry in West Africa. At the end of the day, the Dutch were in possession of some Portuguese settlements but the Portuguese were firmly in charge in Angola and Benguela, and the islands of São Tomé and Príncipe, thanks to the intervention of the force from Rio de Janeiro in 1648. The Portuguese were to lay the groundwork for the future Portuguese Guinea. The Azores were exceptional in that, despite repeated attacks by French, English, and Dutch from the 1530s through to 1712, when Jacques Cassart sacked Ribeira Grande, the Portuguese maintained their possession.

On the other side of the Atlantic, the Portuguese enjoyed more sustained successes. French interlopers under Villegaignon were ousted from their settlement of France Antarctique and from the Bay of Guanabara by 1567. After a decade, which had included the founding of São Luís (1594) in Maranhão and a presence in Paraíba, the French finally surrendered in 1615. This did not dissuade an attack on Rio de Janeiro in 1710 under Du Clerc, which failed, and successful attack and short occupation (September-November 1711) of René Duguay-Trouin. The English were limited to strafing coastal settlements and attacking vessels in the 1580s and 1590s and never got a foothold in Portuguese America, other than some trading posts in the Amazon in the 1590s and from which they were expelled in 1625. This trading activity in the Amazon also involved the Dutch over about the same period with the same outcome. Elsewhere the Dutch were more menacing. They held Salvador for less than a year (1624-25), but did come to control much of the north-east from Sergipe to the Maranhão from 1630-54, when they were ousted.

The eighteenth century held some respite for the Portuguese.

But in 1822, Brazil, her largest and richest colony, became independent after providing history with two examples of the relocation of power and authority. The first was in 1763 when the capital was transferred from Salvador to Rio de Janeiro. The second was in 1807-1808. The evacuation of the royal court in late 1807 from Lisbon, as the result of the Napoleonic invasion, led to its establishment in Rio de Janeiro. This gave rise to the unique circumstance of a colony being the seat of the royal court of a European nation. Not only did the arrival of the court result in an influx of people to Rio de Janeiro but the decree of 28 January 1808, opening the ports of Brazil to international trade, heralded an era of burgeoning imports and exports and a flood of European scientific expeditions, and paved the way for European migration to Brazil in the nineteenth century. The Portuguese move beyond Europe, which had begun in the fifteenth century, was to leave a legacy of momentum in America four centuries later. The fleet which had carried the Portuguese court to Brazil numbered eight ships-of-the-line, from three to five frigates, two to four brigs, and a storeship. This was accompanied from Portugal by twenty to twenty-five commercial vessels of the Brazil fleet and there were more vessels from Brazilian ports which joined the fleet and contributed to the spectacular arrival in the Bay of Guanabara. Ships and the sea were inalienable parts of the history of Portugal and her presence in the world.[22]

CHAPTER II
MOVERS: CARAVELS, CARRACKS, CARAVANS, CANOES, AND CARTS

The sea provided the nexus for this far-flung world and it is the sea which provides the context for this story of a world on the move. To the Portuguese must go the credit for initiating regular deep-water traffic between the north and south Atlantic, between the African Atlantic and South America, between western Europe and West Africa, and inter-oceanically between the Atlantic and the Indian Ocean. Once beyond the Cape of Good Hope, the Portuguese were entering a world of well-established and intensive maritime connections from East Africa and the Arabian Sea as far as Indonesia. Whereas contacts between Africa, Europe, India, and East Asia, predated the opening of the Cape of Good Hope route by Vasco da Gama, this sea route to the Indies contributed to more intensive and regular contacts and exchanges between East and West. It also significantly collapsed the time frame which had hitherto prevailed for most exchanges between western Europe and India and points further east. This new chronology also applied to maritime routes between Portugal and West Africa. Furthermore, the use of vessels brought about a revolution in the increased volume of merchandise which could be transported.

The *náo*, or carrack, plying the route from Europe to India and thence to Malacca, China, and Japan had antecedents in the Italian merchant vessels of the later Middle Ages, but the Portuguese had placed their own imprint on them. They usually had four decks, high poop and forecastle, were broad in the beam, and grew to be unmanageably large and heavy to the point of disaster when overloaded or with a badly distributed cargo of pepper and spices. Homeward-bound, pepper was stowed on the lower two decks, there were cabins on the third deck, and the fourth deck and superstructure were used for privately owned chests and bales. The deck was cluttered with cargo. Carracks did not get much bigger than the mammoth *Madre de Deus* which was captured by the English homeward bound from India in 1592 and was estimated to be of 1,600 tons. The French traveller François Pyrard de Laval referred to four vessels, each of 2,000 tons, arriving in Goa in 1609. In the early seventeenth century, Dutch and English predations led the Portuguese to switch from the large 'black ships' to smaller, speedier, galliots (*galiotas*) of 200-400 tons for the Macao to Nagasaki run. Although the term 'galleon' (*galeão*) was sometimes used interchangeably with *náo*, galleons were usually smaller and in the 600 ton bracket. The same ambiguity applied to the designation *fragata* which originally applied to smaller vessels of 100-200 tons, but in the seventeenth and eighteenth centuries came to be applied to larger vessels. The best vessels were built in India of teak and in Brazil from native hardwoods, both of which were superior to Portuguese pine and oak.[23]

For other trading routes, the Portuguese came to depend on the caravel. Early explorations down the African coast had been in the small *barcas* and *barinéis*, combining limited sail area with rowers. Owing its genesis to the Arab dhow, the development of the lateen rigged caravel in the 1440s, with stern-rudder, and of some sixty tons, had been the critical first step in an ever-evolving naval architecture and technology. Capable of sailing within five points off the wind, and not merely with the wind astern, the caravel was to become the vessel of choice for exploration and rapid transportation and evolved to the point of being equally suitable for both coastal and fluvial navigation as well as blue water sailing. Such might have two or three (and occasionally four) masts and be rigged with combinations of square (*velas redondas*) and triangular (lateen) sails, developed a stern castle, and were used in exploratory coastal excursions in the fifteenth and sixteenth centuries. The rig could be adapted to the needs of the day. Lateen rig was good for coastal, estuarine, and river sailing, whereas a square rig was preferable for running before the wind on ocean legs. The caravel was used in trade to the Moroccan ports of Safim and Arzila where the Portuguese maintained factories and in the Portuguese Atlantic for trade between Europe and Africa, Europe and Brazil, and Brazil and Africa. Caravels grew in size from the 100-150 tons burthen of the sixteenth century to double the size in the seventeenth century, as much for self-preservation from the Dutch as for commercial reasons.[24] There was also a host of smaller vessels – *patachos, navetas, fragatas, bergantins, fragatins,* and *galiotas* – which were used for sending urgent dispatches, transporting soldiers, or carrying smaller or perishable cargoes, where speed was of the essence.

In addition to these boats developed by the Portuguese, the Portuguese were also open to using non-European vessels. No sooner had Afonso de Albuquerque taken Malacca in 1511, than he chartered a junk to carry merchandise for barter or sale in the Moluccas. Numerous fleets of junks, under Portuguese and local commands, left Malacca for the Bandas and the Moluccas yearly over the next decade. Ocean-going junks were also freighted by the Portuguese for the Macao-Japan voyages. In the Straits of Malacca, they used oared galleys in the shallow waters and, to evade the Dutch East India Company blockade on Goa, the Portuguese resorted to indigenous craft to bring in foodstuffs.[25]

The Portuguese rang the changes on the pros and cons of individual vessels as opposed to fleets, of private vessels and those under crown control, and of free trade and regulated trade. At various times, the crown experimented with exclusive State control over all aspects of trade, private companies, and chartered trading companies. As we shall see later, crown monopolies on some commodities and regulation of routes was not tantamount to exclusion of individuals, provided they entered into the requisite contracts or received the necessary permissions. The Portuguese crown might sell permits for trade to the Red Sea, grant licences for the import of spices, or farm out routes and commodities, but such regulatory measures were of limited effectiveness. Whether ships travelled singly or in convoys depended on a variety of factors: crown control, capital raising capability of individuals, threats posed by pirates or the Dutch, and the factors of time and distance which varied from route to route.

The two major long distance routes of the Portuguese world were the *carreira da India* and the *carreira do Brasil*. Between 1500 and 1635, at least 912 vessels left the Tagus for Indian Ocean ports, which included East Africa and Hormuz as well as India. In the same period, at least 550 left India and Malacca for Lisbon. The larger and heavier vessels of the *carreira da India* generally travelled in fleets. Such fleets averaged seven vessels annually throughout the sixteenth century, dropping to five for the years 1600-1650, and a mere two to three for the remainder of the century. There were also the annual crown voyages from Goa and Cochin to the Spice Islands, inaugurated in 1523 and abolished in 1610. One vessel went to Ternate for cloves, the other to Banda for nutmeg and mace. There was also the annual 'Great Ship' or large merchant vessel, to be replaced by smaller vessels after 1618, which plied annually between Macao and Japan between 1555 and 1639.[26] In the case of the *carreira do Brasil*, no such heavy investment in vessels or crews was necessary as for the India run, and this permitted more captains to enter Atlantic routes than the Indian Ocean. Also, there was not the same commitment of time necessary as for the round trip to India. During the sixteenth and early seventeenth centuries, captains sailed at will and paid the price in losses at the hands of pirates and the Dutch. The Brazil Company (incorporated, 1649) promoted armed convoys and the collecting of vessels into fleets. A royal order of 1660 forbad individual voyages, and the fleet system with accompanying warships survived the abolition of the company in 1720. In the eighteenth century, the Brazil fleets left Lisbon for Rio de Janeiro, Bahia, and Recife in three convoys. The fleet system was abolished in 1765 but briefly restored from 1797-1801. During the late seventeenth and eighteenth centuries, fleets from Brazil could count as many as 100 vessels, making them the largest in the world for that period. As regards Brazilian trade to West Africa, this was intensive but irregular. Between 1743 and 1756, the crown set the number of vessels at twenty-four *per annum* for the round trip. Although trading companies for the East India trade (Companhia do Comércio da India Oriental; chartered, 1628; collapsed, 1633) and West African trade (Companhia de Cachéu e Rios de Guiné, 1676; Companhia do Cabo Verde e Cachéu, 1696-1703) in the seventeenth century were short-lived, those for Brazil were more successful. The Brazil Company never lived up to its billing of putting to sea thirty-six warships which would be responsible for all Luso-Brazilian commerce. In the following century, the monopolistic trading companies (Companhia Geral do Grão-Pará e Maranhão and Companhia Geral de Pernambuco e Paraíba), although lasting less than a quarter of a century, were fairly successful.[27]

Shipping from Portugal was not limited to the India run and the Brazil run. With the building of São Jorge da Mina (1482), the route from Portugal to West Africa took on new importance. In the first third of the sixteenth century, as many as twelve to fifteen caravels loaded with gold and other commodities travelled each year from the Gulf of Guinea to Lisbon. Outward-bound from Lisbon, these and others carried goods for sale and barter. With the development of the ports of Luanda and Benguela, the trade shifted to Angola. There were also vessels travelling regularly from Lisbon to Madeira and, somewhat less intensively, to the Cape Verdes and Azores. In the fifteenth and sixteenth centuries, there was intensive trade with Morocco, which diminished after the Portuguese losses of all but Ceuta, Tangiers, and Mazagão by 1550. Lisbon was also the end port for vessels travelling to northern Europe. In the 1530s, there were two fleets annually to Antwerp and in the second half of the century direct trade was established between Lisbon and Danzig.[28] Finally, there was the traffic between West Africa and Brazil and *vice versa*, sometimes part of a triangular trade which included Lisbon, but frequently without an European component.

Although the Cape route was the most spectacular in terms of length, duration, and the opening of a new era in East-West relations, it was rivalled, and even exceeded in terms of sheer profitability, by intra-Asian routes. The word 'profitability' should be emphasized because, unlike the *carreira da India*, *carreira do Brasil*, and the Brazil-West Africa routes, whose vessels carried commodities and people, vessels on the intra-Asian routes and the Indian Ocean primarily transported merchandise. These routes radiated out from Goa, Malacca, and Macao, and an estimate of their complexity can be gauged from the fact that in 1570 there were some twenty-seven *carreiras*. These included: from Goa to Hormuz, Mozambique, Ceylon, Moluccas, Coromandel, Bay of Bengal, and Malacca; from Malacca to Siam, Macao, Japan, Burma, Moluccas, and Bandas; from Macao to Japan, Indonesia, Siam, and Timor. Portuguese determination to reach the source of more valuable spices such as cinnamon (Ceylon), cloves (Moluccas), and nutmeg and mace (Bandas), or luxuries such as sandalwood from Timor, silk from China, or lacquer from Pegu, led to variations on these trade routes. In the early seventeenth century, there was a flourishing Portuguese trade from Macao, Malacca, and Coromandel coast ports to Makassar on the south-westerly point of Sulawesi in the Celebes, with between ten and twenty-two Portuguese vessels annually trading Chinese silks and Indian textiles for sandalwood from Timor, cloves from the Moluccas, and diamonds from Borneo. Vitorino Magalhães Godinho and Luís Filipe Thomaz have issued timely reminders that the impression has been left that the Portuguese dominated the spice trade from the Moluccas. While this held true among European carriers, Thomaz has pointed out that the bulk of the spice production of the Moluccas was never carried to Europe but was distributed to markets in Asia. In addition to these trade routes, the Portuguese also maintained patrols for the coast from Mozambique to the Red Sea (based on Malindi), and at the entrance to the Persian Gulf based on Hormuz.[29]

Vessels sailing on these long and medium distance routes did not have *carte blanche* to come and go as their captains pleased. Briefly put, sailing times and routes were determined by wind systems and currents in the Atlantic and by seasonal monsoons from the Cape of Good Hope to Japan and the Moluccas. Winds and currents of the North Atlantic gyre circulate in a clockwise direction and those of the South Atlantic counter-clockwise.

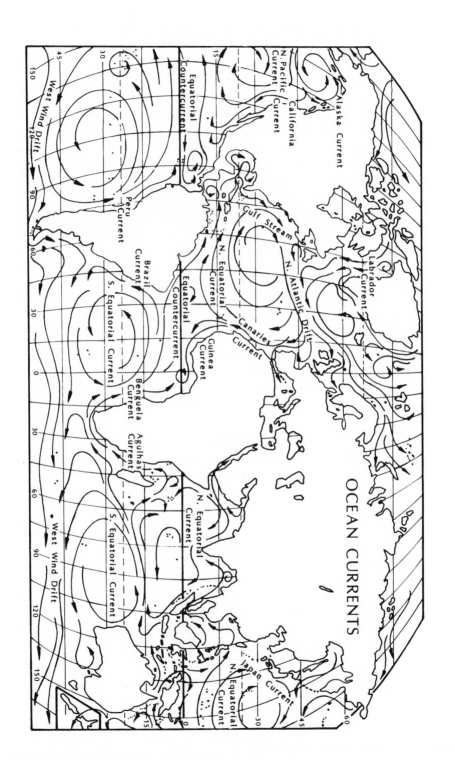

OCEAN CURRENTS

There is the hazard of the doldrums, the equatorial low pressure zone, to be avoided at all costs. From Lisbon to the Atlantic islands there are seasonally variable wind systems. From Lisbon to Madeira was a comparatively easy voyage driven by winds from the north or north-west; the return journey took advantage of the south-westerlies which predominated in the winter months. Since they are located virtually due west of Lisbon and some 900 miles from the coast of Portugal, passage from Lisbon to the Azores was more difficult outward because of the westerlies and north-westerlies, but these facilitated passage on the homeward leg. Vessels homeward-bound from West Africa might sail on a north-westerly course to catch the westerlies. The run from Portugal to Brazil called other factors into consideration. The north-east trades made for an easy run from Lisbon to northern Brazil, but passage southwards beyond Cape São Roque was extraordinarily hazardous. There was a critical distinction between the east-west coast (Ceará, Maranhão, Pará) and the north-south coast (Cape São Roque to Río de la Plata). In practical terms, this meant that it was shorter and safer to sail from Lisbon to São Luís than from São Luís to Salvador. There is also the strong Brazil current running south along the coast. For coastal shipping, the north-east monsoon (October to April) permitted sailing from Pernambuco to Salvador in four to five days, and the south-east monsoon (April to October) permitted the return voyage.[30]

For the Brazil run, according to one eighteenth-century sea dog, vessels should leave Lisbon between 15 and 25 October and arrive in Pernambuco before 15 December; from there to Salvador was less than a week, and New Year's Eve should find the vessels in the Bay of Guanabara. The crown attempted (1632 and 1690) to set schedules but captains cocked a snook at such schedules, preferring to sail in small groups rather than fleets. In the eighteenth century, most fleets from Lisbon destined for Salvador or Pernambuco left Lisbon in April, and those for Rio in March, April, or May. Homeward-bound there was greater irregularity. October was the month for the greatest numbers of vessels from Brazil arriving in the Tagus but, with the exception of June, vessels from Salvador put into the Tagus every month of the year. Of vessels homeward bound from Rio, most arrived in the Tagus in August and October, those from Pernambuco in

July and August, and from the Maranhão in December and January. For the period 1712-66, 31 per cent of vessels leaving Lisbon for Brazil did so in April (and, in decreasing order, March, May, December, January, February). As for arrival in Lisbon from Brazil, most favoured months in decreasing order were October, August, December, and January. Sailing times from Portugal varied, depending on the destination in Brazil. From Lisbon to São Luís in the Maranhão took about five weeks, whereas from Lisbon to Recife was sixty days, to Salvador seventy, and eighty or ninety for Rio de Janeiro. Homeward-bound from Recife was about seventy-five days, Salvador eighty-four, and Rio ninety-seven for fleets, and some two to three weeks less for single vessels. Once stays in Brazilian ports were added, a round trip Lisbon-Pernambuco-Lisbon could range between seven months and a year, Salvador about seven or eight months, and Rio de Janeiro about a year. Voyages between West African ports and Brazil took between thirty and fifty days. From Angola to Pernambuco was about thirty-five days, forty to Salvador, and fifty to Rio. There was no perceptible change in sailing times between the sixteenth and eighteenth centuries. From Lisbon to the Cape Verdes was a mere two weeks of sailing, and forty-five days to São Jorge da Mina. Turning northwards, from Lisbon to La Rochelle took about a week and to Amsterdam or Antwerp two weeks. In the 1530s and 1540s, two fleets annually sailed from Lisbon to Antwerp arriving in May/June and in October/December.[31]

Although delayed departures could lead to being becalmed in the equatorial zone outward-bound or harried by winter gales in the latitude of the Azores homeward-bound, generally the Atlantic offered more flexibility and was more forgiving than the Indian Ocean and South China Sea. India-bound vessels sailed south to Madeira and then were carried by the north-east trades and Canary current. They headed south-east and south from the Cape Verdes and then swept westwards to avoid the doldrums and toward the coast of Pernambuco south of Cape São Roque. Here they picked up the south Atlantic gyre and Brazil current. The south-east trades carried them further west to about 20° South, when they picked up the southern westerly winds which would carry them east-south-east round the Cape of Good Hope. From the Cape the choice lay between the Mozambique

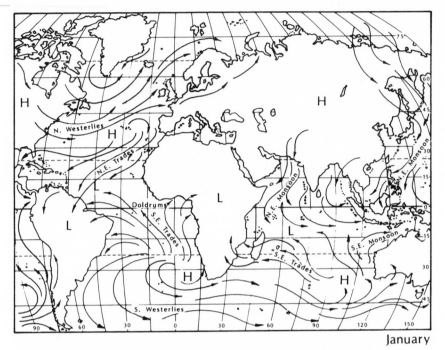

January

GLOBAL WIND & PRESSURE PATTERNS

July

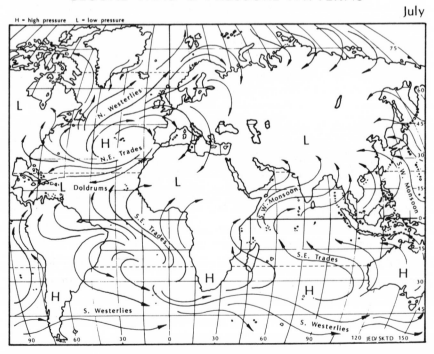

channel calling at Mozambique island, or sailing south of Madagascar and heading north-east and then east to India. Once in the Indian Ocean, progress was determined by the monsoon systems. Briefly put, the south-west monsoon (summer) lasts from the end of May to September; and from October to April the winds blow from the north-east. To catch the monsoon, vessels to the west coast of India left Portugal in late February, March, and April, to cross the equator before June and to arrive in Cochin or Goa between August and October. Cochin was the major port initially for the Portuguese, but Goa was the administrative centre of Portuguese India. Vessels bound for Cochin made up their cargo of pepper at Quilon but later the fleet from Portugal of some four vessels would divide, with two going to Goa and two to Cochin. From 1584, Goa was the first port of call for vessels which loaded there or went on to Cochin to load. This ended in 1611 because of Dutch threats. Homeward-bound, ideally carracks left Cochin and Goa in late December or January. Returning vessels more or less sailed their outward route in reverse as far as the Cape of Good Hope and then were carried by south-easterlies toward the north-west to the equator. Here the doldrums occasioned delay and vessels were subsequently compelled to tack because of north-easterly winds. Then the high pressure system would take them to the Azores. Way-stations homeward-bound were Mozambique, St Helena, or the Azores. Increasingly, in the eighteenth century, Indiamen put into a Brazilian port homeward-bound. The voyage to India could range between four months and eighteen months. From Lisbon to Goa usually took six to eight months each way without stop. This would be extended if vessels touched at Mozambique, or wintered there, outward-bound. Homeward-bound, a late departure from India could result in delays occasioned by wintering at Mozambique, running into rough weather at the Cape in May or June, putting into a Brazilian port for repairs or provisions, or into the Azores.

In the case of the Goa-Macao-Japan run, sailing schedules were at the mercy of a different set of monsoons and could also fall victim to delays in acquiring cargoes. Captains-major of the Japan voyages would ensure that their annual carrack left Goa in April or May. Usually a stop was made at Malacca and, if there were no delays, the carrack would arrive in Macao in June or

August. Here the vessel might stay as little as a few weeks or as much as a year if it missed the south-west monsoon in the China Sea or the biannual (June and January) silk fairs at Canton. If so, it would catch the monsoon in June-August of the following year. Sailing time from Macao to Japan (Bungo, Hizen, and Omura; after 1571, Nagasaki) was between two weeks and a month. In late October or November, the onset of the north-east monsoon permitted departure from Japan for Macao any time before the following March. Under ideal conditions the Goa-Macao-Japan-Goa voyage was six months, but not always fair weather sailing. In July 1564 the *Santa Cruz* bound from Macao to Japan hit heavy weather, only partly tempered by the Jesuit Baltazar da Costa's action in throwing into the sea a harpoon to whose cord he had attached holy relics. The voyage took forty-two days. If there were delays occasioned by missing the monsoon in Malacca or Macao, or in assembling a cargo, the round trip Goa-Japan-Goa could be as long as three years. If the Lisbon-Goa leg was extended to include Japan, anywhere between eighteen months and five years could elapse before a sailor from Lisbon again set foot on his native soil.[32]

Monsoons also determined schedules for vessels between Malacca and Banda, and Banda and Ternate in the Moluccas. Vessels left Malacca in January, arrived in Banda in February, departed in July and were back in Malacca by August. To continue to Ternate, vessels left Banda in the period May-July and arrived in Ternate in June-August. Homeward-bound, a vessel could not leave Ternate until the following January and then had to wait in Banda until July when the monsoon would permit return to Malacca. From the mid-1520s, a shorter route (Borneo, Ambon) was used from Malacca to Ternate and Tidor, which cut the round trip voyage to some ten and a half months. After 1523, the State organized two annual voyages from the west coast of India. Vessels left Goa or Cochin in April or May and arrived in Malacca at the end of May or June. That vessel whose destination was Ternate, left Malacca in mid-August and arrived in October. The other for Banda weighed anchor in Malacca the following January and arrived in Banda the following month. After loading cloves in the Moluccas, the first vessel departed for Malacca in mid-February with the south-east monsoon, stayed in Malacca from June-November, and unloaded its cargo in Cochin the

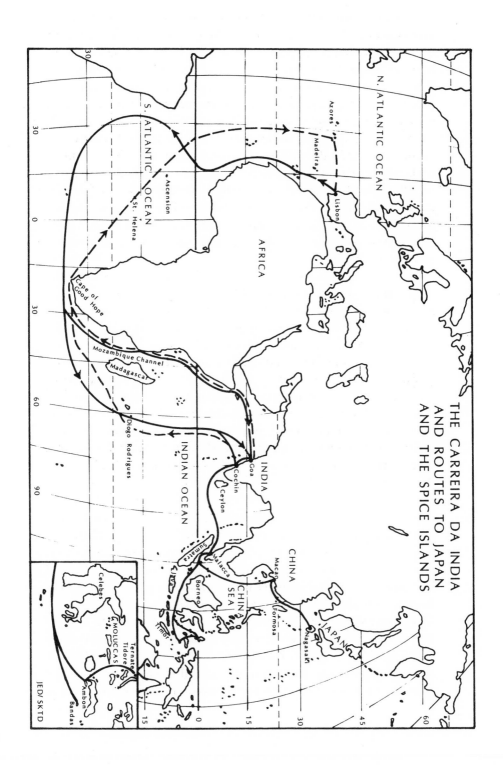

THE CARREIRA DA INDIA
AND ROUTES TO JAPAN
AND THE SPICE ISLANDS

N. ATLANTIC OCEAN

Azores

Madeira

Lisbon

AFRICA

S. ATLANTIC OCEAN

Ascension

St. Helena

Cape of
Good Hope

Mozambique Channel

Madagascar

Diogo Rodrigues

INDIAN OCEAN

Goa

Cochin

Ceylon

INDIA

Sumatra

Malacca

Borneo

CHINA SEA

Macao

Formosa

CHINA

JAPAN

Nagasaki

Celebes

Ternate
Tidore
MOLUCCAS

Ambon

Bandas

JED/ SKTD

beginning of the following January. If it continued to Goa, its arrival would be in mid-March. The other vessel, loaded with nutmeg and mace, departed Banda in July, stopped over in Malacca from August to mid-November, and would anchor in Cochin or Goa about the same time as the vessel from the Moluccas. The time spent on such voyages varied wildly, depending on failure to catch the monsoons but, if all went well, the following gives an indication: Malacca-Banda-Malacca, 7-8 months; Malacca-Banda-Ternate-Banda-Malacca, 19-20 months; Malacca-Ternate/Tidor-Malacca (via Borneo, Ambon), 10-11 months; Goa/Cochin-Malacca-Moluccas-Malacca-Goa/Cochin, between 23 (via Borneo) or 30 months (via Banda); Goa/Cochin-Malacca-Banda-Malacca-Cochin/Goa, 23 months. In other words, the round trip from Goa-Moluccas-Goa was even more protracted than Lisbon-Goa-Lisbon.[33]

The emphasis given to these medium or long distance blue water routes does not exhaust the myriad of variations of routes followed by vessels. Two aspects merit comment: islands and coastal trade. In the annals of European discovery, the Portuguese 'discovered' the archipelagos of Madeira, the Azores, and Cape Verdes, and the islands of São Tomé, Príncipe, Ascension, St Helena, Trindade, Tristão da Cunha, Gonçalo Álvares (later Gough island), and Fernão de Noronha. Vasco da Gama touched some islands on the East African coast on his first voyage and the roster was completed by Cabral outward-bound from Brazil to India. The Portuguese explored the Maldives and Ceylon (1505), Bay of Bengal, Sumatra, Java, Borneo, the Bandas, and Moluccas. All of this had been achieved before 1515. But it was Madeira, the Azores, and Cape Verdes, and São Tomé and Príncipe in the Gulf of Guinea, which took on special importance for the Portuguese in settlement and commercial terms. In addition to engaging in a thriving inter-insular trade, Madeira, the Azores, and Cape Verdes were hubs for a series of complex commercial networks. As such they were points of articulation between the North and South Atlantic, North and South America and the Caribbean, Africa and America, Africa and Europe, and Europe and America. Furthermore, especially in the case of the Azores and Cape Verdes, their strategic locations made them important as way-stations for Indiamen and Brazil fleets. In the case of Madeira for sugar, and the Azores for wheat, they became major producers. The Azores in particular, and Madeira and the Cape Verdes to a lesser degree, provided settlers for Brazil. On the Cape Verdes, São Tomé, and Príncipe, converged products of the three continents bordering the Atlantic. They also played key roles in the passage of slaves from the African mainland and subsequent distribution to Europe and the Americas. The islands of the East African coast, most notably Mozambique, were markets rather than points of articulation. This was also the case of islands of the Indian Ocean and China Sea and beyond – Ceylon, the islands of Indonesia, the Lesser Sunda, and the Celebes. One exception was Makassar in the Celebes which was used by the Portuguese for a trade which flourished in the first quarter of the seventeenth century, attracting Portuguese vessels from Macao, Malacca, and even the ports of Coromandel, to exchange Chinese silks and Indian textiles for sandalwood from Timor, cloves from the Moluccas, and diamonds from Borneo.[34]

Not surprisingly, in view of the fact that the maritime routes of the Portuguese caravels and carracks took them to ports which themselves had subsidiary transportation and communication networks with smaller ports, coastal shipping took on extraordinary importance. This played an important role in the transportation of commodities. Sometimes the Portuguese themselves engaged in such trade, whereas sometimes it was in the hands of indigenous peoples. The Portuguese engaged in coastal trade in Morocco and the Maghreb and their explorations and early commerce along the coast of West Africa had been essentially coastal. In the Bight of Benin and further south, there is little indication that the Portuguese themselves engaged in coastal trade other than to anchor offshore and engage in barter with coastal villages. The Venetian Alvise da Cà da Mosto who travelled along the coast of Senegal in the mid-fifteenth century commented that there had been no coastal trade prior to the arrival of the Portuguese and that the locals used canoes (*almadie*) which carried only three or four people.[35] As regards East Africa, coastal trade was Muslim dominated. Red Sea traders, interested in Monomotapa gold, had established bases along 'the gold route' on the coast from Mogadishu to Sofala or on islands before the arrival of the Portuguese. Portuguese factories were staging points for the collection of commodities, rather than forming part of a coastal trade network. On the west coast of India, Goa and Cochin in particular were entrepôts of Portuguese commerce to and from both east and west, and for the trans-shipment of goods received from, and for transportation to, other west coast Portuguese enclaves (Diu, Daman, Bassein, Chaul, Cannanore, Cranganore, Quilon), Ceylon, the Bay of Bengal (St Thome of Meliapore, Hooghly), and further afield to Hormuz, East Africa, and China. In the second half of the sixteenth-century, caravans (*cafilas*) of small ships on the west coast of India brought cargoes to Goa for trans-shipment to Lisbon. In Ceylon, the Portuguese presence may have stimulated a coastal trade which did not previously exist. But, in all these cases, few Portuguese themselves were engaged in coastal trade. One exception was China. Despite imperial prohibitions, Portuguese engaged in coastal trade which was tantamount to smuggling in the provinces of Fukien and Chêkiang until 1547.[36]

In Portuguese America, it was a very different story. The major ports of Belém do Pará, São Luís do Maranhão, Pernambuco, Salvador, and Rio de Janeiro, engaged primarily in oceanic trade. But they, and the smaller ports of Fortaleza, Ilhéus, Vitória, Angra dos Reis, Parati, Santos, and São Francisco do Sul, were also the scenes for a very active coastal trade. A visitor to colonial Salvador noted the diversity of shipping in the Bay of All Saints: carracks from India and caravels from West Africa and from Portuguese ports. In addition to these blue water vessels, there was the full range of brigantines, sloops, smacks, *faluas*, *saveiros*, *jangadas*, and canoes. Writing in 1587, Gabriel Soares de Sousa had noted that every plantation of the Recôncavo of Bahia itself maintained at least four vessels and that, should it have been necessary to mobilize maritime resources in an emergency, a governor-general could have counted on mustering a marine force of some 1,400 vessels in the bay. Two centuries later (1759), the military engineer, José António Caldas, put at 2,500 those vessels engaged in trade between the ports of the Recôncavo and estimated that on any given day some 1,000 of these could be seen in the harbour of Salvador. To the south, Parati, Angra dos Reis, and Santos were in daily communication with Rio de Janeiro. This coastal trade falls roughly into three categories. First, trade of a highly local nature in the delivery of perishable provisions or foodstuffs to a local port, and which might involve a combination of coastal and river routes. Secondly, that coastal trade which was essentially the redistribution of commodities brought to major Brazilian ports from Europe and Africa and which were then trans-shipped to smaller vessels. Thirdly, the carrying trade in products which were region-specific: for example, salted beef from Ceará or tallow from Rio Grande do Sul. Finally, there was a lively coastal trade in contraband goods to vessels of other nationalities off-shore, and between ports of the south of Brazil and Río de la Plata.[37]

The safe havens which were the departure and arrival points for this ebb and flow which characterized the Portuguese world ranged from the superb anchorages provided by the estuary of the Tagus, Bay of All Saints, Bay of Guanabara, broad bay of Paranaguá, estuaries of the Mandavi and Pearl rivers, and the deep harbour of Nagasaki, to less than desirable anchorages in roadsteads or in the lee of protecting promontories or islands. Although Lisbon and, to a significantly lesser degree, Oporto, were the ports in Portugal most frequented by Indiamen and vessels of the Atlantic routes, brief reference to any atlas reveals the numerous ports dotting the Portuguese coastline: Caminha, Viana do Castelo, Aveiro, Setúbal, Lagos, and Faro. Vessels from all these ports appear on shipping records to and from West Africa, the Atlantic islands, and Brazil. In Brazil the Portuguese faced no prior claimants to ports. Any opposition which they did experience to establishing port facilities came not from the indigenous peoples but from European rivals, most notably the French in the sixteenth century.

Elsewhere, the Portuguese confronted entrenched local political, religious, and commercial interests, which led to each situation having to be assessed on its own merits. Options open to the Portuguese ranged from warfare to negotiation or withdrawal. In West Africa, the Portuguese had to deal with chiefs of states, sometimes of the stature of that of Benin. In East Africa, rulers of the city-states of Mozambique, Kilwa, Mombasa, Malindi, and Pate, reacted in different ways to Portuguese interest and intrusion. Alliance with the sultan of Malindi, backed up by forts at Sofala, Mozambique, and Mombasa, was the foundation of the Portuguese presence in East Africa. Some rulers rejected Portuguese overtures, others reached working arrangements, and still others found themselves manipulated by the Portuguese who took advantage of local rivalries (as between the sultans of Malindi and Mombasa or the Samorim of Calicut and the Raja of Cochin). The Portuguese negotiated with Hindu rajas and Muslim sultans in India, Hindu rulers in Ceylon, and Muslim sultans in the Malay peninsula, Indonesia, Ternate, and Tidor. The Portuguese imposed their presence through warfare in the case of the deep-water port of Goa, seized by Afonso de Albuquerque from the sultan of Bijapur (1510), Malacca (1511), and Hormuz (1515). At an early date Goa became more important to the Portuguese than the older Portuguese settlements at Cochin and Cannanore, and Cochin was favoured over the more northerly Cannanore. By mid-sixteenth century, Goa was well established and well fortified as the political and commercial centre of Portuguese India. Macao and Nagasaki were distinctive in that the impetus for a Portuguese presence came not from the crown but from merchants or missionaries. There are several versions of how the Portuguese came to be granted permission to establish themselves in Macao in 1555-57. One is that it was an act of gratitude by Cantonese authorities for Portuguese help in defeating a local pirate or ridding the area of robbers, for which it was notorious. Another is that the Cantonese sought Portuguese trade, conditional on payment of custom dues and agreement not to build a fort. Geoffrey Scammell has referred to this as 'the only Asian city truly created by Portugal'. In Japan, in 1569 the Jesuit Gaspar Vilela was invited by a convert, who was a vassal of the Christian *daimyo* Omura Sumitada, to a fishing village called Nagasaki. In short order, the Jesuit built a chapel, converted the populace from Buddhism to Catholicism and, in 1571, the first Portuguese carrack from Goa dropped anchor. In 1580 the *daimyo* deeded Nagasaki and the neighbouring fortress of Mogi to the Jesuits. This was the sole sovereign territory held by the Jesuits or, to put it in the words (1580) of Alexander Valignano, S.J. : 'The lord of the soil gave them to us in perpetuity and virtually unconditionally as regards the Company.' With the exception of Brazil, Macao, and Nagasaki, the Portuguese arrived in ports which were already well-established entrepôts.[38]

The arrival of Vasco da Gama in Calicut heralded in a new era of European maritime trade to India and the East, but the seaborne route around the Cape of Good Hope did not totally supersede the old caravan land-based routes between Europe and Asia. In various combinations, these included the Euphrates valley – the oldest and the most direct route until contacts between East and West were interrupted by the Mongol invasion and then Ottoman empire – the Red Sea, Persian Gulf, or the Caspian. The Euphrates valley route was extensively used and continued to be so until the end of the eighteenth century. There were the exclusively terrestrial routes through Tabriz to Central Asia or the more popular land/sea route to and from Europe through Persia, the Persian Gulf, or the Red Sea. Of these, the Red Sea route had two major drawbacks: difficult navigation, and delays in trans-shipment from the larger Indian Ocean vessels to smaller vessels. Its advantage was that the land portage from Suez to Cairo was much shorter, and thus less costly, than either the Persian Gulf route or the Euphrates valley route from Basra to Aleppo. There were several land/sea options, according to a seventeenth-century Portuguese Jesuit. The shortest was by ship from India to Bab-el Mandeb, transferring to another vessel to Suez, overland to Cairo, down the Nile to Alexandria, and thence by boat to Lisbon, probably via Marseille. Longer but safer was the overland/river route through Persia, namely Bandar 'Abbas (Gombroon), Lar, and Shiraz and thence either to Romus, Laxa, Baghdad, Aleppo, and on to Alexandretta or Damascus; or from Shiraz to Isfahan, Tabriz, Smyrna, Baghdad, and Aleppo. More frequented, but dangerous because of desert Arabs, was the route through Basra and up the Euphrates to Hait and Baghdad and thence to Damascus or Aleppo. Later these overland routes were to be popular with British East India Company officials going to, or returning from, India. The 'Great Desert Route' led directly from Aleppo to Basra; the 'Little Desert Route' made for Baghdad and then by river to Basra. These overland routes were to last until the advent of steam vessels; the opening of the Suez canal (1869) sounded their death knell.[39]

These were not abandoned because of the opening of the Cape route (*Rota do Cabo*), but tended to be used by individuals or small parties of merchants. No land/sea route was free from attacks by desert Arabs or Muscat Arabs, expenses of transfers, difficulty of finding passages or joining a caravan, and risks of navigation in the Red Sea or Indian Ocean. Before the traveller secured passage, there could be interminable delays which offset

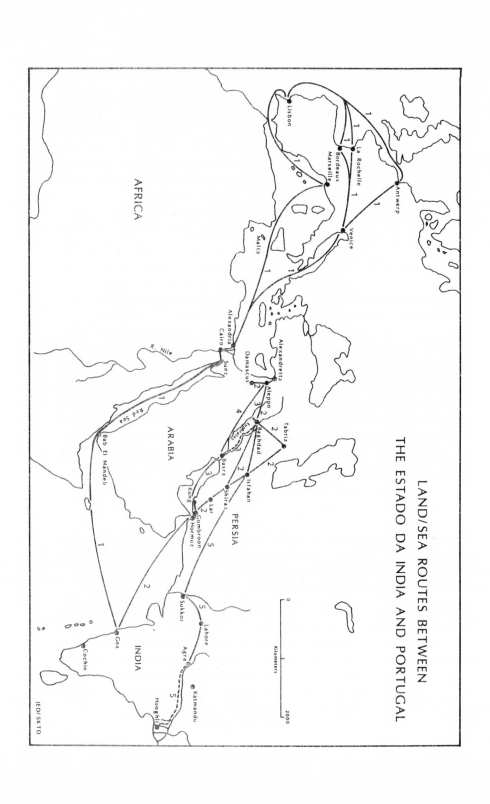

LAND/SEA ROUTES BETWEEN
THE ESTADO DA INDIA AND PORTUGAL

any advantages of time over the longer Cape Route. The Portuguese were probably the first Europeans to use the short-cut to India of which the Aleppo-Basra caravan route along the Euphrates valley was part. Pero de Covilhã, returning from Hormuz to Cairo in 1487, may have followed this route. The land/sea route through Aleppo and Basra was also often used by couriers carrying letters and for rapid delivery of dispatches carrying sensitive information or instructions, and which were in code. This was especially the case in the seventeenth century, when Dutch and Arabs made the sea route to Persia from India unsafe for the Portuguese.[40]

The first recorded overland (1513) journey from the Red Sea to Portugal was by one Fernão Dias, a Muslim who had deserted to the Portuguese. Disguised as an escaped slave, he was dispatched by Afonso de Albuquerque to the king and not only arrived safely in Portugal but made it back to India. A decade later the Portuguese, António Tenreiro, was the first European to record his crossing (1523) of the desert from Aleppo to Basra and the first to make the return journey in 1528. Tenreiro spoke Persian and Arabic. On this return journey, he carried dispatches from the Portuguese governor of Hormuz advising Dom João III that the governor of India, Dom Nuno da Cunha, was in Malindi and that the sultan of Egypt had resolved against sending an expeditionary force to India. Tenreiro was to deliver them in Lisbon three months later, but only after an eventful journey. In Basra, Tenreiro missed the Aleppo-bound caravan. Nothing daunted, he hired two camels and, with an Arab companion, rode across the desert in twenty-two days (including a halt of eight days because of an injured camel) and caught up with the caravan a week out of Aleppo. Tenreiro's *Itinerário* was published in 1560 and João de Barros and Diogo do Couto noted his exploits in their *Décadas*. Diogo do Couto also referred to a 1565 crossing from Basra by Portuguese led by António Teixeira and there were doubtless others in the sixteenth century.

In the seventeenth century, English and Italians *inter alia*, joined Portuguese on this Arabian desert route. Among the Portuguese were Pedro Teixeira (1604-05) coming from India, and friar Gaspar de São Bernardino (1606-07), both of whom crossed the desert and left narratives. Pedro Teixeira had intended to sail up the Euphrates but, learning in Basra that the river would not be navigable for some months, joined a *cafila* or caravan. After a journey of slightly over five months, riding a camel and carried in camel panniers, and including a wedding and attack by thieves, he reached Aleppo. The Franciscan Gaspar de São Bernardino was returning to Portugal after missionary service in India. He survived shipwreck off Madagascar and was taken by the locals to Mombasa, from where he travelled on to Malindi. Here he was taken by the *cafres* to their sultan at Pate, where he was graciously received. From Pate, the friar travelled to the Red Sea and Persian Gulf and then overland, finally realizing his dream of visiting the holy places of Palestine before embarking for Europe. His *Itinerario da India por terra até este reino de Portugal, com a descrição de Jerusalém* (Lisbon, 1611) was written at the suggestion of Margaret of Austria, queen of King Philip III, who had received the itinerant friar in Madrid and to whom he dedicated his account. That this desert route was frequented by Portuguese was evidenced by the 1622 report of the English consul in Aleppo in which he noted: 'four Portugal fathers have arrived here from Goa, sent with letters to their King'.[41]

If Teixeira's account is somewhat dry of tone and content, not the same can be said of Manuel Godinho's *Relação do novo caminho que fez per terra e mar vindo da India para Portugal no anno de 1663* (Lisbon, 1665), a delightful personal narrative by an astute observer. As a young Jesuit, Godinho had left Portugal for India in 1655 and was charged by the viceroy of India, António de Mello de Castro, to be the courier for an important message to King Dom Afonso VI advising against the cession of Bombay to England. Leaving Bassein, he travelled to Daman and to Surat, under Mughal sovereignty. He sailed to Bandar 'Abbas, overland to Kung, and then by sea to Basra. Rather than wait in Basra for a boat to carry him to Baghdad, or for caravan protection in crossing the desert, Godinho set off by horse with three companions and for part of the journey was accompanied by three Arabs. From Baghdad, he travelled to Ana, Aleppo, and Alexandretta, taking boat for Marseille, crossing to La Rochelle, and thence by boat to Cascais at the mouth of the Tagus. He rubbed shoulders with a French bishop *en route* to China, and his travel companions included a Persian Muslim and a Hindu brahmin. Not only did Godinho describe customs and rituals of Hindus and Muslims, landscapes, cities, commerce, and diet, fruits, and dress, but also incidents such as a fight between a tiger and a wild boar near the Euphrates. Remarkably even-handed in many regards, Godinho could be critical, as in his description of Persian women (chapter 13), 'tall, hefty, and more fond of frippery than women of any other nation ... of rough mien and ill natured'.[42]

These overland routes underline an important aspect of the Portuguese overseas: namely, that the emphasis on the seaborne and maritime component should not lead one to the belief that the Portuguese presence was limited to forts, trading factories, and settlement enclaves. The maritime commercial component remained strong, but in India, Africa, and America, the Portuguese had territorial holdings. It is often difficult to establish precisely the nature of Portuguese authority, to distinguish between suzerainty and sovereignty, and it is probably better to forsake legalistic definitions and refer to 'spheres of influence'. In India, Portugal had control over Goa and its islands, the neighbouring mainland areas of Bardez and Salsette, and (until 1740) some 1500 square miles between Bombay and Daman (*governo do norte*). In the sixteenth and seventeenth centuries, much of Ceylon was effectively under Portuguese control. In East Africa, the Zambezi had afforded the Portuguese access to the hinterland of their coastal settlements in Mozambique, Sofala, and Quelimane. After setbacks and failures, trading posts had been established at Sena, Tete, and Zumbo (the last, c.1716 by a Goanese) on the Zambezi. The more determined settled on lands granted by the Monomotapa and the Portuguese crown and were known as *prazeiros* (holders of entailed estates). While disease, small numbers and local politics were strong constraints on settlement, the Portuguese had lands and exerted considerable influence inland as far as present-day Zimbabwe. Seventeenth-century settlement proposals were not implemented. In the 1870s and 1880s, the Portuguese of the Zambezi launched a campaign which, if successful, could have given them much of what is now Zimbabwe. The British Ultimatum of 1890 denied Portuguese hopes of larger territorial holdings in Central Africa but did confirm the territories historically occupied by the *prazeiros* as Portuguese.[43] Apart from the limited terrorial extent of the Atlantic islands of Madeira, Azores, and Cape Verdes, it was only in Angola and Brazil that the Portuguese had extensive contiguous territorial possessions.

This raises the question of transportation within these areas. In the case of many of the Portuguese territories in Africa, this was determined less by man than by insects. Animals for transportation could not be used in those areas which were infested by the tsetse fly. On the fringes of such areas, as elsewhere, mules and donkeys were used for transportation. From the sixteenth century onwards, horses had been imported from Europe and the Cape Verdes into Senegambia, but these were limited to military use. Camels were used in the desert and along the sahal and pack oxen for local transportation, but donkeys were the animals most extensively used for carrying goods in the savannah and even beyond the tsetse line. In Angola, porters were the most used form of transportation. A caravan comprised from between twenty to one hundred porters, carrying bales on their heads or slung from poles on their shoulders. The heaviest loads were slung from poles carried by one or two pairs of carriers. Travel rarely exceeded seven miles a day. The trails were such as to permit movement only in single file. Only in the early nineteenth century did the Lisbon authorities encourage the formation of herds of horses and mules near Luanda. Oxen were used only in areas which were reasonably healthy for livestock, such as east of Anbaca. The same situation prevailed in East Africa. Except where rivers were available, transport of goods was on the heads of local carriers, and caravans of porters followed narrow paths in single file. Apart from hazards such as attacks by animals, crossing crocodile-infested rivers, and dense forest and bush, there were delays occasioned by the need to receive permission from each chief or headman before crossing his territory.[44]

Until the eighteenth century, the situation was not much better in colonial Brazil. Even the term 'road' was something of a misnomer. Often so narrow that movement was only possible in single file, these were unpaved tracks, subject to being washed out by floods or torrential rains. Rivers had to be forded, or passage negotiated with a ferryman. Roads over the Serra da Mantiqueira were steep, hazardous, and with precipitous drop-offs. The only coastal route was from Maranhão to Pernambuco. In the north-east, roads linked Piauí, Maranhão, Ceará, and the São Francisco river. A route through the *sertão* linked Bahia to the Maranhão. With the gold strikes in Minas

Gerais in the 1690s, slowly roads were developed from Rio de Janeiro, São Paulo, and Bahia. These were to be complemented by further roads to Goiás and the overland route from Vila Boa to Cuiabá in Mato Grosso. Also of the eighteenth century were routes from São Paulo south to Santa Catarina, Curitiba, and Rio Grande. Even as late as the eighteenth century, until the development of roads such as to permit the use of animals, Indians and African slaves carried packs on their heads and backs from Rio de Janeiro to Minas Gerais. Pack mules came into use, but it was some time before roads were such as to permit wheeled vehicles. Even then, slaves were preferred for the transportation of valuable or fragile objects. Mules became the backbone of middle and long distance transportation in colonial Brazil. The demand stimulated a new economy in Rio Grande and the south and a well established link between that region and Minas Gerais, Goiás, and Mato Grosso, and even extending to Potosí. One shortcoming of mules was their limited carrying capabilities and the necessity of balancing the panniers. Inevitably this led to slow progress. The *tropeiros*, or drovers, not only drove herds of mules but were carriers of merchandise, tools, and messages. The wooden-wheeled ox-carts, with posts at the sides to keep in the loads of cane and other commodities, and which were so prominent in the paintings of the seventeenth-century Dutch artist Frans Post, were used only for local transportation.[45]

Transportation in urban areas in Brazil was primitive. Transportation of persons was in a sedan chair (*palanquim* or *cadeirinha*) carried on the shoulders of black slaves. The decoration or simplicity of such chairs reflected the social and financial standing of the occupant. The basic design was a chair of wickerwork (preferable for lightness) or of wood. The chair had a high back and was placed on a board to which was attached a foot-rest. An oblong wooden top provided stability and the opportunity to decorate the chair with lavish gilding and carved flowers. Coats of arms might also be added. A curtain, no less lavishly decorated and embroidered, protected the occupant from sun and stares. Two fashioned carrying handles protruded some six feet in front and behind. Such elaborate chairs were more prevalent in Rio de Janeiro than Salvador, whose topography and steep *ladeiras* made passage difficult. For the same reason, Bahians were slower than *cariocas* to adopt the new form of transportation which made its appearance after the arrival of the court. This was the chaise, a carriage which was often heavily decorated. There were more rustic variations on both forms of transportation. A hammock (*rede*) or litter of fibre or cotton net could be slung from a single bamboo borne on the shoulders of two slaves and with a cloth thrown over the pole to conceal the occupant. Or simple carts were improved by the addition of a roof and curtains on the sides.[46]

Slaves, both male and female, transported on their heads a wide variety of containers and their contents: earthenware jars of milk, metal jugs of liquids, trays of foodstuffs or fish, baskets of sugar-cane, vegetables, and fruit, cages of birds, and small wooden casks or piles of hats. Other methods of transportation demanded team work. In the late colonial era, blacks assembled on the corner of the Rua Direita or Rua da Alfandega in Rio de Janeiro and waited for work. Each *cangeiro* (or *gangeiro*) had a wooden pole, some nine to twelve feet long, to which leather thongs were attached. These were used to carry heavy weights or casks. The thongs were wrapped around the load in such a way that, when suspended from one or more such poles, the weight would be evenly distributed. Working in teams of from two to eight, blacks carried large crates and casks in this manner. With a pole over one shoulder, the other arm on a team-mate's shoulder for support and balance, such groups transported their loads, often to an African chant. A team effort was also required to transport heavy loads which had been placed on a roughly con-structed dolly or flat-bed (*piolho*) with solid wooden wheels resting on concavities formed of the axle-trees which also re-volved. Teams of from four to eight blacks pushing and pulling such unwieldy and noisy vehicles were common sights in colo-nial cities.[47]

Rivers played an extraordinarily important role in the move-ment of persons and commodities in the Portuguese overseas empire. As there was a symbiotic relationship between coastal trade and oceanic trade, so too was there a relationship between oceanic trade and fluvial transportation. The peninsula on which Macao was settled was on the estuary of the Pearl river with easy access to Canton and this and the West river were part of inter-locking river systems and of coastal trade to the myriad of islands off the China coast. Old Goa was on an island bordered by two rivers: the Mandāvi to the north and the Zuari to the south. The magnificent harbour between the promontories of Bardez and Salsette was further enhanced by numerous navigable rivers which intersected the Velhas and Novas Conquistas. Along the coast were waterways leading inland both to the north and to the south of Goa. Locally produced goods were transported down rivers, trans-shipped for passage to Goa, where they were further trans-shipped to the Indiamen, and a similar process in reverse took place with goods from Europe. But it was in Africa and Brazil that broad, long, navigable rivers took on exceptional importance both for access to the interior and passage of people and commodities.

The Senegal, Cacheu, Gambia, Niger, Congo, Cuanza, and Zambezi, were navigable rivers which permitted the Portuguese to penetrate into the African continent and trade in the second half of the fifteenth century. Diogo Cão probed the mouth of the Congo river (1482-83) and on his 1485-86 voyage sailed 100 miles upstream. The combinations of tide and seasonal currents were tricky and to these could be added the hazard of floating islands of rushes swept along on the deep central channel. Portuguese captains looking for slave cargoes frequented the estuaries of rivers such as the Senegal where slaves from up-country were trans-shipped or delivered. Duarte Pacheco Pereira in his *Esmeraldo de Situ Orbis*, had cautioned captains wishing to enter the river Senegal to exercise caution at the bar and be aware of changing channels, unusual tidal directions, and seasonal differences. He noted that Portuguese vessels only went as far as the kingdom of Tucurol to barter. Both mighty rivers, the Senegal was navigable from the coast for 580 miles to the Felu falls, whereas the tidal Gambia was navigable only for some 290 miles before the Barrakunda rapids. From the mouth of the Gambia as far south as Sierra Leone, there was a profusion of rivers at whose mouths the Portuguese engaged in commerce, sailed inland to fluvial ports, and traded at inland fairs on the Senegal and Rio Grande. As early as 1456 the Portuguese sailed up the Gambia to trade at the fairs at Cantor which were held from June to September. Indeed, until 1586, the Portuguese had a factory there, according to one source. Portuguese sailed as far as 450 miles upstream to the fluvial port of Jagrançura. In the sixteenth and seventeenth centuries, there were settlements of Portuguese along the Gambia. Further south, Portuguese penetrated inland from the coast by the 'rivers of Guinea' such as the Casamance and São Domingos. The five 'slave rivers' of the Bight of Benin were certainly visited by the Portuguese from the 1480s, but problems of navigability may have meant that the Portuguese did not penetrate far up such rivers. Notwithstanding such river ventures, on the whole the Portuguese preferred either to trade from their vessels which remained on the coast, or through their trading posts. Factories at Arguim, Cantor on the upper Gambia, in Sierra Leone, and forts at Axim and São Jorge, were collecting points for much river and coastal trade but many declined in importance after the mid-sixteenth century. Nevertheless, in the nineteenth century Cape Verdeans continued to trade with rivers of Upper Guinea (Casamance, Cacheu, Buba and Geba) as they had three hundred years earlier, and had trading posts at the highest tidal points of such rivers. So common was their presence as traders (mostly in slaves) that, already in the sixteenth century, the coast came to be known as the 'rivers of Cape Verde', here referring to the archipelago and not the promontory in Senegal. In East Africa, although early Portuguese pioneers followed the different branches of the Zambezi and its tributaries inland, exports from the Portuguese settlements on the Zambezi, and even less on the Pungue and Buzi rivers where there sporadically were factories, were too small as to make them of great importance. In the sixteenth century, an annual vessel with cloth and glass beads sailed from Chaul to Mozambique, where the cargo was trans-shipped to a pinnace for the coastal trip and then up the Zambezi river to Sena.[48]

It was in America that the Portuguese were to find and to use the most extensive and best interlocking network of river systems. Looking from north to south, there are the major river systems of the Amazon-Madeira with tributaries such as the Tapajós, the Araguaia-Tocantins, and the Paraguay-Paraná. There is a host of other major rivers, of varying degrees of navigability, which provided access from the coast to the interior. These include (from north to south): Parnaiba, São Francisco, Paraguaçú, Rio das Contas, Rio Pardo, Jequitinhonha, Doce and Paraíba do Sul. As we shall see later, river systems were to play an extraordinarily critical role in the economic development and settlement of Goiás and Mato Grosso. In the colony, rivers were important not only for transportation of people and goods over long distances, but for shorter local and regional communication and transportation. In Pernambuco, for example, the only effective mode of transportation of goods and people was along the Beberibe and Capiberibe rivers.

The importance of rivers to the Portuguese in Africa and Brazil raises the question of modes of transportation. In general it would be true to say that the Portuguese used indigenous craft, but there were instances where they introduced designs from Portugal and even apparently developed vessels to meet local demands. On the Zambezi, the Portuguese freighted river boats and used canoes extensively. Duarte Pacheco Pereira had described the prevalence of canoes in West Africa and noted very large canoes on the Rio Real (eastern delta of the Niger) capable of carrying eighty men. On the Guinea coast, a distinction was made between those who remained on rivers and lagoons and those who sailed out from the coast and fished. In West Africa, canoes predominated and on the Congo at least such transportation was cheaper than employing porters, once the initial outlay had been made. The most durable were made of mahogany with a life of as much as fifteen years. It took several months from cutting of a suitable tree to conclusion. These canoes ranged from the small nine-foot craft for local travel or negotiating swamps, to trading canoes as long as sixty feet. On the Gambia, the Portuguese used waterborne routes extensively and caravels could sail up-stream. Here there occurred an interesting instance of the bringing together of Portuguese and indigenous African building techniques. Essentially, the Portuguese contribution was sails and rigging and the result was a larger version of fishing boats used for surf fishing. A descendant of this design was photographed by Philip Curtin in the 1960s at Nomi on the north bank of the Gambia. The Senegal, because of current and unfavourable winds, was more difficult. But before the arrival of the Europeans, canoes had been developed and a seventeenth-century report stated these had a capacity of about fourteen English tons burden.[49]

In Brazil, in the Bay of All Saints and the wider sections of the river São Francisco for example, the Portuguese used vessels of Portuguese design: *faluas* and *saveiros*. Such vessels could be used on the lower stretches of the numerous navigable rivers of

Brazil, until that point when swiftness of current, inadequate depth, narrowness, or falls, prevented their passage. It would seem that in the eighteenth century the Portuguese were using in Brazil a vessel of their own creation. This was the *pelota*, made of hide. They also built river boats and rafts, but generally adopted the use of indigenous canoes. These fell roughly into two categories: the more fragile carried at most three or four paddlers but were ideal for negotiating narrow or shallow rivers, and larger canoes hollowed out of tree trunks and pointed at both ends. The latter could be used on coastal waters and rivers and, in addition to paddlers, could be equipped with sails of cotton or vegetable fibres and rigging made out of vines. That these could be substantial was apparent to Martim Afonso de Sousa who sailed into the Bay of All Saints in 1531 and witnessed indigenous warfare carried out from canoes, each carrying some sixty warriors. It was these larger canoes (*canoas de casca*), some up to forty-five feet long and six feet wide, which were used on the Amazon and its tributaries by Portuguese missionaries and colonists, often to subdue indigenous peoples. They were especially effective in flood waters and were easy to beach. The Luso-Spanish combined force, which routed English and Dutch interlopers in the Amazon in 1623, travelled in canoes from Pará through the forested channels west of Marajó island. In the 1720s, disillusioned by their failure to find gold in Goiás, five *paulistas* and fourteen Indians descended the 1,200 miles of the Tocantins river by canoe and reached Belém. The gold-bearing region of Mato Grosso could only be effectively reached by use of the interlocking rivers and portages from the Tietê to the Cuiabá. The whole journey took some five to seven months to cover 2,200 miles and the larger canoes (rarely exceeding forty feet in length and five feet in breadth) in convoy could each carry as much as three hundred *arrobas* (about 4,425 kilos) and as many as twenty passengers in addition to crew (one or two pilots, bow oarsman, five rowers). Before leaving the subject of canoes in Brazil, it should be noted that slaves imported from West Africa, most notably the Minas, were already adept at the construction and sailing of canoes and presumably brought such skills to Brazil. From descriptions of West Africa in the sixteenth and seventeenth centuries and those for colonial Brazil, there was not a marked difference in construction techniques of canoes in the two continents and both were pointed at bow and stern. In Brazil a less common form of transport was the *jangada*, which comprised several rounded pieces of wood lashed together to form a raft. At a pinch, bundles of reeds could be lashed together with lianas. Although in mid-seventeenth century, men from the *bandeira* of António Raposo Tavares descended the Amazon on such rafts, clearly they were unsuitable for rivers with underwater obstacles, and had limited carrying capacity. Only in the south did the use of *jangadas* persist, on the rivers Uruguay and Paraná.[50]

We have seen that the routes followed by the Portuguese were maritime, terrestrial, and fluvial. The vehicles they employed ranged from the enormous carracks of the *carreira da India* to hollowed-out canoes in Africa and Brazil, and the animals included camels, horses, donkeys, mules, and oxen. Such vessels and animals permitted the Portuguese to transport goods locally, and across and between continents. Those vessels which carried the Portuguese beyond the Pillars of Hercules contributed to the ebb and flow of humanity between metropolis and empire, and within and between Africa, Asia and America.

CHAPTER III
FLUX AND REFLUX OF PEOPLE

(i) Migrants and Settlers

Vessels bound for Portuguese India and Portuguese America carried substantial numbers of people – a fact often overlooked because of the emphasis placed on their carrying capacity homeward-bound, laden with pepper, spices, sugar, and gold. An Indiaman, in addition to a crew of some 120 but which could climb to as many as 200, carried anywhere between 500 and 1,100 passengers of various categories outward-bound. In addition to soldiers for garrisons of India, which could number 700-800 on a single vessel, and other travellers, as many as 400 to 500 slaves might be taken aboard in Mozambique. One sombre side of this enormous carrying capacity was that on some voyages there was as much as fifty per cent mortality outward-bound attributable to exposure to extremes of climate, lack of hygiene on board, putrified water and rancid food, and the fact that many persons were diseased prior to embarkation. Homeward-bound, there were usually fewer but better-heeled passengers. These included merchants and their slaves, officials of church and State, and perhaps the viceroy or the archbishop of Goa accompanied by their retinues and servants. With the addition of children, slaves, soldiers, and women, the numbers on some homeward-bound vessels approximated those carried to India. Some vessels, especially in the eighteenth century, put into Brazilian ports homeward-bound. The heavy mortality and large numbers of those who had to be taken to the hospital of the Santa Casa da Misericórdia or placed under private medical supervision, reflected the gruelling nature of the voyage across two oceans.[51]

Vessels on the Brazil run could not match the carrying capacity of their Indian Ocean counterparts, but there was a steady flow of people from Portugal to Brazil and back. This increased in the eighteenth century and Portugal faced the potentially disastrous demographic results of gold rush fever. By 1709, the population of the northern provinces in particular had been depleted to the point that Dom João V reiterated earlier orders that intending travellers should have passports, obtainable from the secretary of state in Lisbon or from the appropriate officials in Oporto and Viana do Castelo. Despite penalties imposed on ships' captains who failed to comply, there was always a way to find a passage. Measures were not strictly enforced at Portuguese ports of departure. In 1733, three vessels arrived in Bahia from Oporto carrying over 700 passengers without the requisite authorization. In 1742 the viceroy of Brazil, the Count of Galvêas, noted the large numbers of migrants arriving from Portugal and the Atlantic islands. Their destinations were Bahia, Pernambuco, São Luís do Maranhão, and especially Rio de Janeiro which offered the shortest route to the mining areas. He estimated that some 1,500 to 1,600 persons left Portugal annually for Brazil, probably a half to a third of those leaving annually during the height of the gold rush years.

Niels Steensgaard has pointed out the impact on collective psychology of 'the annual spectacle of the return of successful and prosperous' from Portuguese India, and how this could serve as an incentive to others to count themselves among the fortunate few. This, of course, also applied to persons returning from Brazil to the mother country. The example of the fortunate stimulated others to emulate their travels and share in the rewards, but also contributed to the depletion of the human resources of one of the smaller countries of Europe.

Portugal counted a population of about 1,000,000 at the beginning of the fifteenth century, between one million and 1.5 million according to the 1527-32 census, and two million by the time of the Restoration in 1640. This number remained fairly constant until 1732, increased to 2,500,000 by 1758, and to about three million at the turn of the nineteenth century. This was in a country whose territorial extent of 35,340 square miles today has altered little since the thirteenth century. What is quite remarkable is that, from such a small demographic base, the Portuguese could be omnipresent in Asia, Africa, and the Americas. The British historian Charles Boxer has suggested that, at the end of the sixteenth century, the number of able-bodied Portuguese overseas did not exceed 10,000. He estimates that every year during that century some 2,400 persons, mostly unmarried young men, left Portugal predominantly bound for Portuguese India. Magalhães Godinho suggests a higher figure of some 3,000 to 4,000 leaving annually, with as many as 8,000 by 1620.

The Portuguese presence in Africa was demographically small. In the Gulf of Guinea this was represented primarily by the fort of São Jorge da Mina, established in 1482 with a garrison of 500 armed men and 100 artisans. This was granted a municipal charter in 1486. But the civilian population both at Elmina and in the half-dozen or so other Portuguese settlements on the Gulf of Guinea probably did not number more than 200 in the sixteenth century. As for the Congo, the number of Portuguese probably did not exceed 100 at any time in the sixteenth century, a number out of proportion to their commercial impact. When Paulo Dias de Novais was granted (1571) his charter for Angola, it had been with the expectation that colonization from Portugal and São Tomé would be encouraged by offers of seeds and plants. Such hopes were not realized. The combination of disease and quick profits from the slave trade was not conducive to the emigration to Angola of families from Portugal. In the 1660s the whole of Angola counted only 326 white households. By 1777 the white population was about 1,581, declining to about 1,000 in the first quarter of the nineteenth century. One success story in terms of population increase was Madeira whose population increased to some 50,000 by 1676. In addition to emigrants from continental Portugal, increases of population in the Atlantic islands, most notably in Madeira and the Azores in the sixteenth century, were to contribute a fair share of migrants to Brazil in the seventeenth and eighteenth centuries. As for the Cape Verdes, in 1582 the islands of Santiago and Fogo counted one hundred white men and about 13,700 African slaves. Moving to East Africa, demographic increase of the white population was curbed by the lack of white women. In 1722, the Portuguese community in Zambezia numbered 300, and in 1802 the number of Portuguese households was put at 283.

Moving across the Indian Ocean, in 1524 there were about 2,500 Portuguese in Goa, and this increased to about 10,000 people of European descent by 1540. In the seventeenth century, the numbers of Portuguese in settlements from Hormuz to Malacca declined. Macao experienced a rapid growth in numbers of Portuguese. The riches and easy life of Macao made it attractive not only to Portuguese from the mother country but also from India. In 1601 there were over 600 Portuguese males capable of bearing arms, and this remained constant into the 1640s. By 1669 there were some 300-320 Portuguese *casados* in Macao. But already the tide was turning to Brazil and, by the end of the seventeenth century, there were probably less than 2,000 white Portuguese in those settlements still remaining in Portuguese hands between East Africa and Macao.[52]

By 1584, the white population of Brazil was about 25,000. The European presence in Portuguese America grew through migration in the sixteenth and seventeenth centuries and, more slowly, through natural reproduction as more white women took up residence in the colony. A greater crown presence, suppression of hostile Indians, and economic upturns, spurred migration to Brazil in the seventeenth and eighteenth centuries. There may have been about 50,000 whites in the mid-seventeenth century. By the 1680s some 2,000 each year were arriving in Brazil from the Atlantic islands and Portugal. Such migration intensified as a result of news of gold strikes. Between 1700 and 1720, emigrants numbered 5,000-6,000 annually, decreasing to some 3,000 to 4,000 annually. These centuries also witnessed increases in the numbers of persons of African origin and descent transported to Brazil: about 560,000 in the seventeenth century and 1,891,400 from 1701-1810. In 1818, the population of Brazil was about 3,805,000. Of these, only an estimated 250,000 were native Americans. Be they of European (1,040,000) or of African (2,515,000) descent, over 93 per cent of the population of Brazil was the product of migration from Europe or Africa over the previous three centuries. This would also apply to Madeira, the Azores, Cape Verdes, São Tomé, and Príncipe, which were uninhabited or virtually uninhabited before the arrival of the Portuguese. This, indeed, was the world the Portuguese created.[53]

The role of the State in sponsoring migration was minimal. One exception concerned sponsored relocation from one part of the Portuguese-speaking world to another, involving the diplomatically, economically and militarily sensitive lands of southern Brazil in the eighteenth century. Already in the seventeenth century, the crown had encouraged migration from Madeira and the Azores to Brazil, but the response had not met expectations and the majority settled in Rio Grande and Santa Catarina. Dom João V pursued this policy more forcefully. The crown sponsored migration from the Azores and Madeira to Santa Catarina in the south of Brazil in the 1740s and early 1750s. What distinguished this official venture was that this migration was of families with the stipulation that the wives be of child-bearing age. This did not reach the projected goal of 4,000 couples. Between 1748 and 1752, 1,057 families, totalling 5,960 people, from the Azores settled in Santa Catarina where there was an increase in population from 4,197 in 1749 to between 6,000 and 7,000 by 1767. Couples from the Azores also settled in Rio Grande do Sul but it is not clear if they were sponsored. After 1808, further incentives were provided to encourage migration from the Atlantic islands to Brazil. Families received financial aid for their first two years in Brazil, lands to cultivate, seeds, farming tools, and draft animals. By a decree of 1813, Dom João VI exempted migrants and their families from military service. Such families were not limited to the south of Brazil, but were spread between Rio de Janeiro, Minas Gerais, Espírito Santo, São Paulo, and Pôrto Seguro. A second example is intriguing, illustrating the close ties between Brazil, by now independent, and Angola. Insurrection in Pernambuco in 1847-48 scared recent Portuguese and other European immigrants to the point that they approached the Portuguese crown for permission to relocate to Angola. This was granted. Between 1849 and 1851, some 497 such migrants from Brazil arrived in Angola and settled in Mossamedes, 200 miles south of Benguela.[54]

It is difficult to estimate the extent of the Portuguese presence in Asia, Africa and America at any single period. But it would be fair to say that the population density of Portuguese in any one of these continents was extraordinarily low, even at the beginning of the nineteenth century. In the preceding four centuries, during which Portugal created and consolidated a far-flung empire, manpower was spread exceptionally thinly in terms of sheer numbers. One characteristic which was not unique to the Portuguese, but distinguished the Portuguese by its prevalence from other European nations overseas, was the predominantly male nature of the outflow of Portuguese from the mother country. A second characteristic was the high incidence of Portuguese who took up residence overseas and spent their lives in the tropics and sub-tropics. These were the *casados* and they settled in India, Macao, Africa, or Brazil and, for the most part, took local females as wives. The resulting progeny were likely to be brought up as Portuguese and Catholics. Thus it was that a small country of limited population was able to maintain a presence, admittedly often merely of a token nature, in so many widely dispersed settlements beyond Europe. The Portuguese also resorted to a second expedient to use to the full their limited human resources in manning garrisons, populating townships, developing commercial ties, administering the thousand-and- one aspects of empire, and making converts for Christianity. This was by moving people, inter- and intracontinentally and across oceans. The result was to create the impression of omnipresence and of numbers far greater than were, in reality, the case.

The Portuguese seaborne empire was characterized by a constant flux and reflux of people. Some were in the service of the crown, others servants of God, others servants of men, others captive of their own self-interest and cupidity, and still others who were essentially part of the flotsam and jetsam of empire. Some travelled voluntarily, whereas others were coerced or forcefully transported against their will. The skill of the crown and of the various councils which administered Portugal overseas – the Casa de Guiné initially, which gave way to the Casa da India, to be replaced (1604) by the Conselho da India e Conquistas Ultramarinas, and finally the Overseas Council in 1642, lay in what we would now call 'maximization' of resources, be these human or technological. Viceroys, governors, judges and magistrates, senior civil servants, captains of fortresses, administrators of factories, and soldiers, were constantly on the move. Let us look at this movement of people between continents and within continents.

(ii) Servants of the Crown

In the sixteenth and even seventeenth centuries, a Portuguese nobleman could earn his spurs on the battlefields of North Africa or India, travel extensively east of Goa on official or semi-official business, and then return to Portugal. Having met the two most important criteria for high office, namely military expertise and nobility – either inherited or through merit – he would be well placed for a posting to Brazil. Typical of the breed was Duarte Coelho Pereira, who served king and country as a soldier in Morocco and West Africa. In 1509 he voyaged to India and saw twenty years in the royal service in India and East Asia. This included three voyages to China, one each to Vietnam and Indonesia, and four to Siam. Pereira was present at the capture of Malacca, was twice ambassador to Siam, and made a diplomatic coup in securing for the Portuguese the right to trade freely at Malacca. He was at the capture of Bintan in 1526. He returned to Portugal and was, in quick succession, Portuguese ambassador to the French court, captain-major of the supply fleet for Elmina, and commander of a coastguard patrol on the Malagueta coast. Coelho Pereira was ideally placed to invest his fortune and stake his reputation in accepting the king's award (1534) of the lord-proprietorship of the newly designated captaincy of Pernambuco in north-east Brazil. For two decades, Duarte Coelho Pereira was a forceful leader who laid the agricultural foundations for the future prosperity of the captaincy. His younger son, Jorge de Albuquerque Coelho (b. 1539), also had an action-filled life in several continents. From the age of twenty to twenty-five he fought the Caeté Indians in Brazil. Travelling to Portugal in 1565, he was on the *Santo António* on a voyage afflicted by storms and pirates and recorded in the *História Trágico-Marítima*. The year 1578 found him on the field of battle at Alcácer-Quibir in North Africa in the honorary post of chief of medical services and as a soldier in the front rank of the 'adventurers'. He was wounded and subsequently was held captive at Fez. Three years later, he inherited the lord-proprietorship of Pernambuco but never returned to Brazil.[55]

A contemporary was Martim Afonso de Sousa who did not allow his success as lord-proprietor of the captaincy of São Vicente to prevent him from leaving Brazil in 1533. As Admiral of the Indian Sea, Afonso de Sousa commanded a fleet of five vessels from Lisbon which arrived in India in 1534. He commanded the Portuguese force which captured Daman, negotiated an agreement with the king of Cambay for the building of a fort at Diu, saw service at Colombo, captured moorish vessels, riches and weapons, and was at the relief of Diu in 1538. When the viceroy refused his request to be permitted to pursue the enemy back to the Straits of Mecca, Afonso de Sousa returned to Lisbon. Ironically, should he have stayed, he would have succeeded to the highest office of the Estado da India because viceroy Dom Garcia de Noronha died on 3 April 1540. As it was, the son of Vasco da Gama, Dom Estêvão, was appointed governor. Martim Afonso de Sousa succeeded him as governor in 1542. A fellow traveller on the fleet taking him to his new posting was Francis Xavier, S.J., and both were detained in Mozambique because of adverse weather. The transition from da Gama to de Sousa was characterized by bitterness. Martim Afonso de Sousa had a chequered record as governor, was victim of a smear campaign over diverting public funds to his own use, and left the post in 1545 weary of office and disillusioned by rampant corruption. Although a military hero in Portugal, Martim Afonso de Sousa spoke out against the North African campaign of Dom Sebastião, was omitted from the expedition to Morocco, and thus did not see service in the name of Portugal in another continent but was also spared the bloodshed of Alcácer-Quibir in 1578.[56]

This multi-continental quality characterized Portuguese in the service of the crown in the sixteenth and seventeenth centuries. Let us take three disparate examples. Immortalized as a navigator and for his epochal voyage of 1519, Fernão de Magalhães also had an earlier military career in the service of Portugal. Born about 1480, he was a page in the service of the queen and then passed to the service of king Dom Manuel. In 1505 Magalhães sailed for India as a soldier, was on an expedition to Sofala and Kilwa in East Africa, fought in the battle against a combined Egyptian-Gujarati force at Diu in 1509, and saw service at the conquest of Malacca in 1511. Already Magalhães had acquired a reputation for his knowledge of navigation and wind systems. In 1513 he sailed for Portugal and saw military service in Azemmour in Morocco before leaving for Seville and service of the king of Spain in 1517. No less familiar with the Indian Ocean and Pacific was Tristão Vaz da Veiga. Born on Madeira, at the age of sixteen (1552) he sailed for India in the royal service. He was present at the siege of Malacca (1574-75), was twice captain-major of the Japan voyage, and was one of the founders of Nagasaki. On his return to Portugal he was given the captaincy of Machico in Madeira. An administrator whose experiences were no less multi-continental but whose career ended disastrously was Dom Jorge de Meneses. His taking office as captain-general in the Moluccas was disputed by his predecessor. Meneses' subsequent exploits included plundering the Spanish fort on Tidor in 1528, forcing the king to pay excessive tribute to Portugal, poisoning the sultan of Ternate, and committing atrocities against the island's populace. He was sent to India in chains, returned to Portugal, and was banished to Brazil where he was killed by Indians in 1537.[57]

Until the mid-seventeenth century, a posting to Brazil or indeed anywhere in the Portuguese Atlantic ranked lower than to Portuguese India. This distinction between Portuguese India and Portuguese America was reflected in the fact that only sporadically before 1720 did the crown's senior representative in Brazil carry the title of viceroy. While not commonplace, it was not unknown for a senior official to serve as viceroy or governor of Portuguese India and subsequently as viceroy or governor-general of Portuguese Brazil. António Teles de Meneses, Count of Vila-Pouca de Aguiar, was governor of India (1639-40) and governor-general of Brazil (1647-50). The first to hold the title of viceroy of Portuguese India and of Brazil was Dom Vasco Mascarenhas, count of Obidos, who was the crown's representative in Goa (1652-53) and in Salvador (1663-67). Dom Pedro António de Noronha, Count of Vila Verde and Marquis of Angeja, was viceroy in Goa from 1693-98 and viceroy of Brazil, 1714-18. Vasco Fernandes Cesar de Meneses, Count of Sabugosa, was viceroy in India from 1712-17 and in Brazil from 1720-35. There were those who moved from west to east. These included António Luís Gonçalves da Câmara Coutinho, governor-general in Brazil (1690-94) and viceroy in India (1698-1701), and Dom Rodrigo da Costa, governor-general in Brazil (1702-05) and subsequently viceroy in India (1707-12). Two Almeidas (unrelated) served as administrators in India and Brazil in the eighteenth century. Dom Pedro de Almeida Portugal, Count of Assumar (and later Marquis of Castelo Novo which title was replaced by that of Marquis of Alorna), was governor of the captaincy of São Paulo and Minas Gerais for the tumultuous years 1717-21 and was appointed – against his will – as viceroy of India for the term 1744-50, where he was exceptionally successful. Dom Lourenço de Almeida spent six years in India where he acquired a wife and a fortune by dealing in diamonds, was a member of the unsuccessful expedition to relieve Mombasa, and served in Brazil as governor of Pernambuco (1715-18) and Minas Gerais (1721-32). Almeida's residence in India made all the more incredible his pleas of ignorance as to the real contents of reports of 'little white stones', whose appearance (1726) in the Serro do Frio region of Brazil had come to the attention of Dom João V and who reprimanded his governor for failing to inform him of the discovery of diamonds. Another governor, this time of the captaincy of São Paulo, was Dom Luís de Mascarenhas (1739-48) who, as Count of Alva, also saw service as viceroy in India from 1754-56.[58]

The close connections between Brazil and Angola were reflected in the careers of two governors who saw service in both continents. During his eighty or so years of life (1602-81/87), Salvador Correia de Sá e Benevides seems to have been in perpetual motion. At the age of twelve he accompanied his grand-father to Brazil in search of gold and silver mines, and learnt to speak the *língua geral* of the Tupi during four years in the south-west before returning to Portugal. In 1618 he accompanied his father who had been appointed commander of the garrison in Rio. For the next five years Correia de Sá remained in Brazil, returning to Portugal in about 1623 as commander of a home-ward-bound convoy from Pernambuco to Lisbon. The following year he commanded a vessel bringing reinforcements to Rio. In March 1625 he skirmished with Dutch vessels under Piet Heyn and was present at the Portuguese recapture of Bahia. The year 1626 or 1627 found him in Madrid, where he received appointment *in perpetuo* as *alcaide-mór* of Rio de Janeiro. By 1628, he was back in Rio de Janeiro. The years 1630-35 found him travelling to Asunción, suppressing the Guaicurú and Paiaguá Indians, crushing the Calchaqui uprising in Tucumán, making an advantageous marriage, travelling to Potosí, and returning to Rio de Janeiro where his father had died during his second term as governor. A visit to Madrid led to Correia de Sá's appointment as governor of Rio de Janeiro, 1637-1643. In 1643 he was at court to clear his name of allegations of abuse of office. He was appointed to the Overseas Council and general of the Brazil fleets. Correia de Sá was involved in the 1645 revolt in Pernambuco against the Dutch. The Dutch presence in Angola demanded resolution. In 1647, Correia de Sá was appointed governor of Rio de Janeiro and captain-general of Angola. In 1648 he had his first taste of Africa, when he led the expeditionary force which recaptured Luanda and expelled the Dutch from Angola. Subsequently, Correia de Sá served as governor of Angola until 1652. After this stint of duty in Africa, he returned to Brazil shortly, accompanied the sugar fleet to Lisbon, commanded the defence of Lisbon, and saw service in the Alentejo, before his appointment in 1658 as captain-general of the southern part of Brazil (*Repartição do Sul*) and general of the Brazil fleet. Only in 1663 did this seasoned soldier and civil servant return to Portugal. One of his last acts was to throw his support behind the creation of Colônia do Sacramento on the Río de la Plata in 1680. But his career could have taken a very different turn if, in late 1645, Dom João IV had accepted his application, endorsed by the Overseas Council, for the post of captain-general of Macao.

Portugal's south Atlantic empire also affords one of the rare instances of a person of African descent occupying high office. This was the mulatto João Fernandes Vieira (c. 1620-81). Born in Madeira, which he left at age ten for Pernambuco, by the age of seventeen he had acquired enough capital by commercial dealings to have his own house. He was friendly with the Dutch commander Jacob Stachouwer, married well, and prospered. Vieira led the 1645 uprising against the Dutch in Pernambuco and distinguished himself, especially in the second battle of Guararapes, in the 'War of Divine Liberty' against the Dutch. He acquired extensive land-holdings and sugar mills taken from the Dutch. Vieira was appointed governor of the captaincy of Paraíba – not a prestigious post – in the north-east of Brazil (1655-57). In 1658 he took office as governor of Angola (1658-61), where he suppressed rebellious chiefs, and forced the king of Congo to live up to agreements made with Salvador Correia de Sá. Vieira strengthened the fortifications of Luanda, raised infantry troops and two troops of cavalry, and created coastal patrols against pirates. His relations with the Jesuits were tainted by allegations that he violated their ecclesiastical immunity. The judicial enquiry into his term alleged abuses of power. This did not prevent his appointment, after his return to Pernambuco, as superintendent of all fortifications on the Brazilian coast from Maranhão to Alagoas. The careers of Salvador Correia de Sá and João Fernandes Vieira fully illustrated the inter-dependence of Portugal, Angola, and Brazil.[59]

There were those who moved from one posting to another within Brazil. A successful governorship could find its reward in promotion to viceroy. André de Mello de Castro, Count of Galvêas, was a calming influence in the ever turbulent captaincy of Minas Gerais, where he served as governor (1732-35) and later enjoyed a long and successful term as viceroy of Brazil from 1735 to 1749. So too did Dom Marcos de Noronha e Brito, sixth Count of Arcos. After serving as first governor of the new captaincy of Goiás (1749-55) he went on to serve as viceroy in Salvador from 1755 to 1760. One of the most distinguished crown servants was Dom Luís de Almeida Portugal, second Marquis of Lavradio, who followed in the footsteps of his predecessor, Dom António Rolim de Moura Tavares, Count of Azambuja, who had been promoted from governor of Bahia to viceroy (1767-69) in Rio de Janeiro. After serving as governor-general of Bahia from 1768 to 1769, where he distinguished himself as a fiscal manager, Lavradio was promoted to be viceroy in Rio de Janeiro. He held this office for ten years, much of them devoted to problems in Rio Grande do Sul and Santa Catarina and Luso-Spanish rivalries in Río de la Plata. Dom Fernando Martins Mascarenhas e Lencastre was governor of Rio de Janeiro 1705-1709, after serving as governor of the captaincy of Pernambuco from 1699 to 1703. José da Silva Paes was interim governor of Rio de Janeiro, organizer of the colonization of Rio Grande, and first governor of Santa Catarina (1739-49). In terms of power and authority, no governor of colonial Brazil rivalled the energetic Gomes Freire de Andrada. He was captain-general of Rio de Janeiro from 1733 to 1763 but, at one time or another, under his jurisdiction fell the captaincies of Minas Gerais, São Paulo, Goiás, Mato Grosso, Santa Catarina, and Rio Grande do Sul. Although never viceroy, Gomes Freire thus exercised jurisdiction over a greater part of Brazil than did his viceregal colleagues in Bahia.[60]

There was one father-son team which vividly illustrates how office-holding, nobility and mobility often went hand-in-hand in much of the Portuguese-speaking world, parts of which preserved a frontier quality well into the eighteenth century. This was António de Albuquerque Coelho de Carvalho and his son António de Albuquerque Coelho. The father was of noble Portuguese ancestry and resided in Brazil prior to his appointment as governor of the province of Maranhão e Grão-Pará 1690-1701. He returned to Portugal and fought in the War of Spanish Succession. Evidently heart and body lay in the tropics for he returned to Brazil and served as governor not only of Rio de Janeiro (1709-10), but also of the newly created captaincy of São Paulo and Minas Gerais (1710-13). As if this were not enough, he crossed the Atlantic to take up a triennial appointment as governor of Angola where he died in 1725. Taking time out from this distinguished career as soldier and governor, António de Albuquerque sired a bastard son by a woman who, to borrow the late Gilberto Freyre's expresssion, epitomized luso-tropicalism, being of white, black, and Amerindian descent. The son was born about 1682 and named after his father. He was schooled in Portugal and in 1700 was packed off to India to cut his teeth as a soldier in search of fame and fortune. He made the rank of marine captain and sailed for Macao in 1706 where – after surviving assassination attempts which led to injuries resulting in amputation of his right arm – he married (1710) a ten-year-old orphan who was also an heiress. She died aged fourteen, after giving birth to the couple's second child. Albuquerque was to return to Goa to clear his name of charges and was appointed governor of Macao. There followed an extraordinary twelve months of travel which included a journey overland to Madras, a voyage to Malacca with an English pilot in a small vessel which Albuquerque had bought, and an adventurous winter in Johore, before he arrived in Macao in May 1718. He discharged his responsibilities magnificently. In 1721 Albuquerque was appointed governor of Timor and Solor where he also served a full three year term. He returned to Macao in 1725 and to Goa the following year. Like his father before him, there was one final trans-oceanic posting. This was in 1728 as governor and captain-general of Pate off East Africa. This was a disaster. Albuquerque failed to carry out his orders to build a fort and abandoned the island. He added to his problems by failing to try to relieve Mombasa which had been recaptured by the Arabs. Back in Goa he defended himself against charges of dereliction of duty and his final service to Portugal was as general of Bardez during the Maratha invasion.[61]

Mobility was also a career characteristic of the Portuguese magistracy. For the most part, these were born in Portugal, graduated from the University of Coimbra with a degree in canon or civil law, completed a stint in Portugal, and then were posted overseas. This could be as *juiz de fora* or *ouvidor* in one of the Atlantic islands, São Tomé or Príncipe, Angola, Brazil or India, with the hope of promotion to one of the supreme appellate courts (*Relação*) overseas (Goa; Salvador, and, after 1752, Rio de Janeiro) as a judge (*desembargador*). For the very few, the final promotion would be to the highest appeals court of the realm, the *Casa de Suplicação* in Lisbon, and subsequent service on the Overseas Council, Desembargo do Paço, or Mesa da Consciencia, also in Lisbon. For the less worthy, there was the consolation of a seat on the *Relação* of Oporto. A collective career profile of 168 judges of the court in Salvador for the period 1609-1758 is revealing as regards promotion and mobility. Of those whose birthplace can be identified (136), all were born in Portugal, with 15 exceptions: 2 in Pernambuco; 7 in Bahia; 1 in Rio de Janeiro; and 5 in the Azores. The 168 had accumulated between them 54 tours of duty outside Portugal before promotion to the high court in Salvador. These were distributed as follows: Goa, 2; Morocco (Mazagão), 1; Cape Verdes, 3; São Tomé, 2; Angola, 8; Brazil, 38 (Bahia, 10; Pernambuco, 8; Paraíba, 4; Sergipe, 4; Rio de Janeiro, 3; Minas Gerais, 2; Piauí, 2; and 1 each in Maranhão, São Paulo, Cuiabá, Alagoas, and Espírito Santo). This suggests that such mobility would fall within one of two spheres, either the Atlantic sphere or the Estado da India, with little exchange between the two, and that service in the colonial judiciary was increasingly a prerequisite for promotion. After their service on the high court of Bahia, eighty-three went on to serve on the court in Oporto. This career mobility also applied to the lesser magistracy, the multitude of *ouvidores* and *juízes de fora*.[62] Civil servants in the Treasury were also moved frequently, with service in Africa, in India, and in East Asia, not being an uncommon career trajectory. This mobility also applied to factors and lower ranking bureaucrats.

Such mobility was a characteristic of persons in the service of the crown. Skilled mariners were always in demand as the Portuguese crossed the oceans and seas of the world. In the early sixteenth century, Francisco Rodrigues showed his piloting skills in the royal service on pioneering Portuguese expeditions from Malacca to the Bandas and Moluccas (1511-12), to the Red Sea (1513), and to the South China Sea when he accompanied to Canton the expedition of Simão Peres de Andrade in 1519.[63]

Despite the hardships of the *carreira da India*, there were those who made a career of maritime service on this route. Two such were João Pereira Corte-Real (c. 1580-1641) and António da Costa de Lemos (1601-51). The former claimed to have rounded the Cape of Good Hope eight times and advanced from soldier to admiral, while being one of the very few to pass the professional examination for pilots on the *carreira*. The latter worked his way up from ordinary seaman to captain during thirty years at sea. Corte-Real and Costa de Lemos were exceptional in that, after a lifetime at sea on the India run, they could retire. A century later, an enterprising variant to retiring from maritime service was provided by one Inácio de Sousa Ferreira. A sometime captain of the *carreira da India*, he forsook the sea and turned to crime in the gold-mining regions of Brazil. Sousa Ferreira became leader of a gang which operated an illegal foundry and mint in Minas Gerais until it was raided by the authorities in 1731.[64] Rodrigues, Corte-Real, Costa de Lemos, and even

Sousa Ferreira, were endowed with skills which made them exceptional. For the most part, ordinary seamen on the *carreira da India* fell victim to shipwreck, disease, or exposure, jumped ship to try their fortune in Portuguese India, or succumbed to the charms of women in Brazil. Dangers from the elements were less on the shorter Atlantic runs, but viceroys and governors constantly faced the problem of under-manned vessels.

One to whom the high seas were familiar was Duarte Pacheco Pereira (c.1450-c.1526). He combined an exceptional knowledge of navigation with the skills of a soldier. In the former capacity he was the leading authority of his day on the west African coast from Morocco to the river Gabon, and was an expert on nautical science in such areas as finding latitude, tides, and instrumentation. In 1498 he was a participant on a mysterious voyage to a 'western region', and sailed with Cabral when he made his landfall on the coast of Brazil in 1500. As a soldier, Pereira saw service at Arzila (1471) in North Africa, sailed for India in 1503 with Albuquerque, led an expedition against the fleet of Calicut, attacked the Samorin in 1504, and brilliantly defended Cochin the same year, before returning to Lisbon in 1505. In 1509 he captured the French pirate Mondragon off Finisterre, captained the Portuguese fleet in the Straits of Gibraltar in 1511, and finally was governor of the fort of São Jorge da Mina from 1520-22. He was ordered back to Lisbon in chains on charges of fraud which were later shown unproven but left him to die in poverty. [65]

Soldiers were a constant presence on vessels. Usually soldiers were poorly trained and had been forced into service as the result of periodic sweeps of the streets and jails of port cities of Portugal and Brazil. It was also alleged that many so-called recruits were not even teenagers, and eight and even six-year-olds were not unknown in the royal service. Conditions on the Indiamen were such that, of 5,228 soldiers who left Lisbon in the quinquennium 1629-34, only 2,495 reached Goa. Others deserted prior to embarkation, died of sickness or exposure, or were shipwrecked. In the Indian Ocean, China Sea, and Pacific of the sixteenth and seventeenth centuries, there were enough enemies of the crown of Portugal to require seaborne expeditionary forces to fight on sea and land, make reprisals against recalcitrant rulers, suppress smugglers, and for escort duties. Soldiers were also shuttled from garrison to garrison as required.

Disease, death, and desertion characterized the military careers of many. Angola, Benguela, and Mozambique were terminal postings for many who succumbed to a variety of maladies. Elsewhere cholera, malaria, and problems attributable to putrid food or unclean water decimated garrisons. Wages, if they were paid, were invariably in arrears. Soldiers with Brazilian experience were shipped to Portuguese garrisons in Angola. Mercenaries enlisted in Portuguese regiments were shipped from East Africa as far as Ceylon. It is not clear how much this policy of transporting soldiers inter-continentally applied also to non-white auxiliaries in Portuguese service. These included persons of African descent in infantry regiments in Brazil, the use of black slaves in Africa, and auxiliary troops of *lascarins* or sepoys in India.[66]

Officers with technical skills were highly prized and were moved from one assignment to another in the Portuguese empire. Two military engineers well illustrate both the opportunities for promotion and for mobility. Although not contemporaries, both saw service in Portuguese America, Africa, and the East. The first was António Coelho Guerreiro who had been born in the Alentejo in mid-seventeenth century and then entered the army, seeing service in Brazil and West Africa, and rising to the rank of captain. He was appointed (1688) colonial secretary in Angola and lived in Luanda before his promotion (1698) to secretary of state in Portuguese India. In 1701 Guerreiro was appointed governor and captain-general of the islands of Timor and Solor where his four year tenure was characterized by continual struggles against the 'Black Portuguese' or *Larantuqueiros* , who waged spirited opposition to any imposition of authority by the viceroy in Goa, and by his refusal to buckle under to the Dutch. Evidently, Guerreiro's performance was sterling enough to be offered the captaincy-general of Zambezia in East Africa, but he turned this down and probably returned to Goa where he died. Another high-flying military engineer was Carlos Julião who rose from the rank of second lieutenant in 1763 to that of colonel by 1805. Julião saw service from one end to the other of the Portuguese seaborne empire but did not become an administrator. From Brazil to East Asia, he distinguished himself variously for heroism under fire at Mazagão in North Africa, for his meticulous reports on the district of Macao, or his assessment of artillery and munitions in the province of Extremadura. As a military engineer, Julião travelled the Portuguese world inspecting and designing army arsenals and military positions. A contemporary, who also saw service in Europe, Portuguese India, and Brazil, was André Ribeiro Coutinho. He fought in the War of the Spanish Succession and was present at the battle of Belgrade before returning to Portugal. With the rank of *sargento- mór* he was assigned to India to teach military science. He returned to Portugal in 1735 and, now with the rank of lieutenant colonel, was dispatched to Sacramento. He died in Rio de Janeiro in 1751 with the rank of colonel. He authored one work on the qualities of the perfect general (1713) and another (1751) on infantry training and tactics.[67]

Cut from a different cloth, but whose military career well demonstrates the mobility required of a soldier in the royal service, was João da Maia da Gama. Born in Aveiro (1673), he studied philosophy at Coimbra but dropped out to sail for India in 1692. Surviving an enforced stay at Mozambique and a hurricane in the Indian Ocean, he arrived in Goa in 1693. Over the next five years da Gama saw action along the Kanara coast against an English vessel, was on a squadron which destroyed three Omani frigates off Rajapur, and served with distinction in the Persian Gulf for two years where he was severely wounded. In 1698 he sailed from Goa on the *São Pedro Gonçalves* which put into Bahia after heavy mortality of almost fifty per cent, and returned to Portugal in 1699. Within a few months, da Gama was captain of a frigate bound for Mombasa but which burnt at Bahia. A replacement sank within the Bay of All Saints, but he swam to safety. Returning to Portugal, da Gama saw distinguished service in the War of the Spanish Succession. He also served in the Portuguese squadron which was part of the force which destroyed the French fleet blockading Gibraltar in 1705. Da Gama then moved to Brazil where he served successively as governor of Paraíba (1708-17) and of Maranhão e Grão-Pará (1722-28), before returning to Portugal where he died in 1731.[68]

João da Maia da Gama has another claim to fame which falls within the compass of the central theme of this book. In his capacity as governor of Maranhão e Grão-Pará, he travelled overland from the Maranhão to Pernambuco in 1728-29. He was not the only senior civil servant to travel extensive distances in the colony. In the 1690s and first decade of the eighteenth century, governors of Rio de Janeiro travelled to the interior to attempt to establish law and order in the mining encampments, settle disputes over mining rights, and quell hostilities between *paulistas* and outsiders (*emboabas*). The creation (1710) of the separate captaincy of São Paulo e Minas Gerais relieved them of this chore. Inspection tours by the governor of São Paulo prior to the elevation of Goiás (1744) and Mato Grosso (1748) to the rank of captaincies with their own governors, also demanded lengthy journeys by water and land. Governors taking up posts in Goiás and Mato Grosso faced lengthy and arduous journeys of several months from the coast or from São Paulo by river and overland before reaching their destinations. The distance from Goiás to Salvador was put at some 400 leagues (about 1,200 miles). When Dom Marcos de Noronha e Brito, Count of Arcos, was promoted from the governorship of Goiás to be viceroy in Salvador, he showed his mettle by covering the distance overland in eleven weeks to take up his appointment in 1755. District magistrates (*ouvidores*) too were required to travel substantial distances to hear cases in the various parts of the judicial district (*comarca*) over which they exercised jurisdiction. *Per diem* allowances were inadequate to meet the costs of horses, fodder, lodging, slaves, and food, to say nothing of the physical demands imposed by weeks in the saddle on rough trails and replacement of clothes and equipment spoilt after several weeks of travel. Not surprisingly, judges tried to find excuses not to meet the requirement that they make a 'visit of correction' (*correição*) to every part of their district once a year to hear cases.

Another form of skill which was highly sought after by the crown was diplomacy. These diplomatic initiatives were apparent in Africa in the early period of contact, but emerged full-blown in India and Asia in the course of the sixteenth and seventeenth centuries. Some were truly diplomatic, whereas others were more in the nature of commercial missions. Some sought to achieve by negotiation rather than warfare well defined Portuguese objectives such as the establishment of a factory or fortress. In the Portuguese Atlantic, the acceleration in the volume and intensity of the slave trade radically altered earlier established relationships, whereas in Portuguese India the advent of the Dutch produced the same result. As early as 1456 Diogo

Gomes and Cà da Mosto signed treaties of 'paz e amistade' with the Mandingas of the Gambia, which had less to do with friendship than acquisition of Africans for transport to Portugal as slaves. On the other hand, the Portuguese mission to the Congo in 1490 achieved a more lasting alliance despite the fact that the partners had different priorities, each weighting very differently the military, commercial, evangelizing, political, and technical components. Embassies to the Ngola (known to the Portuguese as the king of Angola) of the kingdom of Ndongo in 1520 and 1559 had a dual agenda of commerce and conversion. The latter was headed by Paulo Dias de Novais, a grandson of Bartolomeu Dias, and included four Jesuits. Neither was successful and the 1559 envoys, lay and clerical, were detained in Angola for several years. In 1571 a Portuguese expeditionary force restored the king of Congo to his throne and military intervention succeeded where diplomacy had failed. This led to the creation of the captaincy of Angola, granted to Novais, and the establishment of Luanda as capital (1576).[69]

Religion motivated the embassy headed by Dom Rodrigo de Lima which finally reached Ethiopia in 1520. This was the culmination of various reports dating back to the time of Pero de Covilhã, and resulting in a rich lode of information and misinformation. Matheus, who was probably Armenian rather than Ethiopian, contributed further to misunderstandings when he was sent to Portugal by Afonso de Albuquerque and was well received by Dom Manuel in 1514. It was Albuquerque who planted in the royal mind the notion of a joint Portuguese-Ethiopian force to overthrow Muslim domination of the Red Sea and even sack Mecca. Matheus accompanied the Portuguese embassy to Ethiopia in 1520, but died before reaching the court. The priest Francisco Álvares, on royal orders, also accompanied the embassy. Álvares' account of the six months journey from Massawa on the west coast of the Red Sea to Shewa in the highlands in 1520 is fascinating. This was a terrible journey over rough stony roads, along deep dry river beds, through deep gullies, along cliffs, through canyons, and over high passes across rugged mountains. All the while, there was the threat of attack by robbers. There are descriptions of cave monasteries and of the monolithic underground churches hewn out of the rock at Lalibela, of sanctuaries with saints' bodies, of prohibitions against females entering certain monasteries, of priests, monks, and nuns, of masses, making of sacramental bread, and fasting. Álvares described baptism, circumcision, marriage, polygamy, and divorce. He was intrigued by herds of large baboons, 'the size of sheep, and from the middle upwards hairy like lions'. He also commented on the everyday lives of people, crops, foods, animals, cattle, and trade in salt and other merchandise. Álvares said mass for Lebna Dengel on Christmas Day and the Portuguese performed a miracle play before the Negus. The priest was a reporter of court life, the political and economic aspects of the kingdom, land charters, its frontiers, and details not only of the Negus but of tribute-paying peoples. This was the first European embassy to reach the court of the Negus and return safely and Álvares' account remains an important source for Ethiopian history.[70]

Commerce was to the fore on the agendas of Portuguese envoys and embassies in India and Asia. After the capture of Malacca, Albuquerque dispatched vessels carrying ambassadors to Pegu and Siam and three vessels under António de Abreu to the Bandas and Moluccas, whence they returned in a junk, with which they had replaced their own old vessel, with a cargo of cloves, nutmeg, and mace. Although the Portuguese participated in long and middle distance trade networks in the Indian Ocean and beyond, they failed to dominate local routes and markets and thus were compelled to achieve working relationships with local producers, suppliers, distributors, and vendors. Although it is often asserted that, by pioneering the Cape route to India, the Portuguese broke the Venetian spice monopoly, this should not be taken to imply that the Portuguese dominated the Asian trade in spices. They did not, remaining comparatively minor players in the overall trade in Asian spices. Co-operation, and not domination, was the Portuguese commercial strategy. Malabar merchants of the sixteenth century provided Portuguese with goods on credit, advanced loans, and even transported merchandise in their own vessels. Portuguese viceroys and other crown officials in Goa had reason to be grateful to *subhedars*, or district officers of the semi-independent *desais* in the region around Goa, for providing commercial, military, social, and political information, and even acting as secret agents for the Portuguese. In Malacca, the Portuguese had to work with a multi-national mercantile community of Chinese, Javanese, Luzonese, and Indians – the latter comprised of Tamil-speaking Hindus and Gujarati Muslims – although it was the Hindu which was to become the most powerful sector after the Portuguese conquest in 1511. It was cooperation and collaboration with this Hindu community in Malacca, which played a prominent role in society and politics as well as commerce, which enabled the Portuguese the quicker to adapt to conditions in south-east Asia. Elsewhere we find locals acting as secret agents for the Portuguese.[71] Although official policy may not have favoured collaborative ventures with Hindus or Muslims or Jews, local reality dictated that Portuguese follow the maxim of the American politician Sam Rayburn to the effect that 'If you want to get along, go along'.

Few can have had such an unlikely preparation for a future commercial embassy as Tomé Pires, son of the apothecary to Dom João II, and himself an apothecary to one of the royal princes. In 1511, when he was in his early 40s, Pires sailed for India as 'factor of the spices' (*feitor das drogarias*) in Cannanore. He made a good enough impression on Afonso de Albuquerque to be sent in 1512 to Malacca to audit and ferret out irregularities by officials in charge of prizes of war. In Malacca, Pires was scrivener and accountant of the factory and 'controller of spices' (*veador das drogarias*) and rapidly acquired wealth. He remained some thirty months in Malacca, interspersed with at least one trip as factor of a fleet to Java. Pires sailed from Malacca for India with the intention of returning to Portugal. But the new governor-general, Lopo Soares de Albergaria, had come out to his posting accompanied by Fernão Peres de Andrade whom Dom Manuel had appointed as captain-major of a fleet to 'discover China'. Andrade was to convey an ambassador to China, and Albergaria selected Pires to head this embassy. Prior to his departure in 1516 from India for China as the first Portuguese ambassador to the imperial court, Tomé Pires had written the *Suma Oriental* which extolled the merits of trade based on the principle of piggy-backing on, rather than working against or dominating, Indian and Asian routes and supply networks. After a delay of nineteen months since leaving Cochin, the squadron carrying Pires arrived off Canton in 1517 and fired a cannon salute which was regarded as a breach of custom by the Chinese. Pires, accompanied by five Portuguese, a Persian from Hormuz, twelve boys, and five interpreters, waited a further fifteen months in Canton before receiving permission to proceed to Beijing. This they did by water and overland. Pires' mission was to establish Sino-Portuguese trade relations. That this failed was attributable less to the merits of the proposed relationship than to protocol blunders by the Portuguese and cultural differences. A letter from Dom Manuel, when translated into Chinese, was not suitably deferential to the emperor. There were breaches of etiquette by the Portuguese in the aftermath of the death of the Zhengde emperor. Also news reached the emperor from the former sultan of Malacca about the Portuguese 'sea-robbers'. The actions of Fernão Peres de Andrade's brother, Simão Peres de Andrade, who sailed into the Pearl River estuary in 1519 confirmed all the bad impressions already gained by the Cantonese of the Portuguese. Andrade started building a stone and wood fort and mounted guns without permission, hanged a sailor (thereby infringing the right of the Cantonese authorities to impose sentence of death), impressed Chinese for labour, disrupted the regular transaction of commerce, and even kidnapped or bought Chinese children as slaves. The arrival of such reports in Beijing undermined any hopes that Pires might have entertained for a successful outcome. Without seeing the emperor, the embassy was sent back to Canton: torture, imprisonment, and execution were their fate. One version recorded Pires' death in 1524. Another – more fanciful version – suggested Pires was banished from Canton to Sampitay, married a Chinese woman, sired a daughter whom Fernão Mendes Pinto met in 1543, and only died in about 1539.[72]

In the 1630s and 1640s, there were several Portuguese trade missions from Macao to Japan to improve or re-establish commercial relations, with mixed results. The union of Spain and Portugal had led to Japanese reprisals in the form of an embargo and detaining of Portuguese vessels arriving in Nagasaki. This action had been provoked by a Spanish captain's capture of a Japanese junk. An embassy from Macao, headed by Dom Gonçalo de Silveira, who had seen a decade of service in the Persian Gulf and been on the expedition to Malacca and Sumatra, left for Nagasaki in 1630. He was to spend four years in Japan and succeeded in having the embargo raised; Portuguese Macao could breathe freely again. But in 1639, two Portuguese vessels were not permitted to unload in Nagasaki and returned to Macao with the news that the Japanese had ordered the cessation of Macao-Nagasaki trade. At least they returned with their lives. Others were not so fortunate. A last-ditch effort in 1640 by Macao took the form of a commercial mission of four leading citizens. This culminated in their imprisonment, sentencing, and execution (4 August) in Nagasaki, together with fifty-seven of their entourage and crew. This year also marked the Edict of 2 August expelling the Portuguese from Japan. This was not quite the end of the Portuguese in Japan. In 1644 the Portuguese nobleman and veteran soldier, Gonçalo de Siqueira de Sousa, sailed from Lisbon heading a royal embassy from Dom João IV to Japan in the hope of reopening commercial ties. After a protracted voyage of extraordinary vicissitudes, the embassy anchored off Nagasaki on 26 July 1647. On 29 August the Portuguese received news that their mission had been rebuffed by the shogun but the embassy was permitted to leave Nagasaki without harm from the some 2,000 vessels which had blockaded the Portuguese in the harbour. [73]

To minimize the likelihood of such set-backs, the Portuguese did come to depend on at least the toleration and even cooperation of local peoples. In Portuguese India, not only did the Portuguese have to deal with the Mughal emperor, the Deccan sultanates such as Bijapur, Ahmadnagar and Golconda before their fall to the Mughals, and the southern Hindu kingdoms of Cochin and Quilon. The Portuguese referred to rajahs or sultans in the vicinity of Portuguese settlements such as Goa, Cochin, Daman, Chaul, and Meliapore as 'neighbour kings' or *reis vizinhos*. It was they who permitted the Portuguese to establish trading factories or build forts in territories under their jurisdiction. The account by Duarte Barbosa (1518), who achieved fame as a linguist, shows how much of his fifteen or sixteen years in the royal service in India as scrivener of the factory at Cannanore was spent as an interpreter and interceding with the local rajah on behalf of the Portuguese. One of his assignments, blending linguistic skills with diplomacy, was to try to persuade the Hindu king of Cochin to convert to Christianity, a task in which neither Barbosa nor Afonso de Albuquerque were successful. After a large Portuguese force under António de Brito obliterated the Spanish factory established in 1521 on Tidor by survivors of Fernão de Magalhães' expedition, de Brito sailed on to Ternate and signed a 'treaty of peace and commerce' with the queen regent which permitted the Portuguese to establish a factory and raise a fort. Negotiations leading to a Portuguese presence in Macao have been discussed. An Indian counterpart was the port of Hooghly, until it was sacked by Mughal troops in 1632. Such acts of collaboration and co-operation were the fruits of diplomatic and commercial embassies, missions, and overtures.[74]

In making overtures or opening negotiations with potentates or leaders, the crown often opted for men of the cloth as well as laymen. Pre-eminent among the former were members of the Society of Jesus and Augustinians. They were accompanied by local interpreters. An idea of the intensity and variety of such embassies, and the travelling they involved, can be gained from the following. Between 1580 and 1605, during the reign of Akbar the Great, the Jesuits undertook three missions to Agra. Between the time of viceroy Dom Francisco Mascarenhas (1581-84) and 1700, viceroys or governors in Goa dispatched no fewer than thirteen embassies headed by Augustinians alone to princes or kings of Persia, Socotra, Achin, and the court of the Mughal emperor. Some were fairly routine, for example to secure releases of prisoners. Others were highly sensitive. Among the most travelled was Friar Luís da Piedade. He was an emissary to the Mughal emperor Aurangzeb on more than one occasion. In 1700 came his most delicate assignment. Two vessels of vassals of the Mughal emperor had been impounded in Goa on the grounds that their captains had infringed the terms of the Portuguese system of passports (*cartazes*). The viceroy ordered they be sold at auction. This provoked protests from provincial governors and vassals of the Mughal emperor on the west coast of India and Mughal threats of invasion of the northern territories. Friar Luís resided in the Mughal court for five months and successfully negotiated reasonable terms for Portuguese commercial access to Mughal-controlled ports and normalization of Mughal-Portuguese relations. The request in 1614 by Shah Abbas I of Persia that neither Jesuits nor Augustinians be sent to his court as envoys was unique, and his negative attitude toward the use of men of the cloth as emissaries was not shared by rulers from the Persian Gulf to Japan.[75]

There were others who had special skills which required travel in the service of the crown or its representatives. These included members of the medical profession and scientists. One such was Garcia d'Orta (1501/2-68), of Spanish Jewish descent, who was a teenage student at the universities of Salamanca and Alcalá de Henares, practised medicine in the small Portuguese frontier town of Castelo de Vide, and moved to Lisbon in 1526 where he came to hold a university chair. In 1534 he sailed for Goa as personal physician to Martim Afonso de Sousa, captain-major of the Indian Ocean and subsequently (1542-45) governor of Portuguese India. D'Orta was physician to several viceroys and governors in Goa, personal physician and friend of the Sultan of Ahmadnagar, and friend and collaborator with Muslims, Hindus, and anyone who could help in his researches on plants and medicine. He was to publish his *Coloquios dos simples* in 1563 in Goa, a landmark in the history of *materia medica* and botany. Less distinguished, but no less travelled than d'Orta, were those surgeons and medical doctors who were posted to garrisons, were in the employ of municipal councils overseas, or were private physicians to governors and viceroys. A graduate of the universities of Evora and Coimbra was Dr Aleixo de Abreu. He was appointed personal physician to the governor of Angola, João Furtado de Mendonça, and resided in Luanda from 1591 to 1604. From Angola, he moved to Salvador to take up appointment as physician to the governor-general, Diogo Botelho. After two years of residence in the Brazilian capital, Abreu returned to Lisbon and wrote (in Latin and Spanish) *Tratado de las siete enfermedades* (Lisbon, 1623).

Requests by overseas governors for medical or technical assistance from Lisbon were often ignored or found a tardy response. When an epidemic of yellow fever in Recife and Salvador erupted in 1685-86, so serious was the mortality among the white population especially that the crown responded immediately to the request by the governor of Pernambuco for an experienced physician. Dr João Ferreira da Rosa, a recent graduate of Coimbra university, was dispatched to Brazil. He arrived in 1687 and studied the fever and treated its victims for five years before returning to Lisbon. Trained medical personnel were in demand overseas for the treatment of soldiers and as appointees by municipal councils who were required to have at least one surgeon and physician on their payroll. One such was the surgeon Francisco da Costa Franco, who was chosen in 1731 by the city council of Salvador to be municipal surgeon. His duties included inspecting vessels arriving from Africa. Prior to this appointment, Costa Franco had served on the vessels of the *carreira da India*, practised medicine in India, and been surgeon of the garrison in Mozambique before coming to Brazil.[76]

Only with the Enlightenment were scientists and naturalists dispatched by the crown to study the flora, fauna, ethnography, and geology of the tropics. Expeditions by crown appointed naturalists in Mozambique and Angola will be discussed later and we may here turn to a closer examination of the travels of Dr Alexandre Rodrigues Ferreira in Brazil from 1783 to 1792. A Bahian by birth, Ferreira graduated from Coimbra, and already during the voyage from Lisbon to Belém do Pará prepared anatomical descriptions and painted watercolours of deep-water and coastal fish. Ferreira travelled extensively in the coastal area of Pará and reported on the cultivation of such export crops as sugar, cocoa, coffee, and indigo. He made shorter trips by canoes on the Tocantins and longer journeys by larger canoes with paddles and sails up the Amazon to Barcelos and to the mouth of the Rio Negro (1784-85). From Barcelos his first trip was along the Rio Negro and its tributaries, visiting the fort of São Gabriel de Marabitanas (1785-86), before returning to Barcelos. The second trip (1786) was from Barcelos to the Rio Branco and involved travel by canoe and overland. Return to Barcelos enabled him to prepare his collected specimens, write reports, and visit the forest Indians. In August 1788, Ferreira departed from Barcelos for his longest journey, namely to Mato Grosso. This he accomplished by following the Rio Madeira and, after numerous portages and explorations of side rivers, reached Vila Bela (current Pôrto Velho) on 3 October 1789. Vila Bela became his base for two years of field trips overland in Mato Grosso and by canoe on the rivers Guaporé, Cuiabá, and upper Paraguay. On 3 October 1791, Ferreira and his companions left Vila Bela and arrived in Belém do Pará three and a half months later. In early 1793, Ferreira was back in Lisbon and received the honours due him for his extraordinary contributions to scientific knowledge. These included the habit of the Order of Christ, appointments and sinecures, and the post of deputy director of the Ajuda museum and gardens.[77]

Ferreira's education exemplified another aspect of movement in the Portuguese world. Given the absence of universities in Portuguese India, Africa, or America before the nineteenth century, there was a reverse migration – albeit small – of male youths who attended institutions of higher education in Europe. In this they were the inheritors of a Portuguese tradition of travel in search of education going back to the fifteenth century, when aspiring students and professors had left Portugal to study at Paris, Louvain, Florence, Siena, Oxford, and Salamanca. As the eighteenth century progressed, there was an increase in the number of Brazilians studying in France, especially medicine at Montpellier. Among the manuscripts of the Torre do Tombo in Lisbon are collections titled 'Leitura dos bacharéis' and 'Assentos de bacharéis' which give biographical details of Brazilians who studied at the University of Coimbra. These can be supplemented from other sources to show that between 1577 and 1822, no less than 2,464 students born in Brazil were matriculated in the University of Coimbra. Numbers increased vertiginously from 13 in the sixteenth century to 354 in the seventeenth century, peaking at 1,753 in the eighteenth century, and 344 in the nineteenth century prior to 1822. In the early nineteenth century, the thirty-three matriculants from the Maranhão included the twins Joaquim Gomes da Silva Belfort (1801) and António Gomes da Silva Belfort (1802) and their relative Joaquim António Vieira Belfort (1801). Many students, drawn from Portuguese territories and settlements overseas, once they had earned degrees in civil or canon law, entered the service of the crown and became part of the magistracy and civil service of Portugal's empire.[78]

Artisans with special skills – stone-masons, carpenters, caulkers, smiths – were moved remorselessly from one centre of activity to the next in the royal service, building, repairing, or supervising work on official residences, barracks, fortresses, trading posts, docks and wharves, mints, bridges, roads, and even water fountains. For the building of the fort of São Jorge da Mina (completed 1482), the Portuguese king dispatched one hundred stonemasons and carpenters from Portugal. Their skills, local labour, and the fact that stones and timbers had already been cut and tiles and bricks already made in Portugal, made for an extraordinarily rapid construction period of a matter of weeks.[79] The

1490 Portuguese mission to Congo also included artisans. On the other side of the Atlantic, when Tomé de Sousa landed on 29 March 1549 in the Bay of All Saints with orders to establish a capital, he brought with him prefabricated materials and a contingent of artisans carefully selected for this purpose. These included carpenters, stone-masons, tile-makers, lime-makers, and workers in wattle-and-daub. Construction was under the direction of the well-known architect and engineer, Luís Dias, who had previously been the master of works at Safim in Morocco.[80]

Given the strongly maritime nature of the Portuguese endeavour overseas, shipyard personnel and shipwrights, master caulkers and craftsmen skilled in naval matters were especially in demand in shipyards in Salvador, Belém do Pará, Rio de Janeiro, Goa, and Cochin. These were recruited in Portugal as well as being moved from one part of empire to another. Naval architects might well see service in Lisbon, Oporto, Salvador, and Goa, and their prestige was such as to merit special privileges. The crown placed emphasis more on skill than national origin. In 1761, Manuel Alvares Barna, a Spaniard, who had extensive prior experience in France and Spain in marine construction, proposed to the king that, should he be appointed to supervise all naval construction in the dockyard in Salvador, there would follow considerable savings to the royal treasury. At the beginning of the nineteenth century, the prince-regent advocated the purchase on the Costa da Mina of young, strong, and intelligent male slaves who would be trained as carpenters for service in the royal naval arsenal in Salvador.[81]

This mobility by artisans with special skills could be harmful to the Portuguese cause. Some artisans possessed skills which might be attractive to local potentates and this was notably the case of gunmakers in Portuguese India. One of the 'neighbouring kings' to Goa was the sultan of Bijapur, known to the Portuguese as the Idalcão. Relations between the Portuguese and the sultan were good and sultan Adil Shah even had an ambassador in Goa. But the sultan was open to temptation in the form of what we would now call technology transfer. This appeared in the 1620s in the form of a Portuguese renegade who was also an artillery foundryman. He offered to cast a large cannon and entered the sultan's service. When viceroy Dom Francisco da Gama heard of this, he charged another renegade also at the sultan's court to murder his fellow Portuguese. Once the assassination had been carried out, the murderer took refuge in Goa, having fulfilled the order of the crown's representative.[82] Somewhat less dramatic were those technicians transported overseas by the Portuguese as foundrymen and minters. Although most were honest, there were instances in Brazil of skilled technicians from the royal mints or foundry houses absconding with dies, or dies which the authorities had failed to destroy. They counterfeited the highly valued gold *dobrões* or certified as genuine bars smelted from untaxed or lesser quality gold.

(iii) Servants of Christ

Such mobility was not limited to laymen in the royal service. Secular clergy, members of monastic orders, and the black robes of the Society of Jesus, were indefatigable in their travels. Still standing today are churches and chapels, testimony to a campaign of conversion which brought Christianity to East and West Africa, India, Ceylon, Malacca, Indochina, Indonesia, Macao and mainland China, Japan, and Brazil. Indeed, it was the Dominicans who pioneered Portuguese settlement on Solor in the Lesser Sunda in the 1560s.[83] Wherever they settled, the Portuguese put an ecclesiastical infrastructure in place. In 1533, a papal bull established the diocese of Goa for all regions east of the Cape of Good Hope. Through another papal bull of 1557, Goa became an archdiocese with Cochin and Malacca as suffragans, later joined by Macao, Funai (Japan), Cranganore, Meliapore, Beijing and Nanjing, and Mozambique. With the establishment of an official Portuguese settlement in Macao, in about 1568 the Bishop of Ethiopia, Dom Belchior Carneiro, moved to the Portuguese enclave and established a Santa Casa da Misericórdia and hospital. In West Africa, the see of São Salvador do Congo was transferred to Luanda in 1676. In Brazil, the bishopric of Salvador was raised to an archiepiscopal see in 1676 and by the end of the colonial period there were eight bishoprics (Rio de Janeiro, São Paulo, Mariana, Pernambuco, Maranhão, Pará, Cuiabá, and Goiás) in the colony.

As had been the case of civil servants, senior ecclesiastical dignitaries moved from one post to another. Portuguese America affords examples of their mobility from one continent to another and within Brazil. Bishops of Malacca and of Macao were promoted to bishoprics in Brazil. Dom Gregório dos Anjos, bishop of Malacca, occupied the see of the Maranhão from 1677 to 1689. Another bishop of Malacca, Dom Miguel de Bulhões e Sousa, served as bishop of Pará from 1749 to 1760. Although he was never to take up office in Brazil, Dom Bartolomeu Mendes dos Reis of the bishopric of Macao, was confirmed in 1772 as bishop of Mariana. In 1820, Dom Fr Joaquim de Nossa Senhora de Nazaré, former prelate in Mozambique, arrived to take up his post as bishop of the Maranhão where he served for three years. The ties between Brazil and Angola, which had been prominent in the crown bureaucracy, had their ecclesiastical parallels. Dom Manuel de Santa Inés was promoted from bishop of Angola to be the archbishop of Brazil (1762-71). Another bishop of Angola, Father António do Desterro, served as bishop of Rio de Janeiro from 1747 to 1773. Dom Luís de Brito Homem was bishop of the Maranhão (1804-13), after having served as bishop of Angola.

There were also promotions within Brazil. In 1738, Dom José Fialho, former bishop of Pernambuco (1725-38), was promoted to be archbishop of Brazil. After serving as bishop of Mariana, Dom Joaquim Borges de Figueiroa moved to the archiepiscopal see in Bahia and served in this capacity from 1773 to 1780. The first incumbent of the newly created (1745) see of Mariana, Fr Manuel da Cruz, travelled overland from São Luís do Maranhão – where he had been bishop for seven years – to Minas Gerais where he resided 1748-64. For such high-ranking ecclesiastics, there appears to have been a lower incidence of promotion from the colony back to Portugal than for their counterparts in the magistracy. Two archbishops of Brazil moved to sees in Portugal. Dom João Franco de Oliveira (archbishop, 1692-1700) moved to the bishopric of Miranda, and Dom José Fialho was promoted (1739) from Bahia to be bishop of Guarda. Fr António de Guadelupe, after fifteen years (1725-40) as bishop of Rio de Janeiro, returned to Portugal to the bishopric of Viseu. Fr João da Cruz served as bishop of Rio de Janeiro 1741-45 and then was appointed to the see of Miranda. Dom Miguel de Bulhões e Sousa, after serving as bishop of Malacca and of Pará, moved back to Portugal as bishop of Leiria. Fr Caetano da Assunção Brandão served as bishop of Pará (1783-89) and returned to

Portugal to take up his post in 1789 as archbishop in Braga. The only posting to Portuguese India from Brazil appears to have been that of Dom Fr Francisco de Assunção e Brito who was bishop of Pernambuco from 1773 to 1783 and then moved to the archiepiscopal see in Goa.[84]

As regards inveterate itinerants, pride of place must go to the members of the Society of Jesus who were – before their expulsion from Portugal and her empire in 1759-60 – to establish missions in India in 1542, in Japan from 1549 to 1650, in Beijing in 1601, in Tongking and Cochinchina (North and South Vietnam) in the seventeenth century, in Abyssinia prior to expulsion in 1633, and in Brazil. Macao was the *point de départ* for missionaries to China, Borneo, Siam, Cochinchina, and throughout south-east Asia. The Spanish-born Francis Xavier, S.J., set the pace. He left Rome in 1540, travelled to Lisbon, and arrived in Goa in 1542. He spent three years on the south-east coast of India and in 1545 travelled from Malacca to the Moluccas. He returned to Goa in 1548. In April 1549 he left Goa for Malacca and arrived in Kagoshima in Japan on 15 August. In the slightly over two years (August 1549-November 1551) in which he was in Japan, he travelled from Kagoshima in the south-west of Kyushu, to Yamaguchi in southern Honshu, on through snow and storms to the imperial court in Kyoto, and back to Yamaguchi. In November 1551 he embarked in Funai in Bungo province for India and the following year died off the China coast. In terms of residence in the East, few could match the lifetime of service of Luís Fróis, S.J. Born in Beja in 1532, he travelled to the East in 1548 and died in Nagasaki in 1597. Fróis wrote copious letters which gave an account of the introduction of Catholicism into Japan and a history of that country.

Jesuit missionaries were often the first Europeans to set foot in regions of Africa, Asia, and South America. Gaspar Pais, S.J., was the first European to reach lake Tana in Ethiopia (1603). Pero Pais, S.J., a Spaniard in Portuguese service, reached the springs of the Blue Nile (1618). Jesuit missionaries reached the interior of Bengal in 1576 and Jesuits came to reside within the Mughal empire. Bento de Góis, S.J., born on the island of São Miguel in the Azores, saw service as soldier of his king and of Christ. He had travelled to India as a soldier and was at the court of Akbar. After taking his vows, in 1602 he left Goa disguised as an

Armenian, crossed the Himalayas, and was the first European to enter China by this route. His journey took five years and he died in China in 1607. António de Andrade, S.J., crossed the Himalayas and was the first European to enter Tibet, whose capital he reached in 1624. Other Jesuits visited Nepal and Bhutan. Francisco de Azevedo, S.J., walked for six months from Agra to Traparang, Leh, and returned. While he did not pioneer new missions, the moves of the future historiographer (*Oriente Conquistado*, Lisbon, 1710) of the Jesuit Province of Goa, Francisco de Sousa, are indicative of this mobility. He was born in 1648 or 1649 on the island of Itaparica in the Bay of All Saints in Brazil, joined the Society of Jesus in Lisbon in 1665, travelled to Goa where he arrived in 1666, and was Superior of the Casa Professa of Goa where he died in 1712. It was administrative rather than directly missionary activity which took another Jesuit, Cristóvão de Gouveia (1542-1622), on a tour of inspection of all Jesuit missions in Brazil in the five years 1583-88.[85]

Remarkable even by the peregrinatory standards of the Society of Jesus was António Vieira, S.J. Born in Lisbon, while a child he accompanied his father to Salvador in Brazil on the latter's appointment as secretary of the high court. António was educated in the Jesuit College in Salvador and entered the Society as a novice in 1623 at the age of fifteen. He was present at the Dutch invasion of Salvador, was transferred to the college in Olinda where he lectured on rhetoric, returned to Salvador – all of this before his ordination in 1634! A brilliant scholar, eloquent preacher, and outspoken on the contemporary political situation and social injustices in the colony, Vieira went to Portugal in 1641 and was appointed court preacher by Dom João IV. From 1646 he travelled on secret diplomatic missions to France, the United Provinces, and Italy. In 1652, Vieira was sent by the Society of Jesus to the Maranhão where he was a missionary for nine years, travelling widely and learning Indian languages. His return to Portugal was in less than glorious circumstances, victim of palace intrigues and his own outspoken beliefs and views. This did not prevent him from residing in Rome from 1669-1675. He returned to his native land, and thence to Salvador in 1681 where he died in 1697. While the peregrinations of António Vieira, S.J., were exceptional because of their extent both within European nations and among regions and peoples of the Amazon, they were not unique among the black robes.[86]

Vieira's travels were matched, and even exceeded in terms of sheer adventure and happenstance, by his contemporary Jerónimo Lobo (1595-1678). Son of the governor of Cape Verde, he entered the Society of Jesus as a novice at the age of fourteen at Coimbra. Lobo was ordained in 1621 and sailed for India the following week, but the fleet departed so late that a decision was taken in the Gulf of Guinea to return to Portugal. The following year, the fleet on which he was a passenger reached Mozambique, where it ran foul of a British and Dutch attack which the fleet survived only to be wrecked because of pilot incompetence. Having finally arrived in Goa in December 1622, already in January 1624 Lobo was on his way to East Africa to join the newly created Ethiopian mission. After landing at Pate he travelled to the mouth of the Juba in Somalia, only to discover that he could not ascend the river to Ethiopia as he had hoped. He left Ampaza for India in April 1624. No slouch he, exactly twelve months later, the intrepid Lobo left Diu for the port of Bailul and crossed the Danakil desert to arrive at the Jesuit mission at Fremona in June 1625. Here he remained nine years until persecution and banishment drove the Society from Ethiopia in 1633. Within two months of his arrival (December 1634) in Goa, Lobo was on the high seas again, this time bound for Lisbon. He was charged with the important mission of inducing the Spanish and Portuguese authorities to dispatch a military expedition to Ethiopia to pave the way for a Jesuit return. Thus began an extraordinary voyage. His vessel was wrecked on the south-east coast of Africa before rounding the Cape, but Lobo reached Luanda in March 1636 in a small boat made by the survivors. He took ship with the retiring governor who was taking slaves to Cartagena. The vessel was captured by the Dutch on the Spanish Main, but Lobo and his companions were put ashore on an island and managed to find their way to Cartagena. From there Lobo travelled to Havana, thence to Cadiz, Seville, Lisbon, and Madrid, before travelling by sea from Barcelona to Genoa to report in Rome. His mission failed in its goal and Lobo returned to Lisbon in 1639, where he presumably wrote up the account of his travels. September 1640 found him in Goa again and he held several offices in Goa and Bassein before his designation in 1647 as Father Provincial. Differences with the viceroy in Goa prevented Lobo from taking up this post and led to his confinement (1648-52), accused of Spanish sympathies. Although restored to his post of prefect of the Casa Professa in Goa and vice-provincial in 1653, this respite was short-lived. In 1655, a new viceroy relegated him to 'the South', and Lobo visited Ceylon and Malacca. In 1657, Lobo returned to Europe and was in Rome and Rouen, rector of the College in Coimbra, and then vice-prefect of the Casa de São Roque (1660-62) where he died in 1678, the last survivor of the Ethiopian mission.[87]

The Jesuits were tireless in their travels by sea and by land, but they were not alone in their evangelizing mission. Friars of the mendicant orders – Franciscans, Dominicans, Augustinians, Carmelites, and a host of others – travelled extensively in Africa, Asia, and America, to convert and to preach. After short-lived and fruitless efforts at evangelization in Benin, in 1538 two Franciscans and a member of the Order of Christ were dispatched to Benin City. Although they were received once by the Oba, rejection followed. The missionaries were not permitted to leave until Dom João III personally authorized their return. Their fate is unknown.[88] The Franciscans came to Goa from Portugal in 1518, to be followed by the Dominicans in 1548, and the Augustinians in 1572. In 1607 the Discalced Augustinians arrived, not directly from Europe but through Persia and Hormuz. The year 1639 marked the arrival in Goa of the Theatines. In Portuguese India, as in Portuguese America, there were frequent complaints of the excessive numbers of friars and the heavy burden monasteries imposed financially on local communities. In 1636 in Goa a meeting was convened of the superiors of all the religious orders to discuss the appropriate numbers for such communities.

To illustrate the mobility of members of religious orders, let us consider one Dominican and one Augustinian. Among the twelve Dominican missionaries who sailed for Goa in 1548 was one Friar Gaspar da Cruz, a native of Evora. He successfully organized a mission on the west coast of India and another at Malacca. Da Cruz's attempt to found a mission in Cambodia failed. In the winter of 1556 he visited Canton for some weeks fruitlessly and returned to Malacca. The next twelve years are a virtual *tabula rasa* as regards his personal life, although at some stage he was in Hormuz. Da Cruz returned to Portugal in 1569 and fell victim the next year to the plague ravaging Lisbon and

Setúbal. His death or his modesty prevented him from accepting the royal appointment as bishop of Malacca. No less mobile was the Augustinian, Sebastião Manrique, a native of Oporto who took holy orders in Goa in 1604. He was in Hooghly in 1612 as a member of the Bengal mission, and was a missionary in the kingdom of Arakan in Burma from 1629-37. He descended the Ganges and travelled along the east coast of India. From 1637 to 1640 he voyaged to the Philippines, where he stayed fourteen months, and on to Macao. Manrique then travelled to Makassar in the Celebes and Bantam. He returned to India for about a year, visiting Patna, the uncompleted Taj Mahal in Agra, and Lahore. Manrique spent the years 1641-43 travelling to Europe through Afghanistan, Persia, and Palestine. In Rome, he put his experiences on paper and they were published in 1649 in Spanish under the title *Itinerario de las Missiones del India Oriental*. In 1669 Manrique was murdered by his Portuguese servant in London, who placed the cadaver in a box which he threw into the Thames. Subsequently, the servant was brought to justice and hanged.[89]

With the establishment by the Portuguese of religious orders overseas, the question arose of the admission of local people. This is not the place to describe the sliding-scale of policies and practices which varied from order to order, and depended on time and place. Let it be said that persons born overseas from Japan to Brazil were accepted as novices and were ordained and led productive and full lives as men of the cloth, without in most cases ever visiting Portugal. Some demonstrated no less mobility than their European-born colleagues. One such was the Franciscan Paulo da Trindade, whose *Conquista Espiritual do Oriente* was a history of the Franciscans in India and Asia in the late sixteenth and seventeenth centuries. Paulo da Trindade was born in Macao about 1570, travelled to Goa to enter the Franciscan Order, was a young cleric in Bassein, rector of a parish in Bardez, was appointed professor of theology at the Franciscan College in Goa, and held numerous positions in Goa before his death in 1651.[90]

In the fifteenth and early sixteenth centuries, young men from Congo and Malabar were brought to Portugal for religious instruction, and some returned to their countries of origin as ordained priests or catechists. Others were trained as secular clergy *in situ*, as was the case in São Tomé, Cabo Verde, Angola, and Goa, rather than being sent to Portugal. Some few blacks from East Africa travelled to Goa or Portugal for training and ordination, but fulfilled their ministries in India rather than returning to Africa. In Japan, only seven Japanese were ordained as secular priests, in addition to seven as Jesuit priests, before persecutions began, and in China the indigenous clergy only numbered seventy-eight in 1810. In both cases instruction occurred in-country. The number of non-European novices or ordained priests travelling beyond their home countries remained very small.[91]

Secular priests and friars were part and parcel of any caravel or carrack leaving Portugal for Africa, India, or Brazil. Some were to perform miracles of conversion and lead holy and pious lives. But many and strong were the temptations of the flesh awaiting them on distant shores, often conveniently remote from their superiors or even the long arm of civil law. In the Estado da India, some secular clergy were notorious for their dedication to Mammon rather than God. They engaged in commerce, amassed material rewards, took concubines, and had as their goal in life not the propagation of the faith but rather a safe return to Portugal personally accompanying a shipment of pepper or spices, a crate of curios or silks, or a lacquered box of jewels. The first half of the eighteenth century witnessed friars sent to Brazil with the explicit charge to collect alms for monasteries and religious houses in Portugal and the Atlantic islands. In this activity they were joined by the secular clergy. Priests and friars were notorious for their persistence in obtaining, by hook or by crook, unauthorized passages to Brazil for no purpose other than to engage in gold and diamond smuggling. Some were even accused of inciting revolt in the backlands. Comparatively few were arrested and returned to the custody of their superiors.

(iv) Servants of Mammon

Commercial gain was a powerful lure and civil servants, soldiers, and men of the cloth alike were not immune to its seductive force. Involvement in trade, be it by the Jesuits in spices, by a captain of a garrison seeking to supplement his salary, or even by a magistrate whose judgment might be swayed by local connections, was often not considered corrupt or immoral by the standards of the age. One exception was in Japan where local expectations as to what constituted proper behaviour by holy men, led to scorn for those Jesuits who engaged overtly in commerce. As for civil servants, although they might be banned from commerce by royal decrees, provided they did not commit excesses or abuse their offices, there was a fair chance they would escape censure. Salaries earned by servants of the crown represented the base line for their income, and it was accepted practice this would be supplemented from other sources. There are numerous instances of public officials who muddied the waters between private and public funds, or were accused of embezzlement or misappropriation of funds in the judicial enquiry at the end of their term of office, but who returned to Portugal and successfully cleared their names and reputations once at court. But this situation could lead to military expeditions motivated more by a personal desire for plunder and booty than the national interest. At a lower level were those who had gone to the Estado da India initially as soldiers, turned to combining soldiering with a little commerce on the side, and finally came to the realization that trade and the allure of a potential fortune were more attractive than service to king and country. If this was the attitude of public officials, it was not surprising that among the *casados* of Portuguese India there should be a marked lack of patriotism as shown by their willingness to put trade before loyalty.[92]

There were those for whom trade and commerce were their sole livelihood. Anticipated profits from gold, slaves, and ivory, led the more rugged Portuguese to travel up the rivers of West Africa in the fifteenth century, and travel up the Zambezi river valley in the sixteenth century. Especially in Zambezia, the few settlements they did establish were fever-ridden. In Zambezia the Portuguese turned to locals, the *mossambazes*, to trade to the more remote areas. Hopes of finding gold and silver led the Portuguese to prospect north of the Zambezi as early as the 1640s and were to culminate with Portuguese penetration into the region which is now Zambia. In the 1690s there were reports of silver deposits having been located at Nhacasse, near Tete, but apparently these were not substantiated although there were isolated reports of finds in the eighteenth century. Gold strikes in Marave country were a different story and inflicted the same socio-economic trauma as those in Brazil. If *sertanejos* fleeing from justice had made the initial strikes, soon there was a gold rush by adventurers, both lay and clerical. In Angola, the more determined of traders pushed eastwards from Luanda to cross the Kasai river and inland from Benguela.

Merchants, traders, and financial speculators were part of any fleet to Portuguese India or Portuguese America. Sometimes they engaged in licit practices, on other occasions they dealt on the wrong side of the law. Some worked for themselves, whereas others were essentially operating on a commission basis. Not infrequently their presence in East Asia led to accusations of extortion, smuggling, contravening local edicts governing trade, and even blatant pillage. Some went it alone, but most Portuguese overseas entered into some form of partnership or relationship with local merchants and entrepreneurs. The fairer sex also could come to play an important role as agents in the transformation of an adventurer/entrepreneur into a business magnate. In Zambezia, by law at least, *prazos* descended only on the distaff side, making the few white women wealthy landholders. A shortage of European males led many to marry Goanese, or marry below their social standing.[93] In Macao, the beauty and the wealth of young heiresses were famed, leading potential suitors to risk death in pursuit of their hands in marriage. In colonial Brazil, there were complaints on the part of aggrieved women that they had been duped into marriage for their wealth or inheritance and then deserted.

One soldier and entrepreneur was Galeote Pereira. On the coast of China in the first half of the sixteenth century, Portuguese smugglers alternately rivalled and collaborated with Japanese pirates and defied imperial decrees forbidding their trading and their presence. Islands and inlets provided refuges from patrol vessels. Pereira was of the provincial gentry of the Beira province in Portugal and sailed for India in 1534, seeing service over the next fourteen years as a soldier in Malacca and Siam and also as captain of Daman. He also made two trading voyages to China between 1539 and 1547 and accompanied Diogo Pereira on a further commercial venture to China in 1548. When Diogo Pereira returned to Malacca, he left some thirty Portuguese, among them Galeote Pereira, and two junks laden with unsold goods off the Fukien coast. In March 1549, these were captured by Chinese coast-guard patrols. The Portuguese and their Chinese accomplices were taken to the provincial capital of Fuzhou where they remained for a year. Some Portuguese and Chinese smugglers were executed. The others were saved from a like fate by the fact that the local viceroy had exceeded his authority and was impeached. The remaining Portuguese went free and were exiled to Guilin. Travel was substantially by river and overland. Here Galeote Pereira stayed for some time before being one of the lucky ones to be smuggled out to the coast and freedom. Galeote Pereira's account reveals him as an impartial and acute observer of Chinese justice and its prison system, but what concerns us here is his account of his travels. He commended the Chinese for the quality of their roads, noted the masonry and unusual construction of the great stone bridges of Fukien, and the walled cities of Fuzhou and Guilin with towers, gate-houses, iron-covered gates, paved streets, and large market places. Pereira was clearly in awe of the network of rivers and tributaries, the variety of river craft, and in particular the breadth of the river at Kan-chou-fu in Kwangsi province and its pontoon bridge of 122 barges. He noted such details as dung-farmers and use of chopsticks, but above all was impressed by the universal civility of the people.[94]

Another Portuguese who appears to have been moved by curiosity, a lust for travel, and who combined royal service with commercial dealings, was the somewhat mysterious Pedro Teixeira. Whatever the circumstances of his birth (devout Catholic or of Portuguese-Jewish stock) and education (a self-described youthful addiction to history), Teixeira exemplifies the opportunism and mobility present for a young man in Portuguese India at the end of the sixteenth century. He probably sailed for India in 1586. Within four months of his arrival in Goa, he accompanied the punitive expedition to Hormuz in 1587. This enabled him to visit Ampaza, Pate, Lamu, Malindi, and Mombasa in East Africa, Socotra at the mouth of the Bay of Aden, and Muscat in the Gulf of Oman. Back in Goa by October 1587, on 4 February 1588 Teixeira was again on the high seas, this time on the fleet to help the besieged Portuguese in Colombo in Ceylon. By the end of March he was back in Goa. It would appear that Teixeira was on the expedition to East Africa to quell the Turkish commander Mír Alí Bey. Leaving Goa in January 1589, this retraced Teixeira's earlier voyage along the East African coast from Ampaza to Mombasa and back to Ampaza, on to Socotra, and back to Goa by 16 May 1589. For the next three years he lived in Cochin and possibly elsewhere on the west coast of India. In 1593 Teixeira sailed for Hormuz where he remained four years and travelled in Persia. In 1597 he resumed his peregrinations, returning to Goa but immediately departing for Malacca where he remained two and a half years. On 1 May 1600, he left Malacca on a pinnace for the Philippines. After less than a month in Manila, Teixeira sailed to New Spain and reached Acapulco on December 1. He rode to Mexico City, which he reached on Christmas Day. Teixeira crossed to the port of Vera Cruz and sailed for Spain on 31 May 1601. Emerging unscathed from near-shipwreck off Cuba and corsairs off the Algarve, Teixeira arrived in Lisbon on 8 October, after a voyage which had taken him as far north as the Newfoundland banks and included San Lúcar and Seville.

There is mystery concerning his true vocation. One scholar opined that Teixeira was a physician, and his display of interest in the natural history of the Malayan archipelago might show a scientific training. He was a good linguist. He also saw military service. Probably, like so many of his age, Teixeira had many irons in the fire, but one such was almost certainly as a trader. After 1589, his lengthy periods of residence in Cochin, Hormuz, and Malacca, his return to Lisbon, subsequent short stay in Goa, and return to Venice and Antwerp, bear the hallmark of a person engaged in some form of business transactions. Otherwise it is difficult to explain how Teixeira came by the large amount of money which he had entrusted to friends in Malacca prior to his departure, and which they were to remit to Lisbon. This failed to arrive and, after eighteen months in Portugal, on 3 March 1603 Teixeira was India-bound, arriving in Goa in October. Evidently his endeavours were rewarded by success, for he remained in Goa for only four months. In February 1604, Teixeira sailed for Hormuz where he remained slightly less than a month before leaving for Basra. Inclement weather, declining provisions, strong currents and head-winds forced a return to Hormuz after five battered weeks in the Gulf. His next attempt was more successful and 7 August found him in Basra. From here he joined a caravan and travelled by the Arabian desert route to Baghdad and Aleppo before taking a boat from Alexandretta to Venice which he finally reached on 11 July 1605. Teixeira had business to transact in Venice and then embarked on the European leg of his travels. These took him through Italy, the Piedmont, Savoy, and across France to Antwerp. Why he should have chosen Antwerp as his final destination is unknown. Was it because of the commercial reputation of the city? Or could it have been because of the community of Jewish exiles there from Spain and Portugal? His translator, William Sinclair, referred to Teixeira as a 'globe-trotter', and his *Narrative of my journey from India to Italy* which started with his departure from Malacca in 1600 and concluded with his arrival in Antwerp holds three qualities of a good travel book: detailed observation, good narrative, and an entertaining read.[95]

There was no such ambiguity as to the prime motivation which led those Portuguese who, at the drop of the proverbial hat or whiff of a rumour, travelled inland from the coast of Brazil from the sixteenth century onwards in search of fabled mountains of silver and deposits of gold. Even prior to the establishment of royal government in Brazil in 1549, already in the 1520s Aleixo Garcia brought back silver samples from the Inca empire. After the death of João Dias de Solis in the Río de la Plata, the survivors had made for Spain but their vessel was wrecked off Santa Catarina. Garcia and eighteen others survived. Garcia headed a small group of Europeans and Indians who left Santa Catarina, crossed the Paraná, ascended the Paraguay, and crossed the Chaco. They entered Incan territory by what is now the province of Chuquisaca in Bolivia. Plunder and robbery ensued. With their spoils, the small group again crossed the heart of South America to the Paraguay. Garcia was to be killed in a Guaraní uprising.

The Amazon river valley was a route preferred by adventurers who ventured out from Portugal in search of gold and silver in South America. In 1536 an expedition headed by Aires da Cunha travelled up the river Maranhão in search of 'infinite quantities of gold' and, presumably, silver. Despite lack of success, reinforcements were dispatched from Lisbon in 1537, but with the same negative results. Francisco de Orellana's descent from Quito in 1541-42 via the rivers Napo and Solimões, had shown the possibilities of a fluvial route from Spanish Peru to the Atlantic seaboard. The more intrepid Portuguese used this exit for contraband silver from Potosí or to escape the clutches of the Spanish authorities. One Portuguese – António de Acosta – was even credited with writing a *Historia de Potosí* which has never been found. In 1558, the Portuguese Henrique Garces discovered mercury in what had by then become Spanish Peru. There were also Portuguese in the Spanish Caribbean in the sixteenth and seventeenth centuries engaging in the slave trade, smuggling, or simply sailors in search of a better future.[96]

During the late sixteenth and seventeenth centuries, the Amazon became an object of officially sponsored exploration. With total justice the Portuguese referred to the main channel as the 'River-Sea'. Into this flowed the major tributaries of the Xingú, Tapajós, Madeira, Negro, Purús, Japurá, Juruá, and Solimões, into which in turn flowed a myriad of other smaller rivers. Orellana's voyage is justly famed. Not so widely known is that Orellana was part of an expedition headed by Gonzalo Pizarro which left Ecuador in February 1541 and reached the mouth of the Amazon in August 1542. Between 1686 and 1724 a remarkable Bohemian-born Jesuit, Samuel Fritz, who had been sent to the Jesuit College in Quito and later was to be Superior of the Amazon Missions, travelled around the Amazon ministering to peoples from the river Napo to the river Negro. In fact, one of his charges was to move the Indians up-river out of the reach of the Portuguese![97] Already the Amazon had become an area disputed by Spanish and Portuguese. In 1638 the Portuguese captain Pedro Teixeira (not to be confused with his globe-trotting namesake), who had distinguished himself attacking Dutch and English settlements on the island of Tucujus, reached Quito after eight months of travelling up the Amazon, its tributaries and the river Quijos, returning by the same route. Teixeira carried sealed orders from the governor of Maranhão to establish a Portuguese settlement west of the line of the Treaty of Tordesillas and flagrantly within Spanish territory. In this, Teixeira was successful and established a Portuguese claim to the upper Amazon. On his return voyage, he was accompanied by a Spanish Jesuit, Cristóbal de Acuña, who wrote an account (published in Madrid in 1641) under the title *Nuevo Descubrimiento del Gran Rio de las Amazonas*. Whether the listings of native peoples, their habits and foods are more attributable to the observations of Teixeira or his Spanish colleague are not known.[98]

Portuguese in search of mineral deposits also travelled overland westwards from the Atlantic coastboard and its immediate hinterland in the latter part of the sixteenth century. One such was Gabriel Soares de Sousa, born in Portugal in the 1540s and who emigrated to Brazil in the late 1560s. He became a successful plantation owner in Bahia and served on the city council in 1580. His brother, João Coelho de Sousa, had discovered mineral deposits in the interior and bequeathed to Gabriel a map allegedly showing their location. After presenting his case at court, in 1590 Gabriel was granted the concession of these and any other strikes he might make. He left Salvador accompanied by 360 followers on an expedition to the upper valley of the river Salitre and in search of the headwaters of the river São Francisco. He died on the return journey and was buried in the Benedictine monastery in Salvador under a tombstone with the inscription 'Here lies a sinner'.[99] More successful was Brás Cubas, captain of São Vicente, who led two expeditions in 1560-62, which discovered precious stones and some gold on Brazilian territory.

For many, however, the incentive lay in the high Andes, namely the Imperial City of Potosí. Salvador Correia de Sá e Benevides was but the most prestigious of the many Portuguese visitors. In the later sixteenth century and seventeenth century, adventurers and traders from southern Brazil crossed the Pampas, Chaco, and finally the Andes to reach Upper Peru. They were known as *peruleiros*. This was the final destination of a commercial network extending from southern Brazil to the Río de la Plata, and in which Tucumán was a critical mid-point. There were also those Portuguese who reached Upper Peru by a northern route, namely by gaining passage on a Spanish vessel to Cartagena, and working their way southwards. Portuguese commercial presence in Peru was such as to lead the Inquisition in Lima, possibly acting in collusion with, or at least carrying out the will of, local merchants who resented this competition, to harass and imprison such Portuguese interlopers described by a contemporary as 'masters of commerce'. The union of the two crowns availed them naught in their captivity.[100]

Portuguese initiatives by land, river, and sea, produced expeditions and individual explorers who, by mid-seventeenth century, had travelled the major river systems of Brazil and had penetrated to the far north, the far south, and a substantial part of the western frontiers of Brazil. In this endeavour, one group stands out. These were the famous or infamous *bandeirantes*, associated with São Paulo in the popular mind and historiography, but also originating from Bahia and Pernambuco. For the most part, they were of mixed Portuguese and Indian parentage. Whereas technically to merit the title of *bandeira*, or flag, the group had to number 250, this was often not the case and such *bandeiras* numbered anywhere from a score to 400. The four prime characteristics of the *bandeirantes* were their mobility, their ability to live off the land, and their reputation as fearless fighters and indefatigable explorers. These characteristics led Portuguese kings to coerce them to participate in expeditions in search of mineral wealth, serve as trackers, hunt down runaway slaves, and engage in attacks on Indian peoples. The most notorious of the breed was arguably Domingos Jorge Velho, who 'civilized' Indian peoples, but whose most famous exploit was eradication of the villages of runaway slaves at Palmares which had defied almost a century of Dutch and Portuguese attacks.

Bandeirantes were independent and had their own interest, and not that of the crown, at heart. Profit was a strong motivating force, whether from Indian slaves or precious metals or stones. Their expeditions in search of one or the other, or preferably both, often lasted several years and took them as far north as the Maranhão, south to the Río de la Plata, and west to within the *cordilleras* of the Andes. The exploits of the *bandeirantes paulistas* have been recounted in multi-volume histories such as that of the Viscount of Taunay, but the scope of their activities can be gauged from three examples. In 1629 António Rapôso Tavares, with some 900 *paulistas* and 3,000 Tupí, attacked Jesuit missions of Guaraní in Guairá. Between 1637 and 1651, he led several expeditions, but it was the last (1648-51) which was the most spectacular in terms of using the intricate fluvial systems of Brazil. He followed the Tietê to the Paraná, ascended the Paraná, Ivenheima, and Miranda rivers, before transferring to overland transportation to reach the Rio Grande. Thence he travelled down the Mamoré and Madeira to the main channel of the Amazon which he followed down to the coast. In 1722, Bartolomeu Bueno da Silva marched with his *bandeira* from São

Paulo to Minas Gerais and continued northwards. A small group canoed down the Tocantins to Belém do Pará, but the main *bandeira* continued on to Cuiabá. Nothing daunted by the incredible hardships and Indian attacks, with but a brief respite to replenish his *bandeira* in São Paulo, Bueno da Silva marched off again to Goiás and struck the gold he had coveted. After significant acts of public service, it was the lure of emeralds of the legendary Marcos de Azeredo and the silver of Sabarabuçú which led Fernão Dias Pais (b. 1608) to defy his sixty-six years and leave the town of São Paulo de Piratininga in 1674 with some 680 men, the majority mixed bloods. For seven years he travelled through the harsh *sertão* of the future captaincies of São Paulo and Minas Gerais and did indeed find some green stones before his death while returning. The stones were examined and found to be tourmalines. Fernão Dias's wish that he be buried in front of the high altar of the Benedictine monastery in São Paulo was honoured. It was another *paulista*, Manuel de Borba Gato, who is credited with the discovery of alluvial gold in the region of Rio das Velhas in the early 1690s, which sparked off the first gold rush in Brazil. With some justification, the British historian and explorer John Hemming has equated the travels of such *paulistas* to the journeys in Africa by Speke or Livingstone.[101]

The *paulistas* played a critical role in pioneering fluvial routes and linking up the two major river systems of Brazil based on the Paraná-Paraguay and the Amazon respectively. As we shall see later, it was they who were to prove consummate watermen in navigating large canoes along the network of rivers leading from São Paulo to Mato Grosso in the 1730s and 1740s. This exploratory impulse was not an exclusively *paulista* prerogative. In 1742 a Portuguese, Manuel Felix de Lima, travelled the rivers of the western periphery of Portuguese America. From the encampment (*arraial*) of São Francisco Xavier, Lima and three Portuguese companions and a small group of *paulistas* and Indians travelled the Mamoré, Guaporé, Beni, Madeira, Amazon, and Tocantins to be the first to travel from Mato Grosso to Pará. Protected by a portrait of Our Lady of Conception, Lima and his companions avoided major disasters, visited Jesuit villages and saw groves of cacao, drank fermented liquor made from maize, and caught fish. Lima was fully conscious of the strategic and political importance of what he had witnessed on the blurred boundaries between Spanish and Portuguese America and had high hopes of royal recognition when he made his report in Lisbon, but these were dashed.[102]

In this movement of Portuguese, it would be erroneous to leave the impression that – with the exception of those who were in the service of State or church – those who left Portugal did so either as a measure of last resort, or were a group of rootless, footloose, and ruthless adventurers. Many on board outward-bound Indiamen or travelling to Brazil, were persons of financial means and of recognizable social stature. There were merchants and investors who had 'arrived' in financial terms, and who voyaged to India to pursue new opportunities. There were those who left Portugal and who clearly were destined to achieve positions of economic, and hence political and social, prominence overseas. Some would head merchant houses in Portuguese India. Others would become future owners of sugar plantations, sugar mills, free-range cattle ranches, and mining enterprises in Brazil. These might be accompanied by, or would be joined by, persons with special skills in management or as accountants and book-keepers. There were also those who would come to own enormous tracts of land and enjoy raw power, but were cut from a different cloth. Such were the *prazeiros* of Zambezia, whose life-styles were akin to the more notorious of the autocratic *poderosos do sertão* ('powerful men of the backlands') in Brazil with private armies, retinues of slaves known as *chicunda*, and who collected tribute as ruthlessly as they suppressed rivals.

Among this flow of humanity, quite remarkable was the mobility shown by artisans. Their movements can be followed because they were required to pass professional examinations and to register with municipal councils before they could ply their trade. Furthermore, as brothers 'of minor condition', they were accepted in the Santa Casa da Misericórdia which kept membership rolls. Not only did artisans move between the towns and cities of Portugal, but also to India, Africa, and Brazil. In Brazil, a high proportion of such artisans originated from the Douro and Minho provinces in Portugal. Building trades predominated, with an incessant demand for stonemasons and carpenters, but there was demand for tailors, shoemakers, and craftsmen skilled as cabinet makers and smiths. Sculptors, gilders and painters were less frequent, and there was the occasional hairdresser or hatter. In 1708 the presence in Salvador of the painter Lourenço Velozo was recorded, interesting in that he had been born in Goa. Within Brazil itself, there was a constant movement of qualified artisans from coastal enclaves to the interior and then either back to the coast or even further to the west. It is evident that artisans who left Portugal for Brazil, did not do so in the expectation of acquiring wealth and returning to their mother country, but had made the commitment to live in the New World. As occurred in all sectors of Portuguese society, the gold rushes exerted a powerful force and artisans flooded to the mining townships to practise their trades. In the case of goldsmiths and foundrymen, they were to be accused of engaging in illicit practices and several decrees expelled them from Minas Gerais with varying degrees of effectiveness.

This exchange of artisans was not limited to the Portuguese. The Portuguese were always appreciative of fine workmanship and creativity. Under Portuguese auspices, the Goan goldsmith Roulu Shet (Raul Chatim in the Portuguese spelling), went to Portugal and remained there for some years in the early sixteenth century. Afonso de Albuquerque started the practice of sending skilled needlewomen from Goa to Portugal to work in the service of the queen. Moving in the other direction, the Portuguese jeweller, Álvaro Mendes, went to India in the mid-sixteenth century. In Salvador in the first half of the eighteenth century, painters included one born in Lombardy and two in France. Italians were particularly prized for their expertise in marine construction and several skilled in careening vessels worked in the port of Salvador.[103]

Many left Portugal in search of fortune, but in the hope of returning to dazzle neighbours and relatives by stories of their experiences and wealth gained in far-off places and to die in the motherland. Few realized these dreams. From adventurer to ex-patriot was an all too easy step. Many were to find themselves inextricably linked to the tropics through emotional or financial investment, through family, or because sickness or lack of financial means made impossible their return to a village in the Beira Alta or Minho. They died far from their places of birth, but as Portuguese and as Catholics.

(v) The Voiceless

This ebb and flow of humanity also had its darker side. From an early date, overseas territories had been regarded as suitable repositories for the undesirables of metropolitan Portugal: convicts, New Christians, gypsies, and even lepers. Reference has been made to the use of *lançados* in West and East Africa, but they were to be found as far away as the Fukien coast of China. Exile (*degrêdo*) from Portugal could be to the Atlantic islands, São Tomé and Príncipe, Africa, Brazil, or even Portuguese India. There was a ranking of places of exile from the acceptable to least desirable: Mazagão in Morocco was close enough to Europe to give hope of return; Angola, Benguela and Mozambique were so unhealthy as to be tantamount to a death sentence; and Brazil, the Maranhão, and India, held little hope of return to Portugal. Governors-general and viceroys of Brazil complained of the revolving door of convicts exiled from Brazil to Angola and Benguela only to escape and return to Brazil by the next vessel. Colônia do Sacramento on the Río de la Plata was also a place of exile from Brazil and deportees there joined with the soldiers of the garrison to desert to Buenos Aires, Spanish territories, or to Rio Grande. In the eighteenth century, the island of Fernão de Noronha and Santa Catarina island were places of exile for those convicted in Brazil.

Degredados were predominantly male. Some were used as unskilled manual labor in the building of forts or, as in the case of the 600 *degredados* accompanying Tomé de Sousa, in the building of the first capital of Brazil. If their number included artisans – especially blacksmiths and masons – these were pressed into the royal service. António Fernandes, ship's carpenter and interpreter at Sofala, was to earn a pardon by such service. Others were sent to man garrisons, such as fort Caconada in Angola. At the first opportunity many jumped ship at an intervening port, whereas others would escape their captors and form part of an ever-moving flotsam and jetsam of deprived humanity which was an inalienable part of empire. Despite their unsavoury reputation, shortage of manpower led the Portuguese crown to view *degredados* as essential vehicles for settlement and colonization. Once they had reached their destination, even murderers, rapists, and arsonists were not further incarcerated or subject to physical constraints. Larceny, fraud, vagrancy, being a public nuisance and agitator, and concubinage, adultery, and sodomy, were the more frequently cited crimes. Convicts engaged in commerce, the slave trade, served in the military, were artisans, farmed, and held positions in the colonial bureaucracy. In mid-eighteenth-century Macao, the Provedor of the prestigious Santa Casa da Misericórdia was a former convict and in the course of the c entury others were to serve on the city council and on the governing body of the Misericórdia. In a classic case of 'setting a thief to catch a thief', they served in the police force in Angola. In Angola, which was a penal colony from the sixteenth century to the nineteenth century not only for convicts from Portugal but also from Brazil, the overall white population was so small (about 300 in 1700) that a disproportionate percentage were convicts. Their influence far outweighed their numbers. Their disruptive practices were not limited to criminal acts against persons but included a 1763 plot to kill the governor and over-throw civil government. Their sacking of the Bakongo capital and an attack on Queen Jinga, among other outrages, severely undermined Portuguese official relations with local leaders. In Mozambique, their presence was to be no less deleterious and demoralizing.[104]

In addition to convicts, there were those who were the victims of society or of persecution. There were the true vagabonds – sometimes able-bodied and sometimes destitute – who drifted from place to place. In this mobility, they were joined by fugitives from the Inquisition and from justice, deserters from military service, and renegade clerics. All constituted a threat to law and order and were the subject of municipal, gubernatorial, and viceregal edicts from Macao to Mato Grosso, but with little result and no effective curbs on their mobility. One group which inspired the ire of monarchs and colonial authorities alike were the sons and daughters of Romany. These were persecuted in Portugal and whole families were deported to Brazil and Angola. Within these countries, they were the victims of further harass-ment by the authorities.[105]

A variant on this theme of exile were those victims of religious persecution who fled from Portugal. Jews and New Christians were deported as 'undesirables' to São Tomé, Cape Verde, and Angola, presumably in the expectation that they would be unlikely to survive the ravages of disease which made Angola into a white man's grave. In 1493, the king ordered that minors, both boys and girls, among the Jews from Castile who had come to Portugal and had remained after the allotted time, be dispatched to São Tomé. Others left Portugal voluntarily. Although Garcia d'Orta was not himself to be named or maimed during his lifetime by the Inquisition, that he was of New Christian or crypto-Jewish descent may have been an important factor in his decision to sail for India. Certainly, his two sisters, who had been imprisoned by the Inquisition in Lisbon, and their husbands and d'Orta's mother, were motivated to leave for fear of further actions. After Garcia d'Orta's death in 1568, relatives in Portugal and India were arrested and imprisoned by the Inquisition and a sister was burnt in an *auto da fé* in Goa in 1569. In 1580 his exhumed remains received the same fate. The eighteenth century physicians, Dr Jacob de Castro Sarmento (1691-1762) and Dr António Nunes Ribeiro Sanches (1699-1782) fled to England to avoid the clutches of the Inquisition and the former was elected a Fellow of the Royal Society.

Whereas many New Christians migrated from Portugal to northern Europe, Portuguese America was also a place of refuge for those willing to risk exposure. That the Inquisition was not formally established in Brazil did not guarantee immunity. Visitations by inquisitors and their representatives were a threat. But some New Christians secured office in church and State. In Brazil there were clandestine communities during the colonial era. Whether they originated in Europe or Brazil is not clear, but some Portuguese New Christians travelled to the Río de la Plata region, Potosí, and Peru, and to the Spanish Caribbean and Venezuela. One such was Luís Francisco Rodrigues. A native of Lisbon, he moved to Seville, served as a page for a gentleman travelling to Cartagena, and then travelled to New Spain with a slave dealer. In the company of a clothing merchant, Rodrigues returned to Cartagena, moved to Panama with another slave dealer, and thence to Peru. His subsequent movements were to Cartagena and Zaragoza. Rodrigues became a merchant and businessman and prospered. In 1624 he appeared before the Inquisition in Cartagena and was condemned to exile for five years and confiscation of a third of his possessions. The exodus of Jews after the expulsion of the Dutch from Brazil was devastating in that not only did they take to the West Indies their capital but also technical knowledge of the processing and refining of sugar. Only in 1773 was the invidious distinction between Old and New Christians abolished. A variant on the theme of religious persecution involved Jesuits who had fallen victims of the wrath of the Marquis of Pombal. They were reduced to the status of convicts and deported from Portugal to Angola.[106]

There were those who forsook their Portuguese heritage and upbringing by happenstance or intentionally. This occurred in Africa, Asia, and Brazil. In Asia, not only did they renounce king and country, but often apostatized. In Brazil, a Portuguese by the name of Diogo Álvares Correia had been shipwrecked on the reefs of Rio Vermelho in about 1510. He was taken in by the local Indians who named him Caramurú (moray). He took as his wife an Indian woman, known to the Portuguese as Catarina de Paraguaçú. They and their numerous offspring lived in a small settlement of Indians and Europeans on the south-eastern promontory of the Bay of All Saints. Later, Álvares Correia was valuable to the Portuguese in their overtures to the Indians. The Portuguese crown had, from an early date, realized this potential for assimilation and had used renegades, known as *lançados*, who were essentially put ashore with the charge to establish local contacts. In some cases, these were successful and they did indeed pave the path for future Portuguese-indigenous relations. In other cases, they simply disappeared. Often, the instant curiosity which they aroused in local populaces could lead to veneration to the point of being ascribed divine status, marriages to the daughters of local chiefs, and positions of power. These were not likely to wish to return to the Portuguese fold and evaded, rather than sought out, Portuguese contacts. Whatever the outcome, this group is yet another part of the Portuguese world on the move.

The one group minimally represented in this flow of humanity was women. In the sixteenth century, the crown adopted (1546) the policy of sending to India 'orphans of the king' (*orfãs delrei*), female orphans of (sometimes barely) marriageable age, who were intended as spouses for public officials or officers of the garrisons. Such a policy was not successful and the flow, which rarely amounted to more than a dozen in an average year, was stopped and only falteringly recontinued until the early eighteenth century. Despite dowries in the form of advancements for future husbands, many potential Portuguese suitors would have preferred cash to the added responsibility of administration or command. In 1594, the crown sent to Angola twelve orphans and reformed prostitutes – the first white women in the colony – all of whom married, but none of whom left offspring. A further fifteen female orphans were sent in mid-seventeenth century. The crown was very conscious of the perennial shortage of white women overseas and made sporadic and understated efforts to remedy the situation. In 1529 the crown ordered that four white women be dispatched from Portugal to Elmina to appease the libido of the fifty-six male inhabitants. The suggestion made by none other than a Jesuit of sixteenth-century Brazil, appalled by concubinage and immorality deriving from the absence of white women in the colony, that prostitutes be sent from Portugal to make honest men though marriage, was not adopted. In 1620, the crown ordered – presumably with the same motivation – that white women hitherto exiled from Portugal to Brazil, should be sent to the Cape Verdes.[107]

Despite severe penalties against port officials and sea captains, women of questionable morality found their way onto carracks and caravels leaving Lisbon. There were strict regulations concerning the passage of unaccompanied women from Portugal unless they were joining spouses overseas. On the outward-bound Indiamen rarely would the number of women exceed a score on a vessel.[108] Be it to India or Brazil, few governors or viceroys brought their wives to their postings. As for Angola, only in 1615 and again in 1773 did a governor bring his wife to the colony. Dom João V pursued a policy of encouraging crown employees to bring their families to Brazil and of favouring married men over bachelors for minor bureaucratic offices, grants of land, and honorary positions in the militia. But the practice persisted for married men in search of fortune in India or Brazil to leave wives and families in Portugal or one of the Atlantic islands, with the intent of returning. In the case of Angola and Zambezia, the major deterrent to white colonization in general, and to the introduction of white women and families in particular, was disease. Homeward-bound, regardless of whether they were white or not, women would usually be accompanied by husbands or relatives. In 1721 and again in 1731,

110

the governor of Minas Gerais advocated the introduction of families from Madeira and the Azores in the hope of increasing the number of white women. This must have enjoyed some modest success. In 1742 the governor of Rio de Janeiro reported that the State had incurred no expenses because migrants were coming to Brazil of their own free will and their costs of transportation had been met by relatives already resident in the mining areas. For a time in the 1730s, even married women or widows found it difficult to gain permission to return to Portugal from Brazil.[109]

The two exceptions to this absence of women on the move concerned colonial Brazil on the one hand and Africa and Brazil on the other. Even the building of convents from the 1670s onwards by town and city councils failed to stem totally the flow of young women from Brazil to Portugal where they would be placed in convents either as novices or simply as paying guests (*pensionistas*) by over-zealous martinets of fathers who preferred this option to that of a daughter making a socially disadvantageous marriage in the colony. That such young women were accompanied by substantial sums of gold, in dust, bar, or coin, to meet the costs of admittance fees and upkeep, represented a severe drain on the colony's economy and coinage, to say nothing of the loss of such young women's potential as procreators in the colony. In 1717, the city council of Salvador reported that between eight and ten white women left Bahia every year for convents in Portugal. This appears to have been a particularly acute problem but was not limited to Brazil. The Augustinian convent of Santa Monica, established in Goa during the tenure of archbishop Dom Aleixo de Meneses (1606-27) for 100 nuns, was grossly to exceed this number. An early eighteenth century description of Macao referred to two convents 'for married Women to retire to, when their Husbands are absent, and orphan Maidens are educated in them till they can catch an Husband', and the nunnery for 'devout Ladies, young or old, that are out of Conceit with the Troubles and Cares of the World'. This applied *mutatis mutandis* to colonial Brazil of the seventeenth and eighteenth centuries, with the exception that the practice of shipping young women back to convents in Portugal was less prevalent from Macao or India than from Portuguese America.[110]

The other exception to this generalization about the comparative paucity of movement by women was, of course, the transport of slaves from West Africa to Brazil which will be discussed later. Suffice it to note that, of slaves transported by the Middle Passage, males predominated over females by better than a 2:1 ratio. A survey of slaves carried by the Companhia do Maranhão during the period 1756-1788, showed that only 38 per cent were females. The reason for this imbalance has been attributed, in part, to African reluctance to export women. The result was that in colonial Brazil, and most especially in the mining regions, there was sexual imbalance between males and females. The 1786 census for Minas Gerais showed that males made up 66.8 per cent of the slave population. To a less marked degree, this sexual imbalance with a predominance of males was also present in regions of plantation economies, whereas urban areas showed less pronounced disequilibrium between male and female slaves.[111] Such imbalance notwithstanding, and despite the shortcomings of the records, as many as one million females could well have been transported from Africa to Brazil in the colonial period.

(vi) Individuals and Groups

In this human flux and reflux, there were distinct differences between the situation east of Malacca, or even of Goa, and the Portuguese Atlantic and Brazil. The former was characterized by the mobility of individuals; the latter by mass movements or, at least, movements of groups. Symptomatic of the former is one of the all-time charlatans of history, but none the less colourful for it. Fernão Mendes Pinto (c.1510-83) described himself as having been shipwrecked, 'thirteen times a prisoner and seventeen a slave' from Arabia Felix to 'the edge of the world'. His penchant for mendacity earned him immortality. As self-described slave, soldier, merchant, pirate, ambassador, doctor, and Jesuit novice, he spent twenty-one years in Asia and produced an account described by a modern commentator as a 'corrosive satire'. For his *Peregrinaçam* (Lisbon, 1614), Mendes Pinto drew on anything he ever saw, read, or heard, about Asia and blended this mixture of fact and fiction into an account of his travels. A reconstruction of his wanderings suggests that, after arrival at

Diu in 1537, he joined a reconnaissance expedition to the Red Sea, stopped over in Ethiopia (unlikely), was captured by the Turks, sold to a Greek Muslim, who sold him to a Jewish merchant, who took him to Hormuz. On his return to India, Mendes Pinto forsook the life of a soldier and thenceforth adopted Malacca as his base. He happily married diplomacy with commerce. He was a roving emissary to the petty kingdoms of Sumatra and to Patani on the Malay Peninsula. Commercial ventures verging on piracy took him to the Gulf of Tongking, Indochina, and the south coast of China. His account of a raid on the emperors' tombs and subsequent shipwreck leading to capture and sentencing to hard labor on the Great Wall of China, is a figment of his imagination. Mendes Pinto returned to Ning-po and closed off this phase by returning to Malacca. We next hear of him as an emissary to Martaban in Burma. He recounts a pepper-buying expedition to Java, shipwreck in the Gulf of Siam, and trips to Batavia, Sunda, and Siam, and indeed probably spent a decade voyaging in the South China Sea as far afield as the Moluccas and as far west as Goa. Mendes Pinto probably made four voyages to Japan, although the weight of evidence is against his claim to be the European 'discoverer'. After twenty-one years overseas, he returned to Portugal in 1558.[112]

However picaresque in tone, mendacious in content, and audacious in its claims the *Peregrinaçam* may be, my purpose here is not to separate the wheat from the chaff but rather to take the *persona* of Pinto as representative of the free-booting, unaccountable, and footloose individuals who were part and parcel of a Portuguese presence in Asia. Pirates, grave robbers, Catholics, or whatever opportunism required of them, they wheeled and dealt their way through East Asia, serving whatever prince or king called on their services and beyond the long arm of Portuguese law or viceregal authority. Such were possessors of a blend of charisma, ruthlessness, and business acumen which virtually guaranteed success or an early death. This endemic individualism, and this restless mobility by land and sea, characterized Portuguese activities on and beyond the peripheries of empire. A substantial part of the male population of the Estado da India was, by virtue of distance or because of their residence in native states and kingdoms, out of touch with Portugal and beyond the effective jurisdiction of the viceroy or governors in Goa or crown officials in Malacca or Macao. But, no less than the *paulistas* or the *lançados*, they possessed skills and contacts which could be valuable to the crown. They were persuaded to undertake diplomatic, commercial, or political missions which were too risky or sensitive for the crown to endorse officially. Once accomplished, there was no further commitment by either party other than that the temporary, impersonal, and ambiguous relationship should have been mutually beneficial to both free-lances and the State.

In contrast to Portuguese India, the Portuguese Atlantic and Portuguese America were the scene of mass movements such as were unknown in Asia. Let us look at four examples, involving different racial types, three of which were involuntary and resulted in genocide and ethnicide.

The story of the Middle Passage has been told often enough. The basic facts are that during the 320 years of the trade from West Africa to Brazil somewhere between 3.5 and 5 million slaves entered Brazil, comprising some 38 per cent of the total trade from West Africa to Europe, the Caribbean, and the American continent. What is not generally appreciated is that before Columbus' landfall in the Bahamas, already (1441), the first black captives from the Saharan coast had been landed in Portugal, and a factory had been established at Arguim for this purpose. For the next two decades the Portuguese traded along the Guinea coast as far as Sierra Leone. After 1471 the Bight of Benin became their major trading area, and centred on the fort of Elmina after 1482. Before the end of the fifteenth century, already institutionalized was the administration, supply net-works, and transportation of slaves from the African continent to Portugal, with São Tomé and Príncipe playing important intermediary roles. With plantation agriculture in Brazil, and later with the labour demands of the mines, this European trade was to pale into insignificance beside the massive forced reloca-tion of Africans to Brazil.

In this migration, the actual crossing of the Atlantic was but one of three phases which started in the interior of Africa and concluded for many far from the ports of disembarkation in Brazil. All involved violent transitions. The first was the trek in caravans, often for weeks over rough terrain and bearing the weight of the *libambo* or iron chain used to link the slaves together, from the place of sale or capture in Africa to the coast. Here they were housed in barracoons, or open-air compounds. A commentator, who knew the process well on both sides of the Atlantic, estimated that almost fifty per cent of those brought from the interior of Africa died prior to embarkation. At the port, they were branded and baptized. The second was the actual crossing to Brazil which, depending on the time of year, weather and provisions, could be a voyage of between thirty-five and fifty days. Mortality was heavy enough fully to merit the characterization of such vessels as coffins (*tumbeiros*). The third phase began with sale in the port cities of Brazil, often to be followed by further travel by foot to a final destination and a life expectancy of seven to ten years in the cane fields or mining. In the sixteenth and seventeenth centuries, probably few slaves were transported more than fifty miles from the coastal enclaves of Brazil and there was no discernible pattern to their movements. But, with the discovery of placer gold deposits in Rio das Velhas in the 1690s, there began a systematic movement of slaves from coastal ports to the interior. Some 341,000 slaves were dispatched between 1698 and 1770 to the gold fields of Minas Gerais alone with peak imports in the late 1730s and early 1740s at 7,360 annually. Albeit at a lesser intensity and over a less protracted span of time, similar mass movements were to occur following news of strikes in Goiás in 1725 and in Mato Grosso in 1718 and 1734. [113]

The next two examples concern the indigenous peoples of America. When the Portuguese made their first landfall in Brazil, Pedro Álvares Cabral and his crew came into contact with the coastal Tupinambá. The scribe Pero Vaz de Caminha, in the first letter from Brazil to Portugal dated 1 May 1500, commented on the Indians' physical beauty, their friendliness, and their suitability for conversion to Christianity. Friendship gave way to barter and barter to slavery. What neither Vaz de Caminha nor his successors realized was the propensity of the Tupinambá for migration. This was to be revealed as the result of the outright war on the Tupinambá launched by the third governor-general of Brazil, Mem de Sá, in the 1570s. Some acquiesced peacefully, others withstood attack, and others died fighting. One group of eighty-four villages comprising some 60,000 people, started a trek from Pernambuco on the coast crossing hundreds of miles of savannah and forest, stopping along the way to grow crops, and eventually reaching the Amazon. Their route took them up the São Francisco river, across northern Mato Grosso, until they reached Spanish settlers near the head-waters of the Madeira. Here they settled until friction with the Spanish led some to descend the entire length of the Madeira to the island of Tupinambarana where Pedro Teixeira and the Jesuit Cristóbal de Acuña encountered them in 1639 on their expedition from Quito to São Luís. These Tupinambá had travelled some 3,500 miles in what must surely be one of the largest overland migrations or exoduses in history. The French surrender of São Luís in 1615 was a disaster for the coastal Tupinambá, who had assisted and trusted the French. The next three years saw war against the Tupinambá in Maranhão and Pará. The threat of death at the hands of the Portuguese spurred some Tupinambá again to migrate, this time to the distant upper reaches of the Tocantins.[114]

This was not the only forced and involuntary migration to which Indians in Brazil were subjected. The hereditary captains had been permitted to transport Indians from Brazil to Portugal but these were in such small numbers as to constitute curiosities rather than a valid labour force. In Brazil, Portuguese settlement brought in its wake the demand for labour. Initially, this was satisfied by sporadic incursions (*entradas*) into the *sertão* to capture Indians and, especially in the seventeenth century, by organized razzias by the *paulistas* to capture Indians for plantation labour. The Brazilian economist Roberto Simonsen estimated at 300,000 the numbers captured by the *bandeiras* in the seventeenth century alone.[115] Such forced relocations of Indians were not the exclusive prerogative of laymen. One problem faced by civil and ecclesiastical authorities in Brazil, in counter-dis-tinction to Peru or Mexico, was that the indigenous population was more mobile and with no discernible centres to equate to a Cuzco or Tenochtitlan. This made more difficult the task of converting an indigenous population dispersed over large areas, and it was more difficult for the colonists to gain access to Indian labour. A solution for cleric and layman alike was to *reduzir*, roughly translated as 'round up', the Indians and, either peacefully or forcefully, congregate them in mission villages (*aldeias*) administered by the Jesuits and religious orders.

The first step in this direction had been taken by Manuel da

Nóbrega in 1553 on the plateau of Piratininga when he had amalgamated three Indian villages. In the new *aldeia* Indians were instructed in Catholicism and, under certain conditions which included payment, could be made available to colonists for labour. Some *aldeias* were totally isolated from contact with colonists, whereas others were on the peripheries of white settlements. The means used to bring Indians to such villages adopted the carrot-and-stick approach, mostly the latter. The will of *paulistas* and army soldiers and officers on such *entradas* or *resgates* often prevailed over, or was acquiesced to by, the accompanying Jesuit fathers. Many religious orders had mission stations in Amazonas, but an indication of the numbers of Indians transported to such villages can be gleaned by reference to the Indian populations of twenty-eight *aldeias* administered by the Society of Jesus in Maranhão and Grão-Pará: 11,000 in 1696, almost doubling to 21,031 by 1730. If, to the 11,000 in 1696 in Maranhão and Grão-Pará, are added a further 15,450 for Jesuit missions in the centre and south of Brazil, the total number of Indians under Jesuit tutelage at the turn of the eighteenth century was about 26,500. In 1750 there was a total of sixty-three mission villages administered by all the religious orders with an Indian population estimated at 50,000.[116]

The fourth mass migration was to the mines in a succession of waves from the mid-1690s onwards: initially to Minas Gerais, then to Mato Grosso (Cuiabá 1718: Guaporé 1734), and Goiás in 1725 , as well as to other areas such as to the interior in Bahia in 1727. Portuguese from Portugal, the Atlantic Islands, and the coastal regions of Brazil converged on the mining areas, creating 'instant' demographic nuclei. Figures are uncertain but an influx of 5,000 in any single year would not be unreasonable for the first half of the eighteenth century. Two main networks of roads were developed to reach Minas Gerais. These have been described elsewhere and suffice it to say here that the first comprised tracks from São Paulo and Rio de Janeiro (*caminho velho* and *caminho novo*, and variations thereon), whereas the second used the river valley of the São Francisco and was known as the *caminho do sertão*. With further strikes in Mato Grosso and Goiás, rivers provided the most feasible mode of travelling, especially for travellers from Rio de Janeiro and São Paulo. After a short overland haul from São Paulo to Pôrto Feliz, travel was in the canoes described earlier along the rivers Tietê, Paraná, Pardo, Anhandui, Aquidauna, and Paraguay to the river Cuiabá. The largest such fleet was in 1726 out of Pôrto Feliz with 305 canoes and more than 3,000 persons, including the governor of São Paulo. Mortality was as high as on the *carreira da India*. Capsizes were frequent because of rapids and submerged rocks. Piranhas, poisonous insects, malaria and a host of other diseases, attacks by animals, and the predations of the Paiaguá and the Guaicurú Indians were life threatening. Before their virtual extinction in 1795, the Guaicurú were credited with the deaths of more than 4,000 Portuguese. In 1720 a complete convoy was wiped out and there were no survivors.[117]

Brazil affords the only instance of widespread internal migration in the Portuguese-speaking world. Only later was there a movement to the interior of Angola. Penetration into the upper reaches of the Zambezi involved comparatively few people. In contrast, in Brazil there are clear population moves from the coastal enclaves to the interior. One seventeenth-century writer described the Portuguese in Brazil as being like crabs, such was their reluctance to leave the coastal areas. But the mobility of the populace, noted by the French artist Auguste de Saint- Hilaire in the early nineteenth century, also characterized the seventeenth and eighteenth centuries. From Salvador, people moved north toward Piauí and the Maranhão. There was a movement of people from Pernambuco into Ceará and along the coast. Already described were the parallel movements from Bahia, Rio de Janeiro, and São Paulo into Minas Gerais, and thence to Goiás by land, and the river routes from São Paulo to Mato Grosso. The Amazon and its tributaries provided other routes for the movement of people. The Tocantins was a route for people and merchandise from Goiás to the Maranhão and Pará. The motivations for such movements of people varied, but may be summed up as cattle raising, gold mining, agriculture and commerce. Some sought to evade creditors, judicial authorities or ecclesiastical inquiries. The most important migratory movement in terms of numbers and compressed period of time was to the mining areas in the first half of the eighteenth century. Less intensive and later were migratory moves to the south: Paraná, Santa Catarina, and Rio Grande do Sul.

The authorities made little effort to curb or direct such migratory movements in colonial Brazil. Three observations may be made. First, migratory movements to the north and west notwithstanding, in 1822 some sixty per cent of the population of Brazil still lived on the littoral, which at most comprised ten per cent of the territory of the colony. Settlements in coastal Pernambuco, the Bay of All Saints, and the Baixada Fluminense made up most of this sixty per cent. Secondly, while nuclei of population were created, for example in Minas Gerais, these were more like archipelagos of settlement in an otherwise uninhabited land. They did not constitute the leading edge of an unbroken moving line of migration to the west. Thirdly, although little studied, reverse migration was more prevalent than is generally appreciated. This might be partial, for example from Goiás back to Minas Gerais, or complete, namely returning from the far west to Rio de Janeiro, Salvador, or São Luís. Such reverse migration could be prompted by crop failures, unrealistic hopes of commercial opportunities, disillusion with speculative mining ventures, or drought as occurred in Ceará in the latter part of the eighteenth century but was a constant hazard in the *sertão* and even along the river São Francisco valley. Manuel Felix de Lima and his companions had been spurred to leave Mato Grosso because of the high cost of food, absence of gold, disillusionment, a sedentary way of life, and the need to escape their creditors.[118]

(vii) Carriers of disease

The people who moved around the Portuguese seaborne empire were also carriers of diseases. The Portuguese themselves were carriers of European pathogens. The global band of the tropics and sub-tropics was conducive to a host of diseases. The Portuguese were both victims and carriers of malaria. Stagnant water on carracks and caravels provided ideal breeding conditions. Blacks transported by the Portuguese from West Africa to Brazil could be carriers, although they themselves developed false immunity and had low-intensity malaria. In the case of the introduction of European pathogens into Asia and Africa, contacts prior to the arrival of the Portuguese would have created varying degrees of immunity among indigenous peoples. With one possible exception, the Portuguese did not introduce new diseases into Eurasia or into Africa. That exception is syphilis, which was probably introduced into western Europe by the return of Columbus' sailors from America in 1493 and spread rapidly. Although the lapse in time between recorded appearances (Barcelona, 1493; Italy, 1494-5) of the disease in Europe and its first appearance in India (1498) would have been time enough for transmission of the disease overland or by travellers by land and sea, sailors on Vasco da Gama's armada which left Lisbon in 1497 and came ashore in Calicut in May of 1498 contributed to the introduction of syphilis into India, if they did not themselves initiate it. The 1505 appearance of syphilis in Canton predated by a year what we know to be the first Portuguese presence in and around Canton, although this would not preclude an unrecorded earlier transmission by Portuguese on a Chinese junk or Chinese contacts with infected Portuguese. When Sebastian del Cano's *Victoria* touched at Timor in January 1522, already syphilis was prevalent, 'that some call the sickness of Saint Job, and they call it the Portuguese sickness'. It may be that the Portuguese introduced yaws into Ceylon. But the whole debate over the transmission of syphilis runs into the difficulty of different treponemas and diseases with similar ulcerative symptoms. The Portuguese contributed to the spread of chiggers from Brazil to Europe and Africa. The slave trade encouraged the spread of yaws from sub-Saharan Africa to Europe and Brazil.[119]

As did the Spanish in the Caribbean, Central America, and South America, the Portuguese introduced into Brazil diseases of Old World origins: plague, typhus, tuberculosis, malaria, yellow fever, influenza, measles, smallpox, and mumps. Although measles, smallpox, and influenza were to be devastating to Indian peoples who had had no prior exposure or resulting immunity, the impact of such diseases on indigenous peoples differed both in intensity and rapidity of transmission in Portuguese America from Spanish America. This was attributable to the characteristics of indigenous peoples in Brazil before the arrival of Cabral in 1500 and to the nature of the Portuguese presence. Although sharing with their counterparts elsewhere in the Americas isolation from extra-continental contacts prior to 1492, native peoples of the region into which the Portuguese intruded differed notably in the following three regards from those encountered by the Spanish in Central America or the Andean area. First, they demonstrated greater mobility both at the time of the arrival of Europeans and afterwards. Secondly, Indian peoples in Brazil did not exhibit that density of population which characterized Indian peoples, especially in and around urban nuclei, in what became Spanish America. Thirdly, the absence of a highly centralized and autocratic leadership structure and hierarchy made the Indians of Brazil less vulnerable than their counterparts in Spanish America to the devastating repercussions of the deaths of their leaders.

These factors at least delayed the gross physical, psychological, and cultural impact of Old World diseases on the indigenous peoples of Brazil. Climatic factors in Brazil may also have conditioned those diseases which were to be more or less prevalent. Furthermore, Portuguese migration to Brazil was sluggish for the first half of the sixteenth century and, even after the establishment of coastal settlements, only slowly were the Portuguese to leave the littoral. Mobility both on the part of Europeans and of native Americans resulted in a lower incidence of prolonged, sustained contact between Indians and Portuguese than between Indians and Spaniards. Also, there was a lower incidence of Indians interbreeding with Europeans and Africans in Portuguese America than in Spanish America. These factors may explain the absence in Portuguese America of reports of mortality among Indians on the scale of those in the Antilles and Central America soon after the Spaniards arrived. Already in 1520, much of the indigenous population of the Greater Antilles and Central America was succumbing to the first pandemic of European origin, whereas only in the 1550s were the Tupinikin and Tupinambá first to be smitten by European diseases transmitted by the Portuguese and French. In the 1590s the French introduced influenza and other European diseases among the Tupinambá of the Maranhão, to be compounded by the arrival of Portuguese military forces.

Smallpox was lethal to Indian peoples. In 1621, a smallpox epidemic eradicated the Indian population of São Luís do Maranhão. In Pará, in 1749 and 1750, Indians succumbed to measles and smallpox. Particularly vulnerable to European diseases, notably smallpox, was the one institution where Europeans came into regular and sustained contact with Indians, namely the mission villages. In the 1630s, whole Indian populations of Jesuit missions on the upper Uruguay died of European epidemics and the Indian population of other Jesuit missions in Paraná and Guairá was halved by typhus and smallpox. In the 1660s, smallpox ravaged Indian communities in the Maranhão. In the Amazon there were to be major smallpox epidemics in the 1740s. The civilian administrators who replaced the Jesuits under the terms of the Directorate legislation of 1757 provided no solutions. Bishop João de São José reported (1762-63) that 60,000 Indians had died of smallpox and measles. Those who fled were carriers of disease. Whereas in Spanish America, it was their very permanence which contributed to the destruction of native peoples by European diseases, in Portuguese America not only were the tempo and intensity of the diffusion of European diseases different. Their own mobility and that of the Europeans made the native Americans both more and less vulnerable to diseases of European origin.[120]

CHAPTER IV
EBB AND FLOW OF COMMODITIES

A visitor to the wharves of sixteenth-century Lisbon, Salvador, Rio de Janeiro, Luanda, Goa, Malacca, Macao, or Nagasaki, would have been acutely aware, by sight, hearing, and smell, of a world characterized not only by the ebb and flow of people, but also of an incredible diversity of merchandise.

Today, we have come to take for granted that a local grocery in Baltimore, Maryland, or in Llangollen in Wales, stocks kiwi fruits from New Zealand, cheese from Switzerland, grapes from Chile, butter from Denmark, tea from China, and meat from Argentina, that the cashier rings up the account on a computer made in Japan, that shops sell dress fabric from Madras and hand-made leather shoes from Italy or Brazil, and that cars on the streets are made in Korea, Japan or Germany. It is easy to believe that this international quality to our everyday life is a product of the post World War II revolution in technology, transportation, and communications, but this is not the case. Six centuries ago, pre-dating the Portuguese invasion of Ceuta (1415) and exploratory voyages down the coast of West Africa and into the Atlantic, there had been avid support by the Portuguese crown for international trade. This was reflected in Genoese and Venetian commercial communities in Lisbon, and direct maritime trade from Portuguese ports to northern Europe and the Mediterranean. Goods such as malaguetta pepper arrived in Portugal from West Africa. Lisbon was to become the most westerly point in Europe for a redistribution network of commodities originating from eastern emporia such as the Persian Gulf, India, Indonesia, China, and Japan, all of which the Portuguese were to come to know so well in the sixteenth century. The age of maritime discoveries and the opening of the sea route to India by Vasco da Gama did not usher in a new age of an influx of commodities hitherto totally unknown to the Portuguese. What it did represent was a new era characterized by greater volume, readier availability, more variety, and eventually lower costs of many imported commodities.

An inhabitant of Lisbon in the mid-sixteenth century would have encountered a diverse array of goods available for purchase and originating from all points of the known world. Some were exotic spices, whereas others were as fundamental to the everyday diet of Portuguese as wheat. Some would scarcely be unloaded before they were dispatched on their way again. Some goods were of poor quality and cheap manufacture and essentially mass produced, whereas others were articles of exquisite workmanship. There were the living and the dead: slaves from Africa, Indians from Brazil, and young boys from India and China brought to Portugal to be lackeys and servants; parrots, civet cats, and monkeys brought home by sailors or merchants as curiosities; and objects which represented the destruction of nature and of the environment such as elephant tusks, seal skins, and export crops cultivated at the cost of the destruction of native forests, soil exhaustion, and erosion. In order to gain an idea of the international quality of such goods, let us join that *lisboeta* as he inspected the cargoes being unloaded on the wharves of Lisbon in the 1550s.

Goods from other parts of Europe fell roughly into two

categories: agricultural products and manufactured goods. Of great importance was wheat, most notably from northern Europe – Ireland, England, Brittany, France, and Flanders, and loaded at ports such as Bristol, Saint-Malo, Dieppe, La Rochelle, Bordeaux, and the Baltic port of Danzig. In the earlier part of the sixteenth century Flanders predominated but, by the second half, there was a shift to French wheat. In lesser quantities, there was wheat from the Mediterranean region, primarily Sicily but also Italy, Turkey, and neighbouring Castile. Although the most important cereal import, wheat was not alone and smaller quantities of rye and other grains also were transported to Lisbon. Commercial rivalries notwithstanding, from Venice came velvets, silks, apparel, glass beads, and faience. England, Ireland, France, and Flanders provided woollen cloths, woollen manufactures, and textiles. Channelled to Lisbon through Antwerp and later Amsterdam were Nürnberg copper utensils, brassware and glass beads from Germany, bronze, brass, and copper in leaf and in objects such as bowls, silver, mercury, tin, lead, arms and armour, artillery guns and munitions, faience, tapestries, cinnabar, textiles, clocks, and furniture. From the Baltic originated amber. From Spain arrived mercury from the Almadén mines and silver from Central and South America.[121]

From ports of Morocco came an even more varied assortment of foods and other commodities. These included barley, wheat, honey, dates, grapes, gum arabic, wax, and indigo. There were also metals: silver, gold, and copper. Much in demand in Portugal and as trade objects which the caravels carried to West Africa, were coral, carpets, faience, wool cloths, textiles, and coloured striped blankets (*alambeis*) which were bought in the ports of Safim and Arzila and woven in Safi, Marrakech, Oran, and elsewhere.[122]

The Atlantic was the source of many commodities available in Lisbon. Most obviously, the sea provided cod from the waters off Newfoundland, tuna and sardines from the Algarve, and flounder and eels from the Moroccan coast. From the sandy shores from southern Morocco to Arguim, Portuguese fishermen brought home catches of mullet, menhaden, and other fish for sale in Lisbon and export. More important were the products of the Atlantic islands: the archipelagos of Madeira, the Azores and, to a lesser degree, the Cape Verdes. Madeira was famous for its sugar, wines, and sweet grapes (*malvasia*). It also supplied woods such as cedars and yews, but more important were the various vegetable dyes and resins used in the textile industry: 'dragon's blood' (*sangue de dragão*), a red resin from the dragon-tree present on Porto Santo; woad (*pastel*); and litmus roccella (*urzela*). Porto Santo also exported barley to Lisbon. The Azores added only wheat and cotton among their exports to Portugal, but otherwise duplicated Madeira in their production of sugar and wine, woad, litmus roccella, and 'dragon's blood'. Goods from the Cape Verdes were less in evidence: salt, maize, and orchil, a lichen which produces a red dye. In addition to these products originating on the islands, we have already seen that Portugal's Atlantic islands were places of exchange for goods from Europe, Africa, and America, and these too arrived on the wharves of Lisbon.[123]

Walking along the docks, the visitor's interest would be aroused by those cargoes being unloaded from ports and trading factories of West Africa. With gum arabic, cotton, and gold, he would already be familiar, but to these were added ivory, malaguetta pepper (red, Cayenne: 'grains of Paradise'), most profuse on the Costa da Malagueta (extending 40 leagues from mata de Santa Maria in the west to Cape Palmas in the east), but also on the upper Gambia, upper Niger, and Sierra Leone, and the long black peppers (*pimenta de rabo* or *pimenta-longa*) from the Gulf of Guinea. His nose would be disturbed by the powerful aroma of musk, which seems to have been much in demand as a heady perfume and possibly as sexual excitant, and live civet cats whose glands produced the greasy secretion. There were the skins of sea lions. Parrots and monkeys were curiosities whose antics provided amusement. Curiosity, revulsion, and compassion would have competed with each other as the visitor watched vessels from São Tomé, the Cape Verdes, and from mainland factories such as Arguim, unloading their cargoes of black slaves mostly from the region between the Senegal and Cape Palmas which comprised Upper Guinea. Numbers arriving in any given year of the 1550s and 1560s could be as high as 1,600 for sale in Lisbon.[124]

The diversity of cargoes from African ports paled beside the richness, volume, and variety of cargoes unloaded from Indiamen returning to Lisbon from Goa and Cochin. Some of the goods they carried did indeed originate from lands bordering the Indian Ocean. From Portuguese trading stations of the Swahili Coast and Mozambique came ebony, gold, ivory, coral, tortoise-shell, ambergris, cloths, trinkets, bracelets, conch shells, alumstone, wine, oil, salt, and hemp. Some Persian silver from Hormuz might find its way back to Portugal, as too did incense and myrrh from Arabia and Cambay (Gujarat). Originating from India were chintzes and cotton and calico cloths from Cambay and, from Malabar, an extraordinary diversity of goods which included pepper, ginger, and cardamom (*cardamomo pequeno*), sealing wax (lac), indigo, tamarind, brazilwood (*Caesalpinia sappan*), zerumbet, dried arecanut, copra, coconut oil, coir, myrobalans, rubies and other precious stones including diamonds from Golconda, ivory, perfumes, furniture, and precious woods. There might also be the occasional elephant and 'white slaves'.[125]

But it was goods from east of Cape Comorin which were most likely to spur his imagination and stimulate taste and smell. First and foremost were the spices: cinnamon (Ceylon); cardamom (*cardamom grande*; Ceylon, Coromandel coast, Siam); cloves (volcanic islands of the Moluccas, but especially Ternate and Tidor); mace and nutmeg (Banda islands). There were the aromatic woods and fragrant gums and resins: sandalwood (especially Timor, but also Coromandel, Siam, and Makassar); two species of aloes wood, differentiated in Malay by the words *gâru* and *calambac* (Gujarat, Bengal, Sumatra, Malacca, Ceylon, Siam and Indochina peninsula); camphor (Borneo, Sumatra, Pacem, China); white and black gum benzoin (the best from Siam and Pegu); and saffron, a colouring agent. In addition to the above, there was a miscellany which included lacquer from Pegu, beeswax from Timor, and sharkskins and deerskins from Siam. From Macao, already there were arriving in Lisbon porcelains, raw and finished silks, gold, mother of pearl, lacquer, gum benzoin, and exotic objects with medicinal uses – musk (from the mountainous northern part of China, eastern Tibet, and Pegu), *pau de china*, whose root was claimed to be an aphrodisiac and cure for venereal diseases, the rhizome galangal which could be used as condiment or medicament, another root zerumbet, and the expensive sorrel rhubarb from China and Tibet. A further some thirty years (1580s) would have to elapse until the first

Portuguese imports of tea into Europe.[126]

In contrast, in the mid-sixteenth century Brazil was still taking second place to 'Golden Goa' in terms of commodities arriving in Lisbon. The two most important were brazilwood and sugar, but fascination with Brazilian parrots or monkeys had not worn thin. Portuguese America well exemplified the shift that was to occur over the next century and the move from the Indian Ocean to the Atlantic as the centre of Portugal's commerce and activities. This change was evidenced on a small scale by the Atlantic islands. By the late seventeenth century Madeira was associated more with wine than sugar. In the Azores, already in the first quarter of the seventeenth century, woad production had declined and wheat was the undisputed major export crop. Of any single factor, the most critical was the arrival of the Dutch in the Indian Ocean, Indonesia, and China Sea in the seventeenth century, which was severely to decrease the Portuguese presence in the east with a parallel rise in the fortunes of the Portuguese in the South Atlantic and in particular in Brazil.

This shift would nowhere have been more apparent than in the port of Lisbon. If the great-great-great-great-great-grand-children of that sixteenth-century *lisboeta* had gone down to the wharves of Lisbon two centuries later, they would not have been overwhelmed by the diversity of items reaching the metropolis from Brazil alone. A total of some thirty-five different products were brought by vessels arriving in Lisbon in 1749 from Pernambuco, Rio de Janeiro, and Grão-Pará and the Maranhão. These included gold (dust, bars, coin), diamonds, ivory, bags of wool, sugar, molasses, tanned hides, sole leather, untanned hides, deerskins, sweetmeats, flour, jacaranda trunks, brazilwood, purpleheart, rods for trelisses, honey, fish oil, baleen, cacao, cloves, coffee, cotton, tortoise-shell, medicinal *drogas*, and 370 slaves. The absence of tobacco is attributable to the fact that there was no fleet from Bahia in 1749.

By the end of the eighteenth century, no less than 125 different products from Brazil were being unloaded in Lisbon. These may be roughly classified under the following headings: twenty-seven different foodstuffs and beverages, including brandy, sugar, rice, coffee, honey, pork, manioc flour, cocoa, tapioca, molasses, sesame, cashew nuts, cloves, beans, and vegetables; twenty-four different skins and hides from oxen, wolves, bears, pumas and other wild cats, sea lions, deer, horses, tapirs, agoutis (type of rodent), foxes, goats, ermines, calves, sheep, and wild pigs; and twenty-nine different drugs (*drogas*), including resins, oils, balsams, roots, gum arabic, Brazilian boxwood or stinkwood (*Euxylophora paraensis*), purpleheart (*pau violeta*), tamarind, medicinal roots, cinchona, indigo, ginger, copahiba oil, nutmeg, and copal. Into the category of miscellaneous, numbering some forty-four items, would fall fish oil, baleen, copra, linen, feathers, tobacco, cotton, carnaúba wax, tortoise-shell, silk cotton trees (*castanha do Maranhão*), vicuña wool, topazes, amethysts, gold, silver, and diamonds. In addition, there were some forty categories of woods in planks and beams, including laurel, jacaranda, cinnamon, rosewood, cedar, and sucupira, and wooden objects such as oars, axles, and barrel staves. In this connection, it is worth remembering that references to brazilwood pre-dated Cabral's landfall in 1500 and referred to the dyewood in regions far from that land that was to be known as Brazil. The change of name from Land of the Holy Cross to Brazil led both laymen such as the historian João de Barros and men of the cloth to denounce the avarice which had led the Portuguese to substitute rough wood for the Holy Cross and dye for the blood of Christ. The *Caesalpinia* tree provided not only the highly prized dye but also a wood which was no less in demand in the making of furniture.[127]

Very few of the commodities arriving on the wharves of Lisbon remained in Portugal. But they did enable Portugal to become a major player in a global network of commodity exchanges and trade networks reaching from Danzig to the Zambezi and Mato Grosso to Manila. Of these goods, those originating in Portugal can be counted on the fingers of two hands: wines, salt, cork, soap, olive oil, fruits, quince marmalade, and sumac. Increasingly, Portugal would be dependent on the re-export of goods from beyond Europe to preserve a balance of payments with her European trading partners. Some of those goods which arrived in the Tagus, were trans-shipped to other European destinations immediately, whereas others remained a matter of days on Portuguese soil. These paid for commodities imported by Portugal and which, in turn, would be bartered and traded around the world. Sixteenth-century records show the degree to which Lisbon was but a halfway point until these imports reached their final destinations elsewhere in Europe. To Spain went slaves from the Gulf of Guinea, brazilwood, woad, indigo, pepper and cloves. Spices would be funnelled to Italy (Venice, Florence, Leghorn) either through Antwerp and later Amsterdam, or via Seville, or through the Straits of Gibraltar to the Mediterranean. Northern Europe in general, and the Low Countries in particular, had an insatiable appetite for malaguetta peppers and *pimenta de rabo* from West Africa, all spices from the Estado da India, brazilwood, sugar, 'dragon's blood' and other dyes from the Azores and Cape Verdes, wines, aromatic woods, pearls and jewels. Items exported from Portugal to London in 1574-76 included a mixture of goods imported into Portugal and domestic products: pepper, cloves, mace, ginger, cinnamon, nutmeg , sugar, brazilwood, molasses, marmalades, calico cloths, oranges, sumac, soap, and salt. In this re-export to Europe in the fifteenth, and especially in the sixteenth century, Portugal could count on trading factors in Seville, London, Venice, Antwerp (until 1540s), and Amsterdam among others, in addition to small colonies of Portuguese especially in Castile, the south and west of England, the Low Countries, France, and Italy.

As England entered the Indian Ocean herself at the end of the century, this shopping list was to change. At the beginning of the seventeenth century, sugar was the most important re-export from Portugal to England, tobacco was in demand, wines and salt had declined, and spices had all but disappeared. By the 1670s English demand for Brazilian sugar and tobacco also declined. The Anglo-French wars increased English demand for wines and the Anglo-Portuguese alliance (especially the terms of the treaties of 1642, 1654, and 1661) led to a more prominent English merchant presence in Portugal and overseas. Whatever Portugal imported, be it spices, perfumed woods, and roots with medicinal properties from Asia, ivory or slaves from Africa, wines from Madeira, or sugar, tobacco, cotton, and dyewoods from Brazil, there was an eager and insatiable market in Europe for these goods from overseas. This international dimension was not to change over the following centuries. For the years 1796-1807, products originating in Brazil and which had been re-exported from Lisbon were finding markets in Hamburg (29.1 per cent), England (24.0 per cent), Italy (20.2 per cent), France (16.0 per cent), Holland (3.7 per cent), Spain (3.5 per cent), Prussia (1.7 per cent), Denmark (0.8 per cent), and Sweden, Russia, Germany, and Barbary less than half a per cent. The products of Brazil played a crucial role in Portugal's balance of payments with other European nations.[128]

Commodities carried from Portugal beyond Europe varied, depending on their destinations and consideration not only as to the nature of the demand but also such factors as whether monetary or non-monetary systems existed, and the best form of exchange in societies where non-metallic money circulated, for example cowrie shells or salt. Beginning in the fifteenth century, goods exported by the Portuguese to Morocco were of European origins: especially cloth from England, Brittany and the Low Countries. Oriental spices had reached Morocco in the fifteenth century, but once the Portuguese had direct access to the sources, they re-exported pepper, cloves and the all-critical lacquer to Morocco. The selection of goods carried by the Portuguese to Senegambia underwent a similar change from the exclusively European to a mix of European, Moroccan and Indian goods. In the 1450s Portuguese vessels had carried knitted caps, English and Irish textiles and cloths, Alentejan blankets, copper pans, brass-ware, lead, glass beads, shaving basins, and tin bracelets. But to these were soon to be added woven cloths, corn, and horses from Morocco, white cloths from India, cowries and other shells. The Portuguese were also the carriers of commodities of African provenance which were in demand elsewhere on the west coast. For example, the Portuguese met the demand in Senegambia for colanuts from Sierra Leone, and sold in Benin bark cloth made in the Congo. At an early date in their commerce in the Bight of Benin, Portuguese discovered that gold on the Costa da Mina could be acquired with beads (known to the Portuguese as *coris*) fashioned from a blue stone veined with red, or the more valuable yellow or grey beads, which were available in Benin and on the Forcados river. With the establishment of trading factories and forts, similar goods made up the cargoes of caravels from Portugal to the Gulf of Guinea and then Angola. To the short-lived (1487-1506/7) Ughoton factory in Benin, the Portuguese brought items for exchange which included manillas (copper initially, and later brass, as African fashions and demand changed), coloured cloth, linen, coral beads, and strings of glass and enamelled beads. Dyed caps, coloured hats, horse-tails and red cloth (symbols of authority and badges of rank respectively), Cambay chintz, and shirts of blue Indian silk, were intended as presents to chiefs rather than for barter. Topping the list of commodities which were exchanged at São Jorge da Mina in 1509 for slaves and gold were Moroccan goods: coloured striped cloths (*alambéis*; Arabic *hambel*), cloth covers (for a table) or cloaks (*alquicés*; Arabic *haik* or *Kissa*), and long shirt-like garments (*aljaravias*; Arabic *djellabas*). Other items included woollen goods, linen cloths, red and blue cloths, blue beads, red seashells, cowrie shells, amber and red coral beads, utensils of copper and bronze, tin bracelets, and white wine. It is noticeable that the most popular object, namely *alambeis*, was not from Portugal but from the Maghreb. This listing was not to alter much for the next century, although the value of certain items was to increase, and by 1522 cowries were to rival manillas in importance as objects for exchange. Items originating in India (silk, chintz, and beads) were often preferred as gifts to chiefs or as more valuable instruments of exchange. In East Africa, cloth was the preferred medium for exchange but glass beads were also acceptable.[129]

Outward-bound to India and to Brazil, vessels carried goods of European provenance. On the *carreira da India* in the sixteenth century, the *náos* carried Spanish silver pieces-of-eight, gold, the much-in-demand copper (from Antwerp and used by the Portuguese in casting bronze cannon in Goa and Macao), lead, tin, quicksilver, cinnabar, worked and natural coral from the Mediterranean, alumstone, Florentine scarlet cloth, Genoese velvet, red cloth from London and Flanders, French and English linens, Portuguese wine, clocks, and low-value European goods such as glassware, trinkets, and even playing cards. As regards Brazil, much had happened since Cabral's early offerings of bells, red caps, copper bracelets, fish-hooks, axes, knives, scissors, mirrors, combs, beads and similar trifles had found ready acceptance by the Indians. An increasing Portuguese presence and development of a monetary economy led vessels of the *carreira do Brasil* to carry from Portugal cargoes of olive oil, flour, codfish, wines, woollens, tools and ironware, manufactured goods, and even such items of dress as wigs and silk stockings.[130]

Portuguese trade from India eastwards beyond Cape Comorin

to Indonesia and the China Sea introduced a different dimension into the origin of commodities carried from Goa or Cochin. To be sure, there were some goods of European origin but these were few and rather specialized in nature. They might include Flemish clocks, wine glasses, crystal, and cloths, for sale in Malacca. To China, much of the cargo carried initially by the Portuguese originated in India such as pepper and ivory, but objects carried from Europe included curiosities such as lenses, timepieces, mechanical devices, and prisms. The same applied to the Macao-Nagasaki vessels, with most of the cargo originating in China, but with some goods of Indian origin, and even fine swords, fire-arms, and other weapons brought from Europe. Goa was a port where East met West. It was a distribution point not only for goods of European origin but for those whose destination was Portugal. From Goa spices and Chinese silks were shipped to Hormuz in exchange for silver or Persian horses which, in turn, would be re-exported to southern India. Textiles from Gujarat and Coromandel were shipped to East Africa in exchange for slaves, gold, and ivory. The Singhalese favoured gold and silver coins, copper, cotton and textiles from Gujarat, and cinnabar. Portuguese fleets from Goa/Cochin to the Bandas and Moluccas carried primarily Gujarati or Bengali cottons, some copper objects, dry goods and knick-knacks, which they exchanged for cloves, nutmeg, and mace, until such time as the loss of the trade to the Javanese and Malayans by the 1570s. From Goa and Cochin the Portuguese carried to Malacca, Cambay linens and Coromandel cotton fabrics, cotton thread, and cotton piece- goods, which would be distributed further by local carriers to Indonesia, Java and Malaya. In Malacca these goods were exchanged by the Portuguese for spices and aromatic woods such as sandalwood, and hides from Siam. These in turn would be exchanged in Macao for raw silks, silk piecegoods, floss, porcelains, musk, and gold. At the final port of call in Japan which, after 1571, was Nagasaki, this cargo was replaced by silver, lacquerware, cabinets, painted screens, kimonos, weapons such as pikes and especially swords, and some gold. Returning to Macao, the silver was used to acquire gold and copper, more silks, musk, porcelain, ivory, and pearls which were carried back to Goa.[131]

Let us take four hypothetical examples to illustrate the global nature of this exchange. Venetian glass beads and Flemish brass pans were imported into Portugal, and crated for transportation to a factory in West Africa. Here they were exchanged for malaguetta pepper, gold, slaves, parrots and monkeys which were carried to Lisbon. The malaguetta pepper was dispatched to Antwerp, the slaves to Genoa, and the gold to Bristol to pay for imported cloth and wheat. Another example concerns bolts of English cloth carried from Lisbon to Morocco. Here they were exchanged for *alambeis*, which were carried back to Portugal and trans-shipped to a caravel bound for the Gulf of Guinea. Here they were used for the purchase of three slaves. One was transported to Portugal, but the other two were re-sold to a ship's captain from Brazil who made payment in rolls of tobacco. These slaves were carried to Bahia, where a miner from Minas Gerais bought one with payment in gold and the other was bought by a planter who made payment in sugar. The cycle was completed with the passage of the sugar and gold to Lisbon, and thence to London. Or, let us take the story of the peregrinations of a Flemish clock. Failing to find a market in Goa, this was carried on to Malacca, there to be exchanged for sandalwood which was carried to Macao. Payment in Macao was made partly in gold. This was carried to Japan and financed the purchase of a rare Namban screen by Kano Domi, depicting the unloading of a Portuguese vessel and the procession of the *Namban-jin* or Barbarians from the South. This was carried back to Goa and on to Lisbon. Finally, there were the cloves from Ternate carried to Malacca and on to Cochin, unloaded in Lisbon and re-loaded on a caravel bound for Morocco; payment was made in wheat which would finally find its way to West Africa and become part of the commodity exchange system of the South Atlantic.

Lisbon was indisputably the commercial centre of this far-flung Portuguese network of trading diasporas, but it was not the sole point of reference nor indeed the final destination or point of origin for many of the commodities carried on the oceans of the world by carracks and caravels. There was substantial movement of commodities carried by Portuguese between Africa, Asia, and the Americas, and which never touched Europe. This movement took three forms: first, commodities transported legally by the Portuguese on crown-sanctioned vessels and on routes which had no European component; secondly, commodities transported by Portuguese, who were essentially free agents and sometimes freebooters, on routes and between ports which were not approved by the crown; thirdly, contraband in goods whose transportation was not authorized by the crown, or whose transportation was legal but subject to regulations and only after payment of taxes or customs dues. Despite the best efforts of the Portuguese crown to ensure that the more profitable and revenue-generating sectors of these commercial exchanges remained royal monopolies, that control over commerce was centralized in Lisbon, and that all factories and forts were under crown control, there were loop-holes which were exploited by the less scrupulous who thereby deprived the crown of revenues which were its due.[132]

Let us look first at Portuguese India and Asia, and then at the Portuguese Atlantic. In East Africa, the Portuguese intrusion was no obstacle to Arab and Swahili traders who continued freely to engage in commerce with the Red Sea, Persian Gulf, and India. From the 1670s, Gujarati and Goan traders invested heavily in Mozambique and it was they, rather than the Portuguese, who reaped much of the financial reward. In the case of Goa, what proportion of goods passing through the port did not reach Europe? Malacca, likewise, was a key hub for a series of interlocking trade networks reaching from Bab-el-Mandeb to Macao and the Moluccas and which the Portuguese could, to some degree, moderate from Malacca. It was also a centre for official and private trade carried out by the Portuguese within and without the Indonesian archipelago.[133] In East Asia, thanks to the Ming dynasty's 'Great Withdrawal' and prohibitions on Chinese trading directly with Japan, the Portuguese (and later the Dutch) stepped into the breach and had a virtual monopoly on this carrying trade between Macao and Nagasaki, based on exchange of Chinese silks, gold, musk, and porcelain for Japanese silver and copper. It has been estimated that the Portuguese were the carriers of between a third and a half of all silk that left China by sea. By the 1630s, silk imports into Japan were more important than gold.[134] When to this are added the commercial networks which extended to Indonesia and even East Africa, and in which Indian textiles played a major role, it can be seen that such was the complementarity of supply and demand at different points on these commercial networks that a European component was superfluous.

There developed Indian Ocean and East Asian counterparts to the triangular trade of the Atlantic, namely Goa/Cochin-Mozambique-Hormuz, Malacca-Macao-Moluccas, and Canton-Macao-Nagasaki. Commodities from Indonesia, China, and Japan arrived in Goa and were further distributed to Portuguese enclaves on the west coast of India, to Portuguese forts and factories in East Africa, or to the Persian Gulf. From Macao and Malacca, Portuguese traded to Siam and Indochina, to Solor, Flores, and Timor, and to Makassar in the Celebes, with or without official approval. The potential profits to be made by those Portuguese who persisted in reaching the sources of more valuable commodities – cinnamon (Ceylon), cloves (Moluccas), nutmeg and mace (Bandas), sandalwood (Timor), and silk (China) – and the ready availability of markets for the sale of such commodities within Asia, were considerable incentives to trade both within and without constraining regulations. As we have seen, the result was that profits and volume of such intra-Asian trading by the Portuguese exceeded those derived from commerce between the west coast of India and Europe.

There were set-backs. The Manchu invasion of China disrupted silk supplies to Canton. Cantonese officials developed xenophobic tendencies, which found their mark in the Portuguese. There were hassles over customs dues. The seventeenth century was characterized by Dutch incursions and inroads onto Portuguese 'turf'. The Shimabara rebellion of 1637-38 spurred the council of state (*roju*) to cut all commercial relations between Nagasaki and Macao and forced the captain-major of the 1639 voyage to leave Japan empty-handed without discharging his cargo. Nothing daunted, enterprising Portuguese sought alternate ventures in the Moluccas and Celebes. Portuguese country traders were hard hit by competition from the Dutch and English East India Companies, Dutch traders with no Company affiliation, and piracy. But, as the Brazilians would say, there was always a *jeito*, which might be roughly translated as 'Where there's a will, there's a way'.[135]

Such initiatives could result in conflicts of interest between the Portuguese crown and those of its representatives intent on preserving a royal monopoly, and Portuguese who wished to engage in free trade, often in collaboration with local merchants and in collusion with Portuguese and local officialdom. Private traders and corrupt officials undermined the crown monopoly of the cinnamon trade from Ceylon. Implementation of a decree of 1614 fixing export quotas of cinnamon from the island was postponed until January 1615 so that local merchants, whose livelihood depended on trade in this commodity, could get rid of their stocks. In the first half of the sixteenth century, the Moluccas were notorious for the veniality of the crown appointees. The arrival of António Galvão in the Moluccas in 1536 to take up his post as administrator of the *capitania* illustrated how such conflicts could come to a head. His baggage included the codification of civil and criminal laws known as the *Ordenações Manuelinas* and the ecclesiastical *Constuituições*. Galvão took as his mission to sweep out corruption and profiteering by civilians and officials alike. He even changed the landscape by creating a Portuguese town of stone and whitewash to replace what had had hitherto possessed all the appearances of an indigenous village. Integrity was not a quality in a crown official at that time and place calculated to endear the incumbent. Galvão received no local support for his house-cleaning, nor did his fellow administrators in the Portuguese overseas civil service welcome a colleague who rocked the boat. Galvão became a sacrificial lamb. The viceroy in Goa relieved him of his command a year early.

The combined circumstances of the fortuitous establishment of the Spanish in the Philippines (Cebu, 1565; Manila, 1571) and the gradual taking over by Javanese and Malayans of the trade in cloves from the Moluccas, led Portuguese in Macao and Malacca to seize the opportunity of engaging in an illegal trade to Manila. Trade between Portuguese and Spanish overseas possessions had been forbidden by a royal order of 1581 and by viceregal decrees issued in Goa and New Spain. The only exception was made for supplies of war *matériel* if so requested by the captain-general of Macao or the governor of the Philippines. Such decrees were ineffectual, undermined not merely by private traders but by officials of Portugal and Spain in Macao and Manila respectively. Portuguese carried from Macao to Manila Chinese silks and Indian cottons and textiles predominantly, but cargoes included beds, secretaries, parlour chairs, finely gilded furniture, amber, musk, pearls, and slaves. These were exchanged for American silver. Indeed in 1589-90, one Dom João da Gama, who had been Captain of Malacca, avoided being sent to Portugal in irons by making a trans-Pacific crossing directly to Acapulco where he was arrested and sent to Seville to stand trial. Other merchants with him were more fortunate and returned to Macao, via Manila, with silver bullion. Thus did the Portuguese trade diaspora truly come to encircle the globe with commodities carried by the Portuguese to Manila being trans-shipped on the galleons to Acapulco for further passage to Peru and to Spain, and goods from Spain being carried by the Portuguese onwards to Macao, Malacca, and even the seat of the Estado da India in Goa. But the appearance of the Spanish in eastern waters carried a price. Not only did they seek direct commercial and diplomatic relations with China but there was a renewal of Spanish interest in the Moluccas. These aspirations led to aggravation and hostilities between Spaniards and Portuguese. By 1640, the Portuguese were to lose both the Manila and Japan routes. [136]

The Atlantic also afforded ample opportunity for contraband. Most draining on the metropolitan economy was the traffic in contraband gold from Brazil to Portugal and England. This could be brashly overt, namely transportation of gold dust and gold bars in pinnaces or even *jangadas* from the Brazilian coast to English vessels hove to off shore. But there was also the gold in dust, coins, and bars, together with diamonds and other precious stones, which were embarked on Lisbon-bound vessels and which were not manifested prior to embarkation nor on board 'before the mast' after sailing, as required by a royal resolution of 17 July 1711. Laws of 1720 and 1734 further required that all such remittances be liable to payment of one per cent *ad valorem*. Contrabandists displayed considerable initiative. Gold was concealed in fire-arms, barrels of molasses, and in hollowed out wooden saints, to say nothing of the nooks and crannies around any vessel. Regulatory measures were largely ineffectual. A 1799 report commented on the enormous quantities of gold in dust and bar as well as precious stones entering Great Britain. [137]

As had been the case in India and Asia, there were trade diasporas in the Atlantic which did not include Europe, whose carriers increasingly were as likely to be Dutch or English as Portuguese, and whose operation was financed by non-metropolitan Portuguese capital. The islands of the Cape Verdes, Madeira, and Azores were at the several cross-roads of the Atlantic, points of convergence for goods originating in, and

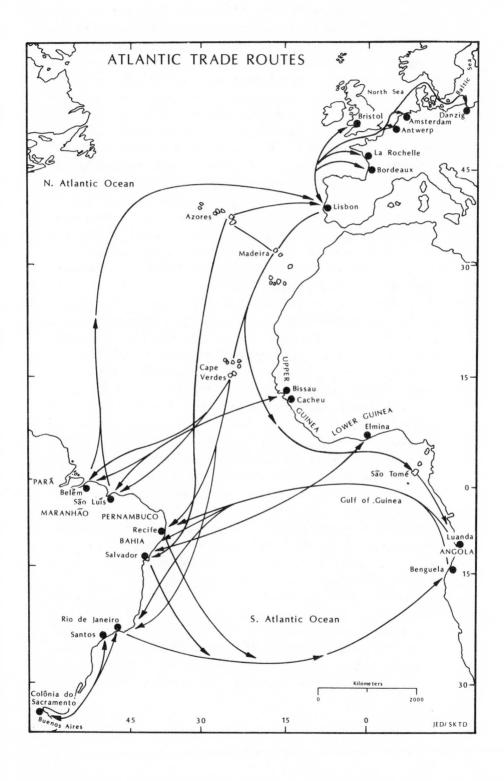

ATLANTIC TRADE ROUTES

N. Atlantic Ocean

North Sea

Baltic Sea

Bristol
Amsterdam
Antwerp
La Rochelle
Bordeaux

45

Azores

Lisbon

Madeira

30

UPPER

Cape
Verdes

Bissau
Cacheu

15

GUINEA

LOWER GUINEA
Elmina

São Tomé

PARÁ

Belém
São Luís
MARANHÃO

Gulf of .Guinea

0

PERNAMBUCO

Recife
BAHIA

Salvador

Luanda
ANGOLA

Benguela

15

Rio de Janeiro

Santos

S. Atlantic Ocean

Colônia do
Sacramento

30

Buenos Aires

45

30

15

0

Kilometers

0   2000

JED/ SKTD

whose final destinations were, Africa, Asia, the Caribbean, and the mainland of North and South America. In the Bight of Benin, from 1493 into the nineteenth century, there was an active commerce between São Tomé and the 'slave rivers', initially in slaves on whose labour the island depended. This was also to be the case of Príncipe after 1500. Brazil was a lively partner in commerce which did not involve the mother country. Homeward-bound East Indiamen put into Rio de Janeiro and Salvador and unloaded substantial quantities of Indian cloth, Chinese silks and porcelain, lacquer objects, and spices, in exchange for contraband tobacco, gold, and diamonds, as well as engaging in legal commerce in sugar, tobacco, hides, and woods. This commerce was significant enough to make the Brazilian ports – most notably Salvador – not mere way-stations for Indiamen returning to Lisbon, but markets in their own right. Bahia was the source for the top quality tobacco leaf 'of the first harvest' (de primeira folha) which was exported to Goa and distributed further. In Macao there was a market for snuff, much in demand for alleged properties of curing diseases of the eyes. Rio de Janeiro, Santos, and ports of southern Brazil in Santa Catarina and Rio Grande de São Pedro were also involved in commodity exchange with the Río de la Plata. This dated back to the mid-1580s and involved African slaves, rice, sugar, dry goods, and European products in exchange for silver originating from Upper Peru as well as products from regions bordering the rivers Uruguay and Paraguay. Not only could the Portuguese count on a ring of rich Portuguese and Spanish contrabandists in Buenos Aires, as well as the collusion of Spanish officials, but in Tucumán there was a strong clique acting in concert with Buenos Aires. There were well developed routes to Chile and Peru for smuggling goods. This illicit trade, centred (after 1680) on Colônia do Sacramento, continued to thrive until 1762 when this outpost was captured by Spanish forces. The price paid by the Portuguese crown lay in loss of revenues from duty payable on such goods.[138]

The Portuguese Atlantic provided the only instance of ties so close between two colonies, that it could be argued that Angola was more dependent on Brazil than on metropolitan Portugal. There was a legal exchange of commodities between the two colonies without there being any need for a European leg, although Angola did also form part of a triangular trade between

Portugal, West Africa, and Brazil. Sugar, sugar-cane brandy, rice, hides, horses, and legal gold were carried from Brazil to Angola in exchange for slaves, ivory, wax, and mats. But it was Brazilian trade to the Gulf of Guinea in general, and Whydah in particular, in the late seventeenth and eighteenth centuries which most exercised the Portuguese crown. In 1721 the Portuguese built a fort at Whydah. This trade could be legal, namely purchase by Brazilians of the much-prized slaves known as Minas, in exchange for tobacco, sugar, and rum. But what angered the crown was the trade in contraband goods from Brazil, primarily Bahia, to Whydah, and the fact that these got into the hands of the Dutch at Elmina and that contraband goods of European provenance entered Brazil through the same intermediary. Furthermore, the islands of São Tomé and Príncipe were frequented by Dutch and English traders. Apart from wringing their hands over the export of contraband gold from Brazil to the Gulf of Guinea, the exchange which most occupied the Portuguese crown in the first half of the eighteenth century was Bahian tobacco for Mina slaves. In vain, did Portuguese kings reprimand civil servants in Angola and Brazil for failing to stop flagrant infractions of the ruling that only third grade tobacco should be sent from Bahia to West Africa. It came to the attention of Dom João V that not only second class, but even first class tobacco was being transported to West Africa from Bahia.[139]

The Brazil-Africa experience differed from that of Portuguese India in this regard. In India, there was a royal monopoly (1624) on the import and commerce of tobacco which was very lucrative to the crown and which, until 1840, took the form of a series of triennial leases of the contract. There was great demand for Bahian tobacco in Portuguese India, in addition to that grown in the territories around Goa. However, although there would have been the potential for a direct Bahia-Goa trade, an initiative which would have found royal support in the eighteenth century, this did not materialize and was opposed by the Tobacco Board (*Junta da Administração do Tabaco*) in Goa. The Board insisted that it was preferable to continue the practice that all such imports be routed through Lisbon to Goa, for further distribution in India. Even after the English took Bombay in 1665 and challenged the Portuguese monopoly, some of the tobacco put on sale by the English in Bombay was of Bahian

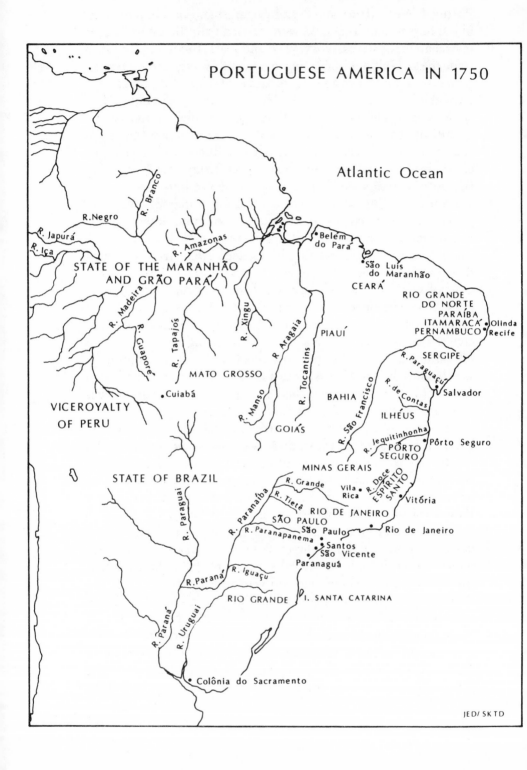

PORTUGUESE AMERICA IN 1750

Atlantic Ocean

R. Branco
R.Negro
R. Japurá
R. Iça
R. Amazonas
• Belém
do Pará

STATE OF THE MARANHÃO
AND GRÃO PARÁ

• São Luís
do Maranhão

CEARÁ

RIO GRANDE
DO NORTE
PARAÍBA
ITAMARACÁ
PERNAMBUCO • Olinda
• Recife

R. Madeira
R. Guaporé
R. Tapajós
R. Xingu
R. Aragaia
R. Tocantins
R. Manso

PIAUÍ

SERGIPE
R. Paraguaçú

MATO GROSSO

• Cuiabá

BAHIA

R. São Francisco
R. de Contas
• Salvador

VICEROYALTY
OF PERU

GOIÁS

ILHÉUS

R. Jequitinhonha
PÔRTO
SEGURO
• Pôrto Seguro

STATE OF BRAZIL

MINAS GERAIS

R. Grande
Vila
Rica
R. Doce
ESPÍRITO
SANTO
• Vitória

R. Paraguai
R. Paranaíba
R. Tietê
RIO DE JANEIRO

SÃO PAULO
R. Paranapanema
• São Paulo
• Rio de Janeiro

• Santos
São Vicente
Paranaguá

R. Paraná
R. Iguaçu
R. Paraná
R. Uruguai

RIO GRANDE
I. SANTA CATARINA

• Colônia do Sacramento

JED/ SKTD

provenance and had been bought by the English in Lisbon. One scholar has gone so far as to assert that this legal trade in tobacco was probably the most revenue-generating item of the overseas trade from Portugal to India and East Asia in the last quarter of the seventeenth century.[140]

Then, as now, it was gold which made the world go round. The Portuguese played their share in the global circulation of this commodity, be it in bars, currency, dust, or nuggets, from the fifteenth to the eighteenth centuries. In the fifteenth century, Portuguese efforts were directed to tapping into the 'golden trade of the Moors', or the gold-bearing caravans crossing the Atlantic Sahara. This led to the establishment of an inland Portuguese factory at Uadam in the Mauretanian Adrar during the reign of Dom João II. Uadam was at the hub of trade betweeen the Atlantic Sahara and Arguim and Timbuktu, but the factory's existence was short-lived. Although the Portuguese were frustrated in their initial hopes of finding an El Dorado in Brazil until the 1690s, already in the 1480s African gold was becoming an export/import commodity and during the reign of Dom Manuel I (1495-1521) the Portuguese were exporting substantial quantities of gold from West Africa through the fort of São Jorge da Mina. This gold exported by the Portuguese through their factories at Arguim off the coast of Mauretania, Cantor on the upper Gambia, Sierra Leone, Axim, and São Jorge da Mina, was destined for Portugal, but much left Portugal to pay for imports, such as corn and manufactured goods, or for items which would be re-exported from Portugal for barter and trade. Gold was to be the *entrée* enabling the Portuguese to become players in the international commerce in the Indian Ocean and beyond, giving the Portuguese who could make purchases in gold rather than goods an edge over Arab traders. Gold from Monomotapa – whose exports exceeded that of Arguim and Elmina – was critically important in providing the Portuguese with a ready means for purchase of Indian textiles or Moluccan spices in the sixteenth and seventeenth centuries, but remained in the Indian Ocean trade diaspora rather than being sent to Portugal.[141]

The conquest of Malacca (1511) enabled the Portuguese to tap into gold supplies which exceeded those of East Africa. These included gold from Sumatra, Java, Borneo, Makassar, and Cochinchina, as well as that produced in the Malayan peninsula.

The Portuguese were the beneficiaries of the imperial ban on trade by Chinese to Japan, the shortage of silver in China which led the Chinese to value silver more highly than gold (of which they produced ample quantities), the Chinese preference for silver over gold, and the Japanese demand for gold as a medium of exchange. At the beginning of the seventeenth century, a gold *peso* in China was worth 5.5 silver *pesos* and might even rise to 7.5 if there were a severe shortage. In Japan, as in Europe, a gold *peso* was worth about 12 silver *pesos*. An overall figure of silver exports by the Portuguese from Japan to China for the years 1546-1638 has been put at between 37 and 41 million *taels* (1,387,500-1,537,500 kilos).[142] This exchange of Chinese gold for Japanese silver from the mines on Honshu provided profits as high as sixty per cent for the Portuguese, and provided them with the means to participate so effectively in Asian networks of trade.

Two centuries and two continents away, it was Brazilian gold which was a lubricant for Portuguese Atlantic commerce, financed the administration of Portugal's south Atlantic empire, and permitted Dom João V to rule as an absolute monarch. It also saved Portugal from a more aggravated balance of payments problem with her trading partners in Europe. But the price exacted on the mother country for this fortuitous windfall of the gold strikes in Brazil was high. Nations other than Portugal were the prime beneficiaries of the flood of Brazilian gold. It has been estimated that from between one-half and three-quarters of all gold entering the Tagus, went to England. Much was squandered on projects of immediate personal gratification rather than on long-term investment in the nation's future, the stimulus for embryonic manufacturing enterprises was weakened (a trend only to be reversed in the 1770s with Pombal's initiatives), the transition from a barter to a monetary economy was slowed, dependency on Great Britain increased, and the State was permitted the luxury of postponing the introduction of much needed reforms.[143]

Gold from these different continents was coined by the Portuguese in their mints in Lisbon, Goa, Cochin, and Brazil, and the currency circulated within and far beyond mother country and overseas holdings. Such coins were accepted as tender by many who neither spoke Portuguese nor adhered to Christianity, and often opposed Portuguese political and commercial aspirations.

48 Plaque (brass) of two Portuguese with
    manillas. Nigerian-Edo. Court of Benin.
    Sixteenth–seventeenth century.
    The Metropolitan Museum of Art, 1991 (1991.17.13).

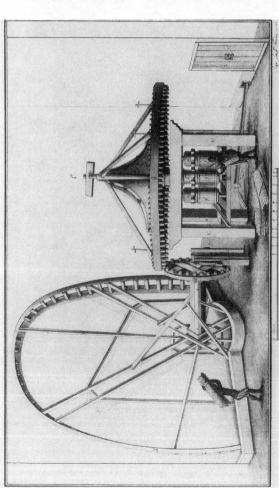

49 (*above*) Mill run by water to crush sugar-cane. Eighteenth-century Brazil.
Alexandre Rodrigues Ferreira, *Viagem filosófica*.

50 (*right*) American Indians chopping down brazilwood tree.
André Thevet, *Les Singularitez de la France Antarctique, autrement nommée Amerique: & de plusieurs Terres & Isles decouvertes de notre temps* (Paris: Héritiers de Maurice de la Porte, 1558).

51　Namban-byobu depicting the Black Ship unloading in Japan. Edo, Ukiyoe school, seventeenth century.
Freer Gallery of Art, Smithsonian Institution, Washington D.C. (65.23)

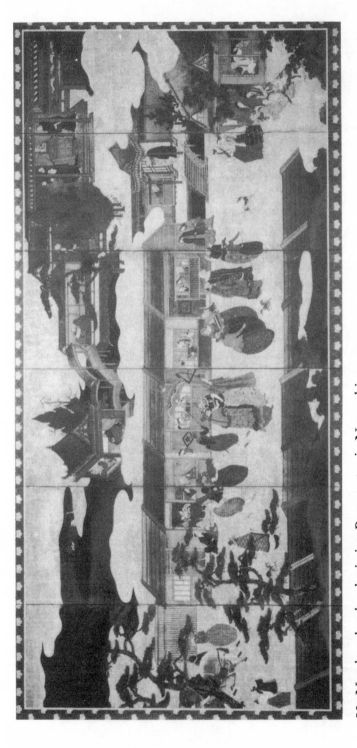

52 Namban-byobu depicting Portuguese in Nagasaki.
Ukiyoe school, seventeenth century.
Freer Gallery of art, Smithsonian Institution, Washington D.C. (65.22)

56 Cocoa plant.
Charles de Rocheforte, *Histoire naturelle et morale des Iles Antilles de l'Amérique* (Rotterdam: Leers, 1681).

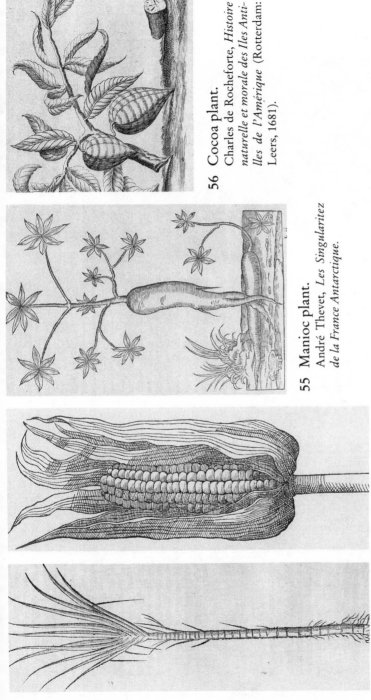

55 Manioc plant.
André Thevet, *Les Singularitez de la France Antarctique.*

53 (*left*) Sugar-cane.
Willem Piso, *Historia Naturalis Brasiliae* (Leiden: F. Hackium, 1648).

54 (*right*) Ear of maize, an illustration for the history of João de Barros.
Giovanni Battista Ramusio, *Navigationi et Viaggi,* (Venice: Giunti, 1606).

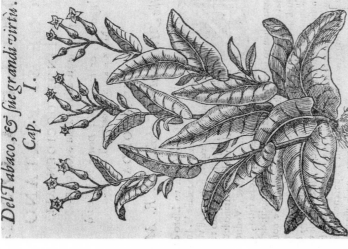

Del Tabaco, & sue grandi virtù.
Cap. I.

Vesta herba, che communemente si chiama Tabaco, è herba molto antica, & conosciuta tra gli In—

59 Tobacco plant.
Garcia d'Orta, *Due libri dell' Historia de
i Semplici, Aromati, e altre cose, che
vengono portate dall' Indie Orientali,
pertinenti alla medicina* (Venice: Ziletti,
1582).

58 Peanut.
Johannes de Laet,
*L'histoire du Nouveau
Monde: ou, descrip-
tion des Indes Occi-
dentales* (Leiden:
Elsevier, 1640).

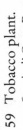

57 Pineapple.
From André Thevet, *Les Singularitez de la France
Antarctique.*

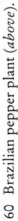

60 Brazilian pepper plant (*above*).

61 Cinnamon plant.
Charles Lécluse (Carolus Clusius), *Aromatum et Simplicium aliquot medicamentorum apud Indios nascientium historia* (Antwerp, 1567).

62 Sapucaia tree of Brazil, showing nuts and blossom.
60 and 62 from Fr. Cristóvão de Lisboa, *História dos animais e árvores do Maranhão. 1624-1627*. Arquivo Histórico Ultramarino, Lisbon.

Iaquas.

Cajus

Mangas

Iambos

Ananas

Gember

Baptista Doeticum fec.

Fructuum Mangas Cajus Iambos Iaquas, et Ananas, qui in India nascuntur qui essusuris, et Zimalkeris, cujus e copia magna illic cultus exoritus viva imago.

De fruyten die in Indien wassen en seer lustelick zyn om te eten als Mangas, Cajus, Iambos Iaquas, en Ananas met die Gember welcke om der menichte wynich geacht is affronterspringe naert leeven gesteld die plaen en wysen.

63 and 64   Trees and plants in Asia, some of American origin (pineapple) and others carried to Brazil (coconut, mango, jack-fruit, pepper) by the Portuguese Jan Huygen van Linschoten, *Histoire de la Navigation … et de son voyage es Indes Orientales,* 3rd edition (Amsterdam, 1638).

65 *Urucuria*, the Brazilian burrowing owl which allegedly would reply to Indians' questions; and *sai*, a species of tanager.
Fr. Cristóvão de Lisboa, *História dos animais e árvores do Maranhão*. Arquivo Histórico Ultramarino, Lisbon.

66 *Urubutinga* or turkey vulture of Brazil.
Alexandre Rodrigues Ferreira, *Viagem filosófica*.

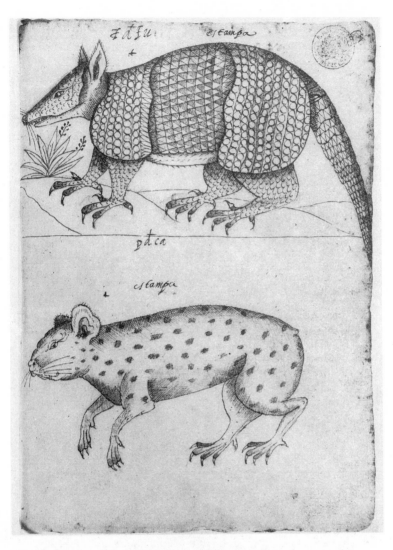

67 Animals of Brazil: the armadillo (*tatu*) and spotted cavy
(*paca*).
Fr. Cristóvão de Lisboa, *História dos animais e árvores do Maranhão*.
Arquivo Histórico Ultramarino, Lisbon.

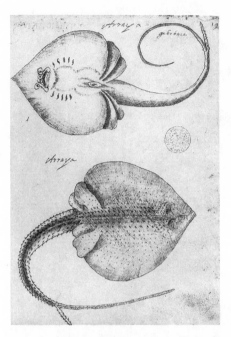

68 *Jarabuibura*, a species
of ray of the
Maranhão.
Fr. Cristóvão de Lisboa,
*História dos animais e
árvores do Maranhão.*
Arquivo Histórico
Ultramarino, Lisbon.

69 Albrecht Dürer's woodcut (1515) of the rhinoceros sent from
Gujarat as a present to King Dom Manuel I of Portugal.

71 Chinoiserie in the choir of the cathedral of Mariana, Minas Gerais. Eighteenth century.

70 Panels with Chinese motifs in the eighteenth-century chapel of Nossa Senhora do O, Sabará, Minas Gerais.

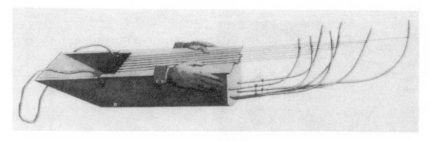

72 *Viola*, musical instrument played by blacks in Brazil.
Alexandre Rodrigues Ferreira, *Viagem filosófica.*

73 Early nineteenth-century water-colour of a porter playing a
musical instrument in Brazil.
Drawing by Guillobel.

74 Coronation of their king by blacks in Brazil. He is carrying a sceptre and wearing a crown, and accompanied by musicians. Late eighteenth century. Water-colour by Carlos Julião.

75 Japanese chest. Momoyama-Edo period, early seventeenth century. Lacquer and inlaid with mother-of-pearl, gold, silver, and gilt-copper. Style and motifs show influence of coastal India.

The Freer Gallery of Art, Smithsonian Institution, Washington, D.C. (79.50).

76 Apotheosis of the Virgin. Indian ink drawing, Mughal (c. 1575-1600). Copy of an engraving made in Germany c.1500. European prints entered the Mughal court during the reign of Akbar (1556-1605) who invited Jesuits to his court to explain Christianity. Mughal artists were influenced by Western styles and techniques.

Arthur M. Sackler Gallery, Smithsonian Institution, Washington, D.C. (Sackler S1990.57).

77 Calligraphy with marginal Christian images. Leaf from the
'Jahangir Album'. Indian painting. Mughal, c.1590.
The Freer Gallery of Art, Smithsonian Institution, Washington, D.C. (Freer
56. 12 verso).

78 Hindus converted to Christianity in Malabar, according to
   tradition by St. Thomas.
   78 and 79 from water-colours by an unknown Portuguese artist, mid-sixteenth
   century. Biblioteca Casanatense, Rome. MS 1889.

79 Portuguese male in India apparently making marriage overtures
   to an Indian woman converted to Christianity. Women are
   dressed in Portuguese style.

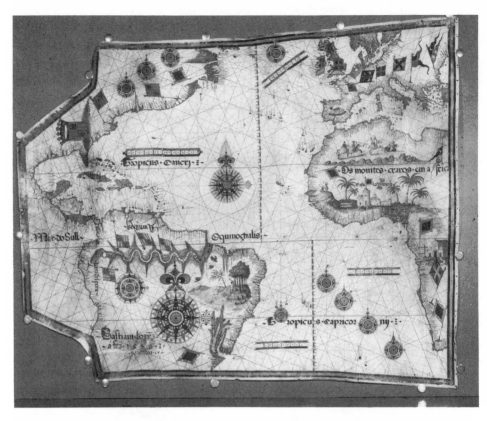

80 Map by the Portuguese cartographer Sebastião Lopes (c.1558), showing coastlines of Europe, West Africa, and America. Note the walled city of Lisbon and fort of São Jorge da Mina.
British Library.

81 Seventeenth-century design for a galleon by Manuel Fernandes.
Livro das traças de carpintaria by Manuel Fernandes, 1616. Biblioteca da Ajuda, Lisbon.

82 Francisco Álvares, *Verdadera Informaçam das terras do Preste Joam* (Lisbon, 1540). Title page.

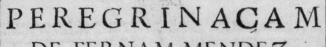

PEREGRINAÇAM
DE FERNAM MENDEZ
PINTO.

EM QVE DA CONTA DE MVYTAS E MVY-
to eſtranhas couſas que vio & ouuio no reyno da China, no da Tar-
taria, no do Sornau, que vulgarmente ſe chama Sião, no do Calami-
nhan, no de Pegù, no de Martauão, & em outros muytos reynos
& ſenhorios das partes Orientais, de que neſtas noſſas
do Occidente ha muyto pouca ou
nenhũa noticia.

E TAMBEM DA CONTA DE MVYTOS CASOS PARTI-
culares que acontecerão aſi a elle como a outras muytas peſſoas. E no fim della trata bre-
uemente de algũas couſas, & da morte do ſanto Padre meſtre Franciſco Xauier,
vnica luz & reſplandor daquellas partes do Oriente, & Reytor
nellas vniuerſal da Companhia de Ieſus.

Eſcrita pelo meſmo Fernão Mendez Pinto.

Dirigido à Catholica Real Mageſtade del Rey dom Felippe o III.
deſte nome noſſo Senhor.

Com licença do ſanto Officio, Ordinario, & Paço.

EM LISBOA. Por Pedro Crasbeeck. Anno 1614.

A cuſta de Belchior ſde Faria Caualeyro da caſa del Rey noſſo
Senhor, & ſeu Liureyro.　　　*Com priuilegio Real.*
Eſtà taixado eſte liuro a 600 reis em papel.

83　Fernão Mendes Pinto, *Peregrinaçam* (Lisbon, 1614). Title page.

84 Allegorical frontispiece to the eighteenth-century *Viagem
filosófica às Capitanias do Grão-Pará, Rio Negro, Mato Grosso
e Cuiabá* by Alexandre Rodrigues Ferreira.

In this regard, the same held true for silver coins of which the first minted outside of Portugal were the *esferas* and *meias esferas* coined in Goa and the *cruzados* coined in Malacca on Albuquerque's order. Copper currency minted in Lisbon had limited circulation. Gold bullion, be it in the form of coins, or bars, or dust, was transported legally and fuelled legitimate commercial enterprises. No less was gold smuggled and the precious metal financed illegal trade and contraband. If illegally exported Guinea gold was carried to Brazil in the seventeenth century to purchase tobacco dipped in molasses so in demand in West Africa, and from Sofala and Mozambique in East Africa by Muslim traders and then Portuguese in the sixteenth and seventeenth centuries, in the eighteenth century it was contraband Brazilian gold which would be one medium for the purchase of slaves. In the first half of the eighteenth century, it was Portugal herself which was the victim of contraband gold running, with English vessels spiriting off from the Tagus to the Thames gold consignments from Brazil. A common thread linking the influx to Portugal of Guinea gold in the sixteenth century and Brazilian gold in the eighteenth century, is the syphoning off of this precious metal to northern Europe.[144]

One aspect of this circulation of bullion concerns the impact of American silver and gold on other parts of the world. This has been studied with relation to Europe and the price revolution spurred in the sixteenth and seventeenth centuries by the influx of silver, especially from New Spain and Potosí. Less studied has been the impact of the export of this bullion from Europe to the East, and for which India was the major recipient. The Portuguese were not alone in such exports and, in the case of India, were to be outdone by gold exports to India by the English East India Company. The result was to bring about a price revolution in India. The Portuguese were also carriers to the East of silver from Spanish America, either via Lisbon and Goa, or as part of the contraband trade with Manila. In both cases, Macao was the final destination. The Indian scholar Irfan Habib has suggested that, of the three precious metals – gold, silver, and copper – it was copper which was the most stable in India in the seventeenth century.[145]

One little-studied player in these global movements of bullion was the secular church and religious orders. They derived funds from a variety of sources. Conquest and conversion led to the acquisition of paddy fields in India, landed estates in Angola and Zambezia, and real estate and plantations in Brazil. Revenues generated from these commercial activities were often spent *in situ* on the maintenance of properties and the institutional needs of the church and religious orders. Other revenues from such commercial ventures were remitted to Lisbon, be they from India, Angola, or Brazil. In addition, the Society of Jesus and religious orders were often placed in the role of executors of wills of Portuguese who died overseas. Once estates had been settled, remittances of bequests were dispatched to relatives, for the most part in Portugal. Another aspect of such remittances was fulfilment of the wishes of the deceased that masses be said for his or her soul in a specific chapel. Monies were sent for the payment of priests and friars saying such masses. In the case of colonial Brazil, and even after the building of convents (the first in 1677 in Salvador), large amounts of gold were dispatched from the colony to Portugal for the initial admission fee and upkeep of young women who were also transported across the Atlantic to live in convents, without necessarily taking their final vows. Finally, both the church and the religious orders undertook to remit consigments of gold, silver, and precious stones on behalf of individuals. Another transaction was remittances from overseas territories to Portugal of monies derived from confiscations by the Inquisition.

The Society of Jesus was very prominent in remittances of bullion from its overseas provinces to Portugal. These derived from agricultural activities in Zambezia, Angola, and Brazil, and from the Society's involvement in trade in East Asia. In the eighteenth century, Jesuit colleges in Brazil regularly remitted gold in coin, bar, and dust, to their procurators in Lisbon or to the Colégio de Santo Antão. Remittances from Jesuit missions in Asia and India were also sent to Portugal on Indiamen which touched at Brazilian ports. To a lesser degree, the religious orders of the Carmelites, Benedictines and Franciscans remitted bullion both of an institutional nature and also acting as agents on behalf of individuals. Individual priests and friars also remitted consignments of bullion, or accompanied such consignments when they returned to Portugal from overseas. Sometimes they were acting on behalf of third parties. On other occasions, such gold represented the fruits of their own commercial acumen despite rulings forbidding such initiatives. In eighteenth-century Brazil, the prospect of tapping into the seemingly endless streams of gold led monasteries and convents in Portugal to dispatch friars to the colony whose charge was to collect alms on behalf of the parent houses in Portugal. Some fulfilled their missions but others remained in Brazil and were the scourge of their provincials and local authorities.

One other institutional participant in the flow of bullion were the brotherhoods of lay men and lay women. Most prominent was the Santa Casa da Misericórdia which counted branches throughout the Portuguese-speaking world. As part of their mission, such branches were executors of wills and in this capacity regularly sent consignments of gold from one branch to another for delivery to heirs or for the saying of masses. The Third Orders of Saint Francis, Saint Dominic, and of the Carmelites, fulfilled a similar role, as too did the numerous branches of the prestigious Irmandade do Santíssimo Sacramento. The Brotherhood of Our Lady of the Rosary, which counted branches in the Atlantic Islands, Angola, Brazil, and in Portugal, and whose membership was predominantly of persons of African descent, also participated in remitting gold.[146]

The Portuguese were active partners in a global circulation of commodities and bullion from the fifteenth century to the eighteenth century. This was primarily by maritime routes and embraced the Atlantic Ocean, Gulf of Guinea, Mediterranean, North Sea, and Baltic, the Indian Ocean, Persian Gulf, Bay of Bengal, and the China Sea, Sea of Japan, and Pacific Ocean. Only in Brazil, and to a less marked degree in Angola and Zambezia, were there to develop overland and fluvial distribution networks. Their trading enterprises brought them into contact with peoples of different religions, cultures, and races, with whom they had to accommodate or at least develop working relationships. The Portuguese carried to Europe the products of plantation economies such as sugar-cane, cotton, and coffee beans, of cultivated plants such as tobacco, cinnamon, cloves, and pepper, or even of wild plants such as cacao beans. Such commodities were for consumption, but a no less fascinating story is that of the Portuguese as disseminators of plants and seeds.

CHAPTER V
DISSEMINATION OF FLORA AND FAUNA

Portuguese participation in these global trade diaspora should not be permitted to overshadow the importance of the Portuguese in what has, in the long run, been a more lasting contribution to the formation of the modern world. Portugal is the sole place of origin of only one plant, namely gorse (*Ulex europaeus*),[147] but the Portuguese were to play a major role as primary and secondary carriers in the global dissemination of cultivated plants. Some were to become major crops in their new habitats. Others were merely relocated from one region to another and, either because of their failure to adapt to their new environment as successfully as had been hoped or because of limited demand, were of lesser importance. In some cases, different dietary habits or inadequate knowledge of how to cultivate a plant or how to process its fruits, determined the degree to which it was accepted in a new location. Given the global quality of the Portuguese enterprise, they were the carriers of plants and vegetables from temperate to tropical climes, and *vice versa*. For the most part, such relocation was by seeds but other possibilities included cuttings or even transporting the whole plant. The hazards of trans-oceanic navigation would certainly have made seeds more viable.

Many of the regions which were the centre of Portuguese activities, lie in the tropics between 23° 27' North and 23° 27' South. The Tropic of Capricorn traversed Portuguese America between Rio de Janeiro (22° 54' S) and Santos (23° 57' S), passed well south of the Kunene River (17° 20' S) which was the southern border of Angola, slightly north of Inhambane on the East African coast of Mozambique, and well south of Portuguese activities in Indonesia. Portugal herself, the Atlantic islands of Madeira and the Azores, and North African outposts, lay north of the Tropic of Cancer which dissects the Red Sea, passing south of Muscat (23° 29' N) on the Gulf of Oman, crossing India from the province of Gujarat to slightly north of the mouths of the Ganges emptying into the Bay of Bengal, and across Asia a mere 20' north of Canton (23° 07'N). In practical terms, the major ports of the Portuguese seaborne empire lay in the tropics, as too did those where they enjoyed trading rights with the exception of Nagasaki. It was precisely those plants of tropical and semi-tropical regions (as opposed to temperate climes) which comprised the greatest variety of flora carried by the Portuguese between tropical Asia, Africa, and America.

The Portuguese were intrigued by the new plants with which they came into contact but produced only one major work. This was Garcia d'Orta's *Colóquios dos simples, e drogas e cousas mediçinais da India*, published in Goa in 1563, a rich compendium of botanical and pharmacological information. This was in part appropriated by the leading European botanist of the age, Charles Lécluse (Carolus Clusius) who published an annotated abridgement under the title *Aromatum et Simplicium aliquot medicamentorum apud Indios nascientium historia* (Antwerp, 1567). These versions appeared in numerous editions and re-editions before the end of the century and were the basis for Italian (1576), French (1602), and English (1604) translations. Lécluse also translated *Tractado de las drogas y medicinas de las*

Indias Orientales (Burgos, 1578) of Cristóvão da Costa, a Portuguese physician and botanist who based his treatise on the *Colóquios* but who had travelled more widely in Asia than d'Orta, visiting Malacca and China, and corrected d'Orta on some points.[148] For Portuguese America, ironically it is to the scientists who came to Dutch Brazil during the administration of Johan Maurits van Nassau-Siegen that we owe major botanical and zoological studies: Georg Markgraf, Willem Pies, and Jan de Laet. Of these, Pies was trained in medicine but was wide ranging in his intellectual curiosity in natural history. Markgraf was the more knowledgeable in zoology and earth and planetary sciences. Markgraf's and Pies' *Historia Naturalis Brasiliae* (Leyden, 1648) describes mammals, birds, amphibious creatures, and fish. Pies' (Latinized as Piso) *De Indiae Utriusque re Naturali et Medica* (Amsterdam, 1658) is a compendium of *materia medica*, tropical medicine, public health, pharmacology, toxicology, botany and zoology. It possesses a strongly practical applicability in its descriptions of plants of commercial importance, both indigenous to Brazil and imported from Africa and Asia, and plants with medicinal qualities. In addition to these scholarly treatises, botanical information, descriptions of crops, and prescriptions based on the medicinal uses of native plants are scattered through many of the geographical accounts, such as those of Duarte Barbosa and Tomé Pires for Asia and in the *Dialogues of the Great Things of Brazil* (*Diálogos das Grandezas do Brasil*). Jesuit letters and writings are mines of information on the flora and fauna of America, Africa, India, and Asia.

There are grounds for believing that – although the sixteenth century was characterized by trading rather than cultivating of spices by the Portuguese – at an early date the Portuguese did conduct experiments into the adaptation of plants to different zones and climates. One such field station could well have been the Cape Verdes, despite their aridity and unstable seasons. Uninhabited prior to settlement by the Portuguese in the 1460s, initially on the largest island of Santiago and then on Fogo, the geographical position of this island group favoured contacts with the Gulf of Guinea, Angola, Brazil, and provisioning of vessels outward and homeward-bound on the India run. Population grew quickly, as too did pastoral and agricultural activities. Native to the islands was orchil, a lichen which produces a red

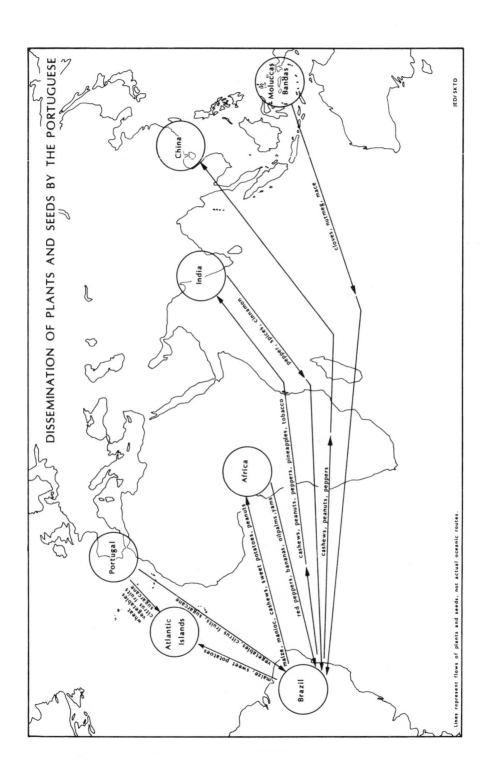

DISSEMINATION OF PLANTS AND SEEDS BY THE PORTUGUESE

Moluccas
Bandas

cloves, nutmeg, mace

China

India

pepper, spices, cinnamon

Africa

red peppers, bananas, oilpalms, yams

maize, manioc, cashews, sweet potatoes, peanuts

cashews, peanuts, peppers, pineapples, tobacco

cashews, peanuts, peppers

Portugal

wheat
vegetables
citrus fruits
sugarcane

vegetables, citrus fruits, sugarcane

Atlantic
Islands

maize, sweet potatoes

Brazil

IED/SKTD

Lines represent flows of plants and seeds, not actual oceanic routes.

dye and for whose export the first royal contract dated from 1469.[149] Grains and root crops of African origin were planted. Maize from America was introduced at the end of the fifteenth century or beginning of the sixteenth century. Later introductions included indigo, cotton, sugar-cane, manioc, and sweet potatoes.

Such experimentation and commercial potential were to lead to State intervention. Royal policy changed as to the desirability of the dissemination of plants from India to America. During the sixteenth century, when Dom Manuel's (1495-1521) top priority had been the strengthening of commercial ties with Asia, royal decrees had been promulgated forbidding the transportation to Brazil of the *drogas da India*, or cultivation of such plants in the New World. Plants which had been brought to Brazil were destroyed. The only plant to escape these sanctions was ginger which, by virtue of being a root, would be less visible to any invading force. But in the late sixteenth century and early seventeenth century, there had been mooted the idea of eliminating Venetian and Dutch competition and of making Portugal independent of Asian sources of spices, by cultivating in Brazil plants of oriental provenance. Considerations which included maintenance of the royal monopoly, apprehension of the challenge presented by a Brazil enriched by cultivating such spices, and of a politico-economic and even religious nature, led to preservation of the *status quo* in crown policy. Similar considerations led the crown to ban exports of ginger from Africa and Brazil and indigo from Brazil because such exports might damage exports from the East Indies or, in the case of indigo, challenge woad production in the Azores. With the gradual loss of Portuguese hegemony in the Indian Ocean and Muslim merchants holding the key to trade in Indonesia and the Spice Islands, Portuguese monarchs appear to have had a change of heart. The loss of Colombo to the Dutch in 1656 not only deprived the Portuguese of access to spices, especially cinnamon from Ceylon, but placed these resources in Dutch hands. In the seventeenth century, not only the Dutch but also the English had direct access to supplies in Asia and transported spices to Europe. Portugal witnessed a decline in her revenues derived from the spice trade, especially pepper.

This spurred the Portuguese crown to action. Two individuals played a major role in pressuring kings to promote the cultivation of oriental plants in Brazil. One was António Vieira, S.J., who advocated such a move in memoranda to Dom João IV. The second was his friend and correspondent, Duarte Ribeiro de Macedo, Portuguese ambassador in Paris (1668-77) and Madrid, who not only supported such an initiative but went so far as to specify how such plants should be packaged (seeds sealed in vials, cuttings in soil in sacks) for transportation from Goa to Bahia. There was also the hope that small-holders in Brazil, who had hitherto been satisfied merely with subsistence agriculture (tobacco and manioc), would diversify and expand into the cultivation of oriental plants. If such a policy succeeded, no longer would the Portuguese be but one of several groups (European and oriental) competing in the spice trade as had hitherto been the case. Given the virtually unlimited lands available for cultivation on a plantation scale in Brazil, cheap labour, and a considerably shorter transit time to European markets, such cultivation in Brazil was highly attractive. Finally, such cultivation could make Portugal less dependent on foreign capital and contribute substantially to improving her balance of payments situation vis-à-vis England especially and other countries of northern Europe.[150]

Keenly conscious of the commercial importance of oriental spices, in 1678 the crown ordered the viceroy in Goa to dispatch plants such as pepper, clove, cinnamon, nutmeg, and ginger, from India to regions more securely under Portuguese control, namely Portuguese America and even metropolitan Portugal and the Atlantic islands. This was to be done as secretly as possible and the governor-general in Bahia was alerted. The viceroy was charged to consult widely as to the most appropriate manner by which to transport seeds, cuttings and plants, to ensure their successful relocation in Brazil. A memorandum of 1681 and royal order of 1691 recommended that experiments be conducted in areas with differing soil conditions and climates, namely Bahia, Pernambuco, the Maranhão, Cape Verde, and Portugal. These were implemented immediately. The governor-general of Brazil (1690-94), António Luís Gonçalves da Câmara Coutinho, actively promoted the cultivation of pepper and cinnamon in regions as diverse as Rio de Janeiro, Pernambuco, and the Maranhão, as well as the Cape Verde islands. Experts on such cultivation were dispatched from India to Brazil. During the seventeenth and eighteenth centuries, there are numerous references in Brazilian archives to the bringing of seeds and plants from the Orient to Brazil. Dom João V (1706-50) took a keen personal interest in the flora of the tropics and and ordered the cultivation in West Africa and Brazil of plants from Asia. In 1707, the king approved payment of a daily stipend to a Franciscan, friar João da Assunção, to come from India to Brazil to instruct in the cultivation of cinnamon and pepper and ordered that local agricultors be advised to attend his seminars.

Neither the cultivation of pepper nor of cinnamon met with the hoped for success. In the late eighteenth century, the naturalist and crown official, Dr Alexandre Rodrigues Ferreira, wrote a memorandum on sending cinnamon trees from the East to Brazil and the care of the plants on board ship. In 1782, the Calced Carmelites in Salvador were reported to have cultivated a pepper plant in their garden in the Hospício do Pilar which bore fruits identical to those of Malabar, but nowhere in Brazil could their success be replicated despite the continued practice of sending pepper seeds and cuttings from India to Brazil and Angola. Kings continued to encourage the cultivation of pepper especially, but also cinnamon, in Brazil throughout the eighteenth century. Cinnamon trees were sent from Lisbon, as too were seeds and instructions. In the 1780s and 1790s governors of Bahia, such as Dom Rodrigo José de Meneses e Castro (1784-88) and Dom Fernando José de Portugal e Castro (1788-1801), promoted the cultivation of pepper and cinnamon and a report from the turn of the century referred to successful cultivation of both pepper and cinnamon in Espírito Santo. Such initiatives met with limited success, essentially because of lack of planter interest in the cultivation of such crops of uncertain financial returns whereas sugar, tobacco, cotton, and coffee were highly lucrative.[151]

The Society of Jesus, with missions in Africa, India, Asia, and Brazil, played a prominent role in experimentation, cultivation, and dissemination of tropical plants. In common with lay persons, Jesuit colleges in India maintained substantial coconut-groves which were revenue-generating. The Dutchman, van Linschoten, commented in the latter part of the sixteenth century on how the Portuguese around Goa leased their coconut trees to *Canarins* and noted the extensive Portuguese holdings of as many as 400 trees. One Jesuit lay brother in Salsette authored the *Arte Palmarica* which recorded his research notes on the yields of different types of coconuts. In Brazil, the Jesuits studied the botany of tropical America. They, and others, were brought to the realization that there grew wild in Brazil, several plants found in the East, or close approximations thereof. Such were gum benzoin trees, first 'discovered' in Porto Seguro in 1650 by an Indian from one of the Jesuit mission villages, and clove plants indigenous to Brazil. The Jesuits themselves used the indigenous plants (*drogas do sertão*) which grew wild in Amazonas, and then experimented successfully with their cultivation. The Jesuits also experimented with different technologies. For example, observing that the use of heavy mortars in hulling rice was destructive, the Jesuits introduced the use of hydraulic and animal energy which was less damaging.

The cultivation of cocoa in the State of Maranhão and in the State of Brazil also was attributable to Jesuit initiative. The story is worth retelling. In 1674, prior to taking up his appointment as rector of the Jesuit College in São Luís do Maranhão, João Felipe Bettendorff, S.J., who had administered the Jesuit missions in Pará, bought the largest canoe he could find and named it *São Inácio*. He travelled by canoe from Pará and brought to São Luís cocoa seeds which were planted. Three years later, so successful had been the new cultivation, that the College had over a thousand cocoa plants. The Jesuits were able to distribute seeds to local people, who welcomed the opportunity such cultivation provided. This preceded a royal order of 1677 to the governor of Maranhão and Pará encouraging such a measure. So successful was the Society in promoting the cultivation of cocoa that already the viceroy in Bahia, Dom Vasco de Mascarenhas, had written (1664) to a Jesuit in Ceará concerning the introduction of cocoa cultivation into the State of Brazil. Cocoa joined cloves, cinnamon, sarsaparilla and certain *drogas do sertão* as sources of revenue for the Society of Jesus.

Jesuits also played a major role in the dissemination of plants from Portugal to Brazil and from India to Brazil. Among the former were oranges, and among the latter jack-fruit. Banned since the time of Dom Manuel, the initiative for the re-introduction of pepper and cinnamon plants from India into Brazil was taken by the Jesuits. António Vieira, S.J., wrote a memorandum to the king advocating such cultivation. In 1682, cultivation of cinnamon was started in the Quinta do Tanque, the country estate officially known as the Casa suburbana de São Cristóvão belonging to the Jesuit College in Bahia, with a cutting and five trees. Success was apparently attributable to elimination by the Jesuits of the scourge of all planters in Brazil, namely ants. The following year ten to twelve pepper plants were also thriving in the Quinta do Tanque garden. In 1688, the king gave a cinnamon tree to the Jesuit father Bettendorff who was returning to the Maranhão. By 1689 the Jesuits in Portuguese America were cultivating numerous cinnamon trees and somewhat fewer pepper shrubs. Cinnamon plants were being transplanted from the Jesuit College in Bahia to the Maranhão in addition to cuttings sent directly from India and Ceylon. Despite conditions which would have favoured their cultivation in the Recôncavo of Bahia, this did not occur, and the only cultivation in Bahia of such plants from India was in the Jesuit Quinta do Tanque. In 1690, two *Canarins* arrived from India specifically to work on the pepper and cinnamon plants under cultivation in this garden. The Society of Jesus was encouraged by the king, who saw in the cultivation of cinnamon in Brazil a means to undercut the revenues which the Dutch derived from their sales of cinnamon from Ceylon. The Jesuits were successful in cultivating cinnamon commercially on plantations but were less successful with pepper. Dom João V tried to encourage the cultivation of such plants in Bahia, the *sertão*, Pernambuco, and in the Maranhão, but apparently apart from the Jesuits there were few takers.[152]

In the case of Europe and Asia, there had been reciprocal contacts overland prior to 27 May, 1498, the date of the arrival of Vasco da Gama in Calicut and which the Indian historian K. M. Panikkar has referred to as a 'turning point' in the history of India and of Europe.[153] North Africa and sub-Saharan West and East Africa had also been tied into such contacts primarily through Mediterranean and Indian Ocean trade. Rare would have been the plant of African, Asian, or European origin, which was totally unknown to the other landmasses of this trilogy. The Portuguese contribution was to turn hearsay or sporadic exposure into everyday reality by commerce or even cultivation. This was the case of spices from the Orient, of whose existence Atlantic Africa was aware, but only with the opening up of trade to India and the Spice Islands by the Portuguese were spices such as cinnamon, ginger, and pepper, to be readily available in West Africa. The role of the Portuguese has been, over a span reaching from the fifteenth to the nineteenth centuries, to disseminate such products and make them available in larger quantities than hitherto to a wider market. Such activity was not limited to spices. Camellia, jack-fruit, rice, coconuts, plantains, mangoes, and citrus plants, all originated in India, the Malay archipelago, Indonesia, or China, and were introduced or reintroduced into Africa and Brazil by the Portuguese in the course of three centuries. As regards tea, in 1801 the governor-general of the Azores sent two boxes of tea plants to Portugal, noting that they grew abundantly on the islands but that nobody knew how to put them to good use. Only after 1808, when he was residing in Brazil, was Dom João VI to be the recipient of tea plants, the gift of the Emperor of China. These were grown around the Lagoa Rodrigo de Freitas in Rio de Janeiro and later were transplanted to the botanical garden in Vila Rica, Minas Gerais.

One *caveat* is in order. Whereas I shall be treating the role of the Portuguese as disseminators, it should be stated unequivocally that by so doing I am not claiming (with some exceptions) for the Portuguese primacy as disseminators of a plant from one region to another. Furthermore, although the pioneering work of Nikolai I. Vavilov has located the principal geographic centres of origin or formation of cultivated plants, there are still problems of differentiating between primary and secondary centres of varietal origin. There is widespread disparity in numbers of plants whose places of origin have been attributed to the Old (Africa, Europe, India, Asia) and New Worlds: of 640 of the most important cultivated plants, only 100 were contributed by the New World and considerably less if each species of the potato is not considered as a separate plant.[154] This caution is inspired by three considerations: first, rarely do documentary data permit accurate dating of the first appearance of a specific plant in a new region; secondly, in many cases the multiplicity of potential routes and carriers precludes attribution of the role of disseminator solely to the Portuguese; thirdly, especially in the case of cereals, contemporary language was imprecise, often applying the same word to different crops or failing to distinguish, for example, between different types of maize or Indian corn (*milho*).

The following discussion will focus on the Portuguese as disseminators of plants throughout the world. But some degree of humility is in order. Long before Europeans started out on their voyages of exploration, peoples of Africa, America, India, Asia, and Polynesia had migrated vast distances by land and water and had been disseminators of seeds and plants. Secondly, although my discussion focuses on human agents acting intentionally in such dispersal, there were probably many cases when this was accidental: on clothes, in packing, in holds or ballast of vessels; or in the wool, hair, or fur of animals and their excreta, and fodder which Europeans carried with them, most notably to America and islands. Nor should it be forgotten that seeds, fruits, and even plants, can be dispersed by the natural forces of water, wind, and by birds. This would probably apply more to wild plants, but not exclusively so.[155]

In the case of the American continent, the Portuguese introduced to Brazil from Europe essentially those same plants and domesticated animals as did the Spaniards for the Caribbean and circum-Caribbean, Central American, and Andean regions. This generalization would apply equally to the dissemination of New World plants to Europe, although here the Spaniards pre-empted the Portuguese. As regards Africa, clearly proximity and intensive maritime contacts between Brazil and West Africa facilitated the ready dissemination of American plants to the African continent. Furthermore, given similar climatic and soil conditions in West Africa and Brazil, success in the cultivation of plants carried across the Atlantic was all but assured. Alternative routes for disseminating plants originating in the Americas to sub-Saharan Africa would have been *via* the regions of the circum-Mediterranean and the Middle East. There were three such routes: from Egypt through Fezzan, Ghat, and Gao to Timbuktu, and subsequent diffusion west and south; or across the Atlantic Sahara, originating from one of several points between Morocco and Tunisia, and either following a route inland from the coast or through the Atlas to Terhazza and Timbuktu or further east through the central Sahara; or *via* the Red Sea or through Arabia and then along the coast of East Africa. In the mid-fifteenth century the noble merchant of Venice, Alvise da Cà da Mosto, noted trade between Cairo and upper Senegal and upper Niger. This route would also have served to bring to sub-Saharan West

Africa commodities from India and Asia.[156]

As regards contacts between America and India and Asia, while it would be tempting to see in the vessels of the *carreira da India* ready vehicles for such dissemination, this was one way: namely from east to west. Only exceptionally did an outward-bound Indiaman put into a Brazilian port, whereas this did occur with increasing frequency homeward-bound in the late seventeenth and eighteenth centuries. Although the Portuguese opening of the Cape of Good Hope route to the East radically altered the intensity, speed, and volume of East-West contacts, we have seen that it did not totally replace the overland or land/sea routes from the Mediterranean and northern Europe. Furthermore, the Pacific offered an easy route for the dissemination of plants, as well as myths and customs, from west to east (*e.g.* bananas, true gourd, coconuts, chickens, and certain beans) and *vice versa* (*e.g.* sweet potatoes, tetraploid cottons). Whether such dissemination was before or after 1492 is not established. Predating by centuries the European 'age of exploration', already from the mainland of south-east Asia and from India there had been the dispersal of domesticated animals, including dogs, fowls, and ducks, as well as of domesticated plants, as far afield as Melanesia, Polynesia, and Micronesia. Similarly, East Africa and the forest peoples of Africa were recipients of crops and domesticated animals from across the Indian Ocean, along a corridor skirting the Arabian Sea away from the cold of a northern route, across the strait of Hormuz, along the southern rim of Arabia, across Bab-el-Mandeb, and thence through northern Ethiopia to Sannar and Sudan and on to the forest lands of sub-Saharan Africa. These included cultivated plantains, bananas, taro, pigs, goats, sheep, cattle, chickens, and some fowl of Asian origins.[157]

Long before that period during which the Portuguese were reaching out to Africa, America, India and Asia, already Islam and Muslim civilization had spread far beyond their origins in the Middle East, and extended from the Maghreb to Indonesia. The period of intense Portuguese initiatives in Africa, America, India and East Asia coincided with all or part of the Ottoman, Safavid and Mughal empires. The Arab trade diaspora gathered greater strength from these empires and the dispersal of New World plants to sub-Saharan Africa, especially East Africa, and to regions bordering on the Indian Ocean and Indonesia, may have been attributable to Arab traders as well as to the Portuguese. Certainly, Muslim traders crossed the Sahara with ease and the empires of Ghana, Mali and Gao were in regular contact with the Mediterranean world. Two exceptions where the ground is firmer are the assertions that the Portuguese introduced manioc to West Africa and were the exclusive carriers of spice plants from Asia to Brazil. If that Genoese sailing in the service of the Catholic kings initiated what Alfred Crosby has referred to as 'The Columbian Exchange', not the same can be said of Vasco da Gama and the aftermath of his landfall at Calicut in 1498. But, that so many Portuguese activities fell within the tropics made inevitable that they would be the disseminators of numerous pantropical plants. Let us now turn to those flora and fauna which the Portuguese transplanted from their places of origin to other parts of the world.

The Portuguese introduced from Europe into Brazil many of those same plants as had the Spanish into North and South America and the Caribbean: wheat, barley, broad bean, sugar cane, chick-pea, melon, onion, radish, cauliflower, cabbage, lettuce, turnip, cucumber, pumpkin, lentil, mint, parsley, dill, coriander, and other vegetables, citrus (orange, grapefruit, lemon, lime), grape vines, fruit trees (pomegranate, pear, fig, peach, quince), and bananas. Some were of Indian or Asian origin or from the Indo-Pacific region. Oranges had been culti-vated in Spain and Portugal before the age of discoveries but a variety – the sweet orange or *laranja da China* – was introduced into Portugal in the first third of the seventeenth century. This variety spread to other countries of western Europe and was to be the basis for the commercial prosperity of São Miguel in the Azores in the eighteenth century, and whose architectural legacies are readily apparent to visitors to Ponta Delgada to-day. Perhaps no commodity of oriental provenance could match sugar-cane (*Saccharum officinarum*) in terms of westwards migration. Its origin has variously been attributed to Polynesia, to the region Vavilov refers to as the Indo-Malayan center of origin (Malay archipelago, Java, Borneo, Sumatra, Philippines, Indochina), and to India. In India, its cultivation was widespread and reached a high level of sophistication, and it was also carried to China. It was brought to Europe by Arab traders, cultivated around Gra-nada in the twelfth century, in the Algarve while still under

Muslim control, and carried to Hispaniola by Columbus on his second voyage. But already it had been cultivated for sixty years by the Portuguese on Madeira, soon to be joined by São Tomé as a major producer, and later in the Azores and Cape Verdes. The Portuguese introduced plantation agriculture and plantation slavery into the American continent with the cultivation of sugar by the proprietary lords of Pernambuco and São Vicente in the 1530s. Subsequently, no single crop was to have such an enduring impact on the Portuguese Atlantic world.[158] In the case of many domesticated animals and fowl, these too had originated in Asia. Long before Columbus' landfall, many had been introduced by the Portuguese from Europe into the Atlantic islands. Whether the maize cultivated in the Azores in the seventeenth century had arrived directly from America or *via* Portugal is not clear. But, in the case of trees on the Azores, in view of the fact that they were densely forested at the time of their discovery by Europeans, the seeds were introduced by birds and not man.[159]

The Portuguese contributed to the diffusion of plants from Africa. Arab control of the trade in the peppers of Guinea and Benin was seriously eroded by the Portuguese in the fifteenth century and their new dominance gave rise to the name Costa da Malagueta or 'Grain Coast' in English, from 'grains of paradise'. Their adoption in cooking in South America was primarily attributable to the Portuguese, and they probably also carried them to India and China. The sixteenth century was also to witness the dissemination of another plant of African (mountain forests of Ethiopia) origin: coffee. Of the four different species of commercial interest, it was the *Coffea arabica* whose cultivation was to be successful in South America in general, but especially in Brazil. The European climate was not suitable for its cultivation, but the Americas proved ideal. Introduced into the Caribbean by the French before 1700, and into Portuguese America by Sargento-mór Francisco de Melo Palheta, who brought seeds from Cayenne in 1727, it was to be grown by the Jesuits in Amazonia by mid-century.[160] Coffee was to be the mainstay of the renaissance of the Brazilian agricultural economy in the nineteenth century. Be their origin in the Malay archipelago or south India, Polynesia or Melanesia, it was on the east coast of Africa that the Portuguese encountered coconuts (*Cocos nucifera*). The Portuguese carried them to West Africa, the Cape Verdes, and thence to Brazil. Coconut palms were introduced into Puerto Rico in 1525, and by the 1580s their presence along the shores of South America was such as to be remarked by voyagers.[161]

The origin of yams (*Dioscorea alata*) is debated. Places of suggested origin are the east coast of the Bay of Bengal and the Malay archipelago, whence they were carried to south-east Asia and the Pacific islands.[162] The greater yam may have been carried to Africa from India by Arab traders, but at least two cultured yams are of African origin – the white and yellow Guinea yams (*Dioscorea rotundata* and *cayenensis*). Yams were but one crop which people of the forest areas in Africa cultivated prior to the arrival of the Portuguese: others included the basic sorghum and millet, the elaeis palm, bananas and plantains.[163] With the exception of sorghum and millet, the Portuguese carried these across the Atlantic. The evidence suggests that yams did not travel beyond the Pacific or Indian oceans until the sixteenth century, when the Portuguese carried them to West Africa, to the Azores, and Brazil. Yams were used as provisions on the Africa to Lisbon route and there was a market for yams in Lisbon in the sixteenth century.[164]

Bananas and plantains had been brought to East Africa and the forest regions before the arrival of Europeans in sub-Saharan Africa and it would seem reasonable to credit the Portuguese with carrying them from Africa to Brazil.[165] Other plants of African origin introduced into colonial Brazil by the Portuguese included certain gourds and squashes and date-palms. The African oil-palm (*Elaeis guineensis*), found between Senegal and Angola and across to the Nile, grew wild or in semi-cultivated groves. It was this palm which led the Portuguese to name Cape Palmas at the meeting of the Grain Coast and the Ivory Coast. In the sixteenth century, palm-oil was being exported to Europe and to America. But only in the twentieth century has oil-palm cultivation in plantations been introduced to Brazil, where the *dendê* oil is used in cooking. By 1945, Brazil had become the leading American producer of palm-oils. Castor-oil plants (*Ricinus communis*), originating in Ethiopia, known in Brazil as *mamona*, also appear to be a recent import to Brazil.[166]

Asia was infinitely richer than Africa in the variety of spices and vegetables. Many had been known in Europe as early as the second or third centuries AD, and had been introduced by Arab traders and middlemen over the intervening centuries. But it was the arrival of Vasco da Gama in Calicut which heralded a new age when the Portuguese were to be prominent in the dissemination of plants from the Asian mainland and the Spice Islands. This was somewhat ironical in that, for the most part, the Portuguese in India and Asia did not themselves cultivate these crops. The list is long and included: pepper (Malabar, Indonesia, Hindustan), ginger (Hindustan), cardamom (Hindustan), cinnamon (Ceylon), nutmeg and mace (Bandas), and cloves (Moluccas). All possessed not only culinary but also medicinal applications. The Portuguese also transported plants within Asia: for example, it was the Portuguese who dispersed clove trees more widely in the Moluccas and introduced these into Ambon.[167] It is difficult to date the introduction of cinnamon into Brazil, but clearly it was being cultivated clandestinely despite sixteenth century royal orders prohibiting this. A royal order of 9 November 1692 authorized such cultivation. Ginger came to Brazil *via* the island of São Tomé in the sixteenth century and thrived so well that in 1578 the king forbad further exports from Brazil or Africa on the grounds that these could undermine the commerce in this commodity from the East. Such royal admonitions were largely ignored. By the early seventeenth century, its cultivation was well established in Bahia. A royal decree of 1671 encouraged this cultivation and the export of ginger to Portugal, and throughout the eighteenth century there were regular consignments of ginger cultivated in the Maranhão. This was not the only case of oriental and African plants (coconuts; Guinea rice) coming to Portuguese America *via* the Cape Verdes or São Tomé.[168] The presence of mango trees in fourteenth-century Mogadishu suggests Arab diffusion, but only with the arrival of Europeans did mangoes gain popularity. The Portuguese have been credited with carrying mango seeds (*Mangifera indica*) to their factories in East Africa and introducing this plant from India into Bahia about 1700, whence the plant was carried to Rio de Janeiro and to Barbados. In general, the cultivation in Brazil of such plants and fruits from India and the East was unsuccessful commercially and Brazil continued throughout the colonial period to import from India spices such as pepper, cinnamon and cloves. Nor was the production (primarily in Pará and the Maranhão from the seventeenth century) or quality of indigenous American variants of cinnamon, clove and pepper sufficient to displace their oriental counterparts in European markets.[169]

As for crops of American origin, the Portuguese were pre-empted by the Spanish in Central America and Andean South America in terms of primacy as disseminators to Europe. For Central America, this generalization would include sweet potatoes, papaya, tobacco, maize, cochineal, tomatoes, cocoa beans, agave, numerous species of beans, vanilla, squashes, capsicums and chillies, and for South America (mostly Colombia, Peru, Ecuador, Bolivia), potatoes, some beans, cotton, tomatoes, pumpkins, cotton (*Gossypium barbadense*), and possibly maize. Those cultivated plants attributed to a Brazilian origin are comparatively few in number, which is surprising given the size of the country and its richness of flora estimated at 40,000 species. The most important are manioc, peanuts, and pineapples – all indigenous to semi-arid areas. Some, such as corn, were cultigens, but when we turn to forest plants the distinction between cultivated and wild is less clear. The six endemic plants are: manioc, peanuts, cacao, rubber, maté and the snail flower. The cultivated fruits number less than ten and include pineapples, Brazil-nuts, cashews (also the Antilles), and jaboticaba.[170] The Portuguese carried some of these plants to the Atlantic Islands, West Africa, and even to Asia.

They were also disseminators of other plants of American, but not necessarily Brazilian, origin. They introduced these plants of American origin to the Atlantic Islands and to West Africa in the sixteenth century: sweet potatoes, peanuts, manioc, maize corn, and possibly capsicums, squashes and pumpkins.[171] The *Agave sisalina* was of Central American origin. The tough fibres extracted from it were essential to the making of ropes and cordage. Plants were carried to Spain before 1561, but the Portuguese may well have introduced it to Fernando Po in the Gulf of Guinea.[172] In the Azores, the agricultural economy was to be transformed by the seventeenth century with the introduction of two crops of American origin: maize and sweet potatoes. Maize and manioc were to enjoy widespread diffusion and assume exceptional importance in the diets of Africans. But the date of introduction, the routes, and the degree of acceptance varied from region to region and crop to crop. For example, Africans of the Upper Guinea coast rapidly adopted maize and sweet potatoes, but were slower to adopt manioc. In the seventeenth and eighteenth centuries, maize cultivation was extensive in northern and central Portugal and had an impact on land use and the cultivation of other cereals (wheat, rye and barley), and may have contributed to population increases.[173]

The problem of primacy becomes compounded by the use of different words at different times and in different regions to describe a plant. Maize is a case in point. In 1502, the Portuguese Valentim Fernandes referred to the presence of *milho zaborro* on the west African coast. In 1520 in Ethiopia, Father Francisco Álvares noted the cultivation of *milho zaborro*. It would seem unlikely that maize could have reached Ethiopia by 1520 and the reference here was probably to millet. But there are doubts on both scores. Before 1550, maize of American origin had been introduced into the Cape Verde islands and West Africa. Whether this was by sea by the Portuguese exclusively, or concurrently with its introduction to the African continent by Arab traders from Egypt and thence to West Africa, is not resolved. In his seventeenth-century compilation, the Dutchman Olfert Dapper credited the Portuguese with bringing it to São Tomé and the Gold Coast. William Bosman, a Dutch factor of Elmina, gave primacy to the Portuguese. Because of its versatility as regards climate and soil conditions, maize proved more reliable in terms of crop production than millet and sorghum. By the seventeenth century, maize of American origin was being cultivated not only in the coastal regions, but inland in the Sudan, Congo, and northern Angola, as well as on the coast of Angola and Benguela. By the 1680s it was cultivated from present-day Liberia to the Niger delta, but primarily between the Gold Coast and Dahomey. It was not pure coincidence that it was precisely these regions which provided substantial numbers of slaves for Brazil. John Barbot noted that maize was a staple diet for slaves transported to America and commented on the profits to be made from its sale to European forts on the west African coast and for the provisioning of slave ships.

There are similar questions about who introduced maize into East Africa and when. A Portuguese source of 1561 referred to maize in Monomotapa. There is a 1634 reference to the growing of maize in the Portuguese settlements in Zanzibar and Pemba to supply the Portuguese garrison at Mombasa. There is support for the notion that the Swahili word for maize, *mhindi*, derives from constantly hearing the Portuguese refer to 'milho da India' ('corn of India'), but this still leaves open the question as to whether this was 'corn of Hindustan', viz the East Indies, or the West Indies. Probably it would be fair to say that, directly or indirectly, the Portuguese were agents in the introduction of maize to East Africa. Obviously this cultivation was not at the same level of intensity as in West Africa and it was only in the nineteenth century that maize was to be widely grown throughout Africa.[174]

Another product of the Brazilian-Paraguayan centre of origin, and domesticated by rain forest Indians in north-eastern South America and the Amazon basin, was the cultigen manioc.[175] This has 'sweet' and 'bitter' varieties and goes under several names: cassava, tapioca, and manihot, or *yuca* in Spanish America. The Indians with whom the Portuguese came into contact were the Tupinambá, for whom manioc had been a staple. The Portuguese not only ate the manioc grown by Indians but themselves learnt to grow it on their plantations and introduced it elsewhere along the Brazilian coast. Sixteenth-century visitors to Brazil, such as the German gunner Hans Staden, the French Franciscan André Thevet, and the Calvinist Jean de Léry, joined Gabriel Soares de Sousa and the author of the *Diálogos das Grandezas do Brasil* in describing and singing the praises of manioc. The Jesuit Fernão Cardim, S.J., who arrived in Brazil in 1583 and was to spend some forty years in the colony as Rector of the Colleges in Salvador and Rio de Janeiro and Provincial of the Society of Jesus in Brazil, described the plant as follows:

The ordinary food of this Country, that serveth for Bread, is called Mandioca, and they are certaine rootes like Carrots though they are greater and longer: these shoot out certaine stemmes or branches, and growe to the height of fifteene spannes. These branches are very tender, and have a white pith within, and at every spanne it hath certaine joynts, and of this bignesse they are broken, and set in the ground as much as is sufficient for to hold them up and within sixe or nine moneths have so big rootes that they serve for food. This Mandioca contayneth many kindes in it selfe, and all are eaten, and they are preserved under the earth three, foure, or unto eight yeeres, and needs no seasoning, for they doe no more but take them out and make fresh meate every day, and the longer they are under the earth the bigger they growe, and yeeld the more...[176]

Manioc shares with maize the quality of versatility in that it grows in poor soils and thus can be planted on the fringes of more fertile lands. Indeed, it grows best in moist, fertile, and deep loamy sands. Drought-resistant, manioc is a plant of the tropics. It can survive virtually anywhere provided the land does not become waterlogged and provided there is no frost. It fully merits its name of *Manihot utilissima*. Although the leaves and young shoots of this largish (five to twelve feet high under cultivation) woody shrub are edible, the Indians had discovered that the roots, which reach two feet in length and from two to six inches in diameter and of which a single plant can yield as much as eight kilograms, provided the best source of food. Furthermore, unlike corn and other grains, as noted by Cardim the roots of cassava do not require immediate harvesting. In practical terms, this makes it ideal for peoples whose crops – as was the case of Brazil and Africa – often fall victim to ants ('The king of Brazil'), or where storage facilities are inadequate. Its high carbohydrate content and very little protein and fat make it of low nutritional value, although it does contain calcium, ascorbic acid, and vitamins.[177]

For once it seems that there is no problem of dating because manioc was not known in Africa before the voyage of Columbus and thus its dissemination is a product of the age of European exploration. It was introduced into the Congo and Angola by the Portuguese in the early sixteenth century. From the earliest successful introduction around the mouth of the Congo, it spread throughout Central Africa. Manioc was also introduced to the Upper Guinea coast in the sixteenth century, but only in the seventeenth century to the islands of São Tomé and Príncipe. Manioc grown in Africa provisioned slave ships to Brazil as well as Europe-bound vessels. During the eighteenth century it was introduced by the Portuguese to Mozambique and to Portuguese enclaves along the coast of East Africa as far north as Mogadishu. But it was not introduced into Goa or the Malabar coast at an early date. Whether it was the Portuguese who carried it to India, Asia, and as far as Indonesia has not been resolved.[178] Maize and cassava were the major foodstuffs at the root of the population explosion in Africa in the nineteenth and twentieth centuries. Today both are staple foods in all of Africa south of the Sahara and Ethiopia and north of the Zambezi.

Peanuts (*Arachis hypogaea*), whose origin has been attributed to Brazil, were valuable dietary additions because of their high protein content and nutritious oil. This crop remained subordinate to maize or manioc, but was also introduced from America to Africa and Asia. Its presence was noted in Senegambia in the 1560s and it may have been used for provisions on the slave ships to America.[179] Probably the Portuguese carried it into the Indian Ocean in the early sixteenth century, but there is some question as to how readily it was accepted for cultivation in India. It was present in China, but whether this was originally attributable to the Portuguese or to trans-Pacific dissemination is also not resolved. In the case of the Portuguese introduction into Africa of the commercial species of vanilla (*Vanilla planifolia*), whose origin lies in Central America but whose plant was not brought from the West Indies to Europe until the nineteenth century, this may have been through São Tomé.

In the carrying of plants to India and Asia, it is more difficult to pin down any specific date or disseminator. Crops of American origin introduced into China included maize, sweet potatoes, Irish potatoes, and peanuts. It does seem certain that the peanut was brought to China by sea in the early sixteenth century. The role of the Portuguese is not clear. Ports of southern Fukien had close trading relations with the Portuguese prior to their arrival in Canton and also with islands of the South China Sea. The Portuguese certainly contributed to the introduction of the peanut, although the evidence points to peanuts being in Canton slightly prior to 1516. The plant may then have been taken to Shanghai from southern Fukien as a by-blow of the coastal cotton trade. Another possibility is that, after their expulsion from Canton in 1522 which led the Portuguese to engage in contraband trade in the ports of southern Fukien such as Chang-chou, Ch'üuan-chou, and Ning-po, the Portuguese brought the peanut to the Hangchou area. By the 1530s, peanuts were grown in regions of the lower Yangtze. Before 1700 some coastal regions already specialized in peanut and peanut-oil production, but peanuts remained an expensive delicacy. Their greater dissemination came in the eighteenth and nineteenth centuries. The presence of the sweet potato was first recorded in Yunnan in the 1560s, which suggests it was imported overland from India and Burma. Independently, about the same time it was introduced into the coastal province of Fukien, which could mean that the Portuguese played a part, and proved popular in the south-eastern coastal provinces. By 1800, with imperial support, sweet potatoes had become a staple in China. Maize too was introduced in the 1530s or 1540s by western tribesmen overland through India and Burma and by coastal routes, with scholars giving precedence to the overland route. In remote Yunnan province its presence was recorded in the sixteenth century. But the people of coastal Fukien and Chekiang preferred rice and sweet potatoes to maize. Only in the eighteenth century did maize become the key crop of the inland Yangtze provinces. By 1800 it was the 'king of crops' of the Han river drainage. Maize and sweet potatoes formed the basis for development of the reddish fertile topsoil of the Yangtze highlands.[180]

Whatever the role of the Portuguese, what is remarkable about these American crops introduced into China in the sixteenth century was how they contributed to spreading utilization of land and contributed decisively to demographic growth. Doubts concerning routes followed by these major crops also apply to the numerous capsicums and chillies which have become a hallmark of the culinary traditions of India and Sri Lanka, and are widely used in southern China. *Capsicum frutescens* and *Capsicum annuum* are both of Central American origin. Their presence was noted in mid-sixteenth-century Goa as 'Pernambuco peppers'. Apparently they were unknown in northern India before the middle of the eighteenth century and only introduced by the Marathas, who were addicted to them. By the 1760s people of Hindustan used such peppers in their food.[181] Such peppers may have been introduced overland to China or through Canton or Macao and sent up country to Hunan and Szechuan.

The Portuguese, by the introduction of crops of American origin, did effect changes in Mughal India. The pineapple was one such. Introduced into the Portuguese enclaves on the west coast in the sixteenth century, by 1700 it was common in Bengal, Gujarat, and Baglana. During the reign of Jahāngīr (1605-1627), the imperial gardens at Agra produced several thousands annually. The Portuguese also introduced papayas and cashew nuts from Brazil in the later sixteenth century, but their cultivation did not spread as rapidly as pineapples. The introduction of potatoes, maize, guavas, and tomatoes into India is of later date, probably after Mughal rule. Whether the presence in India of guava (*Psidium guayava*), another fruit of Central American origin but found throughout tropical America, is attributable to the Portuguese as carriers is not known. Habib doubts its presence until after the Mughal period. There are better grounds for crediting the Spaniards with introducing it into the Philippines at an early date. There could have been carryings in either direction between Malaya and India. On the Malabar coast it was known as 'pear' from the Portuguese *pera*.[182]

There were other crops of American origin – maize, manioc, sweet potatoes, peanuts, pumpkins, squashes, and chillies – in India, Indonesia, and China, as early as the sixteenth century. Who carried them there, by what routes, and precisely when, remains a mystery. The Spanish introduced maize into the Marianas (former Ladrones) by 1601. Only in the late seventeenth or eighteenth centuries did the cultivation of American staples such as maize, manioc, and sweet potatoes, become widespread. Habib states maize was 'probably unknown' in India in the seventeenth century and its spread was primarily in the nineteenth century.[183]

In some instances, there is uncertainty as to the attribution of any single place of origin. The pineapple (*Ananas comosa*) is a case in point. Pineapples were being cultivated in the coastal lowlands of Peru and in the Caribbean before Columbus' first exposure to them in 1492. But there were also reports of their existence from northern Brazil and the Orinoco at very early dates, and Vavilov suggests a Brazilian-Paraguayan centre of origin. Supporting the Brazilian claim is the name *nana* learnt by the Portuguese from the Tupi. On the other hand, Spaniards in the West Indies called them *pinas* because the fruit reminded them of a pine-cone. To the Spaniards must go the credit for appreciating this refreshing fruit and for carrying pineapples to Europe. But there is little doubt that it was the Portuguese who took pineapples from America to West Africa and further east because these were known throughout Asia by the end of the sixteenth century. The name by which this fruit was known in Brazil, *ananás*, was to be taken over in Persian and in local dialects of India.[184]

In some cases, genesis has been attributed to more than one region of America. This applies to cocoa, rubber, and cotton. *Theobroma cacao* had its prime place of origin in Central America and a secondary centre in the Amazon valley. Cocoa plants were indigenous to the Amazon Valley and upper Orinoco and were known to Brazilian Indians before the arrival of Europeans. The beans were used by the Aztecs as coins in Central America, whence cocoa was introduced into Europe in the 1520s. In the case of Brazil, we are talking about the *Forastero* type of cocoa. The fruit has a hard, smooth, surface, and the beans are flat and bitter and of a deep violet colour. The *Forastero* is hardier and has greater yield than the superior Central American *Crioullo* type which the Spaniards disseminated. Its dispersal beyond the jungle areas of Brazil and as an export commodity (c. 1650) was attributable initially to Portuguese missionaries and hunters. It was grown commercially in Bahia, whose production came to exceed that of Pará, and West Africa. In the sixty years preceding Brazil's independence in 1822, over half of Pará's exports were of cocoa, but these mostly came from wild and not cultivated sources. The Portuguese introduced cocoa into Príncipe and São Tomé in the early nineteenth century.[185]

Rubber derived from latex extracted from the *Hevea brasiliensis* was known in pre-columbian Central America – in fact, Olmec means 'dweller in the land of rubber' – and the Andes, but it probably originated in the Amazon valley rain forest. There are European references of the first half of the sixteenth century to its presence. With the gradual penetration of the Amazon by Portuguese, they noted latex as one of several commodities collected by Indians from the forest. In 1743, the French scientist Charles de la Condamine who was conducting research on measuring the equator, during his travels across Brazil from Quito noted its presence in the Amazon. He saw Indians extracting the liquid from the tree and noted how, on coagulation, this produced a substance of both exceptional elasticity and impermeability. The Indians named this *caoutchouc* and from it the Omagua made boots which kept out water, balls which regained their shape after being squeezed, and syringes with wooden tubes (whence the Portuguese *seringueiro*, or 'squirt-maker', for the collector). La Condamine was intrigued enough to carry samples back to France. By the nineteenth century its properties were well known in Europe and a wide range of applications had been discovered. Rubber was not developed as a plantation economy in colonial Brazil but, in 1755, King Dom José I sent several pairs of the royal boots to Pará to be coated with latex, as too 2,000 soldiers' haversacks for the same purpose! It was not until such technical advances as impregnation of textiles with rubber (1823) and discovery of the vulcanization process by Charles Goodyear (1839), that the seeds were sowed for the Brazilian boom from 1850-1920. This was one case of dissemination which the Portuguese were to rue. In 1876, Henry Wickham made the famous 'seed snatch' which led to successful *hevea* cultivation in Kew Gardens and subsequent highly successful cultivation in Britain's Asian protectorates which undermined the Brazilian industry.[186]

One scholar (Vavilov) has attributed the origin of tree cotton to India (*Gossypium arboreum*) and of *Gossypium herbaceum* to Central Asia, whereas another (Hobhouse) credits Egypt with origin and subsequent diffusion westwards to Spain, which it reached about AD 900, and eastwards to China, Japan, and Korea, which it reached some 400 years later. *Gossypium herbaceum*, which the Portuguese introduced into Madeira and the Azores, had been in short supply, was expensive, and had short strands. The cotton indigenous to Central America, the upland cotton (*Gossypium hirsutum*), was stronger, of intermediate coarseness, and had longer strands. From the Pacific coast of South America originated *Gossypium barbadense*, with longer strands, known as Sea Island cotton. Early travellers to Brazil encountered cotton in both cultivated and wild forms.[187] Cotton floss of one species or another was known in sixteenth-century Europe, and probably the Portuguese carried it beyond the shores of Brazil. It reached India and the Indian and Pacific Oceans, date and carrier unknown. Within Brazil, cotton was a labour-intensive crop and was cultivated in the north initially, and subsequently in every province from Pará to Rio de Janeiro. It only became important as an export crop in the 1770s. The fortuitous combination of the demands of the Industrial Revolution and disruption to world supply caused by the Civil War in the United States contributed to Brazil's leading role as a cotton exporter in the nineteenth century.

172

Indubitably of American provenance, the origins of tobacco have been attributed to Central America (*Nicotiana rustica*) and to the Andean areas of South America (*Nicotiana tabacum*), and the common tobacco may in fact be a hybrid. Who first carried it to Europe is not known: seed was in Spain by about 1520. After the Spaniards had established themselves in the Philippines, seed was taken from Mexico and planted in Luzon. Already in 1548 plants were in Portugal, where the French ambassador Jean Nicot was later (1560) to see tobacco growing in the royal garden and grew it in his own garden. Many were its uses and the claims made of it. Called by the Portuguese *erva santa*, the leaves could be chewed, smoked, taken as snuff, or boiled. It served as a medium of exchange and was alleged to have nutritional as well as medicinal qualities in curing ulcers. It was claimed to cure convulsions in children and externally the leaves were used in the cure of orchitis. The Spaniards did not promote smoking tobacco and this was left to the English, Dutch and, to a lesser extent, the Portuguese. The Portuguese carried the plant to the Persian Gulf and India, and the Bahian export market extended to Africa, Europe, and even as far north as the St Lawrence valley. Writing in 1711, the Italian Jesuit known under his pseudonym of André João Antonil commented that if it had been sugar that had made Brazil known in Europe, it was tobacco which had made Bahia famous in 'all the four corners of the world'. It could well have been Bahian tobacco which was smoked in the Manchu court in Beijing.[188]

It is generally accepted that the Portuguese introduced the tobacco plant and knowledge of its properties into the Deccan in the sixteenth century. News reached the Mughal court through pilgrims returning from Mecca. Akbar the Great (1556-1605) was presented with a hookah by an envoy returning from Bijapur. Tobacco provoked much discussion at the imperial court. Jahāngīr (1605-1627) prohibited its use, and one source says the lips of the addicts of Lahore were cut off for disregarding this order. Aurangzeb forbad its cultivation by a 1659 order. Such orders were ineffectual. Rich and poor alike had become addicted. Its rapid acceptance and cultivation were pronounced in the seventeenth century. Tobacco was cultivated in the neighbouring regions of Goa such as Balagate, Panani, and Calicut, as well as elsewhere in India. In the early seventeenth century it was being grown inland in Bijapur, villages near Surat and in Golconda, and it spread inland to Sambhal and Bihar by the mid-seventeenth century. Long before the end of Aurangzeb's reign (1707), tobacco smoking was commonplace, either in the form of a pipe or cheroot, on the west coast and in northern India. Probably the Portuguese carried it to Malacca and it was from the Portuguese that the Malays adopted it into their language. One scholar has written that 'among the American plants that have migrated into India, tobacco is the most significant, because of great economic and commercial value'.[189] The first tobacco arrived in Japan at the end of the sixteenth century and was being grown in the islands by 1605. As had been the experience of Mughal India, official prohibitions on health grounds proved ineffective. Men and women became addicted, smoking the leaf in long pipes or very short metal pipes depending on whether they were inside or outside. The new habit was depicted on the painted Namban screens.[190]

Three fruits of American origins and well known to Brazilian Indians in the colonial era, were all jungle fruits: cashew (*Anacardium occidentale*; Panama, Antilles); the passion-flower (*Passiflora ligularis*; Peru, Ecuador, Bolivia), found also in southern Brazil and so named by the Portuguese because of the plant's alleged similarity to symbols of the passion of Christ and known in Portuguese as *maracujá*; and annatto (*Bixa orellana*; Central America), a plant used for its yellowish-red dye by the Indians for colouring and also as protection against mosquitoes, in addition to being a condiment. Cashews were disseminated by the Portuguese. Apparently, they developed a taste for the nut and in the sixteenth and early seventeenth centuries carried it not only to Portugal but the seeds to Cape Verde, Africa, Goa, Malacca, and other of their settlements. Passion fruit was cultivated in Europe by the 1730s and by the nineteenth century was running wild in India, Ceylon, and China. The fruit had also been introduced, possibly by the Portuguese, into West Africa. Annatto was taken by the Spaniards across the Pacific to the Philippines and possibly the Moluccas. Its introduction into India was more likely to have been from the west and thence to Java. Neither the dates of introduction, nor the identity of the disseminators, have been recorded.[191]

Finally, it should not be forgotten that, in addition to being the disseminators of American plants beyond the American continent, the Portuguese were disseminators of plants within Brazil. This applied to manioc which had initially been cultivated by native Americans but whose use and cultivation by Europeans spread throughout the colony. Although Bahia remained the tobacco capital of Brazil, the plant was cultivated elsewhere. Maranhão was joined by São Vicente and other captaincies in the cultivation of cotton. Already reference has been made to the cultivation of cacao in Amazonas initially, and only later were plants to be carried to Bahia. Indigo, grown initially in Pará, was transplanted to Cabo Frio and elsewhere. The cultivation of coffee, introduced into the Maranhão in 1727, spread to Rio Negro, Pará and Piauí, but half a century was to elapse before its introduction into Rio de Janeiro and the Bay of Guanabara, and later to the valley of the Paraíba.

It is against this backcloth of the important role played by the Portuguese in the dissemination of plants globally, that the questions can fairly be asked. Did they reap the fruits of the seeds they had carried? What was their contribution to demographic growth globally? As regards the first, with the exception of plantation crops – sugar, cotton, coffee – to which should be added tobacco and cacao, the general answer is probably that the rewards were not commensurate with the effort. In some cases, the plants were of limited commercial value. In others, the requisite financial investment was not forthcoming to make their cultivation commercially viable. Nor, in most cases, did the Portuguese display any special desire to promote themselves the cultivation of such crops of American origin beyond the American continent. As regards the second question, Alfred Crosby has argued persuasively that global demographic growth since 1492 was attributable to the dissemination of foodstuffs from America to Europe, Africa, and Asia, this growth being one biological consequence of the Columbus landfall.[192] Of the crops which he has designated as staples – maize, potatoes, sweet potatoes, beans, and manioc – the Portuguese carried some to Europe, but it would be exaggerated to attribute to the Portuguese a role in the slow but steady acceptance of maize in southern Europe in the late seventeenth and eighteenth centuries, or of the potato in Ireland in the seventeenth century and elsewhere by the nineteenth century. In Africa, the Portuguese may have played a significant role in the introduction of maize and manioc, and the resulting demographic repercussions which have been described by Murdock. The evidence for the introduction into China of maize, peanuts, and sweet potatoes, is not such as definitively to establish the importance of the role of the Portuguese as carriers of these plants and their contribution to demographic growth in China.

Perhaps most critical was that crown interest in improving yields or disseminating plants was sporadic rather than sustained. Even in Brazil, whose agricultural products were in the long run the most productive sector of the export economy, and on which both the welfare of the colony and the metropolis depended, there seems to have been little interest in upgrading the quality of production of specific crops to get greater yields. Suggestions on how to improve yields and for the commercial development of crops in Brazil, made by the author of the *Diálogos das Grandezas do Brasil* in the early seventeenth century, fell on deaf ears. Those academies which came into being in the eighteenth century were of a literary bent, rather than scientific. In Portugal, there was a botanical garden in existence at the Palace of Ajuda in the time of the Marquis of Pombal. This had been created for the specific purpose of studying tropical crops and agronomy. One director was Dr Alexandre Rodrigues Ferreira. He led one of three scientific expeditions to Portuguese colonies in Brazil, Mozambique, and Angola, to collect specimens for the botanical garden and Natural History Museum, both of which were in Lisbon. His expedition (which is discussed on p. 84) was to Brazil where, between 1783 and 1792, he travelled in Pará, on the Rio Negro, and in Mato Grosso.

The African expeditions were to Mozambique and Angola. That to Mozambique (1783-1793) was headed by Ferreira's fellow student at Coimbra, Manuel Galvão da Silva, who combined the knowledge of a trained naturalist with the skills of a civil servant as secretary to the government of the captaincy-general of Mozambique. In the latter capacity, he was to be frequently frustrated and even was placed temporarily under 'ceremonial detention'. He only arrived in Mozambique after a detour to Goa to study the flora and fauna about which he wrote a report and sent to Lisbon a herbarium of thirty-five plant specimens. Apparently, he also sent samples of fish and invertebrates from Goa to Ajuda. Da Silva travelled on the mainland near Mozambique Island, and made extensive research trips to Rios de Sena, Tete, and as far as Manica. His research was hampered by sickness and administrative chores and he dispatched few specimens to Lisbon. His mineral samples were of more importance than the natural history specimens, which included two barrels of fish in alcohol and the head of a hippopotamus. As regards collecting birds, he noted how difficult they were to catch and proposed purchasing them from locals. His contemporary, Joaquim José da Silva, held the same dual posts in Angola from 1783-1808. A native of Rio de Janeiro, he too had studied at Coimbra. He became thoroughly conversant with all regions of Angola and sent mineral, flora and fauna specimens to Lisbon. These included seven ribs of a manatee, peculiar to rivers of that part of the coast, at least one crocodile, and live animals.

Although these expeditions had mixed successes, that of Ferreira was especially productive, resulting in copious reports and watercolours. For Africa, the collections and reports of Joaquim José da Silva for Angola were superior to the results derived from Mozambique. The overall results were revealing as to the riches of the natural history of Portuguese America and Portuguese Africa. The European scientific community was fascinated to the point of undertaking expeditions to Brazil, especially in the nineteenth century. In all cases, the best of whatever collections had been housed at the Natural History Museum at the Palace of Ajuda were plundered by Etienne Geoffroy Saint-Hilaire and shipped to the Musée d' Histoire Naturelle in Paris in 1808.

How effective this crown initiative was in giving an incentive to tropical agriculture in the colonies was questionable. Most benefits seem to have remained within the scientific community in Portugal and their colleagues elsewhere in Europe. Even there, the reports were not published in a timely manner and the pioneering nature of their researches not recognized. Publications of the Royal Academy of Sciences, founded in Lisbon in 1779, had little resonance in Brazil. Nor, apparently, did the crown-sponsored publication (1798-1806) of the ten volumes of *O Fazendeiro do Brazil* by friar José Mariano da Conceição Veloso. This was of limited originality but was important as a compilation of current information mostly translated from English and French on tropical agriculture. Not only did Veloso recommend improvements in current crops in Brazil, but suggested new crops which could profitably be introduced.[193]

Not only were the Portuguese the movers of plants and seeds *per se*, but also vehicles for the transfer of the requisite processing knowledge. In Brazil, the Portuguese had used Indians to collect *drogas do sertão* such as cacao, vanilla, and sarsaparilla. Some of the plants carried by the Portuguese from Brazil to other continents required sophisticated processing which, presumably, the Portuguese had learnt from the Indians. Let us take four cases. Two examples come from the jungle areas of Brazil: cocoa and rubber. Cocoa pods have to be split open, the beans extracted from the whitish slimy liquid, dried, and finally roasted before being ground into a paste. As such it can be made into packets and sold. Indians of Central and South America had mastered the art of extracting the sap from rubber trees, heating it over a fire, and then out of the coagulated substance making rubber objects or making it into balls for sale. The pods or beans of the vanilla vine also require curing or 'sweating' and drying over a period of several months before the initially tasteless beans will release their flavour. This realization had dawned on the Indians who had developed a technique for transforming the seed pods from being odourless into something aromatic and flavourful. Bitter manioc provides the fourth example. The root has to be washed to remove the poisonous prussic or hydrocyanic acid. The Indians of the Amazon had developed the technique of removing the prussic acid by leaching, rotting, and heating. This technique was described by Fernão Cardim in his 1584 treatise:

> Of these rootes crushed and grated they make a Meale that is eaten, it is also layd in steepe till it corrupt, and then cleansed and crushed, they make also a Flowre, and certaine Cakes like children very white and delicate. This roote after it is steeped in water, made in balls with the hands, they set it upon hurdles at the smoake, where it drieth in such manner that it is kept without corrupting, as long as they list, and after scraped and stamped in certaine great trayes, and sifted, there remayneth a Flowre whiter than of Wheate...

Cardim described the flour known in Brazil as *farinha de*

mandioca which is prepared by soaking, peeling and scraping freshly dug roots and then grating them into a pulp and passing this through a sieve. This is toasted or dried in the sun and then pounded into powder. It was this technology developed by native Americans which the Portuguese carried to West Africa along with the cassava shrub.[194]

An extension of such technical knowledge lies in the pharmaceutical applications of flora. The exemplar of this was Dr Garcia d'Orta who resided in Goa for some thirty years prior to his death in 1568 and authored the *Coloquios dos simples, e drogas e cousas mediçinais da India* (Goa, 1563). The fifty-seven *colóquios* are mostly on the pharmaceutical and medical applications of plants. A contemporary in Goa at St Paul's College was the Florentine Jesuit Gaspar Antonio (died 1684), doctor and author of treatises on medicine, who developed a formula for the making of *pedras cordiais* which were exported to Portugal and Brazil and were alleged to alleviate leprosy, anaemia, fevers, and even melancholia and depression. In Brazil, the Jesuit Fernão Cardim had credited manioc, dried in the smoke of a fire, with being an effective remedy against poisons, especially snake venom. In his account of travelling from Quito to Pará in 1639, the Spanish Jesuit who accompanied Pedro Teixeira also noted the presence of drugs with medicinal applications.[195]

A variant on the movement of flora for cultivation and commercial purposes was the need to provide provisions for ships' complements on the longer routes. In the Atlantic the Portuguese turned otherwise uninhabited islands into sources for foodstuffs. One such landfall was Saint Helena some 1,140 miles west of the coast of southern Angola and 1,800 miles from South America. This was a provisioning point for homeward-bound Indiamen. The Portuguese cultivated fruit trees and other vegetables and introduced swine and goats onto the uninhabited island. Its disputed (between Dutch and English, the latter having built a fort there in 1658) international status was ended by the royal charter of 1673 which declared the English East India Company as 'true and absolute lords and proprietors'. Farther north and west was Sable Island off the coast of Nova Scotia which the Portuguese (possibly as early as the 1520s by João Álvares Fagundes) stocked with swine and cattle in the sixteenth century and which ran wild. Traditionally, the island of

Barbados which was still uninhabited at the beginning of the seventeenth century, also owed its herds of wild pigs to the Portuguese.[196]

The Portuguese did not have exclusive access to these island deposits, and seamen of other nations availed themselves of such meat on the hoof and crops. Sable Island was to be important to Sir Humfry Gilbert on his second and final voyage (1583), when he hoped to found a colony in fabled Norumbega. After taking possession of Newfoundland for England, he left St John's on 20 August 1583, and his three vessels made for Sable Island to stock up on fresh meat. Wind, rain, and fog slowed their progress. *Delight* ran aground on the shoals off Sable Island with loss of life, and no landing could be effected on the island. Running short on provisions and dispirited, the two remaining vessels turned for home. Gilbert died when the *Squirrel* was swamped north of the Azores.[197]

By its very location, St Helena was likely to be more frequented and this could lead to friction between rival nationalities. Portuguese and Dutch put into St Helena regularly homeward-bound from the East, and could spend several weeks refitting vessels, repairing rigging, and taking on provisions and water. The homeward-bound Portuguese fleet which had left Cochin between Christmas Day 1599 and 15 January 1600, arrived off St Helena on 25 April and found two Dutch vessels already taking water. Shots were exchanged for some twenty-four hours until the Portuguese prevailed and the Dutch fled. Two other Dutch vessels under the command of Wybrand van Warwijck homeward-bound from Bantam, and who had anticipated a rendezvous with the other two vessels expelled by the Portuguese, only reached St Helena on 17 May 1600. They were prevented from landing because of the Portuguese presence and were forced to weigh anchor again on 22 May.[198]

The ebb and flow of flora was complemented by movement of fauna by the Portuguese. As regards the introduction of new species of domestic animals, this was only significant from Europe to America and here the Spaniards took the lead. It was they who introduced animals and fowl (some originating in India and Asia) – horses, asses, mules, donkeys, cattle, oxen, sheep, pigs, goats, chickens, geese, dogs, and cats – to the Caribbean and to the American continent extraordinarily soon after Columbus' landfall on 12 October 1492. The Portuguese were the first to introduce some of the above species to the Atlantic islands (Madeira, 1420; Azores, 1430s; Cape Verdes, 1460s), and to São Tomé and Príncipe in the Gulf of Guinea. Cattle were raised for meat, which could be salted, and milk, from which cheese could be made, as well as giving such by-products as tallow and hides. As regards the American continent, the Portuguese delayed intensive introduction of such species to Brazil until after the establishment of crown government in 1549 could provide the necessary incentives for settlement and a modicum of security. With the exception of sheep, which never found in Portuguese America that success they enjoyed in Mexico or Peru, all other species thrived in Brazil. Inevitably, some experimentation had to take place before finding that species or breed most appropriate to regional conditions of climate, rainfall, soil, degree of sun or shade, and nutrition. Apart from their nutritional value, some of these animals were critical to the economic development of Brazil. Oxen were essential in moving crates of sugar and heavy cargoes, turning the crushing rollers of sugar mills, and providing the energy for ploughing. Mules and donkeys were the backbone of middle and long-distance transportation. Open range cattle ranching opened up the interior of Brazil, and encouraged the development of the north and south, and provided hides which were exported and also were used to wrap tobacco and bundles.[199] Pigs became a staple in the diet of all, but especially in the mining regions. And horses not only provided rapid transportation and communication, and a mode of coping with cattle dispersed over vast ranges of the *sertão*, but eligibility to ride such noble beasts divided a slave from his owner and ownership of a horse was the *sine qua non* of the gentry and landed nobility of Brazil.

Another aspect of this movement of animals lay in their quality as exotica or collectables. The Portuguese were neither the first nor the last to be fascinated by animals from foreign parts. About the same time as the Portuguese were conquering Ceuta, Chinese expeditions under Chêng Ho brought back for the imperial zoo from East Africa, Hormuz, and Aden, such exotica as tigers, lions, ostriches and, most fantastic of all, a giraffe.[200] The Portuguese, for their part, brought to Lisbon from Africa and Brazil, monkeys, humming birds, and parrots. Animals also made good presents. In 1505, a present in the form of a caparisoned horse was delivered in the name of Dom Manuel to the chief of Ughoton in Benin. In East Asia, Japanese Namban screens depict arrivals of the Portuguese in Nagasaki and the mandatory formal processions by the captain-major to the *daimyo* or even *xogun* which often included horses, hunting hounds, camels, cheetahs, mules, peacocks, and elephants.[201]

Dom João II, 'the perfect prince', was but the first in a long line of Portuguese monarchs to be fascinated by the flora and fauna of Asia, Africa, and America. Kings ordered that animals and birds be dispatched to Lisbon, many arriving as carcasses or bundles of feathers or fur after gruelling trans-oceanic voyages. Kings were also recipients of gifts from potentates and emperors as far away as China and the Moluccas. Few gifts could match the rhinoceros sent in 1513 from Gujarat as a present to Dom Manuel. Working from a sketch, Albrecht Dürer immortalized this animal in a somewhat fanciful engraving. An elephant was sent to Portugal from Cannanore in 1510. From Cochin, two were sent in 1512, one in 1513, and three in 1515. Philip III of Portugal was not immune to this fad. He wanted an elephant and a female rhinoceros and ordered these and other wild animals from East Africa, Arabia, and Persia, elephants from Ceylon, or tigers from India. He expressed the wish for such animals and rare birds as 'an ornament of my court'. The exuberance in the sixteenth century for the exotica of Brazil was to give way by the eighteenth century to requests by King Dom João V for the sending of birds from Brazil to Lisbon. Special instructions were given to viceroys as to how this could be accomplished with least loss of life, cages were constructed for this purpose, and captains were ordered to take every reasonable measure to ensure that their cargoes arrived alive. This was a thankless task. In 1782, the governor of Angola, José Gonçalo da Câmara, informed the minister in Lisbon of the results of his efforts to collect and send live specimens to Lisbon. Not surprisingly, animals and large numbers of birds which were consigned from Luanda to Lisbon died during a passage which included stops in Salvador or Pernambuco to unload cargoes of slaves. This was a forceful reminder that those vessels which were critical in the dissemination and dispersal of plants, were also the carriers of people throughout the Portuguese-speaking world.[202]

CHAPTER VI
TRANSMISSION OF STYLES, MORES, AND IDEAS

There are aspects of this mobility which are often ignored, namely, cultural, linguistic, and intellectual diffusion. Be it in Africa, India or Brazil, the Portuguese put an indelible urban imprint on those places they settled. In some cases they had a *tabula rasa*, as at São Jorge da Mina which was not only a fort but, by 1486, had a municipal charter. In Mozambique and in Timor, they transformed the pre-Portuguese settlements into Portuguese towns replete with churches and streets. Prior to the arrival of the Portuguese, settlement in Cochin was around the port with the temple and royal palace as the major landmarks. With the arrival of the Portuguese, this was referred to as *Cochim de cima* (the current Mattanchery) and the Portuguese established their own settlement (the present Fort Cochin) some distance away. Goa underwent a radical transformation from native plan to a fair approximation of a European Renaissance city. In America, whereas the Spaniards had often located their cities on the sites of their pre-columbian predecessors (as at Tenochtitlan), the Portuguese were compelled to start *ab initio*. Contrary to what is generally believed, the Portuguese were no less urban planners than the Spaniards. Frequently, expansion beyond the limits originally envisaged, coupled with difficulties of topography (Salvador being the classic case), resulted in a town or city where passage was difficult, houses were built too closely together, and inadequate sanitation brought problems of public health. This did not prevent Portuguese kings from holding firm to the belief that the creation of towns would encourage a more stable, productive, and loyal populace.

Some 250 miles from the Atlantic coast, in the interior of Brazil, are two townships: Diamantina and Sabará. In the first is a street called Macao de Cima (Upper Macao); in the second, the chapel of Nossa Senhora do O clearly shows oriental influences, as does the presence of chinoiserie in the cathedral of Mariana. Ivory crucifixes from Goa reached São Luís do Maranhão in the seventeenth century, and porcelain tableware from the East and Indo-Portuguese bronze weights were in use in eighteenth-century Minas Gerais. These examples underline the close ties between two peripheries of the Portuguese seaborne empire, and the fact that styles and influences were transported between Asia, Africa, America and Europe. There is a certain irony in that the style which came to be designated as Manueline was essentially a hybrid of the Portuguese Gothic and the plateresque, but much of the characteristic syncretic quality was attributable to its Gothic structure which combined the traditional with new decorative forms and symbols derived from Portuguese discoveries and encounters with other peoples, other lands, and other flora. The distinctive style, so apparent in Portugal in (*inter alia*) the church of Jesus at Setúbal (finished 1492), the Jerónimos and the Tôrre (1515) at Belém, at Tomar, the unfinished chapels of Batalha, and at the royal palace at Evora, was then carried overseas by the Portuguese, back to those very regions which had contributed to the formation of this style in Portugal. Motifs derived from Indian art are apparent in Tomar, most notably the windows of Diogo de Arruda. His brother Francisco de Arruda drew on his own experience in Morocco when commissioned to design the Tôrre de Belém, which reflects Moorish styles and even incorporates a rhinoceros into the decorations. Existing examples of this style overseas include a church in Cochin with a Manueline portal and the chapel of N. S. do Baluarte in Mozambique. The exception to this diffusion of the Manueline style from Portugal appears to be Brazil. However, the Jesuit style of architecture, which bears many points in common with Portuguese *chão* architecture, was readily apparent in Portuguese churches from Brazil to Macao.

This transmission was not limited to architectural styles and decorative motifs, but also included materials available to artists in their creations. From Asia, Africa, and America, the Portuguese brought to Europe an infinite variety of precious stones, ivory, gold, silver, and fine woods. The monstrance attributed to Gil Vicente was made of East African gold and was laden with rubies and other precious stones from India. Gold poured into Portugal, most notably from Brazil. Churches were transformed by gilded ceilings, pillars and altars, and gold monstrances, altar pieces, and crucifixes. The library at the University of Coimbra, built between 1716 and 1723, reflected in its gilded work and fine woods, the 'golden age' of Brazil. The fever of construction in Portugal in the early eighteenth century, as shown by the monastery of Mafra (1717-1730), was underwritten financially by Brazilian gold. Stone quarried and cut in Portugal was also carried overseas, as ballast in vessels. In Salvador, the church of the Jesuit College, later to be the cathedral, was constructed (1657-1672) of such stone as was the façade of the Carmelite church in Belém do Pará. More beautiful was the church of Nossa Senhora da Conceição da Praia in Salvador (begun 1739, completed 1850),[203] the finest example of the Joanine style (*estilo joanino*) in Brazil. All the stone known as *lioz*, a kind of cream-coloured limestone with rose veins but with the appearance of marble, came from a quarry outside Lisbon and was pre-cut in Portugal in accordance with the plans. It was then shipped as ballast to Bahia.

The Portuguese role was not limited to making available new media for artistic expression and new objects which could be incorporated into artistic creations. It extended to the creation of new art forms which represented the blending of European and non-European styles and artistic traditions. A melding of the styles of Portugal and India is readily apparent in the magnificent pieces referred to under the generic name of Indo-Portuguese art. This has been described by Carmo Azevedo as an art where themes and treatment are Portuguese, whereas the inspiration and decorative spirit are Indian. Although there is no technical reason to limit the designation 'Indo-Portuguese', traditionally this has been applied to furniture, tapestry, embroidery, printed or painted textiles, and work in silver and gold and the decorative arts, rather than to architecture. This appreciation of fine art could clash with the official policy of promoting Christianity. In 1546, the king ordered viceroy Dom João de Castro to forbid Hindu artists from making or painting likenesses of Christ or the saints and the archbishop of Goa forbade Christians to commission works of religious art from Hindu craftsmen. Rarely were the Portuguese the vehicles for bringing together artistic traditions which resulted in new art forms, without the European component, for example African-Indian, Indian-Chinese, or African-native American.

The Portuguese were not unappreciative of the skilled craftsmanship of peoples of other religions and nations. Afonso de Albuquerque sent a dagger made by a Goan goldsmith to Dom Manuel. In India, not only did the Portuguese decorate homes, palaces, and even churches with locally made objects but, on their return to Portugal, they often carried articles of Indian workmanship. These included finely carved cabinets, tables, chairs, secretaries and beds, sometimes with inlays of ivory or ebony; tapestries, wall-hangings, bed coverings, and other worked cloth which included embroidered vestments for church dignitaries as well as for secular self-adornment; a wide range of jewellery, ranging from the sacred to the profane, and incorporating precious stones; and, finally, works in lacquer or ceramic.[204] Many of these remain in private collections in Portugal, but a visit to the Museu de Arte Antiga in Lisbon provides a wonderful introduction to the role of the Portuguese as connoisseurs of beautiful objects and their role in bringing such objects to Europe and, to a lesser extent, to Brazil where examples of Indo-Portuguese art are to be seen in port cities and in the interior to this day. Portuguese returned to Europe from China and Japan with objects such as porcelains, silks, painted screens, and lacquer-ware. Given the paucity of Portuguese in East or

West Africa, and the fact that the majority were unlikely to return to Portugal with *objets d'art* to decorate a mansion or *solar*, those objects which were carried back to Portugal from Africa were more likely to fall under the category of curios. In the case of Brazil, during the colonial period churches and religious brother-hoods followed the practice of commissioning statuary in the mother country. Those objects of Brazilian origin carried to Por-tugal included gold jewellery and furniture, but in few cases would the contribution (if any) of the craftsmanship of non-European artists or artisans have been identifiable as such because of the anonymity surrounding many such skilled workers.

Such dissemination was not limited to the decorative arts and architecture. Mores were extended beyond their place of origin. This is not the place for a lengthy discussion of cultural and behavioural synthesis brought about by the Portuguese through-out the world, but it should be pointed out that during five centuries of interaction with other peoples, Portuguese policies and practices ranged between respect and tolerance for local customs and outright intolerance and even draconic acts of sup-pression of local ways of life. Policies of Christianization and Lusitanization – depending on local authorities and their zeal for implementation – could lead to unyielding imposition of Portu-guese practices on local populaces, even in such personal matters as diet, dress, and selection of marriage partners. From two or more distinctive cultures, of which one was the Portuguese, could emerge parallel cultures, each evolving in its own distinc-tive way. Sometimes there was little or no interaction between the Portuguese and the non-Portuguese. Other times there occurred a meeting of the two distinctive patterns of mores, only for this to be abruptly terminated by official prohibition. Such prohibitions were more likely to originate with non-European (and non-Christian) leaders or chieftains than by decrees of the Portuguese crown and were accompanied by severe sanctions and punishments of infractors or backsliders. Usually, there would slowly occur at least toleration for, and even acceptance of, European mores. Schedules for such toleration or acceptance were unpredictable: they might occur virtually from one day to the next, or take years of co-existence. The same held true for rejection or expulsion, which might take the form of a slow campaign of attrition or represent a sudden change of policy on the part of a local leader. Some Portuguese mores were accepted, whereas others were rejected for no readily apparent reason.

In India, there were parallel policies in the early years. On the one hand, Afonso de Albuquerque (governor, 1509-15) was careful not to interfere in local living styles and Hindu religious ceremonies, with the exception of Sati which he banned (with limited success, as shown by further gubernatorial decrees banning this practice and resolutions by Provincial Councils of 1575 and 1585). On the other hand, he did promote inter-marriage between Portuguese men and Muslim widows, their daughters and light-skinned Aryan women converted to Catholicism. Each such couple received a piece of land, a house, horse, cattle, and actual currency. The Inquisition established in Goa in 1560 characterized as heretical any vestige of Hinduism. Converts were banned from using Hindu names, attending any Hindu ceremony even including weddings, engaging the services of a Hindu doctor or midwife, wearing the *dhoti* or *choli*, or planting *tulsi*. In the seventeenth century, Portuguese men were permitted to marry Brahmin and Kshatriya women. There slowly evolved easier fluidity between the two cultures and one can refer to an Indo-Portuguese culture and mores.[205]

Elsewhere, the Portuguese crown sought to offset the shortage of European women by officially or unofficially encouraging marriages with native women, or at least casting a blind eye to such liaisons. But cohabitation or sexual intercourse does not translate into cultural penetration. One example of short-lived but intensive Portuguese cultural influence was in the Congo. The Congo provided an extreme case of Europeanization by the ruling classes from about 1490-1530. Kings took names associated with the Portuguese monarchy, the court was revamped along Portuguese lines, tribal laws were replaced by those of Portugal masquerading as traditional Congolese laws, the elites embraced Christianity, and European dress and some manners became the fad. No less than modern day academics from Third World countries who attend institutions of higher education in the First World and then find difficulty in re-adapting to their countries of origin, or applying the skills they have learnt, so too did young Congolese who travelled to the University of Coimbra in the sixteenth century find themselves and their skills irrelevant on their return. Another instance of short-lived but intense Portuguese impact was in Japan, where there was the adoption of ruffs and the Indo-Portuguese baggy pantaloons, and carrying of long handkerchiefs.[206]

The Portuguese were the transmitters of European mores to other continents, of mores of non-European provenance to Europe, and even of mores between Africa, Asia, and America. Let us illustrate each category by reference to specific examples. Into the first category would fall the imposition on native Americans, Africans in Africa, and persons of African descent in Brazil, of dress to which they were not accustomed. This was the case – perhaps the most egregious example – of native Americans in mission villages but applied equally in the secular arena and to slave dress. In Brazil, this could be carried to the point where a favourite slave, or *mucama*, would rival and even exceed the wife of her owner in terms of finery and self-adornment, or where free men of colour might appear as imitations of European fops. Leaders of gangs of porters in late colonial Rio de Janeiro adopted the practice of wearing top-hats, presumably no less a symbol of authority than had been the red cloths or caps so in demand in West Africa in the sixteenth century. In the service of Christ or king, non-Europeans were obliged to conform to European practices by wearing the appropriate dress or uniforms. As regards diet, most notably in Brazil, the Portuguese wrought changes in the diets of persons of African descent who had been transported to the New World. But any dietary modifications of European origin were minimal in the case of native Americans and Africans, and peoples of India, China, or Japan were little effected as regards diet by European imports. One aspect of the introduction of new mores which the Portuguese must have rued, derived from the introduction and dissemination of the horse in Brazil. The Portuguese could not have envisaged that this noble steed, when placed in the skilled hands of the Guaicurú, would make this Indian people one of the most feared as the Portuguese moved to the west in search of gold. Indeed, of the animals introduced by the Portuguese into colonial Brazil only the horse was to find acceptance among some Indian peoples. Pack animals were to be important only in those parts of Africa not affected by the tsetse fly and in Brazil, but had little or no impact on mores in the Estado da India.

The transmission of non-European practices into Portugal

from overseas comprises the second category. Clearly, dietary modifications played an important role, the results of the importation of spices from India, sugar from Brazil, or peppers from West Africa. To these can be added modifications resulting from the importation of maize and other products of American, African, or Asian origins. The degree to which the impact of such imports on the diet of Portuguese was generalized or limited by class or financial means, and the timetable for acceptance or rejection of such imports, and why, would be interesting themes for future research. Within this category fall changes of sartorial fashion attributable to access to cloths, silks, or objects of self-adornment, which were imported into Portugal. Although the Portuguese appear to have been less addicted to tobacco than were the Dutch and English, the taking of snuff and smoking of tobacco was introduced into Portugal. The *palanquim*, or sedan chair, imported from the East, found ready acceptance on the cobbled streets of Lisbon.

Particularly intriguing is the role of the Portuguese as disseminators of customs between Africa, Asia, and America. Dietary modifications attributable to the Portuguese have been discussed and include the introduction of maize and manioc into Africa, and of foodstuffs of African or Asian origin into Brazil. Brazilian tobacco, of which the best came from the Recôncavo of Bahia, found ready acceptance in far-off lands: in West Africa among chieftains, merchants and slaves, in India among coolies and at courts, and among all classes in China. Be it chewed, snuffed, or smoked in a pipe, Brazilian tobacco created addicts among indigenous peoples wherever the Portuguese travelled or traded. It was the Portuguese who introduced firearms into the island of Tanegashima. Within a short time not only the Tanegashimans but other islanders had learnt to manufacture muskets and firearms. The Portuguese were also to be the vehicles for European influence on Japanese sword-fittings. Mahendra Chodankar has pointed out how the introduction of Christianity could bring about modifications in self-adornment. Whereas Hindu or Muslim jewellery prevailed before the arrival of the Portuguese in India, on being converted to Christianity, Indian women changed their taste in jewellery so as clearly to distinguish themselves. Some of this jewellery worn by converts was derived from local art forms, whereas others

190

showed Portuguese influence. These included crosses or pendants depicting Christ on the cross, chains of gold coins, gold hair combs, and a distinctive ring known as a *marker*.[207]

If there was any one group of people on whom the Portuguese were to have most effect it would be on persons of African descent, and less in their places of origin than in the New World. In the case of Africa as a whole, but especially markedly in East Africa, the Portuguese had remarkably little cultural impact either in terms of mores or of religion. Indeed, the reverse was more likely to be the case with the Africanization of Portuguese migrants and colonists and their adoption of African customs. Whereas perhaps nowhere in the Americas did African mores, language, diet, religious beliefs, and values survive the restrictive, oppressive, and destructive pressures of slavery as much as in Brazil, no other people with whom the Portuguese came into contact throughout the world adopted so completely Portuguese language, Portuguese mores, and Catholicism, as did persons of African descent in Brazil. Clearly the yoke of slavery was a weighty influence on such adoption, but Portuguese and European visitors to the colony commentated on the sincerity and devotion of persons of African descent in their adherence to Catholicism.

Turning from mores to language, what is truly amazing is the manner in which the Portuguese language was carried beyond the bounds of the confined area of Portugal to the uttermost ends of the earth and the sheer endurance to our own days of this linguistic legacy. Today, among languages of European origin, Portuguese (186 million) ranks third only to English (487 million) and Spanish (401 million) in numbers of speakers in the world. Far behind come French at 126 million, German at 124 million, and Italian at 62 million. There is a certain irony in that Dutch, the language of those who ousted the Portuguese from their pre-eminence in the East in the seventeenth century, is spoken in the contemporary world by a ninth (21 million) of those who speak Portuguese. Portuguese is the official language of continental Portugal and of Portugal beyond Europe (Azores, Madeira, Macao), and of the sovereign nations of Brazil, Angola, Cape Verde, Guinea-Bissau, São Tomé and Príncipe, and Mozambique. That Columbus wrote Castilian using Portuguese spelling, suggests he spoke Portuguese before Spanish. Already, by 1500, Portuguese was the *lingua franca* of West Africa and in the sixteenth and seventeenth centuries was to become the *lingua franca* of the west coast of India, and of much of the coastal regions of Asia and Africa, as well as of Brazil, and of islands of the Atlantic and Indian Oceans and the China Sea. In many parts of the world, the Portuguese came into contact with multi-lingual communities. Especially in India and beyond, the Portuguese were forced to learn the local languages of trade. In India, Afonso de Albuquerque considered the Portuguese language as a suitable vehicle to acculturate the locals to a Portuguese *modus vivendi*. One scholar has referred to the way in Goa, every effort was made – by *ferro, fogo, e sangue* ('iron, fire, and blood') – to replace Konkani by Portuguese, and Sanskrit by Latin.[208] In Portuguese India, as elsewhere, a knowledge of Portuguese was a prerequisite to enter the service of church or state. It was Portuguese, rather than Malay or other oriental languages, which was the language of long distance trade from Japan to Mozambique. The Dutch and English were initially compelled to do business in Portuguese in India and East Asia.

This was a two-way process of linguistic exchange: Portuguese words entered local languages on the one hand, and local words entered Portuguese. In addition to theological and specialized terms, some everyday domestic words entered the Japanese language: *tabako* (Port. *tabaco*; Eng. tobacco), *kappa* (Port. *capa*; Eng. straw cape), *botan* (Port. *botão*; Eng. button), *pan* (Port. *pão*; Eng. bread), *karumeru* (Port. *caramelo*; Eng. caramel). The most extensive example of the latter is provided by Brazil where numerous words of native American and African languages have been incorporated into Portuguese. The *Crioulo* of the Cape Verdes is a fusion of African languages (which predominate) and Portuguese and, although still in a process of evolution, has become a vehicle for literary expression. As regards oriental languages, it would appear that Portuguese incorporated a higher incidence of local words than *vice versa*, although there are numerous examples of Portuguese words in Konkani, Marathi, Sinhala, Tamil, Malayan, and other Asian vernaculars to-day. There was also the emergence of a Portuguese creole or patois. Even in the twentieth century a Portuguese patois was still spoken in Malacca and Malabar. Ironically, although there was never a Portuguese presence in

Batavia, household slaves imported from the Bay of Bengal brought with them a form of Portuguese creole which was adopted by some Dutch and half-castes born in Batavia, even to the exclusion of their mother-language. For some time after the Dutch expelled the Portuguese from Ceylon in 1658, they were forced to use Portuguese in official dealings with Sinhalese officials and Portuguese continued to be used in missionary activities. To this day, the settlement of Batticaloa and its environs continues to be Portuguese-speaking. Be it in Brazil, West Africa, or Asia, Portuguese successfully fought off the challenge of the Dutch language in the seventeenth century.[209] Ironically, given the fact that they were probably the most brilliant and polyglot of linguists to emerge from Portugal, the Jesuits resorted to the use of Tupi rather than teaching Portuguese to their charges in the mission villages of Brazil.

This dispersion of language is not limited to metropolitan Portuguese. The Indo-Portuguese dialect also travelled far and wide, under its own sails, as it were: from Daman and Diu to Sri Lanka and Malacca. The dialect of Macao also shows Indo-Portuguese influence. Nor was the Portuguese role as linguistic disseminators limited to the vernacular. Latin, although used solely within the religious context, was introduced by Portuguese missionaries into Africa, Asia, and South America, and converts were required to have a working knowledge of this language. This included the use of Latin in religious hymns in the parochial schools of Portuguese India in the 1530s. In Jesuit colleges from Macao to the Maranhão, pupils learnt both Latin and Portuguese. In Japan, the introduction of the printing press in 1590 led to some theological terms being transliterated from Latin into Japanese.[210] An aside concerns some of the earliest written records by westerners of non-European languages. These took the form of word lists and grammars drawn up by religious, in which the Jesuits were to the fore but not alone, and laymen, and which constitute a base for historical linguistics of some peoples of Africa, Asia and America.[211]

The Portuguese were also the transmitters of a different medium of expression: music. This applied to instrumentation, singing and, to a lesser degree, dancing. Throughout the Portuguese world, the transmission of European music was initially tied to conversion to Christianity. The Portuguese exported plainsong or Gregorian chant from Europe in the sixteenth century and the Portuguese were to be the vehicles for a new polyphony (or 'counterpoint'). In Jesuit colleges, students were introduced to instrumental music and singing. In India, parish schools taught musical training which included singing and playing of the violin and organ. In the case of European wood-wind instruments, these were introduced into Goa in the nineteenth century, as too were brass-winds such as trombones and tubas. European motets were exported and underwent modifications in Portuguese India. Goan composers of Christian religious music also wrote secular music which introduced western harmony. The *moda*, *fado*, and Portuguese regional and popular music were exported to India, but had less impact on Goan music.[212]

A world away, in Portuguese America, the Portuguese were instrumental in the introduction of not merely one, but two, musical traditions, namely the African and the European. In the case of African music, some of the ethnic (*nações*) differences – which were to be preserved so strongly in the New World and manifested themselves in colonial Brazil in the form of lay brotherhoods, petty commerce, patterns of labour, and even marriage and godparenthood – also found expression in different musical traditions reflecting Bantu, Sudanese, and even Islamic influences. This legacy was not only of secular music but also music associated with religious ceremonies. Although prohibited under the general rubric of witchcraft (*feitiçaria*), such ceremonies of African provenance did occur during the colonial period. More evident to any visitor to Brazil, and cause for concern to authorities, was the prevalence of African dance which was carried to Brazil. This musical diaspora applied equally to African instruments for which there are descriptions or pictures of some twenty different instruments in colonial Brazil. In the case of the dissemination of a European musical tradition, much of what has been said about the Estado da India applies equally to Portuguese America. The Jesuits and the Catholic church played an important role in the diffusion of religious music, and there were ample opportunities in the colony for the playing of secular music which accompanied public processions, be these for Corpus Christi, the arrival of a governor or bishop, or municipal festivities. In terms of more popular music, the music of the Beira and Minho was brought to Brazil and their influence was stronger than that of other parts of Portugal, not surprisingly given the overwhelming predominance of migrants from the north of Portugal to colonial Brazil. The arrival of the royal court marked the beginning of secular musical patronage in late colonial Brazil but the emergence of a Brazilian style of music was not at the expense of a total severance with the Portuguese legacy.

In the history of early modern Europe, the Portuguese played a role in contributing to the whittling away of the world of fantasy created by Europeans vis-à-vis peoples and lands and fauna of Africa, India and Asia, and later of America. A world inhabited by giants and lilliputians and human aberrations ranging from people with a single eye on their foreheads, to men with their faces on their chests and canine heads on human bodies, gave way to new understanding and knowledge based on eyewitness accounts and direct experience. The Portuguese contributed to the transition from the late Middle Ages to the Renaissance and to the revolution in European thought and humanism in the sixteenth century. Experiences and knowledge of Asia, Africa, and America by the Portuguese were funnelled through Lisbon, were widely disseminated and eagerly received, and had an impact on the intellectual life of sixteenth- and seventeenth-century Europe. The *Verdadera Informacam das Terras do Preste Joam* of father Francisco Álvares, describing Ethiopia in the 1520s and published in Portugal in 1540, was to enjoy translation into Italian (1550; 1554), French (1556; 1558), Castilian (1557; 1561; 1588), German (1566; 1576), and English (1625).[213]

While this holds true in the broad sweep, less easy to assess is whether the information and quality of reporting by the Portuguese were commensurate with their experiences. Or, to put it differently, were there missed opportunities? It would be easy to specify instances where a traveller glossed over the details of a voyage or journey, leaving the reader feeling 'if only'. Yet one can turn to Francisco Álvares for Ethiopia, to Tomé Pires for commercial reporting from the Red Sea to Japan, to Gabriel Soares de Sousa for late sixteenth-century Brazil, or to Manuel Godinho's account of his travels from India to Europe, as exemplars of the fruits of keen observation, intellectual curiosity, and detailed commentary. Travellers left rich accounts which dwell on the physical world: landscapes, cities, natural phenomena, flora and fauna; the human world of people and their cultures, economies, mores; and forms of governance or religion. Such accounts by laymen have their counterparts in the copious writings by men of the cloth. Letters and treatises penned by the Jesuits from missions in India, Africa, Asia, and Brazil, to Portugal and to Rome, played a major role in disseminating not only details of religious, political, commercial, social, linguistic, and ethnographic interest, but served to introduce Europeans to what were, for them, different attitudes, different approaches, different values, and different priorities.

Before the 'philosophical journeys' of the Enlightenment, individual Portuguese, both laymen and religious, demonstrated an interest in the practice of medicine, *materia medica*, botany, geology, zoology, and pharmacology. Garcia d'Orta was clearly fascinated by Indian medical practices and the medical applications of flora. Moreover, in the *Colóquios*, he cast himself in the role of the practitioner speaking from the position of what he had observed and advocated the importance of knowledge based on experience over knowledge acquired through books alone. His contribution lay in his descriptions of plants, their places of origin and availability, and the therapeutic benefits to be derived from them. In the *Colóquios*, he was describing plants and their medical uses and providing his readership with clinical descriptions of diseases (such as Asiatic cholera) unknown to physicians in Europe. D'Orta had no inhibitions in faulting Galen, based on his own experiences, but did not himself formulate new medical theories. Dr Aleixo de Abreu, who practised medicine in Portugal, Angola, and Brazil at the end of the sixteenth century and first years of the seventeenth, described three tropical parasites. Although credited by one scholar as 'the author of the earliest book on tropical medicine', Abreu remained Galenic in his approach to medicine. Dr Simão Pinheiro Morão, author of two works on medicine in Brazil, did not rise above the descriptive or critical, rejected empiricism, and his only sally into speculation concerned the impact of metereological phenomena on bodily humours.[214] In common with fellow medical practitioners in the tropics and sub-tropics, Abreu and Morão remained humouralists who ignored climate and the environment as factors in medicine. Their impact on medical theories and on the dissemination of ideas was minimal, and the contributions to medical sciences by João Rodrigues de Castelo Branco and Garcia d'Orta in the sixteenth century and of Zacuto Lusitano in the seventeenth century were descriptive rather than theoretical.

Accounts by religious and laymen from the sixteenth to the nineteenth centuries abound with descriptions of peoples, diseases, and the flora and fauna of Asia, Africa, and America. In the sixteenth century, already João de Barros had described scurvy, Gabriel Soares de Sousa described the *mal do bicho*, and missionaries throughout the world were reporting on the diseases most prevalent in their regions. In Brazil, the Jesuits José de Anchieta and Fernão Cardim in the late sixteenth century recorded detailed descriptions, especially of animals hitherto unknown to Europeans such as agoutis, pacas, armadillos, saki monkeys, howling monkeys, and marmosets. In his *Historia da Provincia Santa Cruz* (1576) and his 'Tratado da Terra do Brasil', Pero de Magalhães Gandavo described not only the indigenous peoples but also the flora, fauna, reptiles and birds of Brazil. Gabriel Soares de Sousa described animals and seventy-eight species of birds. Fr Cristóvão de Lisboa depicted flora and fauna of Brazil in his *História dos animais e árvores do Maranhão* of the early seventeenth century and the *Diálogos das Grandezas do Brasil*, attributed to Ambrósio Fernandes Brandão, attempted to describe the birds, fishes, and animals of Brazil in accordance with the elements. In south-east Africa, Fr João dos Santos described eighty-seven species of animals and species of fish such as the dipnous fish. António de Oliveira Cadornega illustrated his *História geral das guerras angolanas* (1680-81) with water colours of flora and of snakes, hippopotami, crocodiles and boars, *inter alia*. Some of these observers, such as Gabriel Soares de Sousa who distinguished between four species of armadillo, and Pe Luís Mariano who noted in 1613 that the monkeys he saw in Madagascar differed from those of continental Africa and India, were groping toward classifications of such fauna. For the most part, such keen observers lacked scientific training and their contributions remained at the descriptive level rather than forming the bases for broader hypotheses. But the objects, which they and others brought back to Portugal, contributed to collections in Portugal (notably that of Dom João V destroyed in the 1755 earthquake) and, where feasible as in the case of geological specimens, were distributed further through Europe. [215]

197

Less clear is the impact 'lived experience' overseas had on the intellectual life of Portugal itself other than in the fields of earth and planetary sciences, cartography, and navigational and other applied nautical skills. Here I have referred to the 'intellectual life' but it should not be lost from sight that this would apply only to men of the cloth and a select group of secular scholars. The average Portuguese on the streets of Lisbon or Oporto, or even in the Portuguese communities in Antwerp or Seville, probably had little interest in, and was even less affected by, either the Portuguese explorations or the new worlds and peoples they revealed to Europe. This may also have applied to the bulk of Portuguese sailing for Africa, the Estado da India, or Brazil, whose interests were solely practical and revolved around either profit or self-advancement.

In the Portuguese seaborne empire, there was little fertile ground either for the generating of ideas or for further disseminating ideas which might have been carried from Europe. Other than the colleges of the Society of Jesus and religious orders, there were no institutions of higher education. The education provided by the Jesuits, especially in Portuguese India and Portuguese America, through their colleges provided a formal setting for the transmission of ideas and concepts, but with a limited audience. Authorized in 1540, the Society of Jesus was part of the Counter Reformation. Its educational policies revolved around the *Ratio Studiorum*. By 1556 there were 110 students in St Paul's College in Goa following a curriculum heavy on the classics. What is interesting is that the transmission of European concepts and philosophies was not merely to the elite. Students at St Paul's included (in addition to Portuguese) Deccanis, Bengalis, Pegus, Gujaratis, Armenians, Malabars, *Canarins*, and Chinese. Such students learnt Latin and Portuguese but preserved their vernacular languages, which made them suitable vehicles for catechizing and acting as carriers of received European ideas to their own peoples. The Dominicans established a college at Goa initially, and later moved it to Panaji and Panelim. Augustinians and Carmelites also maintained colleges in Portuguese India until their extinction, effective in 1835. In Japan, the Jesuit seminaries educated young men, usually of noble and samurai stock, as future acolytes. The Jesuits and other religious orders established colleges and schools elsewhere in Portuguese Africa and America. In Salvador, the Jesuit College offered a primary education and an advanced curriculum consisting of Letters (Latin, grammar, rhetoric, poetry, history), Arts (philosophy and science), and theology. In 1689 the king had intervened to order the Jesuits to continue to admit *moços pardos* to their school in Bahia. A Jesuit publication of 1940 listed the following institutions of the Society established between 1540 and 1759: 77 colleges (Portugal, 22; Azores and Madeira, 4; Angola and Mozambique, 3; India and Thailand, 29; Macao and China, 3; Japan, 4; Brazil,12), 2 universities, and 9 printing presses.[216]

The real question lies in the nature of the audience for the Jesuits and other missionaries because, if there were to be any dissemination of European ideas and classical learning or if Europeans were to be the recipients of concepts or philosophies from beyond Europe, the disseminators would for the most part be men of the cloth. In the case of America and Africa, the Portuguese were entering regions where the intellectual tradition and corpus of philosophy were less developed than in the highly sophisticated milieux of India and China with millenial traditions of intellectual and cultural refinement. They also came into contact with Islam, Buddhism, Hinduism, and Confucionism, whose philosophical tenets were all pervasive and guided all aspects of their adherents' lives. In India, missionaries were exposed to ideas from religious literature in Sanskrit and Marathi. In China and Japan, they were exposed to Buddhism, Confucionism, and Taoism. But the results of such exposure to other philosophies and the opportunities to disseminate European philosophies were limited. First, although missionaries might be present in the Mughal court and be received in Beijing or Kyoto and by sultans and kings, for the most part they failed to engage in intellectual exercises and dialogue with the intellectual elites. One of the rare instances, possibly unique, of the dissemination of European ideas beyond the religious sphere and actually reaching an indigenous intellectual élite, occurred in China. The Italian Jesuit, Matteo Ricci, tested his Chinese language skills by authoring a book of maxims on friendship based on the classics and church fathers and also discussed with Chinese scholars his theories on memory and the practice of mnemonics. Ricci's use of four images derived from the Bible was preserved by a Chinese publisher eager to include samples of Western art and handwriting in a collection entitled 'The Ink Garden'. Ricci's ideas and this collection circulated among the Ming dynasty's élite. In the sixteenth and seventeenth centuries, the mathematical skills of Jesuits such as Tomás Pereira and Simão Rodrigues were also to receive imperial recognition in China.[217]

As Charles Boxer has pointed out, Portuguese missionaries in Asia did not recognize as soon as did their Spanish counterparts in Mexico and Peru the importance of studying the religions and philosophies of those whom they hoped to convert to Christianity. Even when such studies were made, they did not see the light of day. Sebastião Gonçalves, S.J. (1561-1640) outlined Hinduism in his *History of Malabar*, ready in 1615, and his fellow Jesuit, Gonçalo Fernandes Trancoso (c. 1521-1621), wrote a detailed treatise finished in 1616 on Hinduism. The former was only published in 1955 and the latter in 1973.[218] Finally, such was the strength of oriental philosophies, that even men of the cloth could not resist their seductive force and became enamoured of the new concepts and dialectics to which they were exposed. But there was little likelihood that, even when such novel ideas were shared with their co-religionists in Europe, they would have any impact on a broader intellectual tradition in Europe. As regards Africa and Brazil, so far removed were the indigenous philosophical, religious, and cultural underpinnings from European counterparts, that there was little intrusion of the European on the African and native American, or *vice versa*. Nor was there exchange of ideas.

To the Portuguese must go the credit for playing a pioneering and major role in the dissemination beyond Europe of the precepts, concepts, and teachings of Christianity. Between 1534, with the establishment of the diocese of Goa, and 1659 with that of Tonkin, a total of ten dioceses were established from East Africa (Ethiopia and Mozambique) to Japan. In Brazil, progress was slower but by the end of the colonial period Portuguese America numbered one archbishopric (whose jurisdiction extended to Angola) and eight episcopal sees. Within eighty years of their arrival in India in the 1540s, the Jesuits had established four provinces in the Estado da India (Goa, which included East Africa and Tibet; Malabar, extending to Indonesia; China; and Japan, which included part of Indonesia and the Celebes), to say nothing of the activities of Franciscans, Dominicans, Augustinians, and Carmelites. In Brazil, the Society of Jesus led the way in missionary activities, although the Franciscans were to be consequential especially in the north. Figures bandied about as to the numbers of conversions are staggering, even if probably exaggerated: 300,000 in Japan (1614) and in China, somewhat less for North and South Vietnam, 200,000 in India, 100,000 in Ceylon, to give an aggregate of some 1,200,000 converts to Christianity from Mozambique to Japan. [219]

The degree of impact, and the degree to which this evangelization was sustained, differed notably in Asia, Africa, and America. In India, many conversions were recorded among farmers and fishermen of the coastal regions. Their degree of understanding of the new philosophy is questionable, many conversions were short-lived, and the beliefs and mores of Hinduism and Buddhism prevailed. Furthermore, toleration for the Malabar rites and Chinese rites represented compromise rather than conversion. There was a certain 'Japanization' of Christianity in Japan and 'Indianization' which reached its extreme form in the person of the Italian Jesuit Robert de' Nobili (1577-1656) who dressed as a Hindu sādhu, called himself a Brahmin, and anointed his body. Finally, Islam and its mores were so strong as to lead previously staunch Catholics to leave the Christian fold and apostatize. Nor could converts ignore the danger represented by expulsions of missionaries from Japan, Ethiopia, and China, frequently associated with persecution and martyrdom. In Africa, before the nineteenth century the Portuguese presence was not such as to make any significant quantitative impact on the conversion of the indigenous population. Be it in the Congo or Mozambique, Christianity existed alongside indigenous religions or there was syncretism. In Africa, the bulk of conversions was of slaves summarily baptized prior to embarkation for America and whose understanding of Christianity would have been superficial at best.

Portuguese America provides both an example of a lost opportunity and of an opportunity seized. To this land, whose territorial extent rivalled that of China, the Portuguese brought Christianity. In the case of the indigenous peoples, the appeal of Christianity remained primarily at the ceremonial level, and it may be questioned how successful the Jesuits and other missionaries were in educating native Americans in the philosophical and religious tenets of Christianity. Portuguese America was remarkable in that the expulsion of the Society of Jesus was attributable not to indigenous opposition or the contrary forces of rival religions, but to the Portuguese themselves, most notably in the person of the marquis of Pombal. As regards persons of African descent, whatever the shortcomings of massed baptism prior to embarkation in Africa, Brazil affords the clearest cut example of the successful and sustained role of the Portuguese in disseminating Christianity to a non-Christian people. Contemporary accounts throughout the colonial era, penned by men of the cloth and laymen, testified to the intensity and sincerity of their religious beliefs by persons of African origin and descent. As Catholics, persons of African descent established lay brotherhoods in Angola, the Atlantic islands, and Brazil, supported the Catholic church with their alms, attended mass, and participated collectively in celebration of the high days of the Catholic calendar. In their wills, free persons and slaves alike ordered that masses be said for their souls and requested that they be accorded a Christian burial. Even the staunchly Protestant Mrs Kindersley, who visited Brazil in the latter part of the eighteenth century, commented favourably on the religious fervour of persons of African descent in Salvador.[220]

Were the Portuguese the originators of ideas and concepts, which they carried with them from Europe overseas? Were they the disseminators to Africa, Asia, and America, of ideas current in Europe of the early modern period? Did they disseminate new (for Europeans) philosophies and concepts with which they came into contact? Were the Portuguese the cultural brokers for the exchange of ideas between Europeans and non-Europeans? To trace the intellectual genealogy of an idea or concept is a daunting task. Humanism in the sixteenth century and the Enlightenment in the eighteenth century were the two eras in which Portugal was to be most engaged in the intellectual life of Europe. In both periods, Portuguese scholars fanned out across Europe, in the earlier age to study at major universities and in the latter to travel, study and observe. Whereas there can be no doubt that the international commercial network of Portugal in Europe, which was firmly in place by the fifteenth century, provided an ambience conducive to the introduction into Portugal of humanism, which enjoyed its most glorious period in the second quarter of the sixteenth century, it is less easy to trace the diffusion from Portugal to Africa, Asia, and America, of an intellectual legacy of equal potency. William Brandon has attempted to demonstrate how reports from America had an impact on the development of social thought and intellectual tradition in early modern Europe with special reference to concepts of liberty, freedom, equality, and attitudes toward property. In the case of New Spain, one can point to how the Spanish conquest of the indigenous peoples was to provoke legalistic, moral and philosophical debate not only in Spain but throughout Europe as to the nature of the Indians and whether they were rational and 'slaves by nature'. [221] It is difficult to find a theme attributable to the Portuguese presence in Africa, Asia, or America, which would have so lasting or so deep a resonance in the mother country.

The impact of Africa, Asia, and America on Portuguese thought and of Portugal on the Western European intellectual tradition of the Renaissance appear to be predominantly in the sciences. Widely recognized as one of the outstanding oceanographers of his day was Dom João de Castro, justly famous for his nautical and navigational knowledge and his contributions to hydrography and meteorology. To the Portuguese must go much of the credit for de-mythifying the Atlantic and transforming it from the unknown to the known and from a region forbidden to man into an ocean crossed routinely and without fanfare. Portugal did contribute decisively to a Europe-wide reassessment of the authority of classical antiquity, placing inherited and hallowed 'truths' under the cold spotlight of 'experienced truths' and scientific deduction. But the centrifugal component, with Portugal at its centre, is missing from the equation once one moves beyond Europe. Clearly, those Portuguese travelling to Asia, Africa and America were not immune to European humanism, the Renaissance, and the Reformation, but we know remarkably little about the intellectual formation even of viceroys, governors, men of the cloth, and the leadership cadre, let alone of sailors, soldiers, and those who made up the bulk of this human world on the move. While there are commentaries on political corruption, institutional incompetence, and immorality, the historian seeks in vain for musings on concepts or philosophies. What was the intellectual baggage carried by the Portuguese overseas? How did their intellectual formation contribute to decision making? It would be fascinating to attempt to unravel the fibres of the skein of ideas and ascertain if Portuguese who saw service as laymen or men of the cloth in Brazil carried home to Europe ideas derived from their American residence, and then carried the hybrid of European and American ideas as part of their intellectual and conceptual baggage when posted to India, Malacca, or Macao. The converse would also hold true. Did Jesuits who preached the Gospel in India, China, Ethiopia, Japan or Brazil enlarge and enrich their views of the world as the result of these experiences? And, when they were posted to a different mission, to what degree did their attitudes and previous experiences mould their subsequent attitudes, actions, and personal philosophies?

What intellectual impact there was, attributable to the Portuguese as disseminators of ideas beyond Europe, varied from region to region. In the case of Africa and Brazil, the Portuguese made little lasting impression on the indigenous populations as far as regards matters of the mind. In Asia, the situation was different, in large part attributable to the introduction of the printing press which decreased the practice of circulating treatises, both devotional and linguistic, in manuscript. Jesuits established the first printing press with movable type in India (Goa) in 1556, where various works were published between 1556 and 1674, in Macao (1588), and in Japan where the printing press functioned from 1590 until 1614. Among the publications of the Goan press were two catechisms in Tamil characters. In Japan, cathecisms were published in romanized Japanese and the press was expanded to include Japanese characters. In addition to catechisms and works primarily of a religious nature (*Flos Sanctorum*) in translation, publications included vocabularies, grammars, and dictionaries. Outstanding in this regard were the Japanese grammars and dictionaries of João Rodriguez Tçuzzu, S.J., a native of the bishopric of Lamego. One exception to devotional or linguistic publications was the appearance (1593) of a Japanese translation of Aesop's *Fables*. In the early seventeenth century printing presses were established at the Jesuit College in Rachol and elsewhere in India. The Portuguese were also the disseminators of European artistic techniques and styles. They carried European paintings and engravings to Akbar's court and these were to be highly influential on Indian painters as shown by miniatures with European motifs. Japanese painters copied European models of Christian subjects, a skill learnt in the Jesuit seminaries and other schools.[222]

The Portuguese also disseminated ideas under the broad rubric of what would now be termed technology transfer and skills, and nowhere more successfully than in Japan. Indeed, as regards the printing press in Japan, by 1610 its operation was turned over to the Japanese. Another skill introduced into Japan by the Jesuits was copper-plate engraving. Well known is the Portuguese introduction of fire-arms to a society whose armed martial arts had been limited to archery and swordsmanship. Less known is the Portuguese introduction of an improved liquidation process, known to the Japanese as *nanbanbuki*, used to refine gold and silver and which was important to the development of new gold mines which came into operation in Japan in the last quarter of the sixteenth century and first quarter of the seventeenth. In Japan, the Portuguese also had a profound influence on geographical knowledge, cartography, and nautical skills. The Portuguese introduced European maps and globes to Japan in the sixteenth century. Taking Portuguese or Indo-Portuguese maps as their models, the Japanese executed portulans and the less specialized world maps depicted on screens in pairs for the eastern and western hemispheres respectively. That the Japanese were eager to keep abreast of European developments in navigation is further shown by an early seventeenth-century Japanese version of a Portuguese pilot book which included sailing directions from Nagasaki, tables for finding the altitude of the sun at noon, and tables of declination. The Jesuits, most notably in the person of Luís de Almeida, also introduced new surgical techniques into Japan. European medicine and surgical procedures were taught to indigenous physicians in the hospitals established by the Portuguese overseas, most notably the Hospital de El-Rei in Goa and Portuguese military hospitals.[223]

The most sustained and most profound dissemination of ideas by the Portuguese was to Brazil. Portugal contributed decisively to the education of Brazilians and there was a substantial Brazilian contribution to higher education and public service in Portugal. Reference has already been made to the large numbers of

Brazilians who travelled to Portugal to attend the University of Coimbra. Few matched in aptitude for languages Tomé Barbosa de Figueiredo, a native of Colônia do Sacramento, who received his law degree in 1774 and was subsequently a magistrate in Celorico da Beira. Figueiredo was credited with a perfect knowledge of Greek, Latin, French, Italian, Spanish, English, Danish, Swedish, German, Dutch, Turkish, Arabic, Russian, and their respective literatures. In the scientific field, Alexandre Rodrigues Ferreira, a Bahian, became deputy director of the Ajuda museum and a leading naturalist of his day. In the later eighteenth century, he was joined in his zoological studies by João Pires Sardinha and Manuel Galvão da Silva. Vicente Coelho de Seabra Silva Teles was appointed to the chair of Geology, Mineralogy, Botany, and Agriculture at Coimbra and was but one of several Brazilians to hold chairs or be on the faculty of the University of Coimbra. The brothers Bartolomeu Lourenço de Gusmão, S.J., and Alexandre de Gusmão, born in Sàntos, were both possessors of extraordinary intellectual brilliance and both attended Coimbra. The elder (1685-1724) was an inventor, primarily famed for being the first to build a working model of the aerostat, but whose skills ranged from engineering (such as raising the Paraguaçú to provide water for the seminary in Bahia) to patents in optics, and who worked in France, England, and the Netherlands. His brother Alexandre (1695-1753) received his doctorate from the University of Paris, was statesman, private secretary to Dom João V, emissary, and architect of the Treaty of Madrid which he saw through to final ratification.

Of those Brazilian-born who returned to Brazil after their education in Portugal, many held public office as judges or entered holy orders. Others were to become luminaries in the cultural history of Brazil. These included Sebastião da Rocha Pita, author of the *História da America Portugueza* (Lisbon, 1730). There was Tomás António Gonzaga (1744-1810), born in Oporto to Brazilian parents, who went to Brazil aged seven, primarily known for the poems of his *Marília de Dirceu* and his satirical *Cartas Chilenas* and who was sentenced to exile in Mozambique for his participation in the Inconfidência Mineira (1789). Another graduate of the University of Coimbra implicated in the Inconfidência was the native of Mariana, Claudio Manuel da Costa (matriculated 1749), who committed suicide or was murdered while under arrest in Ouro Prêto. José de Santa Rita Durão, born in Cata Preta in Minas Gerais, received his degree in theology from Coimbra in 1756, fled from Portugal to Spain and Italy for political reasons, and penned the epic poem *Caramurú* (1781). Another poet, José Basilio da Gama (1740-95), born in São José del Rei, was famed for his *Uruguai* (1769). A contemporary *mineiro* was Manuel Inácio da Silva Alvarenga, who attended Coimbra (matriculated 1768), and penned the verses contained in *O Desertor das Letras* ridiculing university organization prior to the reforms of Pombal, whom he praised. On his return to Brazil, Silva Alvarenga was professor of rhetoric and poetry in Rio de Janeiro, was one of the founders of the Arcádia Ultramarina, and even a prime mover behind the foundation of a public theatre in the Brazilian capital. Bridging the colonial era and the dawn of the Empire in Brazil, was Hipólito José da Costa Pereira Furtado de Mendonça (1774-1823), a native of Colônia do Sacramento, who was a diplomat, better known as the editor of the *Correio Brasiliense ou Armazem Literario* published in London, and who was to be a force in the independence movement in Brazil. It would be easy to extend this list of individuals, but the point to emphasize is that there was a flow of students from Brazil who travelled to Europe to receive an education, some of whom returned to their home lands and were disseminators of European ideas, whereas others contributed to the intellectual life of Portugal. Some few achieved European- wide recognition as scholars and intellectuals.[224]

The impact of the Enlightenment on Portugal and the influx of foreign ideas brought by the *estrangeirados*, as they came to be known, on Portuguese territories overseas was to be pronounced and nowhere more than in Brazil. In education, Luís António Vernei's *Verdadeiro Método de Estudar* (1746) and António Nunes Ribeiro Sanches' *Cartas sobre a Educação da Mocidade* (Paris, 1760) were the basis for Pombaline reforms at all levels. New philosophies and concepts radiated out from Coimbra. Brazilians who had studied and travelled in Europe returned home with new ideas. In Brazil, they found fertile soil in the academies, salons, and *tertúlias literárias* which sprang up in cities in the eighteenth century and which were meeting places for the revitalized intellectual life of the colony. Many endorsed the physiocrat doctrines in vogue in Europe and with which Brazilian intellectuals became familiar through a thriving, if sometimes clandestine, book-trade. Private libraries were built up and reflected in their titles European thinkers of the seventeenth and eighteenth centuries. There was an effort to improve education in the wake of the expulsion of the Jesuits. There was greater emphasis on geometry, experimental physics and the sciences, as exemplified by the seminary established in 1800 in Olinda by the Bishop of Pernambuco, José Joaquim de Azeredo Coutinho, and on knowledge of English and French. The early nineteenth century witnessed the arrival of printing presses which further contributed to the dissemination of ideas from Europe.

Among such influences, that of France, where many Brazilian students attended universities, was the most powerful. The causes and implications of the French Revolution were not lost on Brazilians who followed its progress avidly and which found its Brazilian commentators from the Maranhão to Rio de Janeiro. Many of the sentiments were to find resonance in the Inconfidência Mineira (1789) and the Revolução dos Alfaiates (1798). In the 1790s, vigorous sanctions and even imprisonment failed to eradicate a readership avid for the works of the *Encyclopédistes*. The Arcádia Ultramarina in Rio de Janeiro was seen as a hotbed for Jacobinic ideas and Manuel Inácio da Silva Alvarenga, one of its founders, was jailed for two years for allegedly espousing such subversive doctrines. Azeredo Coutinho, who graduated from Coimbra in 1780, was but one of many Brazilian intellectuals such as the Bahian José da Silva Lisboa who were admirers of Adam Smith whose theses were applied to Brazil. Locke and Burke were also translated into Portuguese and received wide dissemination. During the eighteenth and early nineteenth centuries, Brazilians, exposed to physiocrat doctrines and sentiments of republicanism evidenced in France and the United States, gained an awareness of the uniqueness of their own land. This found expression in increased nativism and the quest for economic, administrative, and social reforms, initially within the context of the Portuguese empire. The move to independence in Brazil was attributable not only to colonial unease with the *status quo*, but largely to the irresistible force exerted by the dissemination of ideas.[225]

CHAPTER VII
MOVEMENT IN WORD AND IMAGE

The modern-day Odysseus can follow in the wakes and foot-steps of the Portuguese and undertake a world tour visiting monuments – churches, fortresses, stately homes, water fount-ains, city chambers – and return home with images of the Portu-guese world captured on film. For the armchair traveller, this world in motion was recorded vividly in literature and iconogra-phy from the fifteenth to the nineteenth century.[226]

There are copious reports, *itinerários*, *cartas*, *relações*, *trata-dos*, and *roteiros* (sailing directions), which describe in words the voyages by land and sea of the Portuguese. Ironically, for two epoch-making voyages – Bartolomeu Dias' opening of the south-east passage around the Cape of Good Hope and Fernão de Magalhães' revelation of the south-west passage – no logbook has survived. For the former we are dependent on João de

Barros' account and for the latter on Pigafetta who at least was a participant. Unfortunately, many of these travel and voyage accounts still remain in manuscript in archives and libraries, but enough have been published to show the wealth of literary sources for Portuguese overseas history. Much of this literature remains unavailable to those not familiar with the Portuguese language and my inevitably rapid survey will draw the reader's attention to some works for which there are English translations. What is readily apparent is that there is an imbalance between the wealth of travel accounts for Portuguese India in the sixteenth and seventeenth centuries and the comparative paucity for Portuguese America at any period.

There were the official and semi-official histories redolent with movement. Gomes Eanes de Zurara (c. 1410-c. 74), a contemporary of the events he was describing, paved the way with his *Chronicle of Guinea* which treated Portuguese ventures down the West African coast. For Portuguese India in the sixteenth century, Fernão Lopes de Castanheda (1499?-1559), Gaspar Correia (c. 1496-c. 1567), and Diogo do Couto (c. 1542/43-1616), all left histories based on residence in India. Castanheda spent some ten years in India (1528-38), whereas Correia spent most of his life in the East, and both shared a propensity for action, battles, and military expeditions. Diogo do Couto spent fifty years in India, as a soldier who saw service in the Red Sea and Persian Gulf, civil servant, private citizen, and keeper of the archives at Goa where he died. His *Décadas da Asia* (Lisbon, 1602-1788), which carry the story of the Portuguese in the East down to 1599, were based on manuscripts and also extensive personal contacts and conversations with the high and lowly, both Portuguese and Asians. Castanheda made a special effort to complement his ten years of residence in India by interviews after his return, when he was a librarian at Coimbra university. But first-hand experience did not necessarily mean accuracy. Gaspar Correia's *Lendas da India* has shortcomings as a historical source but is characterized by a vivid and intense style which is well suited to his subject matter. António Bocarro was archivist at Goa and in 1631 became chronicler of Portuguese India. His *Description* was precisely what its title implied, a description of fortresses, cities and towns. He added a further *Década*, and wrote a history of the Moluccas. Damião de Góis

(1502-74), keeper of the archives in Lisbon and panegyrist of Dom Manuel, and João de Barros (c. 1496-1570), 'the Portuguese Livy', used reports from the field and documents translated from oriental languages. João de Barros was uniquely in touch with what was happening overseas as a member of the royal household during the golden age of Portugal, which embraced the reigns of Dom Manuel I (1495-1521) and Dom João III (1521-57). He had voyaged to the fort of São Jorge da Mina on the Guinea coast probably on an official tour of inspection, was treasurer concurrently of the Casa da India, Casa da Mina and Casa de Ceuta in Lisbon (1525-28) and long-serving factor of the Casa de Guiné e da India from 1533-67. As a recipient of a donatary captaincy in the Maranhão in Brazil, in 1535 and again in 1556 he organized colonizing expeditions which both failed. Didactic and epic, rich in detail and based on first-hand oral accounts and extensive documentation, his *Décadas da Asia* 'like an enormous radar screen, reflect the entire scope of Portuguese expansion from the Maranhão to the Moluccas'. [227] Treating the conquest, navigation, and commerce of Portuguese India, the *Décadas* range from Guinea to China and from the fourteenth century to 1538, although Barros clearly updated the manuscripts as new information became available. They were published in 1552, 1553, 1563, and 1615 respectively.

Portuguese missionaries alone generated an enormous literature: annual letters of the Jesuits; letters forwarded to Lisbon, Evora, and Coimbra by Jesuits in the field; correspondence to the general in Rome; chronicles and histories of religious orders and of the Society of Jesus. These are immensely valuable not only for missionary history but for the history of local leaders, politics, economies, societies and mores, although one should remind the reader that the authors did have a cause to plead and adhered fairly well to Francis Xavier's recommendation to his fellow Jesuits that such letters should be edifying. For example, Sebastião Gonçalves' (c. 1555-1619) history of the Jesuits in India includes descriptions of civil customs, dress, marriage practices, religious ceremonies, temples, gods, and even the caste system. What is remarkable is his high regard for the integrity of Brahmins. For China, there is the sixteenth-century account (Evora, 1569) of the Dominican Gaspar da Cruz based partly on his limited personal experiences of Canton which he complemented by using translations of Chinese state papers while drawing heavily on Galeote Pereira's account.[228] This does not prevent him from discussing craftsmen, dress of both sexes, food, and music which he appreciated. The letters of the Jesuits in Brazil give a broad view of the land, climate, crops, and people in the sixteenth century and relations between the Portuguese and Indians and Portuguese and French.[229] For sheer adventure and detailed description, it is difficult to better the Jesuit Jerónimo Lobo's robustly written *Itinerário* which first appeared in French (1728) published at The Hague and was translated into English by none other than Samuel Johnson and published (London 1735) under the title *A Voyage to Abyssinia, by Father Jerome Lobo, a Portuguese Jesuit.*[230]

There are other travel accounts by sea and land of which the liveliest must be Fernão Mendes Pinto's *Peregrinaçam* (1614). This is a long saga of arrivals and departures (often hasty), embarkations and disembarkations, shipwrecks, riding mules in Ethiopia or well-groomed horses in China, joining a merchant caravan in Persia, or sailing through the jungles of Sumatra. Although his truthfulness may be called into question, the text is full of action and movement. Solely maritime, most moving is the literature of shipwreck which tells of maritime disasters (which ran as high as 25 per cent) on the India run between 1550 and 1650. These were individual pamphlets sold in bookshops and were immensely popular, attributable in no small part to the realism of their descriptions which were written by the survivors themselves or as told to a contemporary who wrote them down. Not only do these illuminate the murkier corners of life on the *náos*, bluntly underscoring the stupidity or blind avarice which led to disaster but, since most of the wrecks ocurred off the coast of south-east Africa, they relate the long trek by the castaways to Sofala and the African peoples with whom they came in contact. A score of these were collected and published under the title *História Trágico-Marítima* in the 1730s.[231]

Accounts of the crossing of the Atlantic are less frequent. One such was the account authored by the Portuguese Jesuit Luís Lopes (1597-1676) who accompanied the 120-strong Azorean contingent from Ilha Terceira sent by King Philip IV to repel the Dutch. This left Ponta Delgada on the island of São Miguel on 25 July 1639 and cast anchor in Bahia on 18 September – a voyage of seventy-six days. Inevitably life on board in the Atlantic was not all that different from the Indian Ocean, but the author had a good eye and lively pen. Religion is prominent in his account with the round of vespers, sermons, confessions and mass. The religious hosted a 'moderate dinner' for the officers: this comprised seven courses with roast and boiled chicken and lamb, hams, sausages, cheese, fruits, an assortment of wines, and cakes and biscuits: 'Of all we ate with due sobriety'. The religious were reconcilers in a major argument and the Jesuit told of a soldier who was tied to the main mast for twenty-four hours for having robbed four *tostões* from a brother to gamble. Lopes sympathized with those soldiers whose accommodations below decks were intolerably hot. Recreation took the form of gambling, singing, dancing, and fishing for sharks and other fish. The Jesuit described the varieties of birds and fish, changing weather, and the problem of taking sightings. One incident was remarkable. Soldiers strung their dirty shirts from a line and trawled these through the water. Seeing the line break, one soldier plunged overboard to rescue his shirt and was not only falling behind the boat but was attacked by a small shark. The captain of infantry hurled a pike which hit the shark near the head and scared it off, enabling the soldier safely to get back to the vessel: 'And this throw by the captain was so successful because he had invoked the intercession of Our Lady of the Rosary.' A second soldier was brash enough to jump overboard to retrieve the pike floating on the water! A prayer was said in thanksgiving for saving the first from certain danger and for not punishing the second as his temerity merited. The shark was later hooked but escaped while being hoisted on deck. This was not the only miraculous occurrence. A lighted grain of powder fell into a powder flask but there was little damage.[232]

Albeit of a different genre, but no less nautical, were written sailing instructions. The classic of the genre was the *Esmeraldo de Situ Orbis* of Duarte Pacheco Pereira, which combines navigational with geographical, historical, and ethnographic observations for the West African coastline as far south as the river Gabon. More exclusively technical was the book drawn up by Francisco Rodrigues, pilot-major of the Portuguese armada which discovered the Bandas and Moluccas in 1512. This contains sailing instructions for the Red Sea, a routing from Malacca to Canton, rules to determine latitude, maps of coasts from Brazil to the Spice Islands, drawings and sketches, and tables of declination. We are well supplied with *roteiros* and *diários de navegação* for the *carreira da India*. The most famous was that made by Dom João de Castro who voyaged from Lisbon to Goa in 1538, and who also left rutters for his voyages from Goa to Diu and to the Red Sea. The earliest *roteiro* for Brazil dates from 1530-32 by Pero Lopes de Sousa who accompanied his brother Martim Afonso de Sousa. Dry reading are the rutters of those pilots who sailed against wind and current to provide a link between Maranhão and Pará on the north coast of Brazil and Rio Grande and Pernambuco. The 1615 account of pilot Manuel Gonçalves from Pernambuco to Maranhão blends the two genres of *roteiro* and *diário de navegação,* or on-board journal. More lively reading is José Gonçalves da Fonseca's account describing a voyage undertaken in 1749, at the express order of the king, by a fleet of canoes from Belém do Pará to Mato Grosso. The reader is carried up the Tocantins, into the main channel of the Amazon, past the mouth of the river Tapajós and the Ilha Tupinambaranas, as far as the Madeira. This river was the fluvial gateway to Mato Grosso which was finally reached in February 1750 by navigating the smaller river Guaporé after a voyage of exactly nine months between departure from Belém and arrival at the port of Pescaria. Portuguese townships and garrisons, Indian river communities, cultivated crops, fish and game, and Jesuit and Capuchin missionaries fill the pages of this first-hand account.[233]

The unofficial terrestrial travels of the Portuguese remain, for the most part untranslated into English. One exception is the admittedly dry account of Pedro Teixeira whose narrative of his journey from India to Italy is largely devoted to his crossing of the Arabian desert from Basra to Bagdad to Aleppo between 2 September 1604 and 12 February 1605. Already Teixeira had resided in Hormuz for some four years and had studied the language and history of Persia. Thus, when he returned in 1604, he was exceptionally well placed to be an informed observer on commerce, crops, topography, fauna, the politics and economics of caravans, caravanserais, and thefts and attacks. Teixeira was not enthused by the diet but, of one such meal, commented: 'But our great piece of civilization was that each had his own spoon.'

This was unusual in a land where it was common for a dozen Arabs to share a communal spoon. His youthful addiction to history was satisfied (at least for him) with his 'Chronicle of the Kings of Ormuz' and 'History of the Kings of Persia', both of which accompanied publication (Antwerp, 1610) of his account of his journey. Teixeira's account shares many points in common with those of his fellow overland travellers, both clerical and lay: detailed observation of people, mores, dress, commodity exchange and production, cities and buildings, modes of transportation, and topography. Surprising to the reader of such narratives (and possibly to the authors themselves) is how comparatively rare are those episodes where the traveller was the victim of hostility or placed in danger. In his travels from India to Portugal in 1663, Manuel Godinho, S.J., praised certain aspects of the lives of non-Christian peoples, notably the Persians, but could be harsh as in his description of yogis in Surat whom he characterized as 'devil's martyrs or even living devils'. A variant on accounts of journeys by individuals is the narrative by Miguel de Castanhoso of the well-equipped military expedition to Abyssinia by Dom Cristóvão da Gama and 400 Portuguese in 1541-43, which led to his death and that of the Turkish leader Imam Ahmad, but did oust the invaders from Ethiopia. Inevitably the campaign dominates the account, but there are interesting asides such as on the celebration of Easter and the description of hippos in the Blue Nile.[234]

Other Portuguese literary sources demonstrate a real effort on the part of laymen as well as clerics to come to some understanding of the economies, administration, and mores of places to which they were posted or where they resided. As soldiers, many showed an interest in military strategy, naval tactics and defences. Others focused on the commercial, as did Tomé Pires in the manuscript he wrote in Malacca and India between 1512 and 1515 prior to his ill-starred embassy to China. The *Suma Oriental*, based on personal observation and reports by others, was a survey of geography, history, and commerce from the Red Sea to Japan, a mine of ethnographical information, and the first description of Malaysia by a European. Galeote Pereira's account of his travails and travels through south China gives a remarkably accurate account of Chinese customs and institutions as recorded by a perceptive observer and a favourable assessment of Chinese justice. Substantially finished in 1516 but with additions over the next two years, was the *Livro das Coisas da India* authored by Duarte Barbosa. Duarte Barbosa made two voyages to India in 1500 and 1511, respectively. During his first residency of some five years he was an interpreter and translator in Cochim and Cananor, returning to Lisbon in 1506. When he returned to India in 1511 it was as chief scribe (*primeiro escrivão*) of the factory in Cananor. After his dismissal from this post by Albuquerque in 1513, he moved to Calicut until about 1520, returning to Cananor where he died in 1545. His *Livro*, which was first published in Italian (Venice, 1563) and became widely known in Europe, was based on notes made in India and during his passages to and from India. It was not a travel narrative but rather a remarkably accurate geographical and ethnographical account of peoples and regions, with emphasis on commodities and commerce, based on personal observation and on all the information that he could obtain. While especially good for Malabar, the *Livro* is a survey of peoples, land, and commerce from the Cape of Good Hope to China.

The iconography of the Portuguese experience is as rich as it is diverse, capturing all aspects of the Portuguese experience in Asia, Africa, and America as recorded in maps, statuary, architectural plans, screens, woodcuts, drawings, and paintings. Our purpose here is not to review this iconography but rather to single out those examples which take movement as their theme. Among the movers of empire, clearly pride of place went to the carracks and caravels. These are depicted on maps, such as that of Juan de la Cosa which shows Portuguese *caravelas latinas* off the west coast of Africa and Cape of Good Hope (1500). Latin caravels off the Costa da Mina appear on the 1516 atlas atributed to Pedro Reinel. A *caravela redonda* with four masts and a *latina* with three masts appear on the plan of the bar of Goa included in the first *Roteiro à Costa da India, de Goa até Diu*, by Dom João de Castro (1538). The *Lendas* of Gaspar Correia carry an illustration of four-masted *caravelas latinas* in sight of the port of Aden, and *caravelas redondas* off Jiddah and in Ceylon. The *Teatrum Orbis Terrarum* of Abraham Ortelius (1570) shows *caravelas latinas* in the Tagus, near the Costa da Mina, in the port of Arzila, and under construction in the shipyard of Goa, and a *caravela redonda* off the Azores. Caravels appear in the early sixteenth-century *Árvore Genealógica da Casa Real Portuguesa*

(British Library), in royal chronicles such as the *Crónica de El-Rei Dom Afonso Henriques* by Duarte Galvão (Biblioteca e Museu Castro Guimarães in Cascais), in the 'Livro das fortalezas de El-Rei Dom Manuel' of the early 16th century, as decorations for illuminated manuscripts, illustrations of chronicles, on coats of arms, and in paintings housed in the Madre de Deus in Lisbon. There are numerous depictions of fleets which sailed for India. One of the best sources is the lavishly illustrated manuscript 'Livro das Armadas', housed in the Academy of Sciences in Lisbon. One such illustration depicts the twelve *caravelas redondas* which sailed for India in 1533 under the command of Dom Pedro de Castelo Branco. The third part of the 'Livro de Lisuarte de Abreu', who sailed for India in 1558, is devoted to depictions of vessels of the *carreira da India* and includes the fleets of Vasco da Gama and Pedro Álvares Cabral. Manuel Fernandes, in his *Livro das Traças de Carpinteria* (1616), a construction manual, showed drawings of the hull, decks, helm, keel, stern post, and ribs of a caravel.[235] Rarely did professional mariners who travelled on such vessels make drawings of their impressions. One exception was the pilot Francisco Rodrigues. Of the drawings accompanying his *Book* (c.1513-14), twenty-four show outlines of beaches and mountains and mountains but forty-five show flora, people, and their houses, temples, village life, and volcanoes. These were made *en route* from Banda to Malacca.

What is no less intriguing is that the artists were drawn from different walks of life, of different levels of artistic competence, and of different nationalities and religions. Let us look at some examples. Early Portuguese contacts on the Bight of Benin, visits by Edo to São Jorge da Mina or São Tomé, and visits by Portuguese to Benin City, provided enough materials for local artists to depict the Portuguese, their mores, and their dress and weapons. Not dissimilar to the celebrations accorded the return of spirits from the dead by revivalist cargo cults in nineteenth-century Melanesia, because they came from across the sea and bore presents the Portuguese were accorded special status as messengers of the god of the sea, Olokun. The Portuguese were portrayed in the Benin bronzes and it has been asserted that the depiction of movement in such art was virtually restricted to depictions of foreigners. Certainly, the Portuguese are often portrayed on a horse or in the presence of horses. This also applied to foreigners depicted on the Bini-Portuguese ivory salt-cellars (c.1525-1600) from Nigeria.[236] For Japan, there is an invaluable illustrative record of the contact, and later periods, between East and West. The Namban screens continued to be produced even after the forced departure of the Portuguese in 1639. These screens prominently depict Portuguese vessels in the harbour of Nagasaki. There are acrobatic sailors in the rigging, missionaries, merchants, black slaves carrying lacquered boxes, or accompanying Persian horses, camels, and even elephants, and the procession from the ship headed by the captain-major on his way to make the formal offering to the local *daimyo* or even *xogun*. The great martyrdom of 1622, Portuguese prisoners on their way to being interrogated, the attack on Hara castle, and Jesuit martyrs, were also depicted by Japanese artists. Themes derived from the experience of the Portuguese overseas were widely disseminated and were reflected in other art forms, notably Flemish tapestries and even Persian carpets which depict Portuguese caravels.

Fascinating are the watercolours in a Portuguese codex of the sixteenth century preserved in Rome and known as the Codex Casanatense. These comprise seventy-six drawings, for the most part depicting people and customs from the Cape of Good Hope to the Persian Gulf, Bengal, Sumatra, Pegu, China, Malacca and the Banda islands. Labourers, washer women, Brahmins, war elephants, self-sacrifice, religious processions, priests and warriors make up this colourful ethnographic record by an eye-witness. For Brazil, there are the landscapes painted by the Dutch – notably Frans Post – in the seventeenth century, depicting land, peoples and the plantations of the north-east, but whose depiction of movement is limited to ox carts, slaves plodding along under burdens, and the occasional festivity of persons of African descent dancing in a village square or on a plantation. Few Portuguese artists were to depict the people of colonial Brazil and fewer still were to breathe any life into what are often formal portraits. Carlos Julião (1740-1811) has left a valuable illustrative record in watercolours of slaves in motion: vending, participating in religious festivals such as of Our Lady of the Rosary, playing musical instruments, and dancing. Taking up this legacy was the Lisbon-born Joaquim Cândido Guillobel who probably accompanied the royal court to Brazil and made some 180 post- card size drawings of blacks in Rio de Janeiro. These are portraits in movement: as vendors and domestic slaves, playing musical instruments, carrying sedan chairs, or leading horses. The nineteenth century was to witness an influx of professional and amateur artists into Brazil, notably French, English, and German, who captured in their paintings the human dynamic of Brazil.[237]

A poignant epilogue to this story of mobility is provided by the depictions and words of the votive offerings made by Portuguese to the Virgin and saints in thanks for miraculous salvation from certain disaster or for bringing them home safe and sound. Lighted candles, sung masses, paid sermons, participation in public processions, and even the building of chapels, were but some of the offerings promised for such protection. The illustrations, many crude, which are the visual expression of this deeply ingrained faith, are living testimony to faith in the miraculous and to the human ability to cope with adversity. Having been saved from certain death, many vowed never again to risk life or limb by land or sea. But this was one vow few could keep. The reader of these early accounts finds the same names occurring and reoccurring in that Portuguese human tide whose ebb and flow swept across the oceans and landmasses of the earth for five centuries.

This Lusitanian world in motion was to have an ineradicable impact on Europe, Asia, Africa, and America. The movement of commodities such as pepper, spices, and sugar, altered the diets of Europeans and their culinary habits. If there are cases where with reasonable confidence it can be asserted that the Portuguese were the first to introduce plants from one region of the world to another, there were other instances when, while lacking primacy, their action was important. The introduction of maize and cassava into West Africa was to have demographic repercussions. In fact, no single nation can rival the Portuguese for having altered, and improved, the diet of so many people by the transplantation of food crops and movement of agricultural products. The culinary implications in India and China of these transfers are as intriguing as they are difficult to attribute to the Portuguese alone. Less speculative are the accompanying instances of technology transfer from America to Africa in terms of processing crops, and from Africa to Brazil in terms of panning for gold and metallurgy. Whereas, for the most part, it was agricultural products which were carried by the Portuguese from Asia and Brazil to Europe, as regards tropical plants few of these passed through Lisbon. Rather, these were shipped by the Portuguese directly from India to Africa and to Brazil, and from Africa to Brazil. Albeit to a lesser degree, the Portuguese carried food products and spices from Brazil to Macao. Brazilian gold had a major impact on the flow of capital in Europe and may have laid the ground work for the Industrial Revolution. Gold, silver, and precious stones from Asia and Brazil not only provided indices for class distinctions and bolstered royal fortunes, but also brought about a transformation in the decorative arts. Cottons, silks, and other fabrics altered modes of dress. Brazilwood and its dye stimulated Flemish industry. In demographic terms, the Portuguese move into the interior of Brazil had a major impact on native American peoples but the greatest impact on the world's demographic history attributable to the Portuguese was the movement of several million persons of African origin to America.

Although it can not be claimed that the Portuguese 'discovered' Africa, Asia, or America, they did play a major role in bringing to the peoples of Europe, Africa, Asia, and America an awareness of each other. This occurred initially in the 'contact period' of European explorations. But what distinguishes the Portuguese from the Spanish, English, French, and Dutch, was that such initial contacts were nurtured into fruitful relationships over several centuries and that they were truly global in nature. The Portuguese altered how the peoples of the world saw themselves in the fifteenth, sixteenth, and seventeenth centuries and, by so doing, they contributed decisively to the formation of the modern world. One man epitomized this remarkable achievement. The man was Luís Vaz de Camões. Like so many of his contemporaries, he experienced the stormy passage of the Cape of Good Hope and shipwreck and the vicissitudes of the life of a soldier. Much of his own life is shrouded in mystery but he had first-hand knowledge of North Africa, the Persian Gulf and Red Sea, India, Indochina, and even the Moluccas. His masterpiece was the epic, Os Lusíadas (1572), a synthesis not only of rewards and hardships, hopes and doubts, illusions and disillusion, but an exaltation of first-hand experience ('longa experiencia') and optimism. Like its creator, the *Lusíadas* travelled far and wide in translation into European languages. Above all, the poem is redolent with force, vigour, and movement as it retells in verse the first voyage of Vasco da Gama to India. In his translation of 1655 Sir Richard Fanshawe captured this vision and energy:

> Thus went we opening those seas, which (save
> Our own) no Nation open'd ere before,
> Seeing those new Isles and clymates near which brave
> Prince Henry shewd unto the world before...
>
> Canto V, 4

CHRONOLOGY

1441	Nuno Tristão reaches Cabo Branco (Cape Blanc) in Mauretania
1445	Establishment of the factory at Arguim, first on the west coast of Africa.
1440s	Beginning of sugar-cane cultivation in Madeira
1450s	Portuguese reach Guinea and Sierra Leone
1452	'Discovery' of islands of Corvo and Flores in the Azores by Diogo de Teive
1452	Ethiopian envoy arrives in Lisbon
1452	18 June. Papal bull *Dum Diversas*
1455	8 January. Papal bull *Romanus Pontifex*
1456	13 March. Papal bull *Inter Caetera*
1450s	Introduction of sugar-cane into the Azores
c.1456	Sighting of the Cape Verdes
1460	Death of Prince Henry
1460s	Settlement of Cape Verde Islands
1460s	Portuguese reach Gulf of Guinea
1460s	Casa da Guiné e da Mina established in Lisbon
1470s	Portuguese cross the equator
1470s	Islands of São Tomé and Príncipe 'discovered' by the Portuguese
1472	Fernão do Pó reaches Bight of Biafra
1480s	Portuguese reach Timbuktu and Mali
1480s	Sugar cultivated in São Tomé
1481	Death of Dom Afonso V; accession of Dom João II
1482	Building of São Jorge da Mina fort on the Gold Coast
1482	River Congo reached by Diogo Cão
1482-3	Diogo Cão reaches 13° S (Cape Santa Maria)
1483/4	Columbus offers services to Dom João II, but is rejected
1485-86	Diogo Cão reaches 22° South (Walvis Bay)
1486	João Afonso de Aveiro received in Benin City.
1487-88	Bartolomeu Dias' expedition rounds the Cape of Good Hope.
1487-92	Pero de Covilhã's sea/overland journeys to west coast of India, Persian Gulf, and East Africa
1490s	Portuguese penetrate into interior of Congo.
1493	March. Columbus puts into Lisbon on return voyage from Antilles
1494	Treaty of Tordesillas
1495	Accession of Dom Manuel I
c.1495 -1500	João Fernandes Lavrador's and Pedro de Barcelos' landfall on Greenland
1497-9	Vasco da Gama's voyage to India. July 1497-May 1499.

1499-1502	Gaspar and Miguel Corte Real reach Newfoundland, Labrador, and Nova Scotia
1500	Pedro Álvares Cabral makes landfall on the coast of Brazil
1500	Madagascar 'discovered' by the Portuguese
1501	Casa da Guiné e India established in Lisbon
c. 1501	Portuguese fishing settlement in Newfoundland
1501/2	Ascension Island and Saint Helena reached by João da Nova's fleet
1502-1503	Second voyage of a fleet commanded by Vasco da Gama to East Africa and Malabar
1502	'Discovery' of Trindade
1502	Cantino world map
1502-3	Trading factories established in Pernambuco and Pôrto Seguro
1503	Building of a castle at Axim in Lower Guinea
1503	'Discovery' of Seychelles
1505	Forts at Sofala and Kilwa
1505	Factory in Ceylon (in Gale). Ended 1508
1506	Tristão da Cunha 'discovered'
1507	Fort built at Mozambique
1510	Capture of Goa by Afonso de Albuquerque
1511	Capture of Malacca by Afonso de Albuquerque
1511/12	Initiation of Portuguese trade from Malacca to the Bandas and Moluccas, 'a viagem das drogas'
1512	Installation of a Portuguese factory at Calicut
1513	Portuguese arrive in China
1513/14	Ethiopian embassy to Portugal
1513/15	João Dias de Solis reconnoitres Brazilian coast from Cabo Santo Agostinho to Río de la Plata; killed by Indians, 1515
1514-15	António Fernandes reaches present-day Zimbabwe and travels in kingdom of Monomotapa
1514	First Portuguese trade mission to China by Jorge Álvares
c. 1515	Introduction of the peanut into China
1515	First Portuguese missionaries arrive in Benin
1515	Capture of Hormuz by Afonso de Albuquerque
1516	Portuguese mission to Canton and Beijing headed by Tomé Pires leaves India
1518	Portuguese fort built in Colombo
1519	Fernão de Magalhães sets sail under the Castilian flag
1519	Fernão de Magalhaes and his crew given sugar-cane in the Bay of Guanabara
1520	Portuguese embassy headed by Rodrigo de Lima to the court of the Negus in Ethiopia

1520s	Attempted settlement on Cape Breton Island
1521	King of Tidor recognizes suzerainty of Spanish king Charles I; Spanish establish a factory, which is eliminated by Portuguese force in 1522
1521	Death of Dom Manuel I; accession of Dom João III
1522	António de Brito signs treaty of peace and commerce with queen of Ternate and builds a fort
1523	António Tenreiro crosses the Arabian desert from Aleppo to Basra
1524	Aleixo Garcia travels from Santa Catarina to the Inca empire.
1525	Estêvão Gomes explores American coast from Newfoundland to the Chesapeake in service of Castile
1529	Sack of Mombasa
1529	Charles V renounces rights to Moluccas
1530s/40s	Introduction of maize into China
1531	Martim Afonso de Sousa arrives in Brazil as lord proprietor of the hereditary captaincy of São Vicente
1533	Portuguese raze Bassein
1534	Dom João III grants hereditary captaincies in Brazil
1533/4	Martim Afonso de Sousa introduces large scale sugar cultivation in São Vicente
1536	Expedition of Aires da Cunha up the river Maranhão
1537	Ceding of Diu to the Portuguese.
1541	Francisco de Orellana travels from the Napo River down to the mouth of the Amazon
1541	Expeditionary force of Dom Cristóvão da Gama to Ethiopia
1542/43	Portuguese arrive in Japan
1542	First Jesuit missionaries arrive in Goa
1542-3	Portuguese pilot João Rodrigues Cabrilho, sailing under Castilian flag, reaches California and explores as far north as San Francisco Bay
1549	Francis Xavier, S.J., founds the Japan Mission
1549	Cessation of distribution of spices through the factory at Antwerp
1549	Governor-general takes up his post in Brazil
1552	Publication of the first volume of João de Barros' *Décadas*
1555-57	Extra-territorial rights granted to use Macao
1557	Death of Dom João III; accession of Dom Sebastião
1559	Annexation of Daman
1559	Embassy of Paulo Dias de Novais to Angola
1560s	Introduction of the sweet potato into China
1567	More permanent colonization of Newfoundland

1570s	Tupinambá travel from Pernambuco to the head-waters of the river Madeira
1571	Portuguese established in Nagasaki
1574	Confirmation of grant of Capitania da Terra Nova to Manuel Corte-Real
1576	Establishment of Luanda
1575	Abandonment of Ternate
1578	Death of Dom Sebastião at Alcácer Quibir
1582	Matteo Ricci arrives in Macao en route to Beijing
1587	*Tratado Descritivo do Brasil* of Gabriel Soares de Sousa
1587-98	Reign of terror in Japan with religious persecution
1580-1640	Union of the crowns of Portugal and Spain
1593	Work begun on Fort Jesus, Mombasa
1602-7	Bento de Góis, S.J., travels from Goa to Tibet and China, crossing the Himalayas
1603	Gaspar Pais, S.J., reaches Lake Tana in Ethiopia
1605	Dutch admiral Steven van der Hagan captures Ambon and Tidor
1606	Pedro Fernandes de Queirós 'discovers' the New Hebrides
1614	Publication of *Peregrinaçam* of Fernão Mendes Pinto
1617	Founding of Benguela by Portuguese in Angola
1618	Pero Pais, S.J., reaches the springs of the Blue Nile
1630-54	Dutch occupation of much of the north-east of Brazil
1630-34	Commercial mission from Macao to Japan headed by Dom Gonçalo de Silveira
1632	Beginning of persecution of Jesuits in Ethiopia
1637-38	Pedro Teixeira explores the Amazon from the Maranhão to Quito
1639	Japanese abolition of trade with Macao
1640	Edict expelling the Portuguese from Japan
1641	Fall of Malacca
1644	Gonçalo de Sequeira e Sousa sails from Lisbon as crown appointed ambassador to Japan
1648	Brazilian relief force expels Dutch from Angola
1648-51	António Raposo Tavares' major expedition to the Amazon basin from São Paulo
1650	Expulsion of Portuguese from Persian Gulf
1656	Death of Dom João IV; accession of Dom Afonso VI
1658	Fall of Ceylon
1663	Dutch capture of Portuguese settlements on the Malabar coast
1664-	Religious persecution of Christians in China
1674	Settlement at Manaus

226

1674	Fernão Dias Paes leaves São Paulo in search of emeralds
1680	Founding of Colônia do Sacramento on the Río de la Plata
1683	Death of Dom Afonso VI; accession of Dom Pedro II
1690s	Strikes of alluvial gold in Minas Gerais
1706	Accession of Dom João V
1718	Gold strikes in Cuiabá
1722	Bartolomeu Bueno da Silva travels from São Paulo to Cuiabá
1725	Gold strikes in Goiás
1734	Gold strikes on river Guaporé in Mato Grosso
1730s	Fluvial travel, the *monções*, from São Paulo to Mato Grosso.
1742	Martim Felix de Lima travels from Mato Grosso to Pará by water.
1750	Death of Dom João V; accession of Dom José I
1750s	Gold rush in Zambezia
1752	200 families from the Azores settle in Rio Grande do Sul
1759/60	Expulsion of Society of Jesus from Portugal and overseas territories
1763	Transfer of capital of Brazil from Salvador to Rio de Janeiro
1777	Death of Dom José I; accession of Dona Maria I. After 1791, her insanity led her son Dom João to govern in her name and, in 1799, formally act as prince-regent.
1807	Embarkation of the Portuguese court for Rio de Janeiro: arrives 1808

NOTES

For complete references, see Bibliography

[1] Succinct surveys of these explorations are: Diffie and Winius, *Foundations of the Portuguese Empire*, especially pp. 57-194; Marques, *History of Portugal*, vol. 1, pp. 145-51, 217-38; for Cão and Dias, see Axelson, *Congo to Cape* and Baião, *História da expansão portuguesa*, vol. 1, pp. 363-80.

[2] Boxer, *Fidalgos in the Far East*, p. 39; McIntyre, *Secret Discovery of Australia*, especially pp. 140-83.

[3] Ryder, *Benin and the Europeans*, pp. 29-32, 46-52; Blake, *Europeans in West Africa*, vol. 1, pp. 114-15; Tracey, *Antonio Fernandes Descobridor do Monomotapa*; Axelson, *South-East Africa*, pp. 137-48; Godlonton, 'The Journeys of Antonio Fernandes', reconstructs Fernandes' journeys differently from Tracey which was the basis for Axelson's account. Between 1510 and 1516, there are numerous references to payments of wages and maintenance of 6 *alqueires* of maize and cash to Fernandes, 'carpinteyro e lingoa desta fortalleza' (Vol. 4, p. 570), see *Documentos sobre os portugueses em Moçambique* vols. 2, 3, and 4; Lobato, *A expansão portuguesa em Moçambique*, vol. 3, p. 219.

⁴ The following account is based on Father Francisco Alvares, *Do Preste Joam das Indias. Verdadera informaçam das terras do Preste Joam* (Lisbon, 1540). I have used the revised English translation, Alvares, *The Prester John of the Indies*, vol. 2, ch. 104. This is a modern edition of the earlier translation and edition (1881) by Lord Stanley of Alderley. See also: Purchas, *Hakluytus Posthumus or Purchas His Pilgrimes*, vol. 7, chap. 5, pp. 1-226; *Asia de João de Barros*, 4 vols., 6th. ed., ed. Hernani Cidade (Lisbon: Agencia Geral das Colónias, 1945-46), *Década* 1, bk. 3, chap. 5. Gaspar Correa, *Lendas da India*. 4 vols. (Lisbon, 1858-64), vol. 3, pp. 28-30, has a slightly different version. For a summary, see Axelson, *South-East Africa*, pp. 23-30.

⁵ Alvares, *The Prester John*, chapter 74, pp. 278-79.

⁶ Rogers, *The Quest for Eastern Christians*, especially pp. 68-70, 86-88, 122-147; Baião, *História da expansão portuguesa*, vol. 2, pp. 273-84; Alvares, *The Prester John* for a full account, soon translated into Spanish, French, German, Italian. Bermudez' embroidered account (*Esta he hua breve relação da embaixada q o Patriarcha dõ Ioão Bermudez trouxe do Emperador da Ethiopia...*) of his mission was published in Lisbon in 1565. A translation is contained in *The Portuguese Embassy to Abyssinia in 1541-1543*. Trans. and ed. Whiteway, pp. 123-257. For commentary on the shortcomings of the 1625 translation in *Purchas His Pilgrimes* (vol. 7, chap. 7, pp. 310-78), the validity of his claim to have been appointed patriarch by the dying *abuna* Marcos at the insistence of Lebna Dengel and subsequent confirmation by Pope Paul lll, and Bermudez' papal appointment as patriarch of Alexandria, see Whiteway, pp. lxxxi-xciii.

⁷ Newitt, *Portuguese Settlement on the Zambesi*, pp. 34-38.

⁸ Boxer, *Fidalgos in the Far East*, p. 19.

⁹ A critical edition by Epiphanio da Silva Dias was published in Lisbon in 1905. References here are to the translation and edition of Kimble, *Esmeraldo de Situ Orbis by Duarte Pacheco Pereira*, chap. 27; see also appendices 1 and 2.

¹⁰ Alvares, *The Prester John*, vol. 1, p. 33.

¹¹ Marques, *History of Portugal*, vol. 1, pp. 133-39; Diffie and Winius, *Foundations of the Portuguese Empire*, pp. 113-43. Luís de Albuquerque has published extensively on all aspects of Portuguese navigation: a starting place is his *Introdução à historia dos descobrimentos* (Coimbra: Atlántida, 1962); Parry, *The Age of Reconnaissance*, pp. 53-113, is a comprehensive introduction to the topic. For Portuguese maps, see Armando Cortesão and A. C. Teixeira da Mota, *Portugaliae Monumenta Cartographica*. 6 vols. (Coimbra 1960-63).

¹² For a separation of the factual from the later imaginary travels, see Rogers, *The Travels of the Infante Dom Pedro of Portugal*.

¹³ Cortesão, *The Suma Oriental of Tomé Pires and The Book of Francisco Rodrigues*, vol. 1, p.lxxviii.

¹⁴ Diffie and Winius, *Foundations of the Portuguese Empire*, p. 363; Arasaratnam, *Merchants, Companies and Commerce on the Coromandel Coast*, pp. 114-15.

¹⁵ Whiteway, *The Portuguese Expedition to Abyssinia*, p. xxvi.

¹⁶ For these, and other examples, see Michael Cooper, S.J., ed., *They Came to Japan*; Gaspar da Cruz, *Tractado em que se cõtam muito por estẽso*

as cousas da China... (1569), ch. 10. I have used the translation of Boxer, *South China in the Sixteenth Century,* p.122.

[17] Gune, 'Source Material from the Goa Archives', especially pp. 22-23; Godinho, *Os descobrimentos e a economia mundial,* vol. 2, p. 526.

[18] Pearson, *Merchants and Rulers in Gujarat,* pp. 67-96.

[19] On this key points strategy and configuration of factories, forts, and trading rights, see Boxer, *Four Centuries of Portuguese Expansion,* pp. 14-16; Marques, *History of Portugal,* vol. 1, pp. 233-37. On forts, Boxer and Azevedo, *Fort Jesus and the Portuguese in Mombasa* and Lawrence, *Trade Castles and Forts of West Africa.* Such studies are sorely lacking for Brazil, where scholarly attention has been obsessed with religious baroque architecture. A distinguished exception is *Real Forte Príncipe da Beira.* Bilingual (English, Portuguese) text. Essay by José Maria de Souza Nunes; cartography and iconography by Isa Adonias (Rio de Janeiro: Spala Editora Ltda., 1985), describing the fort raised on the banks of the Guaporé river in the late eighteenth century.

[20] Boxer, 'Salvador Correia de Sá e Benevides' and, by the same author, *Golden Age of Brazil,* pp. 84-105.

[21] On Luso-Dutch rivalries and Portuguese decline in the East, see Boxer, *Portuguese Seaborne Empire,* pp. 106-49.

[22] Manchester, 'The Transfer of the Portuguese Court to Rio de Janeiro'.

[23] Steensgaard, 'The Return Cargoes of the *Carreira*', especially pp. 25-28; Boxer, 'The *Carreira da India*', especially pp. 34-42.

[24] Diffie and Winius, *Foundations of the Portuguese Empire,* pp. 118-19; Parry, *Age of Reconnaissance,* pp. 65-67; Denoix 'Caractéristiques des navires'; Fonseca, *A caravela portuguesa,* pp. 391-456. On the ship yard in Bahia, see Lapa, *A Bahia e a Carreira da India,* pp. 51-138.

[25] Godinho, *Os descobrimentos e a economia mundial,* vol. 2, pp. 174-75; Boxer, *Fidalgos in the Far East,* pp. 27-28; George B. Souza, *Survival of Empire,* p. 173.

[26] Godinho, *Os descobrimentos e a economia mundial,* vol. 2, pp. 77-78, 205; Disney, 'The Portuguese Empire', p. 152; Diffie and Winius, *Foundations of the Portuguese Empire,* pp. 373-74; Boxer, *The Great Ship from Amacon.*

[27] Boxer, *Portuguese Seaborne Empire,* pp. 224-227; Andrews, *Elizabethan Privateering,* pp. 133, 220-221; Boxer, 'English Shipping in the Brazil Trade' and 'Padre Antonio Vieira, S.J., and the Institution of the Brazil Company'; Winius, 'Two Lusitanian Variations on a Dutch Theme'; Disney, *Twilight of the Pepper Empire,* describes the antecedents, existence, and failure of the Portuguese India Company.

[28] Godinho, *Os descobrimentos e a economia mundial,* vol. 1, p. 189; vol. 2, pp. 226-34.

[29] This description is based on Marques, *History of Portugal,* vol. 1, pp. 342-43; Godinho, *Os descobrimentos e a economia mundial,* vol. 2, pp. 173-213; Pearson, *Merchants and Rulers,* pp. 36-39; Boxer, *Fidalgos in the Far East,* pp. 177-78; see Thomaz, 'Portuguese Sources on Sixteenth Century Indian Economic History', especially pp. 101-102. Godinho (vol. 2, p. 199) suggests that in the 1540s only 1/12th or 1/14 of clove production from the Moluccas rounded the Cape, and about 1/7th of mace and nutmeg from the Bandas.

[30] Mauro, *Le Portugal et l'Atlantique*, pp. 13-27; Boxer, *Golden Age of Brazil*, pp. 273-274.

[31] Mauro, *Le Portugal et l'Atlantique*, pp. 25-27, 70-74, 171; Pinto, *O ouro brasileiro*, pp. 133-85; Godinho, *Os descobrimentos e a economia mundial*, vol. 1, p. 22-23; vol. 2, p. 228.

[32] Boxer, *Fidalgos in the Far East*, pp. 15-16; for hazards, see accounts of three voyages between 1564 and 1620 translated in Boxer, *The Great Ship from Amacon*, pp. 309-15.

[33] Godinho, *Os descobrimentos e a economia mundial*, vol. 2, pp. 194-95.

[34] Duncan, *Atlantic Islands*; Matos, *Transportes e comunicações*, pp. 340-50; Vieira, *O Comércio inter-insular*; essays in *Os Açores e o Atlântico*; Boxer, *Fidalgos in the Far East*, pp. 177-78; Sutherland, 'Eastern Emporium and Company Town' for Makassar in the 18th. century, in Broeze, *Brides of the Sea*, especially pp. 98-114.

[35] Ryder, *Benin and the Europeans*, pp. 24 et seq.; *Voyages of Cadamosto*, ed. Crone, p. 34.

[36] Mathew, *Portuguese Trade*, pp. 146-49; Pearson, *Merchants and Rulers*, pp. 45-47; Chang, *Sino-Portuguese Trade*, pp. 69-72; Ptak, *Portugal in China*, pp. 29-39.

[37] Russell-Wood, 'Ports of Colonial Brazil', p. 217.

[38] Scammell, *World Encompassed*, p. 241; Braga, *Western Pioneers*; Carvalho e Rego, *Macau*, p. 8; Chang, *Sino-Portuguese Trade*, pp. 88-93; Boxer, *Christian Century in Japan*, pp. 100-101. The port cities of the Portuguese overseas have yet to receive from historians the attention they merit; see Mathew and Ahmad, *Emergence of Cochin*; Russell-Wood, 'Ports of Colonial Brazil'; Pearson, *Coastal Western India*, pp. 67-92. See also essays in Broeze, *Brides of the Sea*. Although focussing on a later period, the essays of S. Arasaratnam on Coromandel, Heather Sutherland on Makassar, and K. Dharmasena on Colombo are of interest to historians of the seventeenth and eighteenth centuries.

[39] Correia-Afonso, 'Manuel Godinho's Alternatives to the Carreira da India', pp. 84-89; Carruthers, *The Desert Route to India*; Furber, 'The Overland Route to India in the Seventeenth and Eighteenth Centuries'. For a survey of Portuguese overland travellers, 1560-1670, see Graça, *A visão do oriente*.

[40] Disney, 'The Portuguese Empire in India', p.152.

[41] Whiteway, *The Rise of Portuguese Power in India*, pp. 53-57; *The Travels of Pedro Teixeira*, trans. Sinclair.

[42] *Relação do novo caminho* (Lisbon, 1665) is now available in a superbly translated and annotated edition: *Intrepid Itinerant. Manuel Godinho and his Journey from India to Portugal in 1663*. Ed. Correia-Afonso.

[43] Newitt, *Portuguese Settlement on the Zambesi*, pp. 76, 312, et seq.

[44] Curtin, *Economic Change in Precolonial Africa*, pp.221-23; Miller, *Way of Death*, pp. 191-93, 649.

[45] Alfredo Ellis, 'O ciclo do muar'; Zemella, *O abastecimento da Capitania das Minas Gerais*, pp. 134-42; Myriam Ellis, *Contribuição ao estudo do abastecimento das áreas mineradoras*; Prado, *Colonial Background of Modern Brazil*, pp. 276-309, is an excellent survey of transportation and communications.

[46] Albeit for Portugal, see descriptions in Matos, *Transportes e comunicações*, pp. 357-75, 411-16.

[47] All modes are extensively illustrated in the paintings of Henry Chamberlain and Thomas Ender.

[48] Godinho, *Os descobrimentos e a economia mundial*, vol. 1, pp. 178, 180,181, 193, 196, 223-25; Davidson, *The Fortunate Isles*, pp. 12-13, 25; Pereira, *Esmeraldo de Situ Orbis*, chapters 26-32; see also the fascinating description of trade networks involving overland and fluvial transportation, in Harms, *River of Wealth, River of Sorrow*; on the Portuguese in the Bight of Benin, see Ryder, *Benin and the Europeans*, pp. 24-28; for Senegambia, see Curtin, *Economic Change*, pp. 84-85,95-100.

[49] Smith, 'The Canoe in West African History'; Harms, *River of Wealth, River of Sorrow*, pp. 48-50, 69; Curtin, *Economic Change*, p. 98, and plate 12; p. 113.

[50] Hemming, *Red Gold*, pp. 35, 225-26, 382-84; Boxer, *Golden Age of Brazil*, pp. 255, 273; Holanda, *Monções*, pp. 19-54.

[51] Boxer, *Tragic History of the Sea*, pp. 9-10; Steensgaard, 'Return Cargoes of the Carreira', pp. 26-28; Russell-Wood, 'Seamen Ashore and Afloat', and *Fidalgos and Philanthropists*, pp. 286-87.

[52] Marques, *History of Portugal*, vol. 1, pp. 166, 238-39, 246-48, 250, 340, 369, 379, 469; Boxer, *Portuguese Seaborne Empire*, pp. 52, 129; Godinho, *Os descobrimentos e a economia mundial*, vol. 2, p. 606; Boxer, *Four Centuries of Portuguese Expansion*, p. 20; Bender, *Angola under the Portuguese*, pp. 20, 63, n. 13; Newitt, *Portuguese Settlement on the Zambesi*, pp. 140-41; Boxer, *Fidalgos in the Far East*, pp. 49,143; G. B. Souza, *Survival of Empire*, pp. 31-33; Steensgaard, 'Return Cargoes of the Carreira', p. 28.

[53] Boxer, *Portuguese Seaborne Empire*, p. 104; Boxer, *Golden Age of Brazil*, p. 10; Marques, *History of Portugal*, vol. 1, p. 435-36; Prado, *Colonial Background*, pp. 25-89; Curtin, *Atlantic Slave Trade*, pp. 119, 216; Burns, *History of Brazil*, p. 103; for other population estimates, see Marcílio, 'Population of Colonial Brazil', pp. 37-63, and Alden, 'Population of Brazil'.

[54] Alden, *Royal Government in Colonial Brazil*, pp. 70-74; Boxer, *Golden Age of Brazil*, pp. 251-54; Russell-Wood, 'Female and Family', pp. 64-65; Bender, *Angola under the Portuguese*, p. 71.

[55] Dutra, 'Duarte Coelho Pereira'; Boxer, 'Jorge de Albuquerque Coelho'.

[56] Danvers, *Portuguese in India*, vol. 1, pp. 405-7, 418, 421-22, 435, 443, 452, 458, 460-67; vol. 2, p. 22. For a negative assessment, see Whiteway, *Rise of Portuguese Power*, pp. 279-90. For a condemning indictment of corruption in Portuguese India (based on first-hand experience from 1585-98), and constructive suggestions as to how this could be remedied, see the manuscript of Francisco Rodrigues Silveira published by A. de S. Costa Lobo under the title *Memórias de um Soldado da India compiladas de um manuscripto portuguez do Museu Britanico* (Lisbon: Imprensa Nacional, 1877; re-edition published by Imprensa Nacional-Casa da Moeda, 1987).

[57] Boxer, *Fidalgos in the Far East*, pp. 37-8; Danvers, *Portuguese in India*, vol. 1, pp. 383, 388-89, 411.

[58] Boxer, *Golden Age of Brazil*, pp. 205-6, 362-64, 368-69; Ferreira Martins, *Os vice-reis da India*.

[59] Boxer, *Salvador de Sá*; Mello, *João Fernandes Vieira*. A useful reference work is Henige, *Colonial Governors from the Fifteenth Century to the Present*, pp. 227-273; see Bardwell, 'The Governors of Portugal's South Atlantic Empire in the Seventeenth Century'.

[60] Varnhagen, *História geral do Brasil*, vol. 5, pp. 243-96; Alden, *Royal Government in Colonial Brazil*.

[61] Boxer, *Fidalgos in the Far East*, pp. 191-2,199-221.

[62] Schwartz, *Sovereignty and Society in Colonial Brazil*, pp. 280-313, 380-95.

[63] Cortesão, *The Suma Oriental*, vol. 1, pp. lxxviii-lxxxviii, and vol. 2, pp. 290-322.

[64] Boxer, *Tragic History of the Sea*, pp. 28-30 and *Golden Age of Brazil*, p. 201-2.

[65] Pereira, *Esmeraldo de Situ Orbis*, pp. xiii-xv.

[66] Pearson, *Coastal Western India*, p. 45; Russell-Wood, *Black Man in Slavery and Freedom*, pp. 83-94; Boxer, *Portuguese Seaborne Empire*, pp. 116-18, 296-303.

[67] Boxer, *Fidalgos in the Far East*, pp.183-88; introduction by da Cunha to Julião, *Riscos Illuminados*.

[68] Boxer, *Golden Age of Brazil*, pp. 365-67.

[69] Godinho, *Os descobrimentos e a economia mundial*, vol. 2, p. 526; Marques, *History of Portugal*, vol. 1, pp. 246-48, 376-77; Randles, *L' ancien royaume du Congo*, pp. 87-114; Boxer, *Portuguese Seaborne Empire*, pp. 100-101.

[70] Alvares, *Prester John of the Indies*.

[71] Ronald Smith, *The First Age of the Portuguese Embassies*; Mathew, 'Indian Merchants and the Portuguese Trade', pp. 2-6; Kulkarni, 'Portuguese in Deccan Politics'; Thomaz, 'Indian Merchant Communities in Malacca', especially pp. 57-62.

[72] Cortesão, *The Suma Oriental*, pp. xviii-lxiii; Boxer, *South China in the Sixteenth Century*, pp. xix-xxi and n. 2; Chang, *Sino-Portuguese Trade*, pp. 38-56.

[73] Boxer, *Fidalgos in the Far East*, pp. 105-7; *Christian Century in Japan*, pp. 383-89; *A Portuguese Embassy*.

[74] Silva Rego, ' The Monsoon Codices', pp. 58-62; Barbosa, *The Book of Duarte Barbosa*; Godinho, *Os descobrimentos e a economia mundial*, vol. 2, pp. 178-79.

[75] Silva Rego, 'The Monsoon Codices', p. 60; Fernandes, 'Augustinians in Goa', pp. 135-37; Boxer, *Portuguese Seaborne Empire*, pp. 123-24.

[76] Boxer, *Two Pioneers of Tropical Medicine*, pp. 7-9; Goodyear, 'Agents of Empire', pp. 93-100, 109-13; Russell-Wood, *Fidalgos and Philanthropists*, pp. 279-80.

[77] Simon, *Scientific Expeditions*, pp. 23-58.

[78] Fonseca, 'Bacharéis brasileiros'; Morais, *Estudantes da Universidade de Coimbra nascidos no Brasil*; Matos, *Les portugais à l'université de Paris*.

[79] Rui de Pina, *Chronica del Rei Dom João II*, chapter 2, translated by Blake, *Europeans in West Africa*, vol. 1, pp. 70-1. Prefabricated stones and

timber were also prepared for the proposed building of a fort at the mouth of the river Senegal in 1488, *idem* p. 84.

[80] Sampaio, *História da fundação da Cidade do Salvador*, pp. 178-81; Calmon, *História da fundação da Bahia*, pp. 123-31.

[81] Lapa, *A Bahia e a Carreira da India*, pp. 112, 114, 116, 121-29.

[82] Silva Rego, 'Monsoon Codices', p. 71.

[83] Boxer, *Fidalgos in the Far East*, pp. 174-75.

[84] Varnhagen, *Historia geral do Brasil*, vol. 5, pp. 296-305.

[85] Marques, *History of Portugal*, vol. 1, pp. 352-3; Borges, 'Jesuit Education in Goa', p. 159; Mundadan, 'Church and Missionary Works', pp. 13-15; Espinosa, 'Gouveia'; Wessels, *Early Jesuit travellers*.

[86] Boxer, *A Great Luso-Brazilian Figure*.

[87] Lobo, *Itinerário* and pp. xxi-xxiv by Beckingham.

[88] Ryder, *Benin and the Europeans*, pp. 71-72.

[89] Silva Rego, 'Monsoon Codices', pp. 69-71; Boxer, *South China in the Sixteenth Century*, pp. lviii-lxii, 47-239; Manrique, *Travels;* Collis, *Land of the Great Image*.

[90] Mundadan, 'Church and Missionary Works', pp. 9-13.

[91] Boxer, *Church Militant in Iberian Expansion*, pp. 2-30.

[92] Pearson, 'Corruption and Corsairs in Western India', pp. 19-22, and 'The People and Politics of Portuguese India', pp. 11-20; Steensgaard has characterized this situation as follows: 'Estado da India's bureaucracy must be regarded as one of the purest examples in history of constitutionally determined corruption', *Asian Trade Revolution*, pp. 93-94.

[93] Isaacman, *Mozambique*, pp. 59-60; Newitt, *Portuguese Settlement on the Zambesi*, pp. 79-84, 97-99; Randles, *The Empire of Monomotapa*, pp. 25-37.

[94] This is based on Boxer, *South China in the Sixteenth Century*, pp. li-lviii, 3-43, and appendix III.

[95] Teixeira, *The Travels of Pedro Teixeira*, and Ferguson's introduction.

[96] Godinho, *Os descobrimentos e a economia mundial*, vol. 1, pp. 425-26; Nowell, 'Aleixo Garcia and the White King'; Hanke, 'The Portuguese in Spanish America'; Keith, 'New World Interlopers'.

[97] An account by the Franciscan friar Gaspar de Carvajal is available in English translation: Medina, *The Discovery of the Amazon According to the Account of Friar Gaspar de Carvajal;* Edmundson, *Journal of the Travels and Labours of Father Samuel Fritz*.

[98] Edmundson, 'The Voyage of Pedro Teixeira on the Amazon'; Acuña, *Voyages and Discoveries in South America*. This was translated from the French translation of 1682. Markham characterized the translation as defective and himself published a version in his edited work *Expeditions into the Valley of the Amazons*, pp. 41-134; see also Hemming, *Red Gold*, pp. 219, 227-28, 230-37.

[99] Silva, *Memórias históricas e políticas*, vol. 1, pp. 452-56.

[100] Cross, 'Commerce and Orthodoxy', p. 151.

[101] Freehafer, 'Domingos Jorge Velho'; Cortesão, *Raposo Tavares;* Hemming, *Red Gold*, pp. 382-84; Cardozo, 'Last Adventure of Fernão Dias Pais'. For an overview with bibliography, see Morse, *The Bandeirantes*.

[102] Southey, *History of Brazil*, part 3, pp. 311-44.

¹⁰³ Ott, *Formação e evolução étnica*, vol. 1, pp. 46-48; vol. 2, pp. 202-11; Lapa, *A Bahia e a carreira da India*, p. 116; Carmo Azevedo, 'Interaction between Indian and Portuguese Art', p. 69.

¹⁰⁴ Bender, *Angola under the Portuguese*, pp. 59-94; Isaacman, *Mozambique*, p. 58; Alden, *Royal Government*, pp. 70-71, 436-37; Boxer, *Portuguese Society in the Tropics*, pp. 62, 119, 197-209.

¹⁰⁵ Russell-Wood, *Fidalgos and Philanthropists*, p. 243.

¹⁰⁶ Boxer, *Two Pioneers of Tropical Medicine*, p.11; Rui de Pina, *Chronica del Rey Dom João 11*, ch. 68, translated in Blake, *Europeans in West Africa*, vol. 1, pp. 86-87; Wiznitzer, *Jews in Colonial Brazil*; Hanke, 'The Portuguese in Spanish America'; Keith, 'New World Interlopers', especially pp. 366-68; Bender, *Angola under the Portuguese*, p. 62, note.

¹⁰⁷ Boxer, *Portuguese Seaborne Empire*, pp. 129-30; Bender, *Angola under the Portuguese*, p. 51; Scammell, *The World Encompassed*, p. 254; Davidson, *The Fortunate Isles*, p. 26.

¹⁰⁸ Boxer, *Tragic History of the Sea*, p. 20.

¹⁰⁹ Russell-Wood, 'Female and Family', pp. 62-4.

¹¹⁰ Russell-Wood, 'Female and Family', p. 63; Silva Rego, 'Monsoon Codices', p. 71; Hamilton, *A New Account of the East Indies*, vol. 2, p. 116.

¹¹¹ Klein, *The Middle Passage*, p. 37 and p. 48 note; for sexual imbalance for the nineteenth century traffic, see Eltis, *Economic Growth*, pp. 69-70, 170, 255-59; Russell-Wood, *Black Man in Slavery and Freedom*, pp. 111-13; Schwartz, *Sugar Plantations*, pp. 346-53; Goulart, *Escravidão africana no Brasil*, pp. 136-71.

¹¹² *Peregrinação* is available in the excellent English translation of Rebecca Catz; for a critical assessment of his travels, purported and otherwise, see Georg Schurhammer, *Fernão Mendes Pinto und seine 'Peregrinaçam'* (Leipzig, 1927) and Boxer, *Christian Century*, pp.18-27 and notes.

¹¹³ For a meticulously researched and moving account of this trade, see Miller, *Way of Death*, especially pp. 140-531; documents translated in Conrad, *Children of God's Fire*, pp. 15-28; Saunders, *A Social History of Black Slaves*, pp. 4-34; Godinho, *Os descobrimentos e a economia mundial*, vol. 2, pp. 520-76; Goulart, *Escravidão africana*, pp. 149-54, 164-66; Klein, *Middle Passage*, especially pp. 23-72; Conrad, *World of Sorrow*, pp. 25-55.

¹¹⁴ Butler, 'Mem de Sá'; Hemming, *Red Gold*, pp. 83-85, 210-15, 230-36. In 1654 those Indians who had sided with the Dutch were forced to flee, *idem*, pp. 310-11.

¹¹⁵ Simonsen, *História económica*, p. 214.

¹¹⁶ Hemming, *Red Gold*, pp. 97-118, 409-43; Boxer, *Golden Age of Brazil*, pp. 290-91; Azevedo, *Os Jesuitas no Grão-Pará*, pp. 228-30; Leite, *História da Companhia de Jesus*, vol. 4, pp. 138-40.

¹¹⁷ Antonil, *Cultura e opulencia*, part 3, ch. 5; Holanda, *Monções*; Hemming, *Red Gold*, pp. 384-401; Russell-Wood, 'Colonial Brazil', pp. 555-58; Davidson, 'How the Brazilian West Was Won'.

¹¹⁸ This is based on Prado, *The Colonial Background*, pp. 25-89. On the frontier, see Russell-Wood, 'Frontiers in Colonial Brazil', especially pp. 29-36; for a broader discussion, see Hennessy, *The Frontier in Latin American History*.

[119] Crosby, *Columbian Exchange*, pp. 122-64, 209; Russell-Wood, *Fidalgos and Philanthropists*, pp. 260-62; Curtin, 'Epidemiology and the Slave Trade'; Freyre, *Masters and the Slaves*, p. 475 n. 204; Pigafetta, *Le voyage et navigation*, chapter 109.

[120] Crosby, *Columbian Exchange*, pp. 35-63; Hemming, *Red Gold*, pp. 87, 122, 139-45, 148, 170, 198-216, 261-63, 274, 338-39, 444-46, 467-68, *inter alia*, and *Amazon Frontier*, p. 55.

[121] Godinho, *Os descobrimentos e a economia mundial*, vol. 1, pp. 323-24; vol. 2, pp. 230, 263-80; Sideri, *Trade and Power,* pp. 18-39; Marques, *Hansa e Portugal na Idade Média.*

[122] Godinho, *Os descobrimentos e a economia mundial*, vol. 1, p. 49; vol. 2, pp. 216-18.

[123] Godinho, *Os descobrimentos e a economia mundial*, vol. 2, pp. 280-95, 391-92, 489-501.

[124] Godinho, *Os descobrimentos e a economia mundial*, vol. 1, pp. 475-85; Curtin, *Atlantic Slave Trade,* pp. 17-21; Saunders, *A Social History of Black Slaves and Freedmen in Portugal*, pp. 19-25, 28-31.

[125] Godinho, *Os descobrimentos e a economia mundial*, vol. 1, pp. 514, 520-22; Mathew, *Portuguese Trade with India*, pp. 123-45; Pearson, *Merchants and Rulers in Gujarat*, p. 36.

[126] Godinho, *Os descobrimentos e a economia mundial*, vol. 1, pp. 514-34; vol.2, pp. 15-30.

[127] An inventory of cargoes of Brazil fleets arriving in Lisbon in 1749, is in Boxer, *Golden Age of Brazil*, pp. 351-53. Listing for the period 1796-1808 from Arruda, *O Brasil no comércio colonial*, pp. 612-16.

[128] Godinho, *Os descobrimentos e a economia mundial*, vol. 2, pp. 220-34; Sideri, *Trade and Power*, pp. 20-26; Arruda, *O Brasil no comércio colonial*, pp. 293-312, and table 49; Marques, 'Notas para a história da feitoria portuguesa na Flandres no século XV', and Corte Real, *A feitoria portuguesa na Andaluzia.*

[129] Godinho, *Os descobrimentos e a economia mundial*, vol. 1, pp. 178-79, 187, 333-34; vol. 2, pp. 216-19, 527; Ryder, *Benin and the Europeans*, pp. 37, 39-65. The first reference to Maldive cowries in the Guinea trade is 1515, but prior to this date shells were used as currency in Benin; see Ryder, *Benin and the Europeans*, pp. 60-61. For identification of Moroccan textiles, see Ricard, *Etudes sur l'histoire des portugais au Maroc*, pp. 81-114, and R. P. A. Dozy, *Dictionnaire détaillé des noms des vêtements chez les Arabes* (Amsterdam: Jean Müller,1845), pp. 383-86.

[130] Godinho, *Os descobrimentos e a economia mundial*, vol. 2, pp. 33-36; Mathew, *Portuguese Trade with India*, pp. 149-56.

[131] This commodity exchange is well described in Scammell, *The World Encompassed*, pp. 241-3; Boxer, *Fidalgos in the Far East*, especially pp. 5-7, 15-16; Godinho, *Os descobrimentos e a economia mundial*, vol. 2, pp. 177, 195, 200, 211; G. B. Souza, *Survival of Empire*, pp. 50-51.

[132] On organization, see Mathew, *Portuguese Trade with India*, pp. 78-112.

[133] Meilink-Roelofsz, *Asian Trade and European Influence*, pp. 136-72; Steensgaard has a lower opinion of Portuguese private trade in Asia than Meilink-Roelofsz. He also states that there is nothing to show that profits

derived from the Estado da India were transferred to Portugal and that the financial basis of the Estado was not the Cape Route but rather its own production and customs dues obtained in the Indian *alfândegas*, *Asian Trade Revolution*, pp. 81-95, especially pp. 88-89, 92-93 and n.106.

[134] G. B. Souza, *Survival of Empire*, pp. 48-58.

[135] Boxer, *Fidalgos in the Far East*, pp. 117-21. The 'country trade' is extensively discussed by G. B. Souza: for a balance sheet, see *Survival of Empire*, especially pp. 171-72.

[136] Godinho, *Os descobrimentos e a economia mundial*, vol. 2, pp. 191-92, 203-05, 208-10; G. B. Souza, *Survival of Empire*, pp. 63-86; Boxer, *Fidalgos in the Far East*, pp. 43-44, 132-38; Schurz, *Manila Galleon*, pp. 129-34, 138-42.

[137] Russell-Wood, 'As frotas de ouro do Brasil', and 'Colonial Brazil: The Gold Cycle, c. 1690-1750', especially pp. 589-93; Boxer, *Golden Age of Brazil*, pp. 58-60; see also Alden, *Royal Government in Colonial Brazil*, pp. 388-417.

[138] Ryder, *Benin and the Europeans*, pp. 34-37, 42-68; Lapa, *A Bahia e a carreira da India*, pp. 253-99; Canabrava, *O comércio português no Rio da Prata*, pp. 79-181; Alden, *Royal Government in Colonial Brazil*, pp. 67-69, 94; Brandão, *Dialogues*, p. 149.

[139] Boxer, *Golden Age of Brazil*, pp. 153-57 and 306; Lugar, 'Portuguese Tobacco Trade', pp. 37-41; Verger, *O fumo da Bahia* and his *Flux et reflux de la traite des nègres*, especially pp. 28-38.

[140] Dias, 'Impact of Tobacco', pp. 224-25.

[141] Godinho, *Os descobrimentos e a economia mundial*, vol. 1, pp. 163, 186-93, 203-43, 271-79 and *O 'Mediterraneo' saariano e as caravanas do ouro*; Randles, *The Empire of Monomotapa*, pp. 52-54, 79-80; Bovill, *Golden Trade of the Moors*, pp. 98-119.

[142] 1609 *memorial* in Boxer, *Christian Century in Japan*, pp. 425-27. From 1629-44, gold in China was worth 1:10 silver, but south of the Yangtze was 1:13, see G. B. Souza, *Survival of Empire*, pp. 53-58.

[143] On balance of payments, see Sideri, *Trade and Power*, especially pp. 45-55.

[144] Godinho, *Os descobrimentos e a economia mundial*, vol. 1, pp. 228-33, 387-89, 437-47; Boxer, *Golden Age of Brazil*, pp. 157-168.

[145] Habib, *Agrarian System of Mughal India*, pp. 392-94; Lipson, *Economic History of England*, vol. 2, pp. 277-82; Boxer, *Great Ship from Amacon*, p. 7.

[146] Russell-Wood, *Santa Casa*, pp. 159-72 and 'Participação religiosa nas consignações de ouro do Brasil para Portugal'; G. B. Souza, *Survival of Empire*, pp. 27-29. See also Mathew, 'Church Economics in the 16th Century Goa'; Alden, 'Economic Aspects of the Expulsion of the Jesuits', especially pp. 26-30.

[147] Vavilov, 'Origin, Variation, Immunity', pp. 36, 37.

[148] Only in 1872 was a second edition of the *Colóquios* published by the Imprensa Nacional, Lisbon. A facsimile of the first edition was published by the Academia das Ciências (Lisbon, 1963). See Boxer, *Two Pioneers of Tropical Medicine*, especially 27-28 on da Costa. An English translation was made by Markham, *Colloquies on the Simples and Drugs of India*. In a

1909 lecture in Goa, Pinto lamented that d'Orta's contribution had been largely unrecognized and that only with British scientists in the nineteenth century had the wealth of medicinal plants in India been appreciated by Europeans, 'Plantas medicinaes'.

[149] Carreira, *The People of the Cape Verde Islands*, p. 8.

[150] Lapa, *O Brasil e as drogas do Oriente*, pp. 7-15, *passim*, the best introduction to this subject; *Diálogos das grandezas do Brasil*, p. 160 *passim*. See also Duarte Ribeiro de Macedo, *Observação sobre a transplantação dos frutos da India ao Brasil* (Paris, 1675) and *Obras inéditas de Duarte Ribeiro de Macedo*. By A. L. Caminha (Lisbon: Impressão Regia, 1817); Bernardino António Gomes, *Memória sobre a canella do Rio de Janeiro offerecida ao Príncipe do Brazil nosso senhor pelo Senado da Camara da mesma cidade no anno de 1798* (Rio de Janeiro: Impressão Régia, c. 1809). This had been commissioned by the Senado da Câmara of Rio de Janeiro.

[151] Lapa, *O Brasil*, pp. 19-22, 27-32.

[152] Linschoten, *The Voyage of John Huyghen van Linschoten to the East Indies*, vol. 1, p. 187; Borges, 'Jesuit Education in Goa', pp. 159, 164 n. 36; Boxer, *Golden Age of Brazil*, p. 291; Leite, *História da Companhia de Jesus no Brasil*, vol. 4, pp. 153-61, vol. 5, p. 161.

[153] Pannikar, *Asia and Western Dominance*, p. 21; Watson, *Agricultural Innovation*.

[154] Vavilov, ' Origin, Variation, Immunity', especially pp.16-45. I have relied on Vavilov's identification of places of origin in the following discussion.

[155] Ridley, *Dispersal of Plants*, especially pp. 628-659.

[156] These routes are clearly described, with maps, in Godinho, *Os descobrimentos e a economia mundial*, vol. 1, pp. 69-83 and 328; vol. 2, p. 376. See also Crosby, *Columbian Exchange*, pp. 188-89. See also *The Voyages of Cadamosto*, ed. Crone, pp. 16-18, 21-22, 25. On trans-Saharan caravan routes, see Murdock, *Africa*, pp. 16-133, map 12, and bibliographies.

[157] Sauer, *Agricultural Origins and Dispersals*, pp. 24-33, 34-36, 40-61; Murdock, *Africa.*, p. 19; Watson, *Agricultural Innovation*, pp. 77-84.

[158] Godinho, *Os descobrimentos e a economia mundial*, vol. 2, pp. 419-78; Hobhouse, *Seeds of Change*, pp. 41-89. See also Rau and Macedo, *O açúcar da Madeira*, pp. 9-43, and Schwartz, *Sugar Plantations in the Formation of Brazilian Society*, pp. 3-27, and extensive bibliography.

[159] Ridley, *Dispersal of Plants*, p. 681.

[160] Williams, *Agronomy of the Major Tropical Crops*, p. 84; Boxer, *Golden Age of Brazil*, p. 291.

[161] For different hypotheses, see: Sauer, *Agricultural Origins and Dispersals*, p. 27; Vavilov, 'Origin, Variation, Immunity', pp. 28, 30; Williams, *Agronomy of the Major Tropical Crops*, p.156; Burkill, *A Dictionary*, vol. 1, pp. 598-99; Godinho, *Os descobrimentos e a economia mundial*, vol. 2, p. 395; Verrill, *Foods America Gave the World*, pp. 111-12. Ridley, *The Dispersal of Plants*, p. 321, is alone in suggesting an American origin in Costa Rica or Panama.

[162] Sauer, *Agricultural Origins and Dispersals*, pp. 26, 34; Vavilov, 'Origin, Variation, Immunity', pp. 27, 29.

[163] Jones, *Manioc in Africa*, p. 71; Murdock, *Africa*, pp. 22-24, and regional surveys on pp. 153-55, 182-83, 206-8, and 234-35. On yams, oil palms and cotton as indigenous to the 'Sudanic complex', see pp. 69-70; also Harlan, *Origins*.

[164] Sauer, *Agricultural Origins and Dispersals*, pp. 26, 34-35; Burkill, *A Dictionary*, vol. 1, pp. 814-815; Murdock, *Africa*, p. 222.

[165] Jones, *Manioc in Africa*, p. 71; Watson, *Agricultural Innovation*, pp. 51-54.

[166] Burkill, *A Dictionary*, vol. 1, pp. 893-900; Williams, *The Agronomy of the Major Tropical Crops*, p. 167; a comprehensive study is C. W. S. Hartley, *The Oil Palm*. (London: Longmans, 1967); Wilson, ed., *New Crops for the New World*, pp. 61-79.

[167] Boxer, *Portuguese Seaborne Empire*, p. 121.

[168] Lapa, *O Brasil*, pp. 14, 23; Godinho, *Os descobrimentos e a economia mundial*, vol. 2, p. 395.

[169] Burkill, *A Dictionary*, vol. 2, p. 1404; Wilson, *New Crops for the New World*, pp. 10-11; Lapa, *O Brasil*, pp. 38-39; Watson, *Agricultural Innovation*, pp. 72-73.

[170] Vavilov, 'Origin, Variation, Immunity', p. 43.

[171] Crosby, *Columbian Exchange*, pp. 185-87; for a listing, without date of introduction, of American species that have become established in Africa, see Murdock, *Africa*, pp. 234-35.

[172] Burkill, *A Dictionary*, vol. 1, pp. 65-66.

[173] Jones, *Manioc in Africa*, p. 74; Crosby, *Columbian Exchange*, p. 179; Marques, *History of Portugal*, vol. 1, p. 272.

[174] Godinho, *Os descobrimentos e a economia mundial*, vol. 2, pp. 362-80; Alvares, *The Prester John of the Indies*, vol. 1, pp. 69 and 136, n. 1.; Wright, 'Maize Names', especially pp. 64-66; Muratori, 'Maize Names'; Boxer, 'Maize Names'; Crosby, *Columbian Exchange*, p. 186. Randles places maize introduction into the Zambezi only in the eighteenth century, *The Empire of Monomotapa*, p. 491. A good introduction to the debate is Miracle, *Maize in Tropical Africa*, pp. 87-100. See also Portères, 'L'introduction du maïs'; Willett, 'The Introduction of Maize'; and Miracle, 'Interpretation of Evidence'. Negating introduction by the Portuguese is Jeffreys, 'How Ancient is West African Maize?'.

[175] Jones, *Manioc in Africa*, p. 28; Godinho, *Os Descobrimentos e a economia mundial*, vol. 2, p. 386.

[176] Cardim, 'A Treatise of Brazil, written by a Portugal which had long lived there', pp. 474-75; for a biographical sketch of this accurate observer, see Espinosa, 'Fernão Cardim, Jesuit Humanist of Colonial Brazil'. For a seventeenth-century eulogy on manioc, see Brandão, *Dialogues*: dialogue 4, pp. 193-98.

[177] Jones, *Manioc in Africa*, pp. 11-17; Crosby, *Columbian Exchange*, pp. 173-74.

[178] Burkill, *A Dictionary*, vol. 2, pp. 1411-13; Jones, *Manioc in Africa*, pp. 31-33, 60-87; Crosby, *Columbian Exchange*, pp. 187-88.

[179] Burkill, *A Dictionary*, vol. 1, pp. 205-7.

[180] Ho, *Studies on the Population of China*, pp. 142-43, 145,147, 149-50,184-89, and 'Introduction of American Food Plants into China'.

[181] Habib, *Agrarian System of Mughal India*, pp. 46-47 and note 83; Andrews, *Peppers*, pp. 5-8.

[182] Habib, *Agrarian System of Mughal India*, p. 50 and note 107, and p. 56; Burkill, *A Dictionary*, vol. 2, pp. 1815-16. Saldanha, 'Plantas exoticas', lists some 45 plants introduced into India by the Portuguese from the Americas, Portugal, Arabia, Mozambique, Malacca, and China.

[183] Habib, *Agrarian System of Mughal India*, p. 38 and note 34; Crosby, *Columbian Exchange*, pp. 192,194-202. Murdock, noting that among the 17 major crops in India, 5 are of African origin – castor, cotton, pearl millet, sesame, and sorghum – observes: 'we cannot escape the conclusion that western India owes its agricultural civilization very largely to importations from Negro Africa', *Africa*, p. 207. These pre-dated the arrival of the Portuguese in the Indian Ocean.

[184] Sauer, *Agricultural Origins*, p. 44; Vavilov, 'Origin, Variation, Immunity', p. 43; Burkill, *A Dictionary*, vol. 2, pp. 148-49; Habib, *Agrarian System of Mughal India*, p. 50, note 101.

[185] Williams, *The Agronomy of the Major Tropical Crops*, p. 97; Burkill, *A Dictionary*, vol. 2, pp. 2147-50; Alden, 'The Significance of Cacao Production in the Amazon Region During the Late Colonial Period'.

[186] Weinstein, *Amazon Rubber Boom*, pp. 8-13; Burkill, *A Dictionary*, vol. 1, pp. 1143-62; Hemming, *Red Gold*, p. 434, and his *Amazon Frontier*, pp. 271-314, in which he concludes that, because the bulk of labour was done by immigrants, the impact of the rubber boom on the indigenous populations was 'not as catastrophic...as might have been expected' (p. 313).

[187] Vavilov, 'Origin, Variation, Immunity', pp. 28, 31; Hobhouse, *Seeds of Change*, p. 142; Burkill, *A Dictionary*, vol. 1, pp. 1106-8.

[188] Vavilov, 'Origin, Variation, Immunity', p. 42; Burkill, *A Dictionary*, vol. 2, pp. 1551-55; Dias, 'Impact of Tobacco on Goa'; Antonil, *Cultura e opulencia do Brasil*, part 2, chap. 1. Antonil stated that its cultivation started in Bahia about a century earlier.

[189] Dias, 'Impact of Tobacco on Goa', p. 222; Habib, *Agrarian System of Mughal India,* pp. 45-46 and notes, p. 94.

[190] Pinto, *Biombos Namban*, p. 14, and illustrations.

[191] Burkill, *A Dictionary*, vol. 1, pp. 143-46, 330-32; vol. 2, pp. 1675-77.

[192] Crosby, *Columbian Exchange*, pp. 165-207.

[193] Simon, *Scientific Expeditions in the Portuguese Overseas Empire*; Ferreira, *Viagem filosófica às capitanias do Grão-Pará, Rio Negro, Mato Grosso e Cuiabá*; Boxer, *Portuguese Seaborne Empire*, p. 198. The results of the Russian expedition to Brazil under botanist Georg Heinrich Langsdorff were still being prepared for publication 150 years later. See Barman, 'The Forgotten Journey'.

[194] Cardim, 'A Treatise' p. 475; Jones, *Manioc in Africa*, pp. 11-15, 28-31; Godinho, *Os descobrimentos e a economia mundial*, vol. 2, p. 388.

[195] Examples in Boxer, *Two Pioneers of Tropical Medicine*, pp. 15-18; Borges, 'Jesuit Education', p. 158; Cardim, 'A Treatise'.

[196] Boxer, *Portuguese Seaborne Empire*, p. 121; Crosby, *Columbian Exchange*, p. 78.

[197] Morison, *European Discovery of America. The Northern Voyages*,

pp. 480, 575-77.

[198] For a commentary on Diogo do Couto's account in *Década* 12, book 4, chapter 13, see *The Travels of Pedro Teixeira*, introduction and notes by Ferguson, pp. lxviii-lxxv.

[199] Antonil, *Cultura e opulencia*, part 4; Poppino, 'Cattle Industry in Colonial Brazil'.

[200] Boorstin, *The Discoverers*, pp. 196-98.

[201] Ryder, *Benin and the Europeans*, p. 41; Pinto, *Biombos Namban*, pp. 36, 37, 38, 40, 42, 50, 51, 64, 65, 66, *inter alia*.

[202] Rego, 'The Monsoon Codices at the National Archives of the Torre do Tombo', pp. 68-69; Mathew, *Portuguese Trade with India*, p. 137; Simon, *Scientific Expeditions*, p. 82.

[203] Smith, 'Nossa Senhora da Conceição da Praia and the Joanine Style in Brazil', and his *The Art of Portugal*.

[204] Carmo Azevedo, 'Interraction between Indian and Portuguese Art'; Varadarajan, 'Indian Textiles in Portuguese Collections', p. 132 *passim*.

[205] Rego, 'The Monsoon Codices', p. 68; Carmo Azevedo, 'Interaction between Indian and Portuguese Art', pp. 69-71.

[206] Balandier, *Daily Life in the Kingdom of the Congo*, and Randles, *L' Ancien Royaume du Congo*; Boxer, 'Some Aspects', pp. 51-53.

[207] Dias, 'Impact of Tobacco on Goa', p. 223; Chodankar, 'Hindu, Christian and Muslim Jewellery in Goa', especially pp. 90-92.

[208] Barros, 'Influence of Foreign Languages', p.167.

[209] Barros, 'Influence of Foreign Languages', pp. 165-67; Boxer, 'Some Aspects of Portuguese Influence in Japan', especially pp. 55-58; *Four Centuries of Portuguese Expansion*, pp. 56-7; and *Portuguese Seaborne Empire*, pp. 126-27; Goonatilleka, 'A Portuguese Creole in Sri Lanka', pp. 147-51. An excellent survey is Lopes, *A expansão da língua portuguesa no oriente*.

[210] Graciete Nogueira Batalha, *Dialeto de Macau*, cited by Carmo Azevedo, 'Interaction between Indian and Portuguese Art', p. 72; Goonatilleka, 'A Portuguese Creole in Sri Lanka', p. 148; Barros, 'Influence of Foreign Languages', p. 165.

[211] Professor J. G. A. Pocock has brought to my attention that, in their transcriptions from Mandarin, French Jesuits of the seventeenth century were following a system established by the Portuguese.

[212] Mascarenhas, 'Impact of the West on Goan Music', pp. 191-97.

[213] Alvarez, *Narrative of the Portuguese Embassy*, pp. v-vi.

[214] Goodyear, 'Agents of Empire', pp. 95-114.

[215] Mendes Correia, 'Influência da expansão ultramarina no progresso científico' in Baião, *História da expansão portuguesa*, vol. 3, pp. 467-76.

[216] *Documenta Indica*, vol. 3, doc. 89, cited by Borges, 'Jesuit Education in Goa', p. 155; Russell-Wood, *Fidalgos and Philanthropists*, pp. 71, 329; Boxer, *Christian Century in Japan*, pp. 205-6, 222-26; Baião, *Expansão portuguesa no mundo*, vol. 3, p. 462.

[217] Spence, *The Memory Palace of Matteo Ricci*.

[218] Boxer, *Church Militant*, pp. 51-52.

[219] Marques, *History of Portugal*, vol. 1, pp. 350-51. For Japan, see Boxer, *Christian Century*, pp. 77-78, 320-21, and his *Church Militant*, pp. 94-112.

[220] Mrs Kindersley, *Letters from the Island of Teneriffe, Brazil, the Cape*

of Good Hope, and the East Indies (London, 1777), p. 50; Russell-Wood, *Black Man in Slavery and Freedom*, pp. 128-60.

[221] Brandon, *New Worlds for Old*; Keen, *The Aztec Image*, pp. 71-309.

[222] For a remarkable example of European influence on Japanese art, see the detail of a Namban screen reproduced in Baião, *História da expansão portuguesa*, vol. 2, opposite p. 168.

[223] Boxer, 'Some Aspects of Portuguese Influence in Japan', especially pp. 21-47; Boxer, *Church Militant*, pp. 41-45; G.B. Souza, *Survival of Empire*, pp. 48, 53; Bowers, *Western Medical Pioneers*, pp. 11-16.

[224] Fonseca, 'Bacharéis brasileiros', especially pp. 113-15.

[225] Excellent syntheses are Burns, 'The Intellectuals as Agents of Change'; Maxwell, 'The Generation of the 1790s'. See also Cruz Costa, *A History of Ideas in Brazil*, especially pp. 26-43 and Mattoso, *Presença francesa*.

[226] The focus of this study is on movement rather than the literature of the Portuguese overseas. For a broader perspective, see Cidade, *A literatura portuguesa e a expansão ultramarina*. See Michael Teague, *In the Wake of the Portuguese Navigators. A Photographic Essay* (Manchester and Lisbon: Carcanet Press and Quetzal Editores, 1988).

[227] Boxer, *João de Barros*, especially pp. 97-129, quotation from p. 99; Boxer, 'Three Historians of Portuguese Asia'; Harrison, 'Five Portuguese Historians'; MacGregor, 'Some Aspects of Portuguese Historical Writing'. See Boxer, *South China in the Sixteenth Century*, pp. 42-239.

[228] Mundahan, 'Church and Missionary Works', pp. 5-9.

[229] Burns, 'The Sixteenth Century Jesuit Letters of Brazil'; the basic published source is Serafim Leite S.J., *Monumenta Brasiliae*. 4 vols (Rome, 1956-60); for India, see António da Silva Rego, ed., *Documentação para a história das missões do padroado português do Oriente. India* (Lisbon, 1947-) and Joseph Wicki, S.J., ed., *Documenta Indica* (Monumenta Historica Societatis Jesu: Rome, 1948-88); for Indonesia, Artur Basílio de Sá, ed., *Documentação para a história das missões do padroado portugues do Oriente. Insulindia*. 5 vols. (Lisbon, 1954-58); and for the Moluccas, Hubert Th. Jacobs, S.J., *Documenta Malucensia* (Monumenta Historica Societatis Jesu: Rome, 1974-).

[230] *The Itinerario of Jeronimo Lobo.* Translated by Donald M. Lockhart.

[231] Six of these have been translated by Boxer, *Tragic History of the Sea* and *Further Selections from the Tragic History of the Sea.*

[232] Mauro, *Le Brésil au XVII siècle*, pp. 13-68.

[233] *O Livro de Francisco Rodrigues*, translated by Armando Cortesão together with the *Suma Oriental* of Tomé Pires; Boxer, 'Portuguese Rutters, 1500-1700'; Humberto Leitão, ed., *Dois roteiros do século XVI, de Manuel Monteiro e Gaspar Ferreira Reimão atribuidos a João Baptista Lavanha*; Henrique Quirino da Fonseca, ed., *Diários de navegação da Carreira da India nos anos de 1595, 1596,1597, 1600 e 1613*; Mauro, *Le Brésil au XVIIe siècle*, pp. 71-104, 111-20. Gonçalves da Fonseca's 'Navegação feita da cidade do Grão-Pará até à bôca do Rio da Madeira pela escolta que por êste rio subio às minas de Mato-Grosso....' was published under a slightly different title by Candido Mendes de Almeida in his *Memorias do Maranhão*. It was translated into English as 'Voyage Made

from the City of the Gram Para to the Mouth of the River Madeira by the Expedition which Ascended This River to the Mines of Mato Grosso....'

[234] For a comprehensive survey of overland travellers see Graça, *A visão do oriente.*

[235] Fonseca, *A Caravela portuguesa*, pp. 406-22, 491-511, and numerous illustrations.

[236] Cole, *Icons*, pp. 142-48, and figure 167; Bassani and Fagg, *Africa and the Renaissance*, p. 150 and illustrations nos. 191, 247-52 and Catalogue raisonné, nos. 119,120,123,124.

[237] This codex has been published under the title *Imagens do oriente no século XVI*; Larsen, *Frans Post*; Julião, *Riscos iluminados*; *Guillobel.*

BIBLIOGRAPHY

With some distinguished exceptions, monographs on the Portuguese world have tended to fragment this achievement, which was truly global and spanned more than five centuries, by focusing either on individual continents, regions, or specific periods. It is ironical that, in dealing with the Portuguese whose own activities were so markedly intercontinental and inter-oceanic, scholars have not exhibited the same broad view as characterized their subjects. If João de Barros brought to his *Décadas* a perspective which would sit well with present advocates of World History, his example has only rarely been followed. The result has been monographs on the Portuguese in India, in Africa, in Japan and in America. Indo-Portuguese and Indian Ocean history have come into their own as fields of scholarly endeavour and this initiative has been institutionalized

244

by the International Seminar of Indo-Portuguese History and the establishment of the Xavier Centre of Historical Research in Goa. Even with the very welcome surge in seeing the Atlantic and the Indian Oceans as entities worthy of scholarly attention, few scholars have shown a willingness to pass from one ocean to another. There remains the critical necessity for scholars of the different regions and periods of Portuguese history to meet, exchange ideas, suggest comparisons, and contribute their tessera to the mosaic which was, and is, the Portuguese-speaking world.

One such work of synthesis is *The Portuguese Seaborne Empire, 1415-1825* by Charles R. Boxer who may justly be regarded as the dean of scholarship on an empire ranging from the Moluccas to Mato Grosso. With a heavy economic focus, the magisterial study of the Portuguese historian Vitorino Magalhães Godinho, *Os descobrimentos e a economia mundial,* is an indispensable source integrating the Portuguese role into a global system of commerce from the fifteenth to the seventeenth centuries. Bailey W. Diffie and George D. Winius, *Foundations of the Portuguese Empire, 1415-1580,* is a chronological survey of the discoveries, with discussion of thorny historical issues and myths, and an analysis emphasizing political and military aspects of the Estado da India ranging from East Africa to Indonesia and treatment of the 'peripheries', namely China and Japan. The bibliography is exhaustive. For bibliography on Portuguese America, the reader is referred to Francis Dutra, *A Guide to the History of Brazil, 1500-1822. A Guide to the Literature in English.*

Books and Articles Cited

Acuña, Cristoval de, *Voyages and Discoveries in South America, the First Up the River of Amazons to Quito in Peru, and Back Again to Brazil* (London: C. Buckley, 1698).

Akinjogbin, I. A., *Dahomey and its Neighbours, 1708-1818* (Cambridge: Cambridge University Press, 1967).

Alden, Dauril, 'Economic Aspects of the Expulsion of the Jesuits from Brazil: A Preliminary Report', in H. H. Keith and S. F. Edwards, eds., *Conflict and Continuity in Brazilian Society* (Columbia: University of South Carolina Press, 1969), pp. 25-65.

Alden, Dauril, 'The Population of Brazil in the Late Eighteenth Century: A Preliminary Survey', *The Hispanic American Historical Review,*

43:2 (May 1963), 173-205.

Alden, Dauril, 'The Significance of Cacao Production in the Amazon Region During the Late Colonial Period', *Proceedings of the American Philosophical Society*, 120:2 (1976), 103-35.

Alden, Dauril, *Royal Government in Colonial Brazil* (Berkeley and Los Angeles: University of California Press, 1984).

Álvares, Francisco, *The Prester John of the Indies. A True Relation of the Lands of the Prester John*. Translation of Lord Stanley of Alderley, revised and edited by C. F. Beckingham and G. W. B. Huntingford. 2 vols. (Cambridge: Cambridge University Press, 1961. Hakluyt Society. 2nd Series. Vols. 114, 115).

Andrews, Jean, *Peppers. The Domesticated Capsicums* (Austin: University of Texas Press, 1984).

Andrews, K. R., *Elizabethan Privateering: English Privateering during the Spanish War, 1585-1603* (Cambridge: Cambridge University Press, 1964).

Antonil, S. J., André João, *Cultura e opulencia do Brasil por suas drogas e minas....*(Lisbon, 1711. French translation and critical commentary by Andrée Mansuy, Paris: Institut des Hautes Études de l'Amérique Latine, 1968).

Arasaratnam, Sinnappah, *Merchants, Companies and Commerce on the Coromandel Coast, 1650-1740* (Delhi: Oxford University Press, 1986).

Arruda, José Jobson de A., *O Brasil no comércio colonial* (São Paulo: Editora Atica, 1980).

Axelson, Eric, *South-East Africa, 1488-1530* (London and New York: Longmans, Green, & Co., 1940).

Axelson, Eric, *Congo to Cape. Early Portuguese Explorers*. Ed. George Woodcock. (New York: Harper & Row, 1973).

Azevedo, Carmo, 'Interaction between Indian and Portuguese Art', in Shirodkar, P. P., ed., *Goa: Cultural Trends (Seminar Papers)* (Panaji-Goa: Directorate of Archives, Archaeology, and Museum, Government of Goa, 1988), pp. 69-76.

Azevedo, João Lúcio de, *Os Jesuitas no Grão-Pará. Suas missões e a colonização*. 2nd ed. (Coimbra, 1930).

Baião, António, Hernani Cidade and Manuel Múrias, directores, *História da expansão portuguesa no mundo*. 3 vols (Lisbon: Editorial Atica, 1937-40).

Balandier, Georges, *Daily Life in the Kingdom of the Kongo from the Sixteenth to the Eighteenth Century*. Translated by Helen Weaver (New York: Pantheon Books, 1968).

Barbosa, Duarte, *The Book of Duarte Barbosa. An Account of the Countries Bordering on the Indian Ocean and their Inhabitants, Written by Duarte Barbosa and Completed about the Year 1518 A. D.*,

Trans. Mansel L. Dames. 2 vols. (London: Hakluyt Society, 1918, 1921. 2nd Series. Vols. 44, 49).

Bardwell, Ross L., 'The Governors of Portugal's South Atlantic Empire in the Seventeenth Century: Social Background, Qualifications, Selection, and Reward' (Ph.D diss., University of California, Santa Barbara, 1974).

Barman, Roderick J., 'The Forgotten Journey: Georg Heinrich Langsdorff and the Russian Imperial Scientific Expedition to Brazil, 1821-1829', *Terrae Incognitae*, 3 (1971), 67-96.

Barros, Joseph, 'Influence of Foreign Languages on Goan Cultural Ethos', in P.P. Shirodkar, ed., *Goa: Cultural Trends* (Panaji-Goa: Directorate of Archives, Archaeology and Museum, 1988), pp. 165-69.

Bassani, Ezio, and William B. Fagg, *Africa and the Renaissance: Art in Ivory* (Munich: The Center for African Art, New York, and Prestel-Verlag, 1988).

Bender, Gerald R., *Angola Under the Portuguese* (Berkeley and Los Angeles: University of California Press, 1978).

Birmingham, David, *Trade and Conflict in Angola* (Oxford: Clarendon Press, 1966).

Blake, John W., translator and editor, *Europeans in West Africa, 1450-1560*. 2 vols. (London: Hakluyt Society, 1942. 2nd Series. Vols. 86, 87).

Boorstin, Daniel J., *The Discoverers* (New York: Random House, 1983).

Borges, Charles J., 'Jesuit Education in Goa (16th-18th Centuries)', in P. P. Shirodkar, ed., *Goa: Cultural Trends* (Panaji-Goa: Directorate of Archives, Archaeology, and Museum, Government of Goa, 1988), pp. 153-64.

Bovill, E. W., *The Golden Trade of the Moors*. Second ed. rev'd (London and New York: Oxford University Press, 1968).

Bowers, John Z., *Western Medical Pioneers in Feudal Japan* (Baltimore and London: The Johns Hopkins Press, 1970).

Boxer, Charles R., *A Portuguese Embassy to Japan (1644-1647)*. Translated from an unpublished Portuguese MS., and other contemporary sources, with commentary and appendices (London: Kegan Paul, Trench, Trubner, & Co., 1928).

Boxer, Charles R., *Fidalgos in the Far East, 1550-1770. Fact and Fancy in the History of Macao* (The Hague: Martinus Nijhoff, 1948).

Boxer, Charles R., *Salvador de Sá and the Struggle for Brazil and Angola, 1602-1686* (London: The Athlone Press, 1952).

Boxer, Charles R., ed., *South China in the Sixteenth Century. Being the Narratives of Galeote Pereira, Fr Gaspar da Cruz, O. P., Fr Martín de Rada, O. E. S. A.(1550-1575)* (London: Hakluyt Society, 1953. 2nd Series. Vol. 106).

Boxer, Charles R. *The Dutch in Brazil, 1624-1654* (Oxford: Clarendon Press, 1957).

Boxer, Charles R., *A Great Luso-Brazilian Figure. Padre António Vieira, S. J., 1608-1697* (London: Hispanic and Luso-Brazilian Councils, 1957).

Boxer, Charles R., ed., *The Tragic History of the Sea, 1589-1622* (Cambridge: Cambridge University Press, 1959. Hakluyt Society, 2nd series. Vol. 112) and *Further Selections from the Tragic History of the Sea, 1559-1565* (Cambridge: Cambridge University Press, 1968. Hakluyt Society. Vol. 132).

Boxer, Charles R., *The Great Ship from Amacon. Annals of Macao and the Old Japan Trade, 1555-1640* (Lisbon: Centro de Estudos Históricos Ultramarinos, 1959; reprinted 1963).

Boxer, Charles R., and Azevedo, Carlos de, *Fort Jesus and the Portuguese in Mombasa, 1593-1729* (London: Hollis & Carter, 1960).

Boxer, Charles R., *Two Pioneers of Tropical Medicine: Garcia d'Orta and Nicolás Monardes* (London: The Hispanic and Luso-Brazilian Councils, 1963).

Boxer, Charles R., *Four Centuries of Portuguese Expansion, 1415-1825: A Succinct Survey* (Johannesburg: Witwatersrand University Press, 1963).

Boxer, Charles R., *Portuguese Society in the Tropics. The Municipal Councils of Goa, Macao, Bahia, and Luanda, 1510-1800* (Madison and Milwaukee: University of Wisconsin Press, 1965).

Boxer, Charles R., *The Christian Century in Japan, 1549-1650* (Berkeley and Los Angeles: University of California Press, 1967).

Boxer, Charles R., *The Golden Age of Brazil, 1695-1750* (Berkeley and Los Angeles: University of California Press, 1969).

Boxer, Charles R., *The Portuguese Seaborne Empire,1415-1825* (London: Hutchinson, & Co. 1969).

Boxer, Charles R., *The Church Militant and Iberian Expansion, 1440-1770* (Baltimore and London: The Johns Hopkins University Press, 1978).

Boxer, Charles R., *João de Barros. Portuguese Humanist and Historian of Asia* (New Delhi: Concept Publishing Company, 1981).

Boxer, Charles R., 'Portuguese roteiros, 1500-1700', *The Mariner's Mirror*, 20: 2 (April 1934), 171-86. Reprinted in *From Lisbon to Goa, 1500-1750* (London: Variorum Reprints, 1984).

Boxer, Charles R., 'Some Aspects of Portuguese Influence in Japan, 1542-1640', *Transactions and Proceedings of the Japan Society of London*, 33 (1936), 13-64. Reprinted in *Portuguese Merchants and Missionaries in Feudal Japan, 1543-1640* (London: Variorum Reprints, 1986).

248

Boxer, Charles R., 'Salvador Correia de Sá e Benevides and the Reconquest of Angola in 1648', *The Hispanic American Historical Review*, 28:4 (November 1948), 483-515.

Boxer, Charles R., 'Padre António Vieira S. J., and the Institution of the Brazil Company in 1649", *The Hispanic American Historical Review*, 29:4 (November 1949), 474-97.

Boxer, Charles R., 'English Shipping in the Brazil Trade, 1640-1665', *The Mariner's Mirror*, 37 (July 1951), 197-230.

Boxer, Charles R., 'Maize Names', *The Uganda Journal*, 16: 2 (September 1952), 178-79.

Boxer, Charles R., 'The Carreira da India (Ships, Men, Cargoes, Voyages)' (Lisbon: O Centro de Estudos Históricos Ultramarinos, 1961), pp. 33-82. Reprinted in *From Lisbon to Goa, 1500-1750. Studies in Portuguese Maritime Enterprise* (London: Variorum Reprints, 1984).

Boxer, Charles R., 'Jorge d'Albuquerque Coelho: A Luso-Brazilian Hero of the Sea, 1539-1602", *Luso-Brazilian Review*, 6:1 (Summer 1969), 3-17.

Braga, José Maria, *The Western Pioneers and their Discovery of Macao* (Macao: Imprensa Nacional, 1949).

Brandão, Ambrósio Fernandes (attributed to), *Diálogos das Grandezas do Brasil*. Introduction by Capistrano de Abreu, notes by Rodolpho Garcia (Rio de Janeiro: Officina Industrial Graphica, 1930). Translated as *Dialogues of the Great Things of Brazil* and annotated by Frederick H. Hall, William F. Harrison and Dorothy W. Welker (Albuquerque: University of New Mexico Press, 1987).

Brandon, William, *New Worlds for Old* (Athens, Ohio, and London: Ohio University Press, 1986).

Broeze, Frank, ed., *Brides of the Sea. Port Cities of Asia from the 16th-20th Centuries* (Honolulu: University of Hawaii Press, 1989).

Burkill, Isaac H., *A Dictionary of the Economic Products of the Malay Peninsula*. 2 vols. (London: Crown Agents for the Colonies, 1935).

Burns, E. Bradford, *A History of Brazil* (New York and London: Columbia University Press, 1970).

Burns, E. Bradford, 'The Sixteenth Century Jesuit Letters of Brazil', *Historical Records and Studies*, 49 (1962), 57-76.

Burns, E. Bradford, 'The Brazilian Jesuit Letters. A Sixteenth Century View of Portuguese America', *Revista da Faculdade de Ciencias*, 39 (1967), 5-15.

Burns, E. Bradford, 'The Intellectuals as Agents of Change and the Independence of Brazil, 1724-1822', in A. J. R. Russell-Wood, ed., *From Colony to Nation. Essays on the Independence of Brazil* (Baltimore and London: The Johns Hopkins University Press, 1975), pp. 211-46.

Butler, Ruth Lapham, 'Mem de Sá, Third Governor-General of Brazil, 1557-1572', *Mid-America*, 26: 2 (April 1944), 111-37.

Calmón, Pedro, *História da fundação da Bahia* (Bahia: Museu do Estado da Bahia, 1949).

Canabrava, Alice P., *O comércio português no Rio da Prata (1580-1640)* (Belo Horizonte and São Paulo: Editora Itatiaia Ltda., and Editora da Universidade de São Paulo, 1984).

Cardim, Fernão, 'A Treatise of Brazil, written by a Portugall which had long lived there', in Purchas, Samuel, *Hakluytus Posthumus or Purchas His Pilgrimes*, vol. 16 (Glasgow: James MacLehose and Sons, 1906) pp. 417-517.

Cardozo, Manuel da Silveira, 'The Last Adventure of Fernão Dias Pais (1674-1681)', *The Hispanic American Historical Review*, 26:4 (November 1946), 467-79.

Carreira, António, *The People of the Cape Verde Islands. Exploitation and Emigration.* Translated from the Portuguese and edited by Christopher Fyfe. (London and Hamden: C. Hurst & Co., and Archon Books, 1982).

Carruthers, Douglas, ed., *The Desert Route to India. Being the Journals of Four Travellers by the Great Desert Caravan Route Between Aleppo and Basra, 1745-1751* (London: Hakluyt Society, 1929. 2nd series. Vol. 63).

Chamberlain, Henry, *Views and Costumes of the City and Neighbourhood of Rio de Janeiro, Brazil, from Drawings Taken by Lieutenant Chamberlain, Royal Artillery, During the Years 1819 and 1820, with Descriptive Explanations* (London: Columbian Press, 1822).

Chang, T'ien-Tsê, *Sino-Portuguese Trade from 1514-1644. A Synthesis of Portuguese and Chinese Sources* (Leyden: A. J. Brill, Ltd., 1934).

Chodankar, Mahendra, 'Hindu, Christian and Muslim Jewellery in Goa', in P. P. Shirodkar, ed., *Goa: Cultural Trends* (Panaji-Goa: Directorate of Archives, Archaeology and Museum, 1988), pp. 77-93.

Cidade, Hernani, *A literatura portuguesa e a expansão ultramarina.* 2 vols. 2nd ed. revised and enlarged (Coimbra: Armenio Amado, 1963, 1964).

Cole, Herbert M., *Icons. Ideals and Power in the Art of Africa* (Washington D.C. and London: Smithsonian Institution Press, 1989).

Collis, Maurice, *The Land of the Great Image, being Experiences of Friar Manrique in Arakan* (New York: Alfred A. Knopf, 1943).

Conrad, Robert E., *Children of God's Fire. A Documentary History of Black Slavery in Brazil* (Princeton: Princeton University Press, 1983).

Conrad, Robert E., *World of Sorrow. The African Slave Trade to Brazil* (Baton Rouge and London: Louisiana State University Press, 1986).

Cooper, Michael, S.J., ed. *They Came to Japan. An Anthology of European Reports on Japan, 1543-1640* (London: Thames and Hudson, 1963).

Correia-Afonso, S. J., John, 'Manuel Godinho's Alternatives to the Carreira da India', in Souza, Teotonio de, ed., *Indo-Portuguese History. Old Issues. New Questions* (New Delhi: Concept Publishing Co., 1985), pp. 84-89.

Correia-Afonso, S. J., John, editor, annotator, and translator, *Intrepid Itinerant. Manuel Godinho and his Journey from India to Portugal in 1663* (Bombay: Oxford University Press, 1990).

Corte Real, Manuel Henrique, *A feitoria portuguesa na Andaluzia, 1500-1532* (Lisbon: Centro de Estudos Históricos, 1967).

Cortesão, Armando, translator and editor, *The Suma Oriental of Tomé Pires...and the Book of Francisco Rodrigues*, 2 vols. (London: Hakluyt Society, 1944. 2nd series. Vols. 89, 90).

Cortesão, Jaime, *Raposo Tavares e a formação territorial do Brasil* (Rio de Janeiro, 1958).

Costa, João Cruz, *A History of Ideas in Brazil. The Development of Philosophy in Brazil and the Evolution of Natural History*. Translated by Suzette Macedo (Berkeley and Los Angeles: University of California Press, 1964).

Crone, Gerald R., ed., *The Voyages of Cadamosto and Other Documents on Western Africa in the Second Half of the Fifteenth Century* (London: Hakluyt Society, 1937. 2nd ser. Vol. 80).

Crosby Jr., Alfred W., *The Columbian Exchange. Biological and Cultural Consequences of 1492* (Westport: Greenwood Publishing Co., 1972).

Cross, Harry E., 'Commerce and Orthodoxy: A Spanish Response to Portuguese Commercial Penetration in the Viceroyalty of Peru, 1580-1640', *The Americas*, 35:2 (October 1978), 151-67.

Curtin, Philip D., *The Atlantic Slave Trade. A Census* (Madison and London: University of Wisconsin Press, 1969).

Curtin, Philip D., *Economic Change in Precolonial Africa. Senegambia in the Era of the Slave Trade* (Madison: University of Wisconsin Press, 1975).

Curtin, Philip D., 'Epidemiology and the Slave Trade', *Political Science Quarterly*, 83: 2 (June 1968), 190-216.

Danvers, Frederick C., *The Portuguese in India*. 2 vols. (London: W.H. Allen & Co., 1894).

Davidson, Basil, *The Fortunate Isles. A Study in African Transformation* (London: Hutchinson, 1989).

Davidson, David M., 'How the Brazilian West Was Won: Freelance and State on the Mato Grosso Frontier, 1737-1752', in Dauril Alden, ed., *Colonial Roots of Modern Brazil* (Berkeley and Los Angeles: University of California Press, 1973), pp. 61-106.

Denoix, L., 'Caractéristiques des navires de l'époque des Grandes Découvertes', in Mollat, Michel, and Adam, Paul, eds., *Les aspects internationaux de la découverte océanique aux XVe et XVIe siècles.* (Paris: S. E. V. P. E. N., 1966), pp. 137-47.

Dias, Bonifacio, 'Impact of Tobacco on Goa (1620-1840)', in P. P. Shirodkar, ed., *Goa: Cultural Trends* (Panaji-Goa: Directorate of Archives, Archaeology, and Museum, Government of Goa, 1988), pp. 222-28.

Diffie, Bailey W., and Winius, George D., *Foundations of the Portuguese Empire, 1415-1580* (Minneapolis: University of Minnesota Press, 1977).

Disney, A. R., *Twilight of the Pepper Empire. Portuguese Trade in Southwest India in the Early Seventeenth Century* (Cambridge: Harvard University Press, 1978).

Disney, A. R., 'The Portuguese Empire in India, c. 1550-1650', in John Correia-Afonso, S. J., ed., *Indo-Portuguese History. Sources and Problems* (Bombay: Oxford University Press, 1981), pp. 148-73.

Documentos sobre os portugueses em Moçambique e na Africa central/ Documents on the Portuguese in Mozambique and Central Africa, 1497-1840. Vols. 2, 3, 4. (National Archives of Rhodesia and Nyasaland/Centro de Estudos Históricos Ultramarinos: Lisbon, 1962-65).

D' Orta, Garcia, *Colloquies on the Simples and Drugs of India.* Edited and annotated by the Conde de Ficalho (Lisbon, 1895). Translated with introduction and index by Sir Clements Markham (London: Henry Sotheran & Co., 1913).

Duncan, Bentley, *Atlantic Islands. Madeira, the Azores and the Cape Verdes in Seventeenth-Century Commerce and Navigation* (Chicago and London: University of Chicago Press, 1972).

Dutra, Francis A., 'Duarte Coelho Pereira, First Lord-Proprietor of Pernambuco: The Beginning of a Dynasty', *The Americas*, 29:4 (April 1973), 415-41.

Edmundson, George, ed., *Journal of the Travels and Labours of Father Samuel Fritz in the River of the Amazons between 1686 and 1723* (London: Hakluyt Society, 1922. 2nd Series. Vol. 51).

Edmundson, George, 'The Voyage of Pedro Teixeira on the Amazon from Pará to Quito and Back, 1637-1639', *Transactions of the Royal Historical Society*, vol.3 (4th series. London 1920), 52-71.

Ellis, Jr., Alfredo, 'O ciclo do muar', *Revista de história*, 1:1 (1950. São Paulo), 73-81.

Ellis, Myriam, *Contribuição ao estudo do abastecimento das áreas mineradoras do Brasil no século XVIII* (Rio de Janeiro, 1961).

Espinosa, J. Manuel, 'Gouveia: Jesuit Lawgiver in Brazil', *Mid-America*, 24:1 (January 1942), 27-60.

Eltis, David, *Economic Growth and the Ending of the Transatlantic Slave Trade* (New York: Oxford University Press, 1987).

Espinosa, J. Manuel, 'Fernão Cardim, Jesuit Humanist of Colonial Brazil', *Mid-America*, 24: 4 (October 1942), 252-71.

Fernandes, Agnelo P., 'Augustinians in Goa', in Shirodkar, P. P., ed., *Goa: Cultural Trends (Seminar Papers)* (Panaji-Goa: Directorate of Archives, Archaeology and Museum, Government of Goa, 1988), pp. 131-40.

Ferreira, Alexandre Rodrigues, *Viagem filosófica às Capitanias do Grão-Pará, Rio Negro, Mato Grosso e Cuiabá*. Vol. 1. Edited by Edgard de Serqueira Falcão (São Paulo: Gráficos Brunner, 1970).

Ferrez, Gilberto, *O Brasil de Thomas Ender 1817* (Rio de Janeiro: Fundação João Moreira Salles, 1976).

Fonseca, Henrique Quirino da, *A caravela portuguesa e a prioridade técnica das navegações henriquinas* (Coimbra: Imprensa da Universidade, 1934).

Fonseca, José Gonçalves da, 'Navegação feita da cidade do Grão-Pará até à bôca do Rio da Madeira pela escolta que por êste rio subio às minas de Mato-Grosso', translated as 'Voyage Made from the City of the Gram Para to the Mouth of the River Madeira by the Expedition which Ascended this River to the Mines of Mato Grosso....', in *Explorations Made in the Valley of the River Madeira, from 1749 to 1868. A Collection of Reports*. Edited and in part translated by George Earl Church (London: Published for the National Bolivian Navigation Company, 1875), pp. 203-355.

Fonseca, Luiza da, 'Bacharéis brasileiros–elementos biográficos (1635-1830)', *Anais. IV Congresso de História Nacional* (Rio de Janeiro: Imprensa Nacional, 1951), vol. 11, pp. 109-405.

Freehafer, Virginia, 'Domingos Jorge Velho. Conqueror of Brazilian Backlands', *The Americas*, 27:2 (October 1970), 161-84.

Freyre, Gilberto, *The Masters and the Slaves. A Study in the Development of Brazilian Civilization*. Translated by Samuel Putnam. 2nd ed., rev'd (New York: Alfred A. Knopf, 1978).

Furber, Holden, 'The Overland Route to India in the Seventeenth and Eighteenth Centuries', *Journal of Indian History*, 29 (1951), 105-33.

Furber, Holden, *Rival Empires of Trade in the Orient, 1600-1800* (Minneapolis: University of Minnesota Press, 1976).

Godinho, Vitorino Magalhães, *O 'Mediterraneo' saariano e as caravanas do ouro* (São Paulo: Coleção da Revista de Historia, 1956).

Godinho, Vitorino Magalhães, *Os descobrimentos e a economia mundial*. 2 vols. (Lisbon: Editora Arcádia, 1963, 1965).

Godlonton, W. A., 'The Journeys of Antonio Fernandes – The First Known European to Find the Monomotapa and to Enter Southern

Rhodesia', *Transactions of the Rhodesia Scientific Association*, vol. 40 (April 1945), 71-103.

Goodyear, James D., 'Agents of Empire: Portuguese Doctors in Colonial Brazil and the Idea of Tropical Disease' (Ph.D diss., The Johns Hopkins University, 1982).

Goonatilleka, M. H., 'A Portuguese Creole in Sri Lanka: A Brief Socio-Linguistic Survey', in Sousa, Teotonio R. de, *Indo-Portuguese History. Old Issues, New Questions* (New Delhi: Concept Publishing Company, 1985), pp. 147-80.

Goulart, Maurício, *Escravidão africana no Brasil (das origens à extinção do tráfico)* (São Paulo: Livraria Martins Editora, 1949.).

Graça, Luís, *A visão do oriente na literatura portuguesa de viagens: os viajantes portugueses e os itinerários terrestres, 1560-1670* (Lisbon: Imprensa Nacional/ Casa da Moeda, 1983).

Guillobel. Usos e costumes do Rio de Janeiro nas figurinhas de Guillobel/ Life and Manners in Rio de Janeiro as Seen in Guillobel's Small Drawings. Texts by Paulo Berger (Curitiba: Kingraf Ltda., 1978).

Gune, V. T., 'Source Material from the Goa Archive', in John Correia-Afonso, S. J., ed., *Indo-Portuguese History. Sources and Problems* (Bombay: Oxford University Press, 1981), pp. 19-33.

Habib, Irfan, *The Agrarian System of Mughal India, 1556-1707* (New York: Asia Publishing House, 1963).

Hamilton, Alexander, *A New Account of the East Indies*. Edited with notes and introduction by Sir William Foster (London: The Argonaut Press, 1930).

Hanke, Lewis, 'The Portuguese in Spanish America, with Special Reference to the Villa Imperial de Potosí', *Revista de Historia de America*, 51 (June 1961), 1-48.

Harlan, Jack R., *et al*, eds, *Origins of African Plant Domestication* (The Hague and Paris: Mouton, 1976).

Harms, Robert W., *River of Wealth, River of Sorrow. The Central Zaire Basin in the Era of the Slave and Ivory Trade, 1500-1891* (New Haven and London: Yale University Press, 1981).

Harrison, J. B., 'Five Portuguese Historians', in C. H. Philips, ed., *Historians of India, Pakistan and Ceylon* (London: Oxford University Press, 1961).

Hemming, John, *Red Gold. The Conquest of the Brazilian Indians, 1500-1760* (Cambridge: Harvard University Press, 1978).

Hemming, John, *Amazon Frontier. The Defeat of the Brazilian Indians* (Cambridge: Harvard University Press, 1987).

Henige, David P. *Colonial Governors from the Fifteenth Century to the Present; A Comprehensive List* (Madison: University of Wisconsin Press, 1970).

Hennessy, Alistair, *The Frontier in Latin American History* (Albuquerque: University of New Mexico Press, 1978).

Ho, Ping-ti, *Studies on the Population of China, 1368-1953* (Cambridge: Harvard University Press, 1959).

Ho, Ping-ti, 'The Introduction of American Food Plants into China', *American Anthropologist*, 57: 2 (1955), 191-201.

Hobhouse, Henry, *Seeds of Change. Five Plants that Transformed Mankind* (London: Sidgwick and Jackson, 1985).

Holanda, Sérgio Buarque de, *Monções* (Rio de Janeiro: Casa do Estudante, 1945).

Isaacman, Allen F., *Mozambique. The Africanization of an European Institution. The Zambesi Prazos, 1750-1902* (Madison and London: University of Wisconsin Press, 1972).

Jeffreys, M. D. W., 'How Ancient is West African Maize?', *Africa*, 33:2 (1963), 115-31.

Jones, William O., *Manioc in Africa* (Stanford: Stanford University Press, 1959).

Julião, Carlos, *Riscos iluminados de figurinhos de brancos e negros dos uzos do Rio de Janeiro e Serro do Frio*. Historical introduction and descriptive catalogue by Lygia da Fonseca Fernandes da Cunha (Rio de Janeiro, 1960).

Keen, Benjamin, *The Aztec Image in Western Thought* (New Brunswick: Rutgers University Press, 1971).

Keith, Henry H., 'New World Interlopers: The Portuguese in the Spanish West Indies, from the Discovery to 1640', *The Americas*, 25: 4 (April 1969), 360-71.

Klein, Herbert S., *The Middle Passage: Comparative Studies in the Atlantic Slave Trade* (Princeton: Princeton University Press, 1978).

Kulkarni, A. R., 'Portuguese in the Deccan Politics: A Study of New Marathi Documents from Lisbon', in Souza, Teotonio R. de, ed., *Indo-Portuguese History. Old Issues. New Questions* (New Delhi: Concept Publishing Co., 1985), pp. 114-22.

Lapa, José Roberto do Amaral, *O Brasil e as drogas do Oriente* (Marília: Faculdade de filosofia, ciências, e letras, 1966).

Lapa, José Roberto do Amaral, *A Bahia e a Carreira da India* (São Paulo: Companhia Editora Nacional, 1968).

Larsen, Erik, *Frans Post. Interprète du Brésil* (Amsterdam, Rio de Janeiro: Colibris Editora Ltda., 1962).

Lawrence, A. W., *Trade Castles and Forts of West Africa* (London: Jonathan Cape, 1963).

Leite, S. J., Serafim, *História da Companhia de Jesus no Brasil*. 10 vols. (Lisbon and Rio de Janeiro: Livraria Portugalia and Civilização Brasileira, and Imprensa Nacional, Rio de Janeiro, 1938-50).

Linschoten, J. H. van, *The Voyage of John Huyghen van Linschoten to the East Indies*, 2 vols. Eds. A. C. Burnell (vol. 1) and P. A. Tiele (vol. 2) (London: Hakluyt Society, 1885. Ser. 1, vols. 70-71).

Lipson, E., *The Economic History of England*. 6th. ed. Vol. 2. *The Age of Mercantilism* (London: Adam and Charles Black, 1956).

Lisboa, Fr Cristóvão de, *História dos animais e árvores do Maranhão*. Notes by Jaime Walter (Lisbon: Arquivo Histórico Ultramarino and Centro de Estudos HistórICas Ultramarinos, 1967).

Lobato, Alexandre, *A expansão portuguesa em Moçambique. 1498-1530*. 4 vols. (Lisbon: Centro de Estudos Históricos Ultramarinos, 1954-59).

Lobo, S.J., Jerónimo, *Itinerário*, translated by Donald M. Lockhart, introduction and notes by C. F. Beckingham, under the title *The Itinerário of Jerónimo Lobo* (London: Hakluyt Society, 1984. 2nd series. Vol. 162).

Lopes, David, *A expansão da língua portuguesa no oriente nos séculos XVI, XVII e XVIII* (Barcelos: Portucalense Editora, Ltda, 1936).

Lugar, Catherine, 'The Portuguese Tobacco Trade and Tobacco Growers of Bahia in the Late Colonial Period', in Dauril Alden and Warren Dean, eds., *Essays Concerning the Socioeconomic History of Brazil and Portuguese India* (Gainesville: University Presses of Florida, 1977), pp. 26-70.

MacGregor, I. A., 'Some Aspects of Portuguese Historical Writing of the Sixteenth and Seventeenth Centuries on South East Asia', in D. G. E. Hall, ed., *Historians of South East Asia* (London: Oxford University Press, 1961), pp. 172-99.

Manchester, Alan K., 'The Transfer of the Portuguese Court to Rio de Janeiro', in Keith, Henry H., and Edwards, S. F., eds., *Conflict and Continuity in Brazilian Society* (Columbia: University of South Carolina Press, 1969), pp. 148-83.

Manrique, Sebastião, *Travels of Fray Sebastien Manrique, 1629-1643. A Translation of the Itinerario de las Missiones Orientales*. Introduction and notes by C. Eckford Luard, assisted by Fr H. Hosten S. J. 2 vols.(Oxford: Hakluyt Society, 1927. Series 2. Vols. 59 and 61).

Marcílio, Maria Luiza, 'The Population of Colonial Brazil', in Leslie Bethell, ed., *The Cambridge History of Latin America*, vol. 2. *Colonial Latin America* (Cambridge: Cambridge University Press, 1984), pp. 37-63.

Markham, Clements R., editor, *Expeditions into the Valley of the Amazons, 1539, 1540, 1639* (London: Hakluyt Society, 1859. 1st Series. Vol. 24).

Marques, A. H. de Oliveira, *Hansa e Portugal na Idade Média* (Lisbon: Tip. Albano Tomás dos Anjos, Ltda,1959).

Marques, A. H. de Oliveira, *History of Portugal*. Vol. 1. *From Lusitania to Empire* (New York and London: Columbia University Press, 1972).

Marques, A. H. de Oliveira, 'Notas para a história da feitoria portuguesa na Flandres no século XV', in his *Ensaios da história medieval portuguesa*. 2nd ed.(Lisbon: Documenta histórica, 1980), pp. 159-93.

Martins, José F. Ferreira, *Os vice-reis da India, 1505-1917* (Lisbon: Imprensa Nacional, 1935).

Mascarenhas, Mira, 'Impact of the West on Goan Music', in P. P. Shirodkar, ed., *Goa: Cultural Trends* (Panaji-Goa: Directorate of Archives, Archaeology and Museum, 1988), pp. 189-204.

Mathew, K. S., *Portuguese Trade with India in the Sixteenth Century* (New Delhi: Manohar Publications, 1983).

Mathew, K. S., and Afzal Ahmad, *Emergence of Cochin in the Pre-Industrial Era: A Study of Portuguese Cochin* (Pondicherry: Pondicherry University, 1990).

Mathew, K. S., 'Indian Merchants and the Portuguese Trade on the Malabar Coast during the Sixteenth Century', in Souza, Teotonio R. de, ed., *Indo-Portuguese History. Old Issues. New Questions* (New Delhi: Concept Publishing Co., 1985), pp. 1-12.

Mathew, K. S., 'Church Economics in the 16th Century Goa', in P. P. Shirodkar, ed., *Goa: Cultural Trends* (Panaji-Goa: Directorate of Archives, Archaeology and Museum, 1988), pp. 123-30.

Mathew, K. S., 'Trade in the Indian Ocean during the Sixteenth Century and the Portuguese', in K. S. Mathew, ed., *Studies in Maritime History* (Pondicherry: Pondicherry University, 1990), pp. 13-28.

Matos, Artur Teodoro de, *Transportes e comunicações em Portugal, Açores e Madeira, 1750-1850* (Ponta Delgada: Universidade dos Açores, 1980).

Matos, Luís de, *Les portugais à l'université de Paris entre 1500 et 1550* (Coimbra: Imprensa da Universidade, 1950).

Mattoso, Katia M. de Queirós, *Presença francesa no movimento democrático baiano de 1798* (Bahia: Editora Itapuã, 1969).

Mauro, Frédéric, *Le Portugal et l'Atlantique au XVIIe siècle (1570-1670). Etude économique* (Paris: S. E. V. P. E. N., 1960).

Mauro, Frédéric, *Le Brésil au XVIIe siècle* (Coimbra, 1961).

Maxwell, Kenneth R., 'The Generation of the 1790s and the Idea of Luso-Brazilian Empire', in Dauril Alden, ed., *Colonial Roots of Modern Brazil* (Berkeley and Los Angeles: University of California Press, 1973), pp.107-44.

McIntyre, Kenneth G., *The Secret Discovery of Australia*. Rev'd ed. (Sydney: Pan Books, 1982).

Medina, José Toribio, *The Discovery of the Amazon According to the Account of Friar Gaspar de Carvajal and Other Documents.* Translated by Bertram E. Lee. Editor H. C. Heaton (New York: American Geographical Society, 1934).

Meilink-Roelofsz, M. A. P., *Asian Trade and European Influence in the Indonesian Archipelago between 1500 and about 1630* (The Hague: Martinus Nijhoff, 1962).

Mello, José António Gonsalves de, *João Fernandes Vieira.* 2 vols. (Recife: Universidade de Recife, 1956).

Miller, Joseph C., *Way of Death. Merchant Capitalism and the Angolan Slave Trade, 1730-1830* (Madison: University of Wisconsin Press, 1988).

Miracle, Marvin P., *Maize in Tropical Africa* (Madison and London: University of Wisconsin Press, 1966).

Miracle, Marvin P., 'Interpretation of Evidence on the Introduction of Maize into West Africa', *Africa*, 33 (April 1963), 132-35.

Miracle, Marvin P., 'The Introduction and Spread of Maize in Africa', *Journal of African History*, 6:1 (1965), 39-55.

Morais, Francisco, *Estudantes da Universidade de Coimbra nascidos no Brasil* (Coimbra: Faculdade de Letras da Universidade de Coimbra, Instituto de Estudos Brasileiros, 1949).

Morison, Samuel Eliot, *The European Discovery of America. The Northern Voyages, A. D. 500 to 1600* (New York: Oxford University Press, 1971).

Morse, Richard M., ed., *The Bandeirantes. The Historical Role of the Brazilian Pathfinders* (New York: Alfred A. Knopf, 1965).

Mundadan, A. Mathias, 'Church and Missionary Works on Indo-Portuguese History', in John Correia-Afonso, S. J., ed., *Indo-Portuguese History. Sources and Problems* (Bombay: Oxford University Press, 1981), pp. 1-18.

Muratori, Carlo, 'Maize Names in History: A Further Discussion', *The Uganda Journal*, 16:1 (March 1952), 76-81.

Murdock, George Peter, *Africa. Its Peoples and Their Culture History* (New York: McGraw Hill, 1959).

Newitt, M. D. D., *Portuguese Settlement on the Zambesi. Exploration, Land Tenure and Colonial Rule in East Africa* (New York: Africana Publishing Co., 1973).

Nowell, Charles E., 'Aleixo Garcia and the White King', *The Hispanic American Historical Review*, 26:4 (November 1946), 450-66.

Os Açores e o Atlântico (Séculos XIV-XVII). Actas do Colóquio Internacional realizado em Angra do Heroísmo de 8 a 13 de Agosto de 1983 (Angra do Heroismo: Instituto Historico da Ilha Terceira, 1984).

Ott, Carlos, *Formação e evolução étnica da Cidade do Salvador*, 2 vols. (Salvador: Prefeitura Municipal do Salvador, 1955, 1957).

Pannikar, K. M., *Asia and Western Dominance* (London: George Allen & Unwin, 1959).

Parry, J. H., *The Age of Reconnaissance* (London: Weidenfeld and Nicholson, 1963).

Pearson, Michael N., *Merchants and Rulers in Gujarat. The Response to the Portuguese in the Sixteenth Century* (Berkeley and Los Angeles: University of California Press, 1976).

Pearson, Michael N., *Coastal Western India. Studies from the Portuguese Records* (New Delhi: Concept Publishing Co., 1981).

Pearson, Michael N., 'The People and Politics of Portuguese India during the Sixteenth and Early Seventeenth Centuries', in Dauril Alden and Warren Dean, eds., *Essays Concerning the Socioeconomic History of Brazil and Portuguese India* (Gainesville: University Presses of Florida, 1977), pp. 1-25.

Pearson, Michael N., 'Corruption and Corsairs in Western India', in Blair B. Kling and M. N. Pearson, eds., *The Age of Partnership. Europeans in Asia before Dominion* (Honolulu: University Press of Hawaii, 1979), pp. 15-41.

Pereira, Duarte Pacheco, *Esmeraldo de Situ Orbis*. Trans. and ed. by George H. T. Kimble (London: Hakluyt Society, 1937. 2nd Series. Vol. 79).

Pigafetta, Antonio, *Le Voyage et navigation faict par les Espaignolz es Isles de Mollucques....* (Paris, 1525). Translated by Paula Spurlin Paige as *The Voyage of Magellan. The Journal of Antonio Pigafetta* (Englewood Cliffs: Prentice Hall, Inc., 1969).

Pinto, Maria Helena Mendes, *Biombos Namban. Namban Screens.* English/Portuguese bilingual edition. (Lisbon: Museu Nacional de Arte Antiga, 1988).

Pinto, Fernão Mendes, *Peregrinaçam* (Lisbon, 1614). Edited and translated by Rebecca D. Catz as *The Travels of Fernão Mendes Pinto* (Chicago and London: University of Chicago Press, 1989).

Pinto, Virgílio Noya, *O ouro brasileiro e o comércio anglo-português.* 2nd. ed., (São Paulo: Editora Nacional, 1979).

Pinto, Viriato João, 'Plantas medicinaes da India', *O Oriente Portuguêz*, 6: 11-12 (Nova Goa, 1909), 361-79.

Poppino, Rollie E., 'Cattle Industry in Colonial Brazil', *Mid-America*, 31:4 (October 1949), 219-47.

Portères, R., 'L'Introduction du maïs en Afrique', *Journal d'Agriculture Tropicale et de Botanique Appliquée*, vol. ii (1955), 221-31.

Prado, Jr., Caio, *The Colonial Background of Modern Brazil.* Translated by Suzette Macedo (Berkeley and Los Angeles: University of

California Press, 1967).

Ptak, Roderich, *Portugal in China. Kurzer Abriss der portugiesisch-chinesischen Beziehungen und der Geschichte Macaus* (Bad Boll: Klemmerberg Verlag, 1980).

Purchas, Samuel, *Hakluytus Posthumus or Purchas His Pilgrimes*. 20 vols. (Glasgow: James MacLehose & Sons., 1905-1907. Hakluyt Society extra series, vols. 14-33).

Randles, W. G. L., *L'ancien royaume du Congo des origines à la fin du XlXe siècle* (Paris, The Hague: Mouton & Co., 1968).

Randles, W. G. L., *The Empire of Monomotapa from the Fifteenth to the Nineteenth Century*. Translated by R. S. Roberts (Gwelo, Zimbabwe: Mambo Press, 1979).

Rau, Virginia, and Macedo, Jorge de, *O açúcar da Madeira nos fins do século XV* (Lisbon: Junta-Geral do Distrito Autónomo do Funchal, 1962).

Rego, António da Silva, 'The Monsoon Codices at the National Archives of the Torre do Tombo', in John Correia-Afonso, S. J., ed., *Indo-Portuguese History. Sources and Problems* (Bombay: Oxford University Press, 1981), pp. 51-71.

Rego, Francisco de Carvalho e, *Macau* (Macau: Imprensa Nacional, 1950).

Ricard, Robert, *Études sur l'histoire des portugais au Maroc* (Coimbra: University of Coimbra, 1955).

Ridley, Henry N., *The Dispersal of Plants throughout the World* (Ashford, Kent: L. Reeve & Co., 1930).

Rogers, Francis M., *The Travels of the Infante Dom Pedro of Portugal* (Cambridge: Harvard University Press, 1961).

Rogers, Francis M., *The Quest for Eastern Christians. Travels and Rumor in the Age of Discovery* (Minneapolis: University of Minnesota Press, 1962).

Russell-Wood, A. J. R., *Fidalgos and Philanthropists. The Santa Casa da Misericórdia of Bahia, 1550-1755* (Berkeley and Los Angeles: University of California Press, 1968).

Russell-Wood, A. J. R., *The Black Man in Slavery and Freedom in Colonial Brazil* (London: The Macmillan Press, 1982).

Russell-Wood, A. J. R., 'Female and Family in the Economy and Society of Colonial Brazil', in Lavrin, Asunción, ed., *Latin American Women. Historical Perspectives* (Westport and London: Greenwood Press, 1978), pp. 60-100.

Russell-Wood, A. J. R., 'As frotas de ouro do Brasil, 1710-1750', *Estudos econômicos*, 13 (São Paulo, 1983), 701-17.

Russell-Wood, A. J. R., 'Seamen Ashore and Afloat: The Social Environment of the Carreira da India, 1550-1750', *The Mariner's Mirror*, 69:1 (February 1983), 35-52.

Russell-Wood, A. J. R., 'Colonial Brazil: The Gold Cycle, c.1690-1750', in Leslie Bethell, ed., *The Cambridge History of Latin America*, vol. 2 (Cambridge: Cambridge University Press, 1984), pp. 547-600.

Russell-Wood, A. J. R., 'Participação religiosa nas consignações do ouro do Brasil para Portugal durante o reino de Dom João V', paper presented to the Congresso Internacional: Portugal no Século XVIII de Dom João V à Revolução Francesa, Lisbon, 1989.

Russell-Wood, A. J. R., 'Frontiers in Colonial Brazil: Reality, Myth, and Metaphor', in Covington, Paula, ed., *Latin American Frontiers, Borders, and Hinterlands: Research Needs and Resources* (Albuquerque: SALALM Secretariat, 1990), pp. 26-61.

Russell-Wood, A. J. R., 'Ports of Colonial Brazil', in Knight, Franklin W., and Liss, Peggy, eds., *Atlantic Port Cities. Economy, Culture, and Society in the Atlantic World, 1650-1850* (Knoxville: University of Tennessee Press, 1991), pp. 196-239.

Ryder, Alan F. C., *Benin and the Europeans, 1485-1897* (New York: Humanities Press, 1969).

Saldanha, M. J. de, 'Plantas exoticas introduzidas na India pelos Portugueses', *O Oriente Portuguêz*, vols. 5 (1908), 213-22, 300-11, and 6 (1909), 152-62, and 224-28.

Sampaio, Theodoro de, *História da fundação da Cidade do Salvador* (Bahia, 1949).

Sauer, Carl O., *Agricultural Origins and Dispersals* (New York: The American Geographical Society, 1952).

Saunders, A. C. de C. M., *A Social History of Black Slaves and Freedmen in Portugal, 1441-1555* (Cambridge: Cambridge University Press, 1982).

Scammell, G. V., *The World Encompassed. The First European Maritime Empires, c. 800-1650* (Berkeley and Los Angeles: University of California Press, 1981).

Schurz, William L., *The Manila Galleon* (New York: E. P. Dutton & Co., 1939).

Schwartz, Stuart B., *Sovereignty and Society in Colonial Brazil. The High Court of Bahia and its Judges, 1609-1751* (Berkeley and Los Angeles: University of California Press, 1973).

Schwartz, Stuart B., *Sugar Plantations in the Formation of Brazilian Society. Bahia, 1550-1835* (Cambridge: Cambridge University Press, 1985).

Sideri, S., *Trade and Power. Informal Colonialism in Anglo-Portuguese Relations* (Rotterdam: Rotterdam University Press, 1970).

Silva, Ignacio Accioli de Cerqueira e, *Memorias historicas e politicas da Provincia da Bahia do Coronel Ignacio Accioli de Cerqueira e Silva. Annotador Dr Braz do Amaral*. 6 vols. (Bahia, 1919-40).

Simon, William J., *Scientific Expeditions in the Portuguese Overseas Territories, 1783-1808* (Lisbon: Instituto de Investigação Científica Tropical, 1983).

Simonsen, Roberto, *História econômica do Brasil, 1500/1820*. 4th. ed. (São Paulo: Companhia Editorial Nacional, 1962).

Smith, Robert, 'The Canoe in West African History', *Journal of African History*, 11: 4 (1970), 515-33.

Smith, Robert C., *The Art of Portugal, 1500-1800* (London: Weidenfeld and Nicholson, 1968).

Smith, Robert C., 'Nossa Senhora da Conceição da Praia and the Joanine Style in Brazil', *Journal of the Society of Architectural Historians*, 15:3 (October 1956), 16-23.

Smith, Ronald Bishop, *The First Age of the Portuguese Embassies, Navigations and Peregrinations to the Kingdoms and Islands of Southeast Asia, 1509-1521* (Bethesda: Decatur Press, 1968).

Southey, Robert, *History of Brazil*. 3 vols. 2nd ed. (New York: Greenwood Press, 1969).

Souza, George Bryan, *The Survival of Empire. Portuguese Trade and Society in China and the South China Sea, 1630-1754* (Cambridge: Cambridge University Press, 1986).

Souza, Teotonio R. de, ed., *Indo-Portuguese History. Old Issues, New Questions* (New Delhi: Concept Publishing Company, 1985).

Spence, Jonathan D., *The Memory Palace of Matteo Ricci* (New York: Viking Penguin Inc., 1984).

Steensgaard, Niels, *The Asian Trade Revolution of the Seventeenth Century. The East India Companies and the Decline of the Caravan Trade* (Chicago and London: University of Chicago Press, 1974).

Steensgaard, Niels, 'The Return Cargoes of the Carreira in the 16th and Early 17th Century', in Souza, Teotonio R. de, ed., *Indo-Portuguese History. Old Issues. New Questions* (New Delhi: Concept Publishing Co.,1985), pp. 13-31.

Teixeira, Pedro, *The Travels of Pedro Teixeira with his 'Kings of Harmuz' and Extracts from his 'Kings of Persia'*. Translated and edited by William F. Sinclair. Notes and introduction by Donald Ferguson (London: Hakluyt Society, 1902. 2nd Series. Vol. 9).

Tomaz, Luís Filipe, 'Portuguese Sources on Sixteenth Century Indian Economic History', in John Correia-Afonso, S. J., ed., *Indo-Portuguese History. Sources and Problems* (Bombay: Oxford University Press, 1981), pp. 99-113.

Tomaz, Luís Filipe, 'The Indian Merchant Communities in Malacca under the Portuguese Rule', in Souza, Teotonio R. de, ed., *Indo-Portuguese History. Old Issues. New Questions* (New Delhi: Concept Publishing Co., 1985), pp. 56-72.

Tracey, Hugh, *António Fernandes Descobridor do Monomotapa, 1514-1515* (Lourenço Marques: Arquivo Histórico de Moçambique, Imprensa Nacional, 1940).

Varadarajan, Lotika, 'Indian Textiles in Portuguese Collections: A Problem of Provenance', in Souza, Teotonio R. de, ed., *Indo- Portuguese History. Old Issues, New Questions* (New Delhi: Concept Publishing Company, 1985), pp. 133-46.

Varnhagen, Francisco A. de, *História geral do Brasil*. 8th ed., 5 vols. (São Paulo; Edições Melhoramentos, 1975).

Vavilov, Nikolai I., 'The Origin, Variation, Immunity and Breeding of Cultivated Plants', *Chronica Botanica*, 13: 1/6 (1949-50), 1-366.

Verger, Pierre, *O fumo da Bahia e o tráfico dos escravos do golfo de Benin* (Salvador: Universidade Federal da Bahia, 1966).

Verger, Pierre, *Flux et reflux de la traite des nègres entre le golfe de Bénin et Bahia de Todos os Santos du dix-septième au dix-neuvième siècle* (Paris: Mouton, 1968).

Verrill, A. Hyatt, *Foods America Gave the World* (Boston: L. C. Page & Co., 1937).

Vieira, Alberto, *O comércio inter-insular nos séculos XV e XVI. Madeira, Açores e Canárias* (Funchal: Centro de Estudos de História do Atlántico, 1987).

Watson, Andrew M., *Agricultural Innovation in the Early Islamic World* (Cambridge: Cambridge University Press, 1983).

Weinstein, Barbara, *The Amazon Rubber Boom, 1850-1920* (Stanford: Stanford University Press, 1983).

Wessel, C. *Early Jesuit Travellers in Central Asia, 1603-1721* (The Hague: Martinus Nijhoff, 1924).

Whiteway, R. S., translator and editor. *The Portuguese Expedition to Abyssinia in 1541-1543 as Narrated by Castanhoso, with some Contemporary Letters, the Short Account of Bermudez, and Certain Extracts from Correa* (London: Hakluyt Society, 1902. 2nd Series. Vol. 10).

Whiteway, R. S., *The Rise of Portuguese Power in India, 1497-1550* (London: Archibald Constable & Co., 1899).

Williams, C. N., *The Agronomy of the Major Tropical Crops* (Kuala Lumpur: Oxford University Press, 1975).

Willett, F., 'The Introduction of Maize into West Africa: An Assessment of Recent Evidence', *Africa*, 32: 1 (January 1962), 1-13.

Wilson, Charles Morrow, ed., *New Crops for the New World* (New York: Macmillan Company, 1945).

Winius, George D., 'Two Lusitanian Variations on a Dutch Theme: Portuguese Companies in Times of Crisis, 1628-1662', in Leonard Blussé and Femme Gaastra, eds., *Companies and Trade* (Leiden:

Leiden University Press, 1981), pp. 119-34.

Wiznitzer, Arnold, *Jews in Colonial Brazil* (New York: Columbia University Press, 1960).

Wright, A. C. A., 'Maize Names as Indicators of Economic Contacts', *The Uganda Journal*, 13:1 (March 1949), 61-81.

Zemella, Mafalda P., *O abastecimento da Capitania das Minas Gerais no século XVlll* (São Paulo: Editora Hucitec, 1990).

A NOTE ON TWO PORTUGUESE ARTISTS

CARLOS JULIÃO was born in Turin in 1740 and died in 1811. He followed a military career rising from second lieutenant to the rank of brigadier on retirement. He saw service in Portugal, India, China, and Brazil, specializing in meticulous plans of fortifications and detailed reports. Forty-three water-colours depict Portuguese, native Americans, and persons of African descent in Rio de Janeiro, Serro do Frio in Minas Gerais, and with themes from Bahia. These paintings are housed in the Iconographic Section of the Division of Rare books, Biblioteca Nacional, Rio de Janeiro. They were published in 1960 by the Biblioteca Nacional as *Riscos iluminados de figurinhos de brancos e negros dos uzos do Rio de Janeiro e Serro do Frio. Aquarelas por Carlos Julião.* Historical introduction and descriptive catalogue by Lygia da Fonseca Fernandes da Cunha.

JOAQUIM CÂNDIDO GUILLOBEL (1787-1859) was born in Lisbon of a French father and Portuguese mother. His father took Portuguese citizenship and held posts in the Lisbon mint, moving to Rio de Janeiro in 1811 to take up a position in the mint. He also owned a button factory in Lisbon where Joaquim worked. Joaquim moved to Rio in 1808 and pursued a military career, seeing service in the Maranhão, and retiring with the rank of colonel in the Imperial Corps of Engineers. He drew maps and designed public works in Rio de Janeiro and the imperial palace at Petropolis. Concurrently with his military career, he studied at the Academia das Belas Artes in Rio de Janeiro. Later he was appointed Professor of Drawing at the Military Academy in Rio de Janeiro and held the Chair of Descriptive Drawing and Military Architecture at the Imperial Military Academy (1836-1852). He was twice married, on both occasions to Brazilian women, who bore twelve children by him, and many of whom achieved distinction in public service. His miniatures, postcard size, depict scenes in the city and environs of Rio de Janeiro. Those in the collection of Cândido Guinle de Paula Machado were published by him under the title *Usos e costumes do Rio de Janeiro nas figurinhas de Guillobel/Life and Manners in Rio de Janeiro as seen in Guillobel's small drawings* (Curitiba: Kingraf Ltda., 1978).

ACKNOWLEDGEMENTS FOR ILLUSTRATIONS

We acknowledge with thanks the sources of the following illustrations:
1 From the Deutsches Historisches Museum, Berlin. Photographed by R. Boemke and D. Nagel; 2, 3, 5, 6 and 7 from Georg Braun and Franz Hogenberg, *Civitates Orbis Terrarum* (Cologne, 1572); 4, 38, 50, 53–56, 58–59, 61, 63–64 and 82–83 from James Ford Bell Library, University of Minnesota; 4 from John Ogilby, *America. Being the Latest and Most Accurate Description of the New World* (London, 1671); 8, 9, 35 and 37 from The Pierpont Morgan Library, New York (M.525); 10, 11, 12, 16, 49, 66, 72 and 84 from Alexandre Rodrigues Ferreira, *Viagem filosófica às Capitanias do Grão-Pará, Rio Negro, Mato Grosso, e Cuiabá* (São Paulo: Gráficos Brunner, 1970); 13–15 from Henry Koster, *Travels in Brazil*, 2 vols. 2nd. edition (London: Longman, Hurst, Rees, Orme, and Brown, 1817); 19, 39, 45, 47 and 78–79 from Biblioteca Casanatense, Rome. MS 1889; 20, 30 and 74 from *Riscos iluminados de figurinhos de brancos e negros dos uzos do Rio de Janeiro e Serro do Frio. Aquarelas por Carlos Julião* (Rio de Janeiro: Livraria São José, 1960); 21, 22 and 28 from Museu da Inconfidencia, Ouro Prêto, #343, 345, 260; 21, 22, 28 and 71 are photographs by Eduardo Tropia; 23–24, 26–27, 29 and 73 from *Usos e costumes do Rio de Janeiro nas figurinhas de Guillobel/ Life and Manners in Rio de Janeiro as seen in Guillobel's small drawings* (Curitiba: Kingraf Ltda., 1978). Collection of Cândido Guinle de Paula Machado; 25, 31–34 and 40 from *Views and Costumes of the City and Neighbourhood of Rio de Janeiro, Brazil, from Drawings taken by Lieutenant Chamberlain, Royal Artillery, During the Years 1819 and 1820* (London: Columbian Press, 1822); plate 36 is from Sloan 197. This and plate 80 are from the British

Library; 41 and 48 from The Metropolitan Museum of Art, Gift of Mr and Mrs Klaus G. Perls 1991 (1991.17.39 and 1991.17.13); 42 (photograph by Jeffrey Ploskonka) and 43 (photograph by Ken Heinen) both from National Museum of African Art, Eliot Elisofon Archives, Smithsonian Institution (85-19-9) and (82-5-3); 44 from The Metropolitan Museum of Art, Louis V. Bell and Rogers Funds, 1972 (1972. 63.); 46 (Freer 60.28), 51 Freer 65.23), 52 (Freer 65.22), 75 (Freer 79.50), 77 (Freer 56.12 verso), courtesy of the Freer Gallery of Art, Smithsonian Institution, Washington D.C.; 50, 55 and 57 reproduced from André Thevet, *Les Singularitez de la France Antarctique* (Paris: Héritiers de Maurice de la Porte, 1558); 53 reproduced from Willem Piso, *Historia Naturalis Brasiliae* (Leiden: F. Hackium, 1648); 54 reproduced from Giovanni Battista Ramusio, *Navigationi et Viaggi*, (Venice: Giunti 1606); 56 reproduced from Charles de Rocheforte, *Histoire naturelle et morale des Iles Antilles de l'Amérique* (Rotterdam: Leers, 1681); 60, 62, 65, 67 and 68 reproduced from Fr. Cristóvão de Lisboa, *História dos animais e árvores do Maranhão. 1624. 1627.* Arquivo Histórico Ultramarino, Lisbon (Lisbon: Arquivo Histórico Ultramarino e Centro de Estudos Históricos Ultramarinos, 1967); 58 reproduced from Johannes de Laet, *L'histoire du Nouveau Monde: ou., description des Indes Occidentales* (Leiden: Elsevier, 1640); 59 and 61 reproduced from Garcia d' Orta, *Due libri dell' Historia de i Semplici, Aromati, e altre cose, che vengono portate dall' Indie Orientali, pertinenti alla medicina* (Venice: Ziletti, 1582); 63 and 64 reproduced from Jan Huyghen van Linschoten, *Histoire de la Navigation ... et de son voyage es Indes Orientales.* 3rd. ed. (Amsterdam, 1638); 70, photograph by Joaquim, Sabará; 76, Arthur M. Sackler Gallery, Smithsonian Institution, Washington D.C. (Sackler S1990.57); 81 reproduced from *Livro das traças de carpintaria* by Manuel Fernandes, 1616. Biblioteca da Ajuda, Lisbon; 82 reproduced from Francisco Álvares, *Verdadera Informaçam das terras do Preste Joam* (Lisbon, 1540); 83 reproduced from Fernão Mendes Pinto, *Peregrinaçam* (Lisbon, 1614).

INDEX

attacks corruption, 79; diplomatic
overtures, 78, 81; sends artisans to
Portugal, 105, 186; and Hindu
customs 188; marriage policy, 188;
promotes Portuguese language,
192; mints coins, 145
Albuquerque Coelho, António de,
70-1
Albuquerque Coelho, Jorge de, 64,
65
Albuquerque Coelho de Carvalho,
António de, 70
Alcácer-Quibir, 65
Alcalá de Henares, 83
Aleppo, 12, 45, 47, 48, 99
Alexandretta, 45, 48, 99
Alexandria, 12, 45
aljarvias, 132
Almadén, 125
Almeida, Lourenço de, 67
Almeida, Luís de, 205
Almeida Portugal, Luís de, 69
Almeida Portugal, Pedro de, 67
aloes wood, 127
alquicés, 132
alumstone, 127, 132
Alvares, Fr Francisco, 13, 16-17, 77-
8, 165, 195; cited, 78
Alvares, Jorge, 3, 9
Alvares Barna, Manuel, 86
Alvares Correia, Diogo, 109
Alvares Fagundes, João, 179
Amazonia: British in, 25, 56, 100;
Dutch in, 25, 56, 100; Luso-
Spanish rivalry, 100; disease, 121,
122; missionaries in, 90-1, 100,
117; indigenous plants, 171. *See
also* Maranhão e Grão-Pará
Amazon river, 54, 57, 84, 99-101,
102, 103, 214
ambassadors and emissaries: African,
11, 13, 14, 19; Portuguese, 4, 12,
13, 14, 16-17, 19, 64, 76-81, 82, 90,
113, 114, 217; priests and friars as,
13, 82, 90, 91. *See also* diplomacy,
gifts
amber, 125, 137
ambergris, 127
Ambon, 6, 38, 40
Amerindians, in Brazil: guides, 18:
technology, 56-7, 166,171, 178-9;
population, 62; relations with

Portuguese, 3, 64, 66, 68, 109,115-
16, 118, 132; relations with
French, 116, 121; relations with
Spanish, 116; scientific interest in,
84; and missionaries, 90, 102, 116-
117, 121-2, 155, 189, 201-2; and
Paulistas, 56, 102, 103, 116, 117;
languages, 90, 193; forced migra-
tion, 115-17; and Old World
diseases, 119, 120-22; barter and
gifts, 132; dress, 189; in Spanish
America, 116, 120-2, 203
Ampaza, 91, 97, 98
Amsterdam, 35, 125, 130
Ana, 48
Anbaca, 50
ancestor worship, 4, 217
Anchieta, José de, 197
Andrade, António de, 90
Andreoni, Giovanni Antonio *see*
Antonil, André João
Anglo-Portuguese treaties, 130
Angola, 11, 14, 19, 21: Dutch attacks,
24, 25, 68; trade, 31, 96; transpor-
tation, 50; Portuguese coloniza-
tion, 60-1, 77; links to Brazil, 62-
3, 67-9, 70, 88, 140-1; bishops, 87,
88; garrisons, 74; place of exile,
106, 107; women, 110; Jesuits, 69,
77, 146, 199; scientific expedition
to, 177; animals of, 182,197
Angra dos Reis, 42
Anjos, Gregório dos, 88
annatto, 174
Annobón, 25
Antonil, André João, 173
Antonio, Gaspar, 179
Antwerp: trade, 31, 35, 98, 99, 125,
130
Arabia, 127
Arabian Desert, routes across, 44-9,
98-9
Araguaia river, 54
Arakan, 93
architecture, 184-5
arecanut, 127
Arguim, 22, 54, 114, 125, 126, 143
arms and armour, 125, 133, 190, 205
Arruda, Diogo de, 184
Arruda, Francisco de, 184
artisans and artists, 60, 85-7, 104-5,
106, 107, 186-7, 217-9

Bombay, 24, 25, 48, 49, 141
Borba Gato, Manuel de, 103
Bordeaux, 125
Borges de Figueiroa, Joaquim, 88
Borneo, 32, 38, 40, 41, 127, 143;
  missionaries, 89
Bosman, William, 165
Boston, 6
botanical gardens, 157, 172, 176
botany, 83,149-50, 196
Botelho, Diogo, 83
Boxer, Charles R., 60, 200
boxwood, 129
bracelets, 127, 131, 132
Braga, 89
Brandon, William, 203
brandy, 128
brassware, 125, 131
Brazil: Amerindians, 3, 18, 56-7, 62,
  64, 66, 68, 84, 90, 102, 103, 109,
  115-17, 118, 119, 120-2, 132, 155,
  166, 171, 178-9, 189, 193, 201-2;
  exploration of, 18, 102-3; forts, 23;
  foreigners, 21, 24, 25, 43, 56, 68,
  69, 90, 100, 105, 121, 150, 166,
  212, 218; independence, 26;
  capitals, 26; royal court, 26; trade
  with West Africa, 31, 140-1;
  transportation, 50-2, 54-7;
  migration to, 41, 59, 61-2, 104-5,
  110-11, 117; internal migration,
  104-5, 115-16, 117-19; coastal
  trade, 42-3; population, 61-2; links
  to Angola, 62-3, 67-70, 88, 140-1;
  lord-proprietorships, 64, 65;
  postings compared to Portuguese
  India, 66, 71-2; governors-general
  and viceroys, 66-7; bishops, 88-9;
  mendicant orders in, 116-7, 121,
  201-2; exile to, 106; Jesuits in, 89,
  90-1, 100, 102, 103, 116-17, 121-2,
  146, 154-6, 161, 166, 185, 193,
  198, 199, 201-2; Jews in, 108-9;
  exports, 128-9,130-1; imports,
  132; plants and seeds brought
  to,152-6, 157, 158, 160-3; plants
  and seeds carried from, 158, 164-
  70, 171, 173-4; introduction
  European animals to, 181; animals
  and birds carried from, 181, 182;
  Chinese influences in, 184;
  persons of African descent, 51, 52,

56, 62, 86, 102, 112,189, 191, 202,
218-9; music, 194-5; intellectual
and cultural life, 206-8; port cities,
42. See also *carreira do Brasil*,
slave trade
Brazil Company, 30, 31
Brazil-nuts, 164
Brazilwood, 127, 128, 129, 130
Bristol, 125
British: attacks on Portuguese, 24, 25,
  28, 75, 91; in Brazil, 25, 56, 100;
  engage in contraband, 138, 141,
  145; recipients of Brazilian gold,
  138, 144, 145; disseminators of
  plants, 172; ideas in Brazil, 208;
  trade with Portugal, 125, 130; in
  India, 141, 143
British Ultimatum, 49
Brito, António de, 81, 82
Brito Homem, Luís de, 88
Brittany, trade with Portugal, 125
bronze objects, 132; cannon, 132;
  Benin bronzes, 217-18
brotherhoods, 147, 187, 202
Buba river, 54
Buddhism, 4, 44, 199, 201
Bueno da Silva, Bartolomeu, 102-3
Buenos Aires, 140
building technique, 85, 86, 185
Bulhões e Sousa, Miguel de, 88
bulls, papal, 13, 87
Bungo, 89
Burke, Edmund, 208
Burma, 32, 93
Bushmen, 4, 12
Buzi river, 54

Cabeza de Vaca, Alvar Núñez, 5
Cabo de Santa Maria, 2
Cabo do Lobo, 2
Cabo Negro, 2
Cabo Padrão (Cape Cross), 2
Cabo Verde *see* Cape Verde islands
cabotage, 41-3, 52, 53, 54
Cabral, Pedro Alvares, 9, 40, 73, 115,
  132, 217
Cabrilho, João Rodrigues, 5
Cacao, 103, 128, 155,164, 171,175,
  178
Cacheu: trade, 31
Cacheu river, 53, 54
Caconada, 106

272

Cà da Mosto, Alvise da, 21, 41, 77, 158
Cadornega, António de Oliveira, 197
Caeté, 64
Cairo, 12, 45, 47, 158
Cajamarca, 14
Calchaqui, 68
Caldas, José António, 42
Calicut, 9, 12, 44, 73, 120
California, 5
Câmara, José Gonçalo da, 182
Câmara Coutinho, António Luís Gonçalves da, 67, 153
Cambay. See Gujarat
Cambodia, 92
camellia, 157
camels, 50
Caminha, 43
Caminha, Pero Vaz de, 115
Camões, Luís Vaz de, 220-1
camphor, 127
Canarins, 154, 156
cangeiro, 52
Cannanore, 12, 13, 42, 44, 79, 81, 182
canoes, 41, 42, 55, 56-7, 84, 103, 117-18, 214
Canton, Portuguese in, 3, 9, 52, 72, 79, 80, 92; silk trade, 38, 136; syphilis introduced to, 120
Cantor, 53, 54, 143
Cão, Diogo, 2, 53
Cape Bojador, 9
Cape Breton island, 9
Cape Guardafui, 19
Cape Nun, 9
Cape of Good Hope route *see carreira da India*
Cape Palmas, 126
Cape São Roque, 34, 35
Cape Verde islands: 'discovery', 9; trade, 31, 40-1, 50, 126; agriculture, 161; sailing time, 35; waystation, 35; emigration from, 41; population of, 61, 62; exile to, 107, 110; plants of African origin to, 152; of American origin, 152; plant adaptation, 150, 152, 153; maize, 165; introduction of animals, 181
Capiberibe river, 55
caps, 131, 132, 189
capsicums *see* peppers

caravels: design, 28-9, 217; disease environment, 119; depictions of, 216-17, 218
cardamom, 127
Cardim, Fernão, 197; quoted, 166-7, 178-9
career mobility: governors and viceroys, 66-71, 75-6; ecclesiastics, 87-89; magistrates, 71-2; mariners, 65-6,72-3; physicians, 83-4 ; soldiers, 64-5, 66, 73-5
Caribbean, 100, 108, 121
Carmelites, 92, 146, 154, 185, 198
carnaúba wax, 129
Carneiro, Belchior, 87
carracks,18, 28, 30, 58-9, 119
carreira da India, 27-8, 30, 35, 37, 72-3, 84, 110, 132, 140; sailing times, 35-7; conditions, 58-9, 73; way-stations, 37, 58, 59, 65, 75, 140, 180; inliterature, 212; impact of, 124
carreira do Brasil, 29, 30-1, 34-5, 40, 59, 132
Cartagena, 91, 101, 108
cartography: Portuguese, 16, 17-18; Japanese, 205; Javanese, 18. See Rutters
carts, 51, 52
Casa de Guiné, 64, 211
Casa de Suplicação, 71
casados, 61, 63, 95
Casamance river, 54
Cascais, 48
cashew nuts, 128, 164, 169-70, 174
Caspian Sea, 45
Cassart, Jacques, 25
cassava *see* manioc
Castanheda, Fernão Lopes de, 210
Castanhoso, Miguel de, 215
Castelo Branco, João Rodrigues de, 197
Castelo Branco, Pedro de, 217
castor-oil, 162
Castro, Baltasar de, 14
Castro, João de, 186, 203, 214, 216
Castro Sarmento, Jacob de, 108
catechisms and catechists, 93-4, 204
Catherine of Braganza, 24
Cayenne, 161
Ceará, 43, 50
Cebu, 137, 216

cedar, 129
Celebes, 32, 41, 93, 136
cereals: imports to Portugal, 125, 126; imports to Brazil, 160; cultivation, 40, 126, 128, 165
Ceuta, 19, 31
Ceylon: Portuguese in, 22, 24, 49, 65, 97, 193; Dutch in, 24, 193; commerce, 15, 32, 41, 42, 127, 133, 137; exploration, 40; yaws introduced into, 120; converts to Christianity, 201. *See also* cinnamon
chaise, 52
Charles I, King of Spain, 5
Charles II, King of England, 24
Chatim, Raul, 105
Chaul, 13, 42, 54, 81
Chêkiang, 42
Chesapeake Bay, 5
chicunda, 104
chiggers, 120
chillies, 164, 169
China: Portuguese trade mission to, 3, 9, 79-80; Portuguese descriptions of, 20, 97, 215-16; expeditions, 181; Portuguese travellers in, 64, 90, 97; missionaries in, 89, 90, 92, 93, 94, 90; Portuguese trade, 96-7, 127-8, 133; Portuguese smugglers in, 42, 96-7, 168; American crops in, 168-9, 170; converts to Christianity, 201; Western ideas introduced into, 199-200, 204; gold in,144. *See also* Canton, Macao
Chinese: pilots, 15, 18; silk, 32; merchants, 79; rites, 201; clergy, 94
chinoiserie, in Brazil,184
Chodankar, Mahendra, 190
cholera, 74
Chosen, 10
Christianity, converts to: 4, 6, 11, 77, 200-202. *See also* Jesuits, missionaries
Cinchona, 129
cinnabar, 125, 132, 133
cinnamon, 32, 127, 129, 130, 137; plants disseminated, 153-4, 155-6, 163
citrus fruits, 160

civet cats, 126
clergy: quality of, 94, 107; non-European, 93-4
clocks, 125, 132, 133
cloth, 125, 127, 130, 132. *See also* silk, textiles
cloves: trade in, 30, 32, 38, 41, 127, 128, 130, 131, 133; plants disseminated, 153-4, 163; American, 155
Cochin: Portuguese in 24, 44, 73, 98; entrepôt, 30, 37, 38, 40, 42, 133; rulers of 81; shipyard 86; see of 87; elephants sent from, 182; Manueline style, 185; Portuguese urban imprint, 183. *See also* *carreira da India*
Cochinchina, 89, 143
cochineal, 164
cocoa *see* cacao
coconut oil, 127
coconuts, 154, 155, 157, 159, 161-2
Codex Casanatense, 218
Coelho, Gonçalo, 3
Coelho de Sousa, João, 101
Coelho Guerreiro, António, 74
coffee, 128, 161, 175
Coimbra: University, 71, 75, 83, 84, 85, 185, 188; Brazilian graduates of, 205-7, 208; Jesuit college, 92
coir, 127
colanuts, 131
Colégio de Santo Antão, 146
Colombo, 22, 24, 65, 97, 156. *See also* Ceylon
Colônia do Sacramento, 68, 75, 106, 140
'Columbian Exchange', 160, 175
Columbus, Christopher, 1-2, 5-6, 120, 160-1, 191
Companhia de Cachéu e Rios de Guiné, 31
Companhia do Cabo Verde e Cachéu, 31
Companhia do Comércio da India Oriental, 31
Companhia Geral de Pernambuco e Paraíba, 31
Companhia Geral do Grão-Pará e Maranhão, 31, 112
compass, 17
Conceição Veloso, Fr José Mariano da, 177

Condamine, Charles de la, 171
Confucianism, 4, 199,
Congo: kingdom of, 3, 11; Christianity introduced into, 3, 93; Portuguese presence in, 14, 19, 60, 69, 77, 86, 188; trade, 131
Congo river, 2, 9, 14, 53, 55
Conselho da India e Conquistas Ultramarinas, 64
Conselho Ultramarino, 64, 66, 71
'Contact period', 3, 4, 15
contraband: Portuguese engaged in, 135; silver from Peru, 100, 140; on China coast, 42, 96-7; in Caribbean, 100; between Macao and Manila, 137-8, 145; Brazilian gold, 94, 138, 140, 145; between Brazil and West Africa, 141; West African gold, 145; Río de la Plata, 43, 101, 140
convents, 111, 146
copahiba oil, 129
copal, 129
copper: trade in, 12, 125, 132, 133, 135; in India,145; objects, 125, 131, 132
copra, 127, 129
coral, 125, 127, 131, 132
cork, 129
Coromandel, 18, 22, 32, 41, 127, 133
Correia, Gaspar, 210, 216
Correia de Sá e Benevides, Salvador, 24, 67-8, 69, 101
Correio Brasiliense, 207
corruption, 65, 73, 87, 94-5, 136-7
Corte-Real, João Pereira, 72
Cortés, Hernán, 5
Cosa, Juan de la, 216
Costa, Baltazar da, 38
Costa, Claudio Manuel da, 206
Costa, Cristóvão da, 150
Costa, Rodrigo de, 67
Costa da Malagueta, 64, 126, 161
Costa da Mina, 86, 131
Costa de Lemos, António da, 72
Costa Franco, Francisco da, 84
cotton: cultivation: Azores, 126; West Africa, 126; Brazil, 128, 129, 175; dissemination, 152, 159, 164, 175; origins and species, 172
cotton goods *see* textiles
'country trade', 134-8

Couto, Diogo do, 47, 210
Covilhã, Pero de, 12, 13, 19, 47, 77
Cranganore, 24, 42, 87
crime and criminals, 11, 24, 106-7, 206
crocodiles, 16, 197
Crosby, Alfred, 160, 175
Cruz, Fr Gaspar da, 20, 92-3, 211-12
Cruz, Fr João da, 88
Cruz, Fr Manuel da, 88
crystal, 133
Cuanza, 53
Cubas, Brás, 101
Cuiabá, 51, 87, 103
Cuiabá river, 56, 84
Cunha, Aires da, 99
Cunha, Nuno da, 47
Cunha, Tristão da, 13
Curitiba, 51
currency: non-metallic, 131, 132, 171; metallic, 133, 144, 145
currents, ocean, 32-7
Curtin, Philip, 55

Daman, 21, 25, 42, 48, 49, 65, 81
Damascus, 45
Danakil desert, 91
Danzig, 31, 125
Dapper, Olfert, 165
dates, 125
David II, Negus, 13, 14, 78
decorative arts, 185-7
deerskins, 127, 128
degredados, 11, 24, 106-7, 206
Del Cano, Sebastian, 120
Denmark, 131
desembargadores, 71-2
Desembargo do Paço, 71
Desterro, Fr António do, 88
Diálogos das Grandezas do Brasil, 150, 166, 176, 197
Diamantina, 184
diamonds: Borneo, 32, 41; Brazilian, 67, 128, 129; Golconda, 127; contraband, 94, 138, 140
Dias, Bartolomeu, 2, 9, 11, 77, 209
Dias, Fernão, 47
Dias, Luís, 86
Dias de Novais, Paulo, 21, 60, 77
Dias Pais, Fernão, 103
Dieppe, 125
diet and dietary preferences, 164, 169, 189, 190, 191. *See also* plants

diplomacy: gaffes, 79, 80. *See also* ambassadors and emissaries
Discalced Augustinians, 92
'discoveries', 15, 40
diseases, 74, 92-3, 119-22, 197
Diu, 21, 42, 65, 66
Dominicans, 87, 92-3, 198
donkeys, 50
D' Orta, Garcia, 83, 108, 149, 150, 179, 196
Douro province, 104
dragon's blood, 126, 130
dress, 132, 188, 189, 190, 191
drogas do sertão, 155, 178
Du Clerc, 25
Duguay-Trouin, René, 24, 25
Dürer, Albrecht, 182
Dutch: attacks on Portuguese, 23-24, 25, 28, 29, 30, 37, 47, 68, 76, 91, 156, 193; in Brazil, 25, 56, 68, 69, 90, 100, 150, 212, 218; in Angola, 24, 25,68; at Elmina, 25, 141; in Gulf of Guinea, 141; scientists, 150; trade rivalry, 128, 136, 138, 152; language, 192-3
Dutch East India Company, 29, 136, 179, 180
dyes: Asian, 127; Atlantic islands, 126, 128, 130, 152; American, 127, 128, 129 130, 174

Eanes, Gil, 9
ebony, 127
education, 198-9, 207, 208. *See also* Coimbra, University of; Jesuits
Egypt, Sultan of, 47, 66
Elena, Queen, 13
elephants, 127, 182
Elmina *see* São Jorge da Mina
emboabas, 76
emeralds, 103
England: Portuguese colonies in, 130
English *see* British
English East India Company, 45, 136, 145, 152, 179
Enlightenment, 207-8
entradas, 116, 117
Espírito Santo, 62, 154
Estado da India: term defined, 20-21; appointments compared with Brazil, 66, 71-2; governors and viceroys, 66-7

Ethiopia: Portuguese contacts with, 12-14, 16-17, 19, 77-8, 215; missionaries, 24, 89, 91; plants indigenous to, 161, 162; maize cultivation in, 165; Portuguese accounts of, 16-17, 77-8, 195
Euphrates valley, 45, 47, 49
Evora, 83
exile: places of, 106-7, 110. See also *Degredados*

factories (trading stations). Portuguese, in Africa, 21, 22, 29, 49, 53, 54, 127, 131-2, 143; Ceylon, 22; Europe, 130; India, 22, 81; Indonesia, 22; Malacca, 79; Ternate 22, 82; Tidor 22. British, 25; Dutch, 25; Muslim, 41; Spanish, 81
faience, 125
Faro, 43
fauna: studies, 150, 176, 177, 197; dispersal of from Asia, 159, 161; from Europe, 158, 180-1; provisioning of vessels, 179-80; as collectables, 181-2; in Brazil, 197; in Africa, 197
feathers, as trade objects,129
Felu falls, 53
Fernandes, António, 11, 14, 106
Fernandes, Manuel, 217
Fernandes, Valentim, 165
Fernandes Brandão, Ambrósio, 197. See also *Diálogos das grandezas do Brasil.*
Fernandes Trancoso, Gonçalo, 200
Fernandes Vieira, João, 68-9
Fernando Pó, 25, 164
Fernão de Noronha, 40, 106
Ferreira da Rosa, João, 83
Fez, 65
Fezzan, 158
Fialho, José, 88
fire-arms, 133, 190, 205
fish: trade in, 125, 132; studies of, 150, 176, 177, 197
fish-hooks, 132
fish oil, 128, 129
Flanders: trade with Portugal, 125, 130; Portuguese in, 130
fleets, 29-31, 34-5
Florence, 85, 130

flour, 128, 132, 178-9
Fogo, 61
Forcados river, 131
Fortaleza, 42
forts, Portuguese: in Africa, 21, 22, 43, 54, 60, 71, 106, 131-2, 141; Atlantic islands, 23; in Brazil, 23, 84; in China, 80; in India, 21, 65, 81; in Japan, 44; Moluccas, 82. *See also* São Jorge da Mina
foundrymen, 72, 86, 87, 105
France: Portuguese in, 85, 130; Portuguese trade with, 35, 125, 130
Franciscan missionaries, 47, 48, 92, 166; history of, 93; remit bullion, 146
Franco de Oliveira, João, 88
Freire de Andrada, Gomes, 70
Fremona, 91
French: in Brazil, 21, 24, 25, 43, 105, 121, 166, 171; relations with Portuguese court, 64; in Straits of Gibraltar 75; pirates, 73; relations with Amerindians, 116, 121; disseminators of plants, 161; ideas in Brazil, 208
Freyre, Gilberto, 70
Fritz, Samuel, 100
Fróis, Luís, 20, 89
Fukien, 42, 97, 106, 168, 169
Funai, 87, 89
Funchal, 13. *See also* Madeira
furniture, 125, 127, 129, 133, 137, 186, 187
Furtado de Mendonça, João, 83
Furtado de Mendonça, Hipólito José da Costa Pereira, 207
Fuzhou, 97

Galangal, 127
galeão, 28
Galvão, António, 137
Galvão, Duarte, 13
Galvão da Silva, Manuel, 176-7, 206
Galvêas, Count of *see* Mello de Castro, André de
Gama, Cristóvão da, 14, 215
Gama, Estêvão da, 65
Gama, Francisco da, 86
Gama, João da, 137-8
Gama, José Basilio da, 207

Gama, Vasco da: places stone pillars, 2-3; voyage of, 9, 18, 27, 40, 120; son of, 65; sailors and syphilis, 120; iconography of fleets of, 217; 'era', 6, 44, 124, 156
Gambia river, 14, 21, 53, 54, 55, 77, 126
Ganges, 93
Gao, 158, 160
Garces, Henrique, 100
Garcia, Aleixo, 14, 99
garrisons, 58, 59, 60, 73-4, 84, 106, 165. *See also* forts, São Jorge da Mina
Geba river, 54
Genoese merchants, 124
geological specimens, 177, 197
Germany, 125, 131
Ghana, 160
Ghat, 158
Gibraltar, Straits of, 75
gifts, 11, 13, 132, 157; 173, 181-2. *See also* ambassadors and emissaries
Gilbert, Humfry, 180
ginger, 127, 129, 130, 152; dissemination of,152, 153, 163
Goa: archives, 21; Portuguese capture of, 18; strategic importance of, 22; Dutch attack on, 25, 29; as entrepôt, 32, 37-8, 41-2, 52-3, 132-4, 135, 136, 140; population of, 61; seat of governors and viceroys, 44, 66-7; shipyard,86; see of, 87, 89; convent, 111; mint, 145; inquisition, 108, 188; Portuguese city, 183-4; hospital, 205; Jesuit college, 198; colleges of other religious orders, 198; and neighbouring areas, 49, 53, 71, 154. See also *carreira da India*, Jesuits
Goanese, in East Africa: 49, 96
Godinho, Manuel, 48-9, 195, 215
Goiás, 18, 51, 54, 56, 69, 76, 87, 103, 115, 117-18
Góis, Bento de, 89-90
Góis, Damião de, 210
Golconda, 81, 127,
gold: Asian, 127, 133, 135, 143-4; East African, 11, 12, 41, 95-6, 127, 133, 143, 185; West African, 11, 19, 31, 126, 131, 143; Japanese, 205; Moroccan trade in, 125;

152-6, 157; American plants introduced to, 169-70, 173-4; art and artifacts, 186, 190, 204-5; European music and instruments introduced to, 194; converts to Christianity, 201; printing press, 204

Indian Ocean: Portuguese navigation in, 18; routes, 32; monsoons, 37; trade diasporas, 136-7. See also *carreira da India*

indigo, 125, 127, 129, 130, 152, 175

Indochina, 127

Indonesia, 32, 64, 133

Indo-Portuguese: artifacts, 184, 186; culture, 188; dialect, 193; dress, 189

Inquisition, 101, 107, 108, 188

Ireland, 125

Irmandade do Santíssimo Sacramento, 147

Isfahan, 45

Islam, 4, 199, 200

islands, importance of, 40-1, 138-40; as provision depots, 179-80. See islands by name

Italian: merchants in Portugal,124; missionaries, 199-200, 201; painters in Brazil, 105

Italy: Portuguese communities in, 130; Portuguese students in, 85; Portuguese trade with, 125, 130

Ivenheima river, 102

ivory, 16, 126, 127, 128, 133

jaboticaba, 164

jacaranda, 128, 129

jack-fruit,157

Jagrançura, 53

Jahāngīr, 169, 173

jangadas, 57

Japan: first Europeans to, 3, 10, 113; Jesuits in, 3, 6, 20, 22, 44, 89, 94, 95, 193, 199, 200, 201, 204, 205, 218; Portuguese ambassadors to, 4, 81; trade missions to, 80-1; descriptions of, 20; Portuguese expelled from, 24, 81; trade, 18, 30, 32, 37-8, 66, 80-1, 133; Portuguese relations with civil authorities, 69; gifts carried by Portuguese, 182; native clergy, 94;

addiction to tobacco, 174; Portuguese influence in, 189, 190, 192, 193, 204, 205; printing press introduced, 204, 205; converts to Christianity, 201; silver and gold, 133, 135, 144, 205. *See also* Nagasaki

Japurá river, 100

Java, 40, 143

Javanese: pilots, 15, 18; merchants, 79, 133

Jequitinhonha river, 54

Jesuits: in Africa, 69, 77, 92, 146, 199; in Bengal, 89; in Bhutan, 90; in Brazil, 89, 90-1, 100, 102, 103, 116-17, 121-2, 146, 154-6, 161, 166, 185, 193, 198, 199, 201-2; in China, 89, 90, 199, 200, 201; in Ethiopia, 89, 91; in India, 89, 91-2, 146, 154-5, 198, 199, 200,201, 204, 205; in Japan, 3, 6, 20, 22, 44, 89, 94, 95, 193, 199, 200, 201, 204, 205, 218; in Moluccas, 89; in Nepal, 90; in Portugal, 92, 146, 199; in Spanish America, 100; in Tibet, 90; in Tongking, 89; as couriers, 48; as emissaries, 82, 90, 91; mobility of, 88-92; relations with civil authorities, 69, 90, 91-2; non-European novices, 93-4; engage in commerce, 94, 146; Pombaline decrees, 109; deporta-tion, 109; bullion remittances, 146; land holdings, 145; property, 146; dissemination of plants, 154-6; botanical studies, 154-5, 156, 161; printing presses, 193, 199, 204, 205; disseminators of music, 194-5; writings, 19, 20, 48-9, 90, 166-7, 196, 197, 199-200, 211, 212; educators, 198-9; disseminators of ideas, 198-202, 204-5

jewellery, 190-1

Jews, 107-9

Jiddah, 12

Jinga, Queen, 107

João II, King, 2, 11, 12, 13, 14, 79, 143, 182

João III, King, 13, 47

João IV, King, 68, 81, 90, 153

João V, King, 59, 62, 141, 144, 154, 182, 197

João VI, King, 62, 157
Johnson, Samuel, 212
Johore, 71
José I, King, 172
Josepe, 12
Juba, 91
juiz de fora, 71, 72
Julião, Carlos, 74-5, 218, 265
junks, Portuguese use of, 29, 78
Juruá river, 100

Kagan, Richard, 6
Kagoshima, 89
Kamaran island, 13
Kanara, 75
Kan-chou-fu, 97
Kasai river, 96
Kilwa, 43, 66
kimonos, 133
Kindersley, Mrs, 202
knives, 132
Kung, 48
Kyoto, 89
Kyushu, 89

Labrador, 9
lacquer and lacquerware, 32, 127, 131, 133
Ladrones, 170
Laet, Jan de, 150
Lagos, 43
Lahore, 93, 173
Lalibela, 77
Lamu, 97
lançados, 14, 106, 109, 114. See *degredados*
language borrowings, 165-6, 170, 174, 192-3
Lar, 45
Larantuqueiros, 74
La Rochelle, 35, 48, 125
lascarins, 74
Latin, 192, 193, 198, 199
Laxa, 45
lead, 131, 132
Lebna Dengel, Negus, 13, 14, 78
Lécluse, Charles, 149
Leghorn, 130
Leh, 90
Leiria, 88
lenses, 133

Leo X, Pope, 13
lepers, 106
Léry, Jean de, 166
Lima, 101
Lima, Manuel Felix de, 103-4, 119
Lima, Rodrigo de, 13, 19, 77,
língua geral, 67
Linschoten, Jan Huighen van, 154
Lin Tin, 3,
Lisboa, Fr António de, 12
Lisboa, Fr Cristóvão de, 197
Lisbon: entrepôt, 31, 34-5, 43, 124-32; foreign merchant communities, 124; plague, 92-3
litmus roccella, 126
'Livro de Lisuarte de Abreu', 217
Livros das Pazes e Tratados da India, 21
Lobo, Jerónimo, 91-2, 212
Locke, John, 208
London, 93, 130, 207
Lopes, Luís, 212-13
Lopes de Sousa, Pero, 214
Louvain, 85
Luanda, 24, 31, 50, 68, 69, 77, 87. See *also* slave trade
Luzon, 173
Luzonese, 79
Luso-Spanish rivalry: in Amazonia, 100; in Río de La Plata, 70, 140 ; for China trade, 137-8
Macao, Portuguese settlement in, 22, 44 ; Dutch attack, 25; commercial entrepôt, 18, 30, 32, 37-8, 40, 52, 127, 133, 135, 137-8, 145; trade missions to Japan, 80-1; population, 61; marriages in 70, 96; convents, 111; Santa Casa da Misericórdia, 87, 107; bishops, 87, 88; market for snuff, 140
mace, trade in: 30, 32, 40, 127, 130, 133
Machico, 66
Madagascar, 12, 37, 48, 197
Madeira, 9; fort, 23; trade, 31, 34, 40-1, 126, 128; emigration from, 41, 61, 62, 111; population, 61; illustrious sons of, 66, 68; agriculture, 125-6, 161; animals introduced to, 181
Madeira river 54, 84, 100, 102, 103, 116

Madras, 71
Madre de Deus, 28
Madrid, Treaty of, 206
Mafra, 185
Magalhães, Fernão de, 3, 5, 11, 66, 82, 209, 210, 216
Magalhães Gandavo, Pero de, 197
Magalhães Godinho, Vitorino, 32, 60
Maghreb, 41
magistrates, 71-2, 76, 85; and commerce, 95
Maia da Gama, João da, 75
maize, cultivation and dissemination of, 152, 164-6, 168, 169, 170, 175
Makassar, 32, 41, 93, 127, 136, 143
Malabar rites, 201
Malacca: Portuguese conquest of, 13, 22; attacked by Dutch, 24, 25; as entrepôt, 15, 18, 29, 32, 37, 38, 40, 127, 133, 135; trading treaty, 64; merchant community, 78-9; factory, 79; see, 87; bishops, 88, 93; mint, 145
malaguetta pepper, 126, 130
malaria, 74, 118, 119, 120
Malay pilots, 15
Mandavi river, 43, 53
Maldives, 40
Mali, 11, 14, 19, 160
Malindi, 2, 18, 19, 24, 32, 43, 44, 47, 48, 97
Mamoré river, 102, 103
Manchus, 136, 173
Mandinga, 21, 77
mangoes, 157, 163
Manica, 177
Manila, 98, 137-8, 145
Manillas, 127, 131, 132
manioc, 152, 160, 164, 166-8, 170, 175, 178-9
manioc flour, 128, 178-9
Manrique, Fr Sebastião, 93
Manuel I, King, 11, 14, 18, 66, 77, 79, 80, 152; and gifts, 13, 181,182, 186
Manueline style, 184-5
Marajó island, 56
Maranhão e Grão-Pará: maritime connections with 34, 35, 214; land routes in, 50; students from, 85; see, 87; bishops, 88; governors, 70, 75; missionaries, 90-1, 100, 117; disease, 121, 122; exports from,

128, 129; plant experiments in, 153; cocoa cultivation in, 155; coffee cultivation in, 175. *See also* Amazonia
Maranhão river, 99
Marathas, 24, 71, 169
Marave, 96
Margaret of Austria, 48
Mariana, 87, 88, 184
Marianas, 170
Mariano, Luís, 197
Markgraf, Georg, 150
marmalades, 129, 130
Marrakech, 125
marriage, 96, 109, 110, 111, 188
Marseille, 45, 48
Mascarenhas, Francisco, 82
Mascarenhas, Luís de, 67
Mascarenhas, Vasco, 66-7, 155
Mascarenhas e Lencastre, Fernando Martins, 70
Massawa, 77
Matabeleland, 12
materia medica, 83, 149-50, 196-7
Matheus, 13, 77
Mato Grosso, 18, 51, 54, 56, 76, 84, 103, 115, 117-18, 214
Mazagão, 31, 74, 106
measles, 120, 121, 122
Mecca, 12
medicinal plants, 127, 128, 129, 173, 179
Medina, 12
Meliapore, 22, 23, 42, 81, 87
Mello de Castro, André de, 59, 69
Mello de Castro, António de, 48
Melo Palheta, Francisco de, 161
Mendaña, Alvaro de, 5
Mendes, Alvaro, 105
Mendes dos Reis, Bartolomeu, 88
Mendes Pinto, Fernão, 80, 112-13, 212
Meneses, Aleixo de, 111
Meneses, António Teles de, 66
Meneses, Jorge de, 66
Meneses, Vasco Fernandes Cesar de, 67
Meneses e Castro, Rodrigo José de, 154
merchants: Gujarati, 79,135; Hindu, 18, 78-9; Italian, 41, 124; Muslim, 18, 23, 41, 78-9, 135, 159-60;

Portuguese, 44, 96, 101,104; partnerships, 96; of Lima, 101; British, 130; Javanese, 133; Malayan, 133
mercury, 100,125, 132
Mesa da Consciencia e Ordens, 71
Mexico City, 98
migration, from Atlantic Islands, 41, 61-2, 110-11, 117; from Portugal, 59-62, 104-5, 117; State sponsorship, 62-3; forced migration of Amerindians, 115-17; within Brazil, 104-5, 115-16, 117-19; within Zambezia, 118. *See also* slave trade, African
milho zaborro, 165
millet, 162, 165
Minas, slaves, 86, 141
Minas Gerais, 51, 62, 69, 72; illegal foundry, 72; migration to, 110-11; slaves, 112, 115. *See also* gold
Ming trade policy, 135
Minho province, 104
mints, 87, 145; clandestine, 72
Mirabilia, 15
Mír Alí Bey, 98
Miranda river, 102
Miranda do Douro, 88
mirrors, 132
Misericórdia, Santa Casa da, 59, 87, 104, 107, 147
missionaries: in Benin, 11, 92; in Bhutan, 90; in Brazil, 89, 90-1, 100, 116-17, 121-2, 201-2; in Burma, 93: in Cambodia, 92; in China, 89, 90, 92, 199-201; in Ethiopia, 89, 91; in India, 89-90, 91-4, 199-201; in Japan, 44, 89, 199-201; in Moluccas, 89; in Nepal, 90; in Persia, 92; in Spanish America, 200; in Tibet, 90; in Tongking, 89; travels of, 89-94; non-European, 93-4; disseminators of ideas, 198-202; writings by, 19, 20, 48-9, 90, 166-7, 196, 197, 199-200, 211-12
mission villages, 102, 116-17, 121-2, 193
Mogadishu, 41, 163, 167
Mogi, 44
molasses, 128, 130
Moluccas: pioneering voyages to, 72;

trade to and from, 9, 18, 29, 30, 32, 38, 40,41, 127, 133, 136; corruption, 137; missionaries in, 89; captain-general of, 66
Mombasa, 24, 43, 44, 48, 67, 71, 97, 98, 165
monasteries, 92, 94
Mondragon, 73
monkeys, 126, 128, 197
Monomotapa, 11-12, 41, 143, 165
monopolies, 29-30, 31, 137, 141
Montarroio, Pero de, 12
Montpellier, 85
mores, 187-91
Morocco: Portuguese forts in, 22, 31; trade with Portugal, 29, 31, 41, 125, 131; Portuguese military campaigns in, 65, 66; goods carried to West Africa, 131,132
mortality: African garrisons, 74; African slave trade, 114-15; Amerindian, 120-22; *carreira da India*, 58-9, 75; by yellow fever in Brazil, 83; by river transportation in Brazil, 118
mossambazes, 95
Mossamedes, 63
mother of pearl, 127
Mount Sinai, 12
Moura Tavares, António Rolim de, 69
Mozambique: attacked, 25, 91; commerce, 32, 41, 54, 135; way-station, 37, 58, 65, 75; garrison, 74, 84; see, 87; bishop, 88; place of exile, 106, 107, 206; trade to Portugal, 127; scientific expedition to, 176-7; town, 183; architecture, 185; fort, 43; hinterland of, 49
Mughal court: Portuguese relations with, 24, 81, 82, 199; Portuguese at court, 89; tobacco at, 173
mules, 50, 51, 181, 182
municipal council *see* Senado da Câmara
Murdock, George Peter, 176
Muscat, 24
music, 193-5
musk: West African, 126; Asian, 127, 133, 135, 137
Muslim: trade, 12, 21, 41; merchants, 18, 23, 41, 78-9, 135, 159-60;

Paranaguá, 43
Parati, 42
Paris, 85, 177
Parnaiba river, 54
parrots, 126, 128
passion fruit, 174
Pate, 24, 43, 48, 71, 91, 97
Patna, 93
pau de China, 127
Paulistas, 56, 57, 76, 102-3, 114, 116, 117
peanuts, 164, 168-9
Pearl river, 3, 43, 52, 80
pearls, 130, 133, 137
Pedro, Prince of Portugal, 17
Pegu, 32, 78, 127
pelota, 56
Pemba, 24, 165
pepper and peppers: of American origin, 164, 169; Asian, trade in, 37, 127, 130, 131, 133; *pimenta de rabo*, 126, 130; malaguetta, 126, 130, 161; dissemination of pepper plants to Brazil, 153-6
Pereira, Diogo, 96
Pereira, Duarte Coelho, 64
Pereira, Duarte Pacheco, 16, 53, 55, 73, 213
Pereira, Galeote, 96-7, 212, 215-6
Pereira, Tomás, 200
Peres, Damião, 12
Peres de Andrade, Fernão, 79
Peres de Andrade, Simão, 72, 80
perfumes, 126,127
Pernambuco: trading company, 31; sailing frequency, 34-5; trade, 42; land routes in, 50; fluvial transportation, 55; migration to, 59; insurrection in, 62; lord-proprietor-ship of, 64, 65; Dutch in, 68, 69, 150, 218; see, 87; bishops, 88, 89; exports from, 128; plant experiments in, 153; sugar-cane cultivation, 161
'Pernambuco peppers', 169
Persia, 45; women of, 49; Portuguese embassies to, 82; missionaries in, 92; Portuguese in, 98; tobacco in, 173; trade to Portugal, 127. *See also* Hormuz
Persian Gulf: trade, 12, 22, 32, 133, 135; routes, 45, 48, 98

Peru, viceroyalty of, 15; 140; Portuguese in, 15, 100, 101, 108, 138
peruleiros, 101. *See also* Peru, Portuguese in
Philip III, King, 5, 48, 182
Philip IV, King, 212
Philippines, 93, 98, 137-8, 173
physicians, 82-3, 98, 149, 150, 196-7
Piauí, 50
Piedade, Fr Luís da, 82
Pies, Willem, 150
Pigafetta, Antonio, 5, 210
pilots: Portuguese, 5, 72, 91, 213-4; non-European, 15, 18. *See also* rutters
pineapples, 164, 169, 170
Pinheiro Mourão, Simão, 196
Pires, Tomé, 79-80, 150, 195, 215
Pires Sardinha, João, 206
Pizarro, Francisco, 5, 14
Pizarro, Gonzalo, 100
plantains, 157, 162
plants: medicinal properties of, 83, 149, 150, 173, 179; experiments in adaptation, 150, 152-5. Origins: African origin, 152, 161, 162; American , 152, 164, 170-3, 174; Asian-Indian, 157, 159,160, 161-2, 162, 172; Brazilian, 164, 171. Dissemination and dispersal by Portuguese: Africa to Brazil, 161-2; India-Brazil, 152-6, 157, 162-3; Portugal to Brazil, 155, 158, 160-1; Portugal to Atlantic islands, 161; Brazil to Atlantic Islands, 164, 165, 168, 174,; Brazil to Europe, 158, 164-5, 174; Brazil to Africa, 158, 164, 165-8, 170, 171, 174; Brazil to India and Asia, 168-70, 174; Brazil to India, 169-70,173-4; Brazil to China, 168-9, 170; Asian-Indian to Africa, 158, 159, 162; Asian-Indian to Pacific islands, 163; intra-Brazilian, 175. Crown policy on dissemination, 152-6, 176-8; Jesuit studies of, 154-6; Old World species, 157; New World species, 157; descriptions of, 197; Spaniards as disseminators, 158, 160, 164, 170, 171, 173, 174; trans-Pacific dissemination, 158, 159

poderosos do sertão, 104
Pombal, Marquis of, 109, 144, 207
Ponce de Leon, Juan, 5
Ponta do Padrão, 2
population: of Portugal, 60, 165; of Portuguese communities overseas, 60-3; growth attributable to dietary changes, 165, 167-8, 169, 175-6
porcelains, 133
pork, 128
Pôrto Feliz, 117, 118
Pôrto Seguro, 3, 62
Pôrto Velho, 84
ports, 42-44, 149
Portugal e Castro, Fernando José de, 154
Portuguese: pilots, 5, 72, 91, 213-4; maritime exploration, 2, 9-10, 40; overland exploration, 11-12, 14-15; 'firsts' by 2, 3, 4, 9-10, 88-9; in the service of Spain, 5, 66; 'age of discovery', 9-11; intelligence gathering, 11-12, 15, 17, 18, 19-20, 78; military offensives 13, 14, 21, 22, 23-4, 64, 65, 66, 73, 77, 97-8; use of native pilots, 15, 18; indigenous military assistance, 18; relations with non-European merchants 18, 78-9, 95, 96-7; relations with rulers in India, 21, 44, 65, 81-2; with rulers in Africa, 21, 43-4, 50, 69, 76-7; relations with Chinese, 79-80, 136; relations with Amerindian peoples, 3, 64, 66, 68, 109, 115-6, 118, 132; relations with Japanese, 44, 80-1, 136; with rulers in Moluccas, 82; European contacts with knowledge, 15, 17; reporting and travel accounts, 19-20, 195-7, 209-15; insensitivity to local mores, 79, 80 'key points' strategy, 21-22; decline of overseas holdings, 23-25; language, 191-3; regulation of sailing and trade, 29-30; of trade, 134-5; Portuguese overseas, 60-3; crown representatives, 66-71, 74, 75; relations with Spain, 70, 137-8; crown sponsored scientific expeditions, 84, 176-7; carriers of diseases, 119-22; dissemination of

plants and seeds, 152-76; dissemminators of fauna, 180-1; disseminators of ideas, 198-208;connoisseurs of art, 186-7; and other cultures and mores, 187-91; language, 191-3. *See also* Lisbon, trade
Post, Frans, 51, 218
potatoes, 164, 170; sweet potatoes, 152, 159, 164, 168, 169, 170
Potosí, 51, 100, 101, 108
prazeiros, 49, 104
prazos, 96
Prester John, 11, 12, 13
'price revolution', 145
priests and friars as emissaries, 13, 82, 90, 91
Príncipe, 25, 40, 41, 62, 106, 114, 140, 141, 167, 171
printing presses, 193, 204, 205
prostitutes, 110
Province of the North(*Governo do norte*), 25, 49
Prussia, 131
Puerto Rico, 161-2 54
purpleheart, 129
Purús river, 100
Pyrard de Laval, François, 28

Queirós, Pedro Fernandes de, 5
Quelimane, 49
Quijos river, 100
Quilon, 37, 42, 81
quincentennials, 3, 6
Quito, 99, 100, 171

Rajapur, 75
Rapôso Tavares, António, 102
Rayburn, Sam: cited, 79
Recife, 83. *See also* Pernambuco
Recôncavo, 42. *See also* Bahia de Todos os Santos, Salvador
Red Sea, 13, 22, 32, 41, 45, 48, 72, 77, 135
Reinel, Pedro, 216
reis vizinhos, 21, 81, 86
relação, 71; Salvador, 71-2; Oporto, 72
religious orders *see* Augustinians, Benedictines, Carmelites, Dominicans, Franciscans, Theatines

religious relics, 13, 38
resins, 126, 127, 129, 130
Revolução dos Alfaiates, 208
rhinoceros, 182, 185
Ribeira Grande, 25
Ribeiro Coutinho, André, 75
Ribeiro de Macedo, Duarte, 153
Ribeiro Sanches, António Nunes, 207
Ricci, Matteo, 199-200
rice, 128, 140, 157
Rio das Contas, 54
Rio das Velhas, 103, 115
Rio de Janeiro, city of: French
    attacks, 24, 25; capital, 26; seat of
    royal court, 26; sailing schedules,
    34-5; overland routes to and from,
    51; transportation in, 51-2;
    African slaves in, 51, 52, 189, 219;
    shipyard, 86; see of, 87; bishops,
    88; imports and exports, 42, 124-
    34; arrival of Indiamen, 140; trade
    to Río de la Plata, 140
Río de la Plata, 5, 99; contraband, 43,
    101, 140; Luso-Spanish rivalries,
    70. See also Colônia do
    Sacramento
Rio Doce, 54
Rio Grande, 102
Rio Grande do Sul, 43, 51, 62, 69, 140
Rio Negro, 84, 100
Rio Pardo, 54
Rio Real, 55
rivers: in Africa, 53-4, 55; in Asia, 52-
    3, 97: in Brazil, 18-19, 54-7, 76,
    99-101, 102-3, 117-18. See
    individual rivers by name.
Roberts, J. M., 4
Rocha Pita, Sebastião da, 206
Rodrigues, Francisco, 72, 213-14, 217
Rodrigues, João, 20
Rodrigues, Luís Francisco, 108
Rodrigues, Simão, 200
Rodrigues Ferreira, Alexandre, 84,
    154, 176, 206
Rodriguez Tçuzzu, João, 204
Rome, 13, 89, 90, 91, 92, 93
Romus, 45
Rosary, Our Lady of the Brother-
    hood of, 147; festival of, 218
rosewood, 129
Rouen, 92
routes: maritime, 12, 15, 18, 27-8, 30-

41, 78, 124, 213-14. See also
    carreirada India; carreira do
    Brasil. Terrestrial: Arabian Desert
    routes, 44-49; trans-Saharan, 11,
    158; India to East Africa, 159.
    Brazilian: overland, 50-1, 117;
    fluvial, 54, 56, 76, 99-101, 102-3,
    117-18
rubber, 164, 171-2, 178
rubies, 127
rum, 141
Russia, 131
rutters, 18, 205, 213-14
rye, 125

Sá, Mem de, 115
Sabará, 184
Sabarabuçú, 103
Sabi river, 12
Sable island, 179, 180
saffron, 127
Safi, 125
Safim, 29, 86, 125
Sahara: routes across, 11, 158
sailing instructions and journals, 212-
    14
Saint Helena island, 9, 37, 40, 179
Saint Helena Bay, 9
Saint-Hilaire, Auguste de, 118
Saint-Hilaire, Etienne Geoffrey, 177
Saint-Malo, 125
Salamanca, 83, 85
Salitre river, 101
Salsette, 49, 53, 154
salt, 126, 127, 129, 130; as currency,
    131
salted beef, 43
Salvador: building of, 86, 106, 184;
    Dutch in, 25, 68, 90, 212; capital,
    26; routes, 34; sailing schedules,
    34, 35; entrepôt, 42, 140; transpor-
    tation, 51-2; entry point for
    migrants, 59; epidemic, 83;
    municipal council, 84; shipyard,
    86, 105; see, 87; archbishops, 88;
    Jesuit College, 90, 156, 185, 199;
    arrival of Indiamen, 140; convent,
    146
Sampitay, 80
sandalwood, 32, 41, 127, 133
San Francisco Bay, 5
San Ildefonso, Treaty of, 25

Persian, 127, 133; in Zambezia, 95; from Morocco, 125; currency, 133; Spanish American, 100, 125, 137, 140, 145; and 'price revolution', 145
Simonsen, Roberto, 116
Sinclair, William, 99
Siqueira de Sousa, Gonçalo de, 81
skins and hides, 127,128-9, 133, 181
'slave rivers', 11, 54, 140
slaves: African, 51, 52, 56, 58, 61, 86, 102, 111-12, 189, 191, 218-9; Amerindian, 51, 102, 116, 203; Asian, 127
slave trade: African to Brazil, 41, 62, 76, 111-12, 114-15, 119, 120, 141, 165, 167,168; to São Tomé and Príncipe, 140; to Portugal, 126, 162, 167; from Brazil to Portugal, 128; redistributed in Lisbon to Spain, 130; East Africa to India, 133; Macao to Manila, 137; to Río de la Plata, 140; provisioning of, 165, 167,168
smallpox, 120-2
Smith, Adam, 208
smuggling see Contraband
Smyrna, 45
snuff, 140, 173
soap, 129, 130
Soares de Albergaria, Lopo, 79
Soares de Sousa, Gabriel, 42, 101, 166, 195, 197
Society of Jesus see Jesuits
Socotra, 13, 82, 98
Sofala, 11, 12, 41, 43, 49, 66
soldiers and mercenaries: Hindu, 18; Portuguese, 24, 58, 59, 73-5, 106, 107; engage in commerce, 94, 95, 96-7
Solimões river, 99, 100
Solis, João Dias de, 5, 14, 99
Solomon Islands, 5
Solor, 71, 74, 87, 136
sorghum, 162, 165
sorrel rhubarb, 127
Soto, Hernando de, 5
Sousa, Francisco de, 90
Sousa, Martim Afonso de, 56, 65, 83, 214
Sousa, Tomé de, 86, 106
Sousa Ferreira, Inácio de, 72, 73

South-east passage, 5
South-west passage, 3, 5
Spain: treaties with Portugal, 25, 100, 206; Portuguese in Spanish service, 5, 66; rivalry with Portugal, 70,138; Portuguese trade with, 125,130, 137-8
Spanish, as disseminators of plants, 158, 160, 164, 170, 171, 173, 174; of fauna, 180-1
Spanish America: Portuguese in, 14-15, 91, 98, 100, 101, 108, 138, 140; Amerindians of, 116, 120-22, 203; missionaries, 200; silver from, 125, 137, 145; Brazil compared to, 120-1, 122, 184; Portuguese missionary activity in Asia compared to, 200
spices: trade, 12, 32, 130, 133; relative importance of Portuguese in trade, 32, 78. See also cardamom, cinnamon, cloves, ginger, mace, nutmeg, pepper
Stachouwer, Jacob, 69
Staden, Hans, 166
Steensgaard, Niels, 59
Stoner Jr., Winifred Sackville, 5
students, 71, 75, 83, 84, 85, 188, 198-9, 205-7, 208
subhedars, 78
sucupira, 129
Suez, 45
sugar-cane: markets for, 130, 140; cultivation, 40, 126, 128, 152, 160-1; dissemination of plant, 160-1
Sulawesi, 32
sumac, 129, 130
Sumatra, 15, 40, 127, 143
Sumitada, Omura, 44
Sunda islands, 15, 41, 87
Surat, 48, 215
Sweden, 131
sweetmeats, 128
sweet potatoes see potatoes
swords, 133, 190
syphilis, 120

Tabriz, 45
Tagus, 43
tallow, 43
Tamão, 3
tamarind, 127

Tana, lake, 89
Tanegashima, 190
Tangiers, 24, 31
Tapajós river, 54, 100
Tapioca, 128
Taunay, Viscount of, 102
Tavares, António Raposo, 57
tea, 128, 157
technology transfer: horticultural, 153-4, 156, 166, 171, 178-9; other, 86, 190, 205
Teixeira, António, 47
Teixeira, Pedro, 47-8, 97-9, 214-5
Teixeira, Pedro, 100-101, 116
Tenreiro, António, 47
Terceira, 23
Terhazza, 158
Ternate, 30, 38, 40, 66, 82, 127
Tete, 49, 95, 177
textiles: Indian, 32, 41, 54, 127, 132, 133, 137; Moroccan, 125, 131, 132
Theatines, 92
Thevet, André, 166
Third Orders, 147
Thomaz, Luís Filipe, 32
Tibet, 10, 14, 127
Tidor, 38, 40, 66, 81, 127
Tietê river, 56, 102
tigers, 16
Timbuktu, 11, 14, 19, 143, 158
Timor, 10, 32, 41, 71, 74, 120, 136; town, 183
tin, 132
tobacco: traded from Brazil,128, 129, 140, 141; English market for, 130, 143; carried to India, 141, 143; to West Africa, 141; plants dissemi-nated, 164, 172-4, 175; addiction to smoking, 173, 174, 190; medicinal claims for, 140,173
Tocantins river, 54, 56, 84, 103, 116, 214
Tomar, 184
tomatoes, 164, 170
Tongking, 89
topazes, 129
Tor, 12
Tordesillas, Treaty of, 100
tortoise-shell, 127, 129
tourmalines, 103
trade: patterns of: East Africa, 11, 127,132, 135, 136; West Africa, 31,

34, 41, 77, 125, 126, 131-2; Spice Islands, 30, 133, 136; Brazil and West Africa, 140-1; Macao and Japan, 30, 133, 135, 136, 144; Macao and Philippines, 137-8; China, 96-7, 127-8, 133; Río de la Plata, 140; Brazil and Portugal, 128-9, 132; Persian Gulf, 12; Morocco and Portugal, 29, 31, 41, 125, 131; Portugal and European markets, 31, 124-5, 129-31; India and Portugal, 126-7, 132; Atlantic islands, 125-6; Atlantic triangular, 29, 31, 40-1, 138-41; Indian Ocean networks, 135-6; Muslim trade diaspora, 159-60; Pacific trade diaspora, 137-8; regulation of, 29-30, 134-5, 138; profitability, 136, 143, 144; relative importance of Portuguese in Asian trade, 32, 135, 144. Commodities, 124-34, 140, 141, 143-7
trade fairs, 12, 38, 53
trade missions, Portuguese, 3, 9, 78-81
trading companies: Dutch, 29, 136, 179, 180; English, 45, 136, 145, 152, 179; Portuguese, 29, 30, 31, 112
transportation: land, 50-2; fluvial, 52-7, 84
Traparang, 90
travel accounts, 47, 77-8, 91-2, 92-3, 97-9, 100-101, 112-13, 195-6, 211-3, 214-6
treaties, 21, 25, 77, 82, 100, 130, 206,
Trindade, 40
Trindade, Fr Paulo da, 93
trinkets, 127
Tristão da Cunha, island, 9, 40
tropeiros, 51
Tucujus river, 100
Tucumán, 68, 101, 140
Tucurol, 53
Tupi language, 170, 193
Tupinambá, 3, 115-16, 121, 170; and manioc, 166
Tupinambaranas island, 116, 214
Tupinikin, 3, 121
Turkey, 125
Turks, 13, 19, 97-8
typhus, 120, 122

Uadam, 143
Ughoton, 11, 131, 182
universities, 71, 75, 83, 84, 85. *See
also* Coimbra, University of
urban landscape, 137, 183-4
Uruguay river, 57

Valignano, Alexander: cited, 44
vanilla, 168, 178
Vavilov, Nikolai I., 157, 160, 170, 172
vegetables, 128, 160, 164
Veiga, Tristão Vaz da, 66
Velho, Domingos Jorge, 102
Velozo, Lourenço, 105
Venezuela, 108
Venice, 78, 99; merchants in Lisbon,
124; Portuguese trade with, 125,
130; trade rivalry, 152
Vera Cruz, 98
Vernei, Luís António, 207
vessels, Portuguese, 18, 28-9, 30, 42,
55-6, 58-9, 119, 216-7; Chinese,
29; Asian indigenous, 29; African,
41, 55, 56-7; native American, 42,
56-7
Vicente, Gil, 185
Viana do Castelo, 43, 59
Victoria, 5, 11, 120
Vieira, António, 90-1, 153, 155
Vieira Belfort, Joaquim António da, 85
Vietnam, 64, 201
Vila Bela, 84
Vila Boa, 51
Vila Rica do Ouro Prêto, 157
Vilela, Gaspar, 44
Villegaignon, Nicolas Durand de, 25
Viseu, 88
Volta river, 14
votive offerings, 219

'War of Divine Liberty', 69
Warwijck, Wybrand van, 180
waxes, 125, 127, 129
way-stations, 35, 37, 40, 58, 59, 140,
180
wheat: cultivation and trade, 40, 125,
126, 128, 160

Whydah, 141
Wickham, Henry, 172
wigs, 132
wind and pressure patterns, 32-8
wines: production and trade in, 126,
127,128,129, 130, 132
woad, 126, 128, 130, 152
women; in Angola, 110; Brazil, 96,
110-11; in Ethiopia, 78; in Macao,
96; in Persia, 49; in Zambezia, 61,
96, 110; absence of narratives by,
20; on Indiamen, 59, 110; as
migrants, 62; orphans, 109-10;
prostitutes, 110; in convents, 111,
146; slaves, 111-12; exiled, 110;
widows, 188; converts to Christianity, 190-1
woods, 126, 128, 129; aromatic,
127,130, 133
wool, 128, 129
woollen goods, 125, 132

Xavier, Francis, 65, 89, 211
Xingú river, 100

Ya' arubi Imans, 24
Yamaguchi, 89
yams, 162
Yangtze, 168,169
yaws, 120
Yellala rapids, 2
yellow fever, 83, 120
Yunnan, 169

Zacato Lusitano, 197
Zagazabo, 13
Zambezi river, 10, 49, 53, 54, 55, 95
Zambezia: Portuguese population of,
61; 74, 95, 118; mineral deposits,
95-6; *prazos*, 96; Goanese in, 49,
96; Jesuits, 146
Zanzibar, 24, 165
Zeila, 12
Zerumbet, 127
Zuari river, 53
Zumbo, 49
Zurara, Gomes Eanes de, 210